With Compliments

from,

Asouaze

12th OCT. 2022

# Learning about
# NDỊ IGBO

Edited by Chinedu Uchechukwu

INTEGRATED WORK SOLUTIONS LIMITED, LAGOS, NIGERIA

PUBLISHER  *Agunze Chib Ikokwu Foundation*

EDITOR  *Chinedu Uchechukwu*

ELECTRONIC PAGE DESIGN/  *Ubong Etuk*
GRAPHIC DESIGN INPUT

PRINTERS  *Integrated Work Solutions Ltd.*
*Lagos, Nigeria. +234(0)803 565 3914*

Printed in the Federal Republic of Nigeria
by
INTEGRATED WORK SOLUTIONS LIMITED, LAGOS, NIGERIA

ISBN: 978-978-991-846-1

# AGUNZE CHIB IKOKWU FOUNDATION (ACIF)

## THE LOGO

The logo is made up of the following components and their meanings. A human figure in supplication to *Chukwu Okike* - God the Creator. The four red circles above the figure represent the Igbo week, the four market days of *Eke, Oye, Afor* and *Nkwo*. They also represent the number *four* in relation to an *Oji Igbo* 'Igbo kola nut' that has four lobes when split and as a result signifies completeness, equity and social justice. The Ivory coloured half of the human figure represents the titled man with his ivory tusk insignia, while the red hallow on the head of the human figure represents the *Nze na Ozo* red chieftaincy cap. The red coloured half of the body signifies the blood which continues to circulate in spite of past and present genocidal killings. Finally, the black intersecting histogram represents the *Nsibidi* symbol of love and unity.

### Vision and Mission

**ACIF** has the *vision* of promoting *Culture and Community Relations*. It takes full cognizance of the fact that culture in its broadest sense, defines a people: their way of life, their generational baton change that is evident in their arts, beliefs, values, customs, language, religion, dressing, and rituals. Such an all-encompassing view of culture is well represented in

Chinua Achebe's *Things Fall Apart*, which unobtrusively captures and presents the Igbo culture within the pre-colonial period. The *mission* of the ACIF is to concretely undertake endeavors that contribute to keeping Igbo language and culture alive and vibrant, both at home in Igbo land and in the diaspora. These include concrete support for educational, social, psychological and institutional endeavours through publications, research projects, workshops and trainings.

### *Learning About Ndị Igbo*

This work marks the onset of many projects and activities, which are yet to be realized through the *Agunze Chib Ikokwu Foundation (ACIF)*. It presents the multifaceted nature of *Ndị Igbo* in their adaptability to whatever environment they find themselves, and the enrichment of the Igbo culture through incorporating some admirable cultural aspects of their host communities such as cuisine, music, arts, fashion, government and law, language etc, whilst still retaining most of their own unique cultural attributes.

The cosmology of Ndị Igbo is such that a little study by her neighbours or other culturally different society they end up in, will not only unveil but completely allay the unjustified fear of them that is usually based on ignorance about their true spiritual essence. They believe in a just and fair world where justice and equity rules, and that what is good for the goose is good for the gander. They are also conscious of and deeply respectful of host communities, and would never aggressively desire to covet and take over the lands of their host. They believe in hardwork and industriousness and crave therefore, for daily blessings of strength, guidance and good fortune; They cherish a good family and family relationships and would sacrifice unconditionally to ensure that they raise a useful set of children or any other ward that is entrusted to them such that, they all would be the pride of society. They endeavor to be worthy ambassadors who would always add value to wherever they call home, even if it's a temporary abode. They fervently believe that the unjust treatment of a brethren equates to the unjust treatment of all and would bond to resist any such evil. That is why the Igbo libation endorses the healthy and progressive well-being of all - *ikwu na Ibe*. To all these and more, those present and partaking in the breaking and sharing of kola nut would always chorus a resounding *Isee!* (the I, is pronounced as the I of *in* and the S E E, as in *say* ).

One who understands the Igbo Culture would cherish the Igbo as a neighbour. This underpins the raison d'etre for the Mission Statement of ACIF which includes the promotion of Culture and Community Relations through using history, art, music and linguistics to reach out to persons of all ages.

The decades of abolition of History as a course of study in Nigerian schools was a grievous travesty to whole generations. The loss of knowledge arising from this grave and mischievous error has bred a crop of Nigerians whose awareness level of the true history of their Fatherland is horrendously under par. They tend to exhibit therefore, crass indifference to matters of State which ordinarily, ought to be stoking their patriotic chord. They are hybrids whose emotions and responses to issues cannot be accurately determined. It would not be too off the mark to say that since 1966, there are millions of citizens suffering from Transgenerational Trauma (coinage of American Psychotherapist Resmaa Menakem : My Grandmother's Hands).

Communities ought to be encouraged to start healing. The negative stories of yesteryears that pitched brother against brother ought to now be set aside. Lessons have been learnt and it's time now to let bygones be bygones. Let communities drum up the positive efforts of our forebears who without much in their favour, were able to bring us all to relate on an even keel with the rest of humanity. By retelling our own history, by evolving our own drama, by encouraging our art, music, festivals and by upholding the family values that are dear to us all, we shall enthrone that egalitarian society which has always been pristine to some of our cultures. On a final note, the noticeable drop in Igbo Language usage amongst first generation Igbos in diaspora calls for attention. Like the Igbo adage recognizes, 'a death blow to one is a death blow to the other.' The Jewish diaspora experience and cultural survival may come in handy. William Safran in his article "The Jewish Diaspora in a Comparative and Theoretical Perspective: Israel Studies, Indiana University Press, Vol 10, Number 1, Spring 2005 pp 36 - 60" pointed out amongst many others, that "they continue to relate, personally or vicariously, to that homeland in one way or another, and their ethno-communal consciousness and solidarity which reach across political boundaries, are importantly defined in terms of the existence of such a relationship. ———-" He also stated that "Their cultural, religious, economic, and political relationships with the homeland are reflected in a significant way in their communal institutions. Ndiigbo refer to this as *Aku luo Uno*. The overall drive, is to leave this world a better place for our children and generations yet unborn and in the words of our Vision Statement, to uphold and reinforce the beauty and richness of Black African History, Culture and Civilization. ■

**CHIBEZE NNAEMEKA IKOKWU KSC.**

# CONTENTS

# DEDICATION

This book is dedicated to my parents,

**CHIEF GODFREY CHIBEZE IKOKWU (ONOWU OBA)**
**&**
**MARGARET NWANYIDINMA IKOKWU, MON (ANUENYI)**

for imbuing the Onowu Ikokwu family dynasty

with the best, our culture has in the offing.

# ACKNOWLEDGEMENT

**I** **AM VERY MUCH INDEBTED TO MY WIFE** Dr. Lady Uchenna Joy Ikokwu and our children, Chaka, Nnaemeka and Mary, Chuka, Adanna and Chieke, and Chioma, for their relentless effort, support and encouragement in ensuring that this book and others begin to get published. Same, goes to our cherished grandchildren Alex, Tobenna, Olanna and Anyanna who added great impetus to the spirit of the work as they helped, to lighten up the mood with their joyousness and enthusiasm.

To Professor Chinedu Uchechukwu (Department of Linguistics, Nnamdi Azikiwe University, Awka) for his immense contribution and the endless hours we spent trying to ensure that this work is brought to fruition, I say a resounding thank you. I would also like to acknowledge all the erudite Chapter Contributors who despite the travails of the period both locally and globally, did a marvelous job in the sourcing of the materials and data needed for each of the chapter topic.

In agreeing with palpable enthusiasm to write the foreward to this book despite his bereavement, His Excellency Dr. Patrick Dele Cole, OFR reinforced his globally recognized scholarly acclaim and interest in matters relating to history, culture, community relations, media, administration, policy making, international relations and diplomacy. I duly extend my gratitude to him.

To sustain cultural awareness across board can be quite tasking, more so, when faced with existential threats. In this regard therefore, I must recognize Ohaneze as the umbrella Igbo cultural organization, the long-standing contributions of groups such as Aka Ikenga - the foremost Igbo Think Tank Association, the U.S.A based World Igbo Congress and the nascent Umu Igbo Unite which is the cultural plank for our First

Generation Umu Igbo America and the future ones. UIU has a National body and State Chapters. I thank them for their tremendous zeal and success in keeping our cultural flag flying.

The largely unrecognized effort of performing cultural groups back in Igboland has to be brought to the fore. To play or perform professionally requires passion, practice sessions and finance. For regular folks seeking their diverse daily income, this can be quite challenging. I have always been amazed at how such groups in Oba, Idemili South Local Government Area of Anambra State where I come from, can forego their work, family responsibilities and leisure to ensure that they never disappoint in their response and performance whenever their services are sought for in what ever guise. It behoves us all in our various domains, to take a greater interest in how best to support and promote these groups either directly or through organizing cultural fiestas and local or inter state competitions. This support must include our citadels of learning where Igbo studies are taught. I must acknowledge the tremendous strides made by our indefatigable multi talented Onyeka Onwenu, Kanayo O. Kanayo, Ebele Okaro Onyiuke and co in sustaining and advancing our cultural heritage via the performing arts and Nollywood.

The pioneer role of Senator Mike Ajegbo - Ede Obosi, in purposefully establishing his state of the art Minaj Cable, Television, Radio and Satellite services in 1994, 1995, 1996 and 1997 respectively in his hometown Obosi, in Idemili North, on a free-to-home basis for the sole aim of advancing amongst other things, cultural education and awareness remains very laudable. Following in the radio media establishment as of 2013, is Pharm. Nnamdi Obi's Odenigbo 99.1 FM Radio Station located also in Obosi. Lately too, Okpataozuora Obi (Cubana) Iyiegbu's support for the performing arts and youth empowerment premised on the plank of community relations is becoming noticeably and commendably impactful. To add further positive impetus to these efforts is why our environment, has to be Peacefully Enabling for sustainability and continuity of our culture.

My gratitude also goes to Dwight Bolden, a Harvard trained erudite African American for his comments, New Jersey based Mrs Uchenna Agbim Nwachukwu (Ugodiya) for her input in the ACIF logo design and Mr. Ubong Etuk of Integrated Works Solutions Ltd for his professional artistic graphic designs and other inputs.

Finally, we give all glory to God for making this effort possible.

**Chibeze Nnaemeka Ikokwu KSC.**

# FOREWORD

**O**NE THING IS CLEAR ABOUT THE IGBOS, by whatever standards there is, they are a remarkable people, strong in will, great in achievement, undeterred by difficulties. What is it that has produced these remarkable people? What keeps them going? How do a people enhance their self-awareness even amidst open hostility, jealousy and outright discrimination? It would seem as if the harder the other peoples in Nigeria beat them, discriminate against them, the more successful they become.

This book gives a peep into the complexity of what makes the igbo character. It starts from a very simple assumption, that education is a key component of development. Education fosters tolerance, it may also foster bigotry, and when you take a people eager to be educated, eager to change their positions in life, eager to find the world and to leave the world a better place than they found it, that inspires.

I've always believed that Nigeria's 256 different ethnic groups must be, no matter how you cut it, eventually a conglomerate of values, some which complement each other and others which discriminate against each other.

But as societies are evolving and changing, perhaps we should look into each ethnic group and find out which values are transferrable. What is it that an Igbo person can teach a non-Igbo so that the life of the non-igbo is better than it was before the encounter and vice versa? What is the diamond nugget in each ethnic group?

It would be, if you like, picking the jewels of the various ethnic groups and finding out how to amalgamate them. Maybe, this is where Nigeria ought to be, and a good place to start is this book. The book deals with a period in the Igbo life which is difficult by any standards but because of the cosmology, because of the world view, because of the art, because of the culture, because of the training, the changes that come with the challenges of modernization are easier to assimilate. We have a remarkable people as our neighbors, the true response to that is not jealousy but to be proud that a neighbor of ours is so well endowed.

It is time for us to appreciate one another. It is time for the Igbos themselves to appreciate themselves. Maybe they are over boisterous but then, who wouldn't be given the talents embedded therein.

The book deals with all the information gathered by the intelligence officers during the old colonial rule. It also deals with the pre-history of the Igbos, the archaeology, their scientific knowledge, knowledge in metallurgy. The book is coming out at the time when the changes within the Nigerian culture viz a viz whether or not we remain one, or whether we break into several parts, that those changes have got to be internalized. It deals with the new knowledge of numeracy, words such as 100, 500, 1 million and 1 billion, have Igbo equivalent which is not the same as many languages.

**Dr. Patrick Dele Cole, OFR**

# PREFACE

The statement, that "Africa had no history", has been used in the past to justify the argument that the presence of Europeans through colonialism marked the onset of the history of Africa. The reactions of various African historians to this statement and the pioneering works of the African historian Kenneth Dike, have all led to a lot of historical works that finally trickled down to the ordinary citizens of a country like Nigeria through the teaching of history in the primary and secondary schools. This has in the past immensely contributed to Nigeria having generations that are highly appreciative of the diversity of the country's geography, cultures and traditions.

However, effective 2009/2010 to 2019, history was removed as a subject from the primary and secondary school curricula by the Federal Government of Nigeria, thereby depriving the upcoming generation of the simple knowledge of the history and development of their villages, their states, and their regions of the country, as well as weakening the impulse to develop a healthy, socialized mind, which would have resulted from this knowledge of the history and diversity of their environment. And as this generation grew physically, so also did their ignorance increase with regard to the geographical and cultural diversity of their country. That is why Nigeria's *The Guardian* concludes that "it would seem that the ban placed on the teaching of history in Nigerian schools was calculated, deliberately or otherwise, to impose collective amnesia on the people and mentally dislocate Nigerians".
(*The Guardian* editorial of 16 May 2021:

https://guardian.ng/opinion/history-and-school-curriculum-matters-arising/). In expressing his frustration about this decision, Prof. Wole Soyinka described the act as "a crime [...] done to our children and our advancement". (https://shadesofnoir.org.uk/history-removed-from-nigerias-school/)

The nature of this crime is gradually manifesting in the new generation of Nigerians in an attitude that can be described as "ahistorical" which, according to *Websters Dictionary* means "not concerned with or related to history, historical development, or tradition" and "historically inaccurate or ignorant". Similar formulations abound in other dictionaries, all of which revolve around "ignorance of the history of past events or traditions that existed before". The new generation of Nigerians can indeed be described as ahistorical, not because they do not want to learn about their history, or because they deliberately have a wrong attitude towards their history, but due to the fact that they have simply been deprived of ten years of being in touch with their history. This new generation can indeed be described as 'historically clean', because they are almost mentally bereft of any idea of their history and culture. The unfortunate and misguided ones in such a generation would of course be easy prey for hateful and destructive manipulations, after all, they don't seem to have strong memories of any form of historical connections. That is the evil that Nigeria perpetrates on itself.

Compare this development in Nigeria with the study of the history of Africa. It took decades and tremendous efforts for African historians to counter the wrong notion that Africa had no past. Also, compare this with the situation in America, where the *African Americans* had to assert the recognition and documentation of their history. Both are highly positive developments. But could we imagine an African American in the appropriate position getting up one day to announce that African

American History should no longer be studied in American schools? Of course, we cannot imagine such. And for Nigeria? We do not need to imagine it at all, because it actually happened when our Federal Government stopped for ten long years the learning of history at those early stages that the children most needed to know the basics about their history, culture and environment.

How should one interpret this development? Should it be seen as an effort to adjust to the colonizer's interpretation that Africa had no history? Or should it be seen as a new ploy to deliberately wipe off the immediate past in the minds of the new generation and replace it with some concoctions of the present? The time to examine the motivation seems to have run out, because what seems to matter now is the deep gap it has created in the minds of the new generation and the need to close the gap. The fact that this new generation lacks cohesion in discussing historical matters or explaining their cultures and traditions are strong indicators of the emerging socio-psycho-historical amnesia.

This condition needs to be addressed in a straightforward manner from various angles and without much technicalities, because the upcoming, new generation must not become specialists in history and other disciplines in order to understand their history, culture and tradition. After all, that early stage at which they should have been introduced to their history was also not the stage for specialists. In the same vein, the present book is also for non-specialists.

The endeavour of the authors in this book is not to completely fill the identified socio-psycho-historical gaps in the minds of the new generation; it is simply a contribution to filling it. Hence, the first part of the book discusses the history of pre-colonial Igbo land and the position of the Igbos in present day Nigeria, while the second part covers the state of the Igbo language (dying or already dead), Igbo art, Igbo music and musical instruments, Igbo festivities and masquerades, and Igbo philosophy. The third part is on what some have often tried to describe as "Igbo mentality" and its effects on the Igbo person's attitude to work. It is, first, an attitude that involves taking others along as one progresses (*onye aghana nwanne ya*); but it also includes going through an apprenticeship (*ịgba boyị*) and endeavouring to have a professional means of livelihood (*Kedụ aka ọlụ gị? Maka na e kelụ ọlụ eke*). The fourth part of the book examines the traditional socio-political institutions and administration, and relates them to the present; while the last part focuses on the long standing intercultural relationships between the Igbo and their immediate neighbours in the South-West and the South-South regions of Nigeria.

Nigeria is diverse, built on diversity, and can be sustained through its diversity, not through suppression or intimidation. Let us celebrate our diversity without harming our individuality.

**Chinedu Uchechukwu**

# Part One

# SOME ASPECTS OF THE HISTORY OF NDI IGBO

# CHAPTER 1

STANLEY J. ONYEMECHALU  &  J. KELECHI UGWUANYI

# Archaeology Of Igbo Land – The Pride Of Our Ancestors And The Joy Of The Living

## Summary

*Many sons and daughters of Igbo extraction are not knowledgeable in the area of the archaeology of Igbo land and the wealth and ingenuity of their ancestors. Although this could be attributed to poor archaeological investigations, the fact that the little available knowledge of the archaeology of Igbo land is often neglected in schools in Igbo land, which further complicates the matter. It is, therefore, not surprising that many indigenes are simply unaware of the usefulness of the rich and invaluable cultural heritage in their locality. Hence, the need for this written intervention which has a threefold purpose. First, it is to serve as a scorecard for the archaeology of Igbo land in highlighting notable archaeological sites and indigenous archaeologists. Secondly, it implicitly answers the question of whether or not the Igbo were savvy enough to engage in technological innovations such as stone, pottery, or metal, working as obtainable in other civilizations. Thirdly, it contributes to the issue of the role of archaeology in identity politics by highlighting how the archaeology of Igbo land contributes to Igbo identity. Finally, it strives to do all these by presenting the little efforts that have been made by foreign and Igbo scholars within the past 65 years.*

## 1. Introduction

The term "archaeology" comes from two Greek words, "*archaios*" meaning "old" or "ancient", and "*logia*", meaning "learning" or "study", both of which may translate to "the study of old or ancient" things. These old or ancient things are accessed by digging them up from the soil, a process called 'archaeological excavation'; while the things archaeologists 'dig up' are referred to as "artifacts" or "fossils". Paradoxically, every material used in the past is also called an artifact. Generally, archaeologists use reconnaissance, mapping, ethnography and excavation to study the past. One of the tools used mostly by Archaeologists to identify the date or age of an artifact is the Radiocarbon (C-14) analysis.

Globally, Archaeology first began around the 15th or 16th century in Europe but the first scientific archaeological research in Nigeria didn't start until around the 20th century, when scholars like Leo Frobenius and Bernard Fagg began investigations in the Western and Northern regions of Nigeria respectively (Lasisi 2018). Thurstan Shaw was the first person to carry out a systematic archaeological (excavation) investigation in Igbo land. It was the sites of Igbo-Isaiah, Igbo-Jonah and Igbo-Richard, where objects of archaeological importance were accidentally discovered in a shrine, a burial chamber and a cache, respectively, during a latrine dig. It is therefore no surprise that many indigenous scholars took after Thurstan Shaw to further explore the archaeological phenomena in the Igbo area.

In Igbo land there are numerous cultural and natural sites and features that show evidence of human habitation in the past. These sites tell the story of the past and present activities of the Igbo people as well as their relationship with the environment. Such sites are found in many places in Igbo land and they range from stone tools factory sites in Ugwuelle-Okigwe to complex metal working sites in many villages/towns in the northern Igbo region. Others are historic buildings, ancient pyramids in Nsude Udi, gazetted national monuments, museums, pottery, arts and crafts centres and so on. The distribution, however, shows that a larger concentration of these sites and features is located on the Nsukka-Okigwe cuesta (Ekechukwu 2009), probably due to the more favourable geo-ecological conditions of the area. As described by Ekechukwu (2009), the Nsukka–Okigwe cuesta comprises a range of green hills that mark the landscape of Igbo land, from the Okigwe scarp lands, the Udi-Awgu highlands to the Nsukka plateaus. This chapter presents these sites and discusses the ways that they contributed to Igbo culture and civilisation. ⌐

## 2. Notable Archaeological Sites in Igbo land

The view that Africans contributed little or nothing to the world's technological inventory, or that they lacked ingenuity has been refuted in various forms. The contribution of Archaeology in Igbo land to refuting this assumption is through the discovery of the evidence of Iron working in Igbo land (Itanyi & Okonkwo 2009), which is one of the various indigenous technologies found in many African communities, in addition to other archaeological sites that are not restricted to iron working.

In the present Igbo land, iron smelting has long gone into oblivion, leaving behind vague memories of its practice and a fast-dying blacksmithing trade. Many indigenes and residents of iron working communities are unable to remember any valuable information about the practice of iron smelting and there have been cases where the people averred that archaeological materials like slag debris, broken pieces of tuyere and furnace walls found in their communities must have grown from the ground (Anozie 1979; Falola 1987). However, in 1976, a group of men from Umundu, who claimed to have assisted their parents in the smelting process, were assembled in the Department of Archaeology, University of

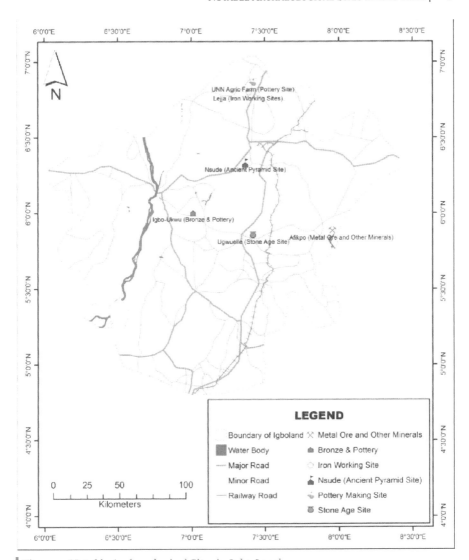

*Figure 1. Notable Archaeological Sites in Igbo Land*

Nigeria, Nsukka for a re-enactment of the iron smelting process (see Okafor 1992). The smelting experiment was 90% success, therefore, proving that those who smelted iron in Igbo land are indigenous. Umundu is in the present day Udenu LGA of Enugu state. Many other villages/towns like Lejja, Opi, Aku, Obimo in the Nsukka cultural area have abundant evidence of iron working industry. The earliest date of the industry is 2000 BC (Eze-Uzomaka 2009). The area has benefited from a lot of archaeological investigations due to its proximity to the University of Nigeria and the Archaeology and Tourism department therein. These archaeological investigations have also gone beyond iron working to other sites that show evidence of pottery making, food production, animal domestication and other endeavours of the pre-colonial Igbo civilisation.

## 2.1 Ugwuelle Stone-Age Site

A stone age site was found in Ugwuelle, an Igbo community in Uturu, Abia State. For clarity, stone ages are considered as an early technological innovation after ages of hunting and gathering; a time when the Homo Erectus human started fabricating stones into shapes for hunting and agricultural purposes. Archaeology categorised stone age into Early Stone Age (ESA), Middle Stone Age (MSA), and Late Stone Age (LSA). The Ugwuelle site is a near combination of MSA and LSA with abundant evidence of stone tools such as handaxes, picks, and cleavers, which goes to show that humans existed in the Igbo area since around 250,000 – 500,000 years ago (see Uzukwu 1997; Ibeanu 2002; Allsworth-Jones 2015). The site was discovered by chance in 1977 when Mrs. Mercy Emezie, a student of Geography at the University of Nigeria, Nsukka reported that she had seen unique stones being fed to crushing machines at a construction site nearby. The information got to the then Department of History within which the Archaeology unit existed, and an archaeologist, the late Fred Anozie, moved swiftly to Ugwuelle to investigate this finding to report back to the department. In his report, he indicated that the stones were indeed lithics belonging to what archaeologists classify as the Acheulean tradition of the MSA. Anozie's report prompted the department to plan and undertake a 'rescue excavation' at the construction site. These efforts yielded lots of stone tools of mostly the MSA and LSA traditions including cleavers, cores, scrapers, handaxes, manuports, flakes, and so on. The site is located within a forest environment surrounded by hills and shrubs with availability of the raw materials - dolerite rocks - useful for the stone tools production. Ugwuelle is a site very unique in the documentation of Igbo development and archaeological history.

## 2.2 The University of Nigeria Agric Farm

Donald Dean Hartle carried out a survey on the University of Nigeria, Nsukka Agricultural Farm (see Anozie 2002). Hartle did not find iron tools in this site, but he was able to use other samples recovered, including lithics, to show that the ESA people may have lived in the Nsukka area at some point in the past. Hartle also used pottery analysis to establish cultural relationship and continuity among those that lived in the area in ESA and those living at the time of the excavation in the 1960s. Chikwendu (2002) noted that the University of Nigeria Farm Site, excavated by Hartle, yielded lots of potsherds that were then dated to about 2,500 BC. This means that people habited in the area and were engaging in domestic and agricultural activities since this period.

## 2.3 The Igbo-Ukwu Sites

Igbo-Ukwu came to limelight after a corpus of bronze materials and beads were accidentally discovered during the construction of a cistern. The finding was reported to the then Antiquities Department of Nigeria (known now as the National Commission for Museums and Monuments (NCMM)) and in 1959, Thurstan Shaw was invited to conduct proper archaeological investigation and excavation at the site (The Telegraph 2013). Shaw carried out more than three excavations in the area between 1959 and 1965. Each site excavated was named after the owner of the compound, Isaiah Anozie, Jonah Anozie, and Richard Anozie. These are the three brothers whose compound became the sites of Igbo-Isaiah (shrine location), Igbo-Jonah (location of a burial chamber), and Igbo-Richard (location of a cache). The report of the excavations revealed extensive bronze works including the famous Bronze roped pot, numerous beads and glass, thousands of pottery wares and some burial and sacred chambers (see Shaw 1970; 1975). The sites exposed to the world the ancient Igbo civilization dating to the 9th century AD; among all the Nigeria's bronze working industries - Ife and Benin, Igbo-Ukwu was the oldest in history.

The complex nature of the bronzes instigated the earlier analysis that claimed that the materials used for their production were imported from outside Nigeria. However, later research found that they are of local origin (see Chikwendu et al. 1989); another study argue that the pottery

*Figure. 2:*
*9th Century*
*Bronze Pot,*
*Igbo-Ukwu*
*(Source:*
*Ochiwar*
*2013, p.4)*

design and motifs relate to the traditional Igbo arts especially in Uli, Anambra state (see Umeji 1985). Even, pots made in Inyi in Enugu state presented similar designs like that of the Igbo-Ukwu bronze roped pot (see Okpoko 1987; Ibeanu 1989). Shaw's excavations at Igbo-Ukwu revolutionised the known history of the Igbo people because it provided the much-needed scientific consolidation for certain historical records. Writing on the importance of the Igbo-Ukwu discovery, Adiele Afigbo argue that by 9th AD, Igbo land was already a space for highly artistic culture centred on the institution of a divine king with high religious ideas that derived its sustenance from an economy based partly on agriculture and partly on wide-ranging commercial contacts with the outside world (see Afigbo 1971).

The complex nature of the bronzes instigated the earlier analysis that claimed that the materials used for their production were imported from outside Nigeria. However, later research found that they are of local origin (see Chikwendu et al. 1989); another study argue that the pottery design and motifs relate to the traditional Igbo arts especially in Uli, Anambra state (see Umeji 1985). Even, pots made in Inyi in Enugu state presented similar designs like that of the Igbo-Ukwu bronze roped pot (see Okpoko 1987; Ibeanu 1989). Shaw's excavations at Igbo-Ukwu revolutionised the known history of the Igbo people because it provided the much-needed scientific consolidation for certain historical records. Writing on the importance of the Igbo-Ukwu discovery, Adiele Afigbo argue that by 9th AD, Igbo land was already a space for highly artistic culture centred on the institution of a divine king with high religious ideas that derived its sustenance from an economy based partly on agriculture and partly on wide-ranging commercial contacts with the outside world (see Afigbo 1971).

### 2.4 Afikpo Archaeological Sites

Extensive archaeological excavations and documentation in Igbo land suggest that the Nsukka–Okigwe–Afikpo cuesta was the origin of Igbo settlement (see Okonkwo and Ikegwu 2020). This position could be attributed to the extensive nature of archaeological research conducted in the area since the inception of archaeology department at UNN. Even though there have been various archaeological investigations in other parts of Igbo land, none has been as extensive as the cases in northern parts of Igbo land. Archaeological investigation in Afikpo is very important because of the connection that the information about metal ore exploitation in the area has on the finished bronze objects of the Igbo-Ukwu excavations (see Craddock et al. 1997). The arguments for local origin of the materials used in the production of Igbo-Ukwu bronzes relied on the information gathered from Afikpo sites (see Chikwendu 1976). It was found that the metal contents of the Igbo-Ukwu bronzes are available in large quantity in Afikpo; and the distance between the two towns would make it easier to source the materials from within. Archaeological information on local mining and uses of the metal ores in Afikpo helped scholars of both Igbo and foreign origin to debunk the earlier assumption that the materials and skills applied in the manufacture of the Igbo-Ukwu bronzes came from outside Igbo land.

Figure 3: Assembled Cylindrical Slags at Otobo-Dunoka, Lejja (Source: Eze-Uzomaka 2009, p. 6)

## 2.5 Iron Working Sites in Lejja and other parts of Igbo Land

Available evidence suggests that extensive iron working, including smelting and smithing took place at Lejja in the deep past. These evidences include cylindrical slag debris, pottery tuyere, iron ores, and furnace walls; their presence tell the story of a once-thriving iron working industry. The popular Otobo Dunoka (village arena of Dunoka) is the location of the iconic square, where giant cylindrical slag blocks numbering over 700 are arranged in a theatre row to serve as seats for village meetings (see Fig. 2). Each of these slag blocks weigh between 34-57kg measuring up to 50cm in diameter with 40cm height (Eze-Uzomaka 2009; Okafor 1999). This prehistoric archaeological iron working site has been dated to 2000 BC (Eze-Uzomaka 2009), a date that placed it among the earliest iron working sites in Africa. Asides Lejja, there are several towns and communities that have evidence of intensive iron smelting activities in the Nsukka area. They include Aku, Obimo, Opi, Owerre-Elu, and so on.

Unsurprisingly, these cylindrical slag debris packed at the village square can still be found intact today for obvious reasons. First, because they are durable and second, because there are taboos preventing their removal, destruction or tampering (Eze-Uzomaka 2010); they have some cultural utilities among the people. A visit to Dunoka and an encounter with the people will take one through numerous extant cultural histories and activities that reflect the place of iron technology in their livelihood.

There have been numerous archaeological investigations at other iron working sites in parts of the Nsukka area. Eze-Uzomaka (2010) studied iron working in Amaovoko as a further research on the iron smelting culture of the Lejja community. Anozie also contributed to the archaeological investigations in Enugu state with major interest in Lejja, Umundu and Ogbodu-Abba (Anozie 1979). Professor Edwin Okafor surveyed many communities in the Nsukka cultural area such as Ede-Oballa, Eha-Alumona, Eha-Ndiagu, Isiakpu, Nru, Opi, Orba, Owerre-Elu and Umundu (see Okafor 1995; 1997). His research was among the earliest attempt to engage "modern scientific techniques to study the Nsukka bloomery iron working", which produced results that point to the indigenous origination of the technology. Outside Nsukka area, Okpoko et. al. (2016) examined the presence of iron working evidence in Okpatu, Udi LGA, Enugu state. They interrogated the origin and the cultural connectedness between the past generations and the current inhabitants. Their study pointed out the peculiarity of standing furnaces still visible in Okpatu. All these efforts by different scholars widened our knowledge of iron technology in Igbo land and used scientifically generated dates and experiments to demonstrate the ingenuity of the past inhabitants of these Igbo communities.

Okonkwo and Ibeanu (2016) studied various sites of indigenous technology in Nigeria but with major focus on these south-eastern communities: Nsukka, Udi, Awka, Opi, Inyi, Igbo-Ukwu, Ugwuelle, Okigwe, Ishiagu, Abakiliki, and Enyigba. The study used archaeological and ethnographic data to identify the extraction methods for some of these raw materials in the past. For iron smelting, particularly, their findings showed that the source of raw materials were from stone ores such as haematite, which were traditionally obtained along the Nsukka-Okigwe escarpment (Umeji, 1985 in Okonkwo & Ibeanu, 2016). It means that the Igbo people were able to engage in extensive iron smelting because of the availability and accessibility of the required raw materials in their environment. Okonkwo and Ibeanu (2016) further noted that the Igbo blacksmiths, who showed mastery over these raw materials, were involved in the iron foundries that helped build many of the railway tracks in Nigeria. It must be noted that the mastery of smelting around the Nsukka-Udi-Okigwe cuesta would have instigated the extensive smithing technology (fabrication of tools) around Awka, Udi, and the Nsukka region.

## 3. The Wealth and Complexity of Pre-colonial Igbo Society

Most people do not know how archaeology contributes to the society. As a result, they are quick to underestimate its relevance to humanity. Ironically, the same set of people are drawn to cultural festivals and exhibitions in museums within and outside Nigeria, and would choose to visit places of historical relevance during holidays with little or no interest in archaeology. For this reason, this section, in addition to mentioning notable Igbo archaeologists, also will highlight the numerous socio-cultural and politico-economic significance of archaeology in Igbo land using evidence obtained from archaeology sites from the area. The section exposes the rich and complex nature of the Igbo society made possible by systematic archaeological investigations.

Archaeological studies in Igbo land show the wealth of the mineral resources in Igbo land that the people have exploited to meet their needs, including food processing as well as the production of metal and stone implements. It is pertinent to note at this point that the wealth and complexity of a society is shown in the connectivity of the materials discovered in an archaeological investigation to its socio-cultural, political, religious and economic activities. Hence, evidence from the sites discussed above will be interpreted to show the presence of these various elements in the wealth and the complexities of living in Igbo society.

### 3.1 Socio-political Organisation

In Igbo-Ukwu, the evidence gathered suggest that the Igbo had a priestly-kingly setup that helped to organize the society. The popular interpretation about the discoveries made in Igbo-Ukwu is that the town was a burial place for the priest kings of Nri, who had burial chambers made for them containing vast amounts of 'goods' for the afterlife (Afigbo

1971; McIntosh 1999). Although such priest-kings did not have the kind of sweeping powers that their counterparts had in other parts of Nigeria, the Igbo people respected them and went as far as to honour them at death. In the case of the iron working site at Lejja, Eze-Uzomaka (2009) noted that on top of the northern edge of the slag embankment in *Otobo Dunoka* village, there is a large cylindrical slag block named *"Eze mkpume"* – king of stones. The specific slag block, according to her, cannot be touched by anyone, since it is a symbol of the authority of the ancestral father of Lejja. The taboo on touching the slag block is also an act of respect shown towards the elders. Also, the seat of the King of Lejja behind this 'king of stones' places him in an ancestral protective position over the other chiefs, as well as the rest of the people gathered in the venue (Eze-Uzomaka 2009). This evidence indicates a practice that recognizes a related kind of priestly-king like in Igbo-Ukwu. Anyone (except the three most senior elders – Eze-Lejja, Eze-Uwani and Eze-Akaibute) who wishes to speak during a meeting must move to the centre of the arena, where there are no cylindrical slag blocks to address the people.

Lejja also tells us about the social cohesive mechanism employed by the Igbo people to foster peace and unity in their communities. Lejja had a mace of authority that was used during meetings. This mace was moulded from a collection of different pieces of iron contributed from the different villages in Lejja. When the mace is old and needs to be replaced, the different villages must contribute a piece of iron each to replace it. The significance in this example from Lejja is that the villages are united through a process that produced their symbol of authority (Eze-Uzomaka 2009). So, the Igbo had respect for constituted authority and their elders. They also organised their society and gathered to deliberate on the common affairs of the communities, usually presided over by a king/chief or a priest. The Lejja iron working site and the Igbo-Ukwu sites show us that the Igbo were also able to designate areas of social, economic and political activities, culminating in a mature level of socio-political organisation as far back as 2000 BC and 9th AD respectively.

## 3.2 Survival and Settlement Pattern

From the archaeological sites in the earlier section, it is evident that ancestors of the Igbo lived in hilly or heavily forested areas. Scholars have also noted that Igbo people lived in groups and in clusters due to the dangers of living in or close to their forest environment (Afigbo 1971; Eze-Uzomaka 2009). This strategy may have led to an increase in the density of the Igbo population, making them one of the most populous ethnic groups in West Africa. In addition, the transcendence from stone tools at Ugwuelle 250,000 years ago, to the smelting of iron to fabricate tools at Lejja around 2000 BC showed a technological progression in the lives of the Igbo people. The new sophisticated iron tools not only helped them to increase their food production to nourish their growing population, but they also proved their quest for food and general survival in the forest. The invention of iron technology also helped the Igbo to clear their forested environment to gain further access to settle in the interior parts. It also enhanced their agricultural inventions, where the domestication of some species of yam is traceable to the tick forest areas of West Africa, part of which was and still being inhabited by the Igbo.

## 3.3 Agriculture and Specialisation

The archaeological sites mentioned above also show evidence of agricultural activities. The findings at all these archaeological sites included pottery, a key component of agricultural activity. Pots were used to water the crops, store seeds and cook the harvested foods. It is also known that, in the early agricultural period, iron implements contributed immensely to the improvement of planting and harvesting processes. De Barros (1985) study of the Bassar observed that the production and use of iron implements, amongst other things, "increased food production through the use of more efficient bush clearing tools, tools which permitted the clearing of forest and increased productivity in areas where stone was not readily available for stone axes". The Igbo landscape is a forest area and the availability of metal-made tools would have helped in the people's agricultural development. This is evident in the remains of extensive iron working industry scattered across Igbo villages/communities. To further demonstrate the importance of iron in agriculture, blacksmiths migrated from their villages to other towns to produce tools and implements for their farm uses.

Also, the Ugwuagu Abandoned Village site in Afikpo presents us with evidence that the Igbo were masters of sedentarism and domestication of plants and animals. The bones of domestic animals recovered, like sheep and dog as well as the presence of potsherds which resemble the "Ehugo Brown Wave" from Ukpa Rock-shelter also lent credence to this fact.

## 3.4  Affluent Economy

Undoubtedly, the way in which the priest-king found in the burial chamber at Igbo-Ukwu was buried showed affluence, luxury and enormous wealth. The burial chamber seemed extravagant but probably because there was enormous wealth from where those burial items came from. Also, the numerous pieces of evidence of domesticated animals gotten from the Ugwuagu site in Afikpo indicate that domestication was done not only for consumption purposes but also for commercial purposes and so they must have engaged in some kinds of trade and exchange of goods and services which resulted in the numerous farm implements found in the site.

Likewise, monetary affluence and an increase in the standard of living could have been some of the results of the large-scale smelting carried out in Lejja in the past. Although smelting did serve as a good source of income that led to material comfort for the smelters, Eze-Uzomaka argues that affluence or wealth was not their prime concern. She believed that the craftsmen and smelters had this "aura" around them that gave them elevated social status and a sort of "power, which bordered on the divine" (Eze-Uzomaka 2009). So, in addition to the monetary benefits, they began to see themselves as traditional custodians of power and authority, and that was more important to them. However, the iron working industries also supplied products within and outside Igbo land, and such level of trading could have provided the smelters and smiths with monetary affluence. The knowledge of iron production alone showed that the Igbo people had wealthy class of peoples. Hence, De Barros' view on the multiple-gainful effects of iron working on a society also applies to the pre-colonial Igbo iron working society. He argued that it "increased food production; increased specialisation and social differentiation, especially the formation of iron working castes or classes; larger and more stable communities due to both increased specialisation and the existence of food surpluses; increased trade due to increased specialisation; and the 'embryonic rise' of modern politics, 'the politics of class differentiation" (De Barros 1985). These explanations counters Eze-Uzomaka's point about the 'aura' of social status and 'divine powers' enjoyed by the smelters that may have obscured their interest on pursuing affluent economy. Even, the 'aura' of social status is in itself a result of affluent economy.


3.5 Religion

Some of the potsherds found at Ugwuagu had sacred paintings and engraving which also indicate a belief in supernatural. Also, the extensive iron working industry that existed in Igbo land was laced with religious practices and observances that shaped the belief system of prehistoric Igbo people. As reported in Njoku (1991), Okafor (1995) and Eze-

Uzomaka (2009), iron workers performed rituals, including offering songs, sacrifices and prayers against evil spirits that could hamper their smooth production process. They also prayed for healing when they suffered injuries or needed cures against certain illnesses. In many cases, the heart of the furnace (for smelters) or the anvil (for the smithers) was a sacred space where they would pour libations and offer sacrifices to further their requests. These are indications of a belief system that is expressed through the material culture. This reverence for supernatural beings also influenced the social and political institutions as the 'God first' ideology usually made possible through the kola nut ritual was always observed before the commencement of any event.

## 3.6 Sophisticated Technological Ingenuity

The stone tools at the Ugwuelle stone age site, the agricultural implements at the Ugwuagu abandoned village site, the bronze objects found in Igbo-Ukwu and the iron tools at the Lejja iron working site as well as other numerous supplementary tools found in association with these major materials shed light on the technological ingenuity and development of the Igbo society. Technology is the practical application of human's knowledge in order to solve problems or to adapt to a given environment. The Igbo people can be said to be very hardworking and pragmatic people who have a nature of stopping at nothing to attain self-dependency and satisfaction. Arguably, it is this technological ingenuity that spurred them onto producing indigenous wonder-ammunitions during Nigeria's civil war that lasted from 1967 to 1970.

## 4. Conclusion

In Igbo land, the basic archaeological time frame encompasses the periods from the Stone Age up to the Metal Age. In this case, the sites discussed above showed a rich progression from the Stone Ages in Ugwuelle (likened to the Acheulian culture) through the bronze working evidence in Igbo-Ukwu to the iron working sites in Lejja and Nsukka environs. These historical antecedents carry with them the evidence of religion, kingship and affluence exemplified in the Igbo-Ukwu discoveries. Also contained in the evidence is the practice of sedentarism and agricultural specialisations found in the abandoned settlement site of Ugwuagu, Afikpo. These archaeological sites shaped the history of the Igbo people as one that did not just exist in a vacuum with only myths and legends. It consolidated on the uniqueness, ingenuity and technological progression of the Igbo civilisation from over 250,000 years ago.

In summary, the study and practice of archaeology in Igbo land have helped to bring to prominence the socio-political and cultural lifestyle of the Igbo, which have inspired the interest of scholars from around the world to come to conduct more studies. However, much more investigation into the prehistoric times of the Igbo is required to situate appropriately the Igbo history in the world history and polity. There is need, therefore, for government and local communities to support more extensive archaeological investigations to augment what was done already to further consolidate the Igbo place in world history and civilisation. Particular attention needs to be paid to the study of the Nsude pyramid, which appears like an archetype of pyramids. Nsude is in the present Udi in Enugu state, where a colonial anthropologist found some sets of pyramids made of mud. Since this discovery was made, no useful research has been conducted to further examine it.

The time is now or never.

## References

Afigbo, A. E. (1971). 'On the threshold of Igbo History: Review of Thurstan Shaw's Igbo- Ukwu', *The Conch* [Special September Issue on Igbo Traditional Life, Culture and Literature], pp. 205-218.

Allsworth-Jones, P. (2015). Ugwuelle-Uturu: A Lithic Exploitation Site in South-East Nigeria. *Journal of African Archaeology*, 13(2). Retrieved from https://doi.org.10.3213/2191-5784-10274.

Anozie, F.N. (1979). Early Iron Technology in Igbo Land. *West African Journal of Archaeology*, 9, 119 – 134.

Anozie, F.N. (2002). Archaeology of Igbo land: The Early Prehistory, in G. E. K. Ofomata (Ed.), *A Survey of the Igbo Nation*. Nigeria: African First Publishers Ltd., pp. 10 - 23.

Chikwendu, V.E., (1976). *Afikpo: Excavations at Ugwuagu Rock Shelter Site (1) and Abandoned Habitation Site (2)*. [PhD Thesis], University of Birmingham. Retrieved from https://elibrary.ru/item.asp?id=7377854

Chikwendu, V. E., Craddock, P. T., Farquhar, R. M., Shaw, T. and Umeji, A. C. (1989). Nigerian Sources of Copper, Lead and Tin for The Igbo-Ukwu Bronzes. *Archaeometry*, 31 (1), 27 – 36. https://doi.org/10.1111/j.1475-4754.1989.tb01053.x

Chikwendu, V.E. (2002). Archaeology of Igbo land: The Later Prehistory, in G. E. K. Ofomata (Ed.), *A Survey of the Igbo Nation*. Nigeria: African First Publishers Ltd., pp. 24 - 38.

Craddock, P., Ambers, J., Hook, D., Farquhar, R., Chikwendu, V. Umeji, A. and Shaw, T. (1997). 'Metal Sources and the Bronzes from Igbo-Ukwu, Nigeria'. *Journal of Field Archaeology*, 24 (4), 405-429. Retrieved from https://www.jstor.org/stable/530674.

De Barros, P. (1985). *The Bassar:*

*Large–scale Iron Producers of the West African Savannah*. Michigan: University Microfilms International, Ann Arbor.

Ekechukwu, L. C. (2009). Pathways for Harnessing the Tourism Potential of Natural and Cultural Sites and Features on The Nsukka-Okigwe Cuesta. *International Journal of Research in Arts and Social Sciences*, 1, 273 – 285.

Eze-Uzomaka, P.I. (2009). Iron Age Archaeology in Lejja, Nigeria. In Pwiti, G. Radimilahy, C. and Macamo S. (eds), *Dimensions of African Archaeology: Studies in the African Past*, Vol. 7, 41 – 51. Dar es Salaam: E & D Vision Pub. Ltd.

Eze-Uzomaka, P.I. (2010). "Excavation of Amaovoko: A Further Study of the Lejja Iron Smelting Culture." In Chami, F.A. and Radimilahy, C. (eds.), *Studies in the African Past. The Journal of African Archaeology Network*, vol. 8, 178 – 191. Dar es Salaam: E & D Vision Pub. Ltd.

Eze-Uzomaka, P. I. (2018). Conceptualizing Time in Archaeology: A Study of the Igbo of Nigeria. *Advances in Sciences and Humanities*. 4 (5), 62-67. https://doi:10.11648/j.ash.20180405.11

Falola, T. (1987). *Britain and Nigeria: Exploitation or Development?* Zed Books: Great Britain.

Hartle, D. D., (1967). Archaeology of Eastern Nigeria. *Nigerian Magazine*, 8 (93), 4.

Ibeanu, A. M. (1989). Inyi: A probable centre for the Igbo-Ukwu pottery. *West African Journal of Archaeology*, 19, 137-159.

Ibeanu, A. M. (2002). Ethnoarchaeological investigations in Okigwe and its environs. *West African Journal of Archaeology*, 32 (1), 25-56.

Itanyi, E. I. and Okonkwo, E. E. (2009). *A Preliminary Report on Recent*

*Archaeological Field School on Iron Working Sites in Nsukka Plateau: Onyohor, Ekwegbe And Obimo, Nigeria.* A paper presented at the West African Archaeological Association (WAAA) Conference, Jos. 25th – 30th October, 2009.

Lasisi, O. B. (2018). *History of Archaeological Research in the Yoruba-Edo Region of Nigeria: New Directions for Urban Earthen works.* Retrieved from http://dx.doi.org/10.21220/s2-1q8z-ex71

McIntosh, S. K. (1999). Pathways to Complexity: An African Perspective. In McIntosh, S. K. (ed.), *Beyond Chiefdoms: Pathways to Complexity in Africa.* Cambridge University Press, Cambridge, pp. 1–30.

Njoku, O. N. (1991). 'Magic, Religion and Iron Technology in Precolonial North-Western Igbo land'. *Journal of Religion in Africa,* 21 (3), 194-215. Retrieved from https://www.jstor.org/stable/1580821

Ochiwar (2013). *Bronze Pot, 9th century, Igbo-Ukwu, Nigeria. [jpg].* Retrieved from https://commons.wikimedia.org/wiki/File :Bronze_pot,_9th_century,_Igbo-Ukwu,_Nigeria.jpg

Okafor, E. E. (1992). *Early Iron Smelting in Nsukka Nigeria: Information from Slags and Residues.* PhD Thesis, University of Sheffield. Retrieved from https://etheses.whiterose.ac.uk/21859/1/70095 7.pdf

Okafor, E. E. (1995). "*Twenty-Five Centuries of Bloomery Iron Smelting in Nigeria*" in Report of the First Meeting of the International Scientific Committee on UNESCOS'S IRON ROADS' Project for Africa; held at the International Conference Centre, Abuja, Nigeria; 23rd-27th February; pp. 75-83.

Okafor, E. E. (1997). "Identification and Composition of Bloomery Slags", *West*

*African Journal of Archaeology,* 27 (2), 32-53.

Okafor, E. E. (1999). "The Relevance of Ethnography for Archaeological Investigation". *International Journal of the Humanities,* 1 & 2, 300-306.

Okonkwo, E. E. and Ibeanu, A.M. (2016). Nigeria's Archaeological Heritage: Resource Exploitation and Technology. *SAGE Open,* 1–7. https://doi.org/10.1177/2158244016651 111.

Okonkwo, E. E. and Ikegwu, J. (2020). A study of Ozizza archaeological and ethnographical sites and features in Ebonyi state of Nigeria: research methodological discussion. *Heliyon,* 6, 1 – 9. Retrieved from https://doi.org/10.1016/j.heliyon.2020.e 03583.

Okpoko, A. I. (1987). Pottery-Making in Igbo land, Eastern Nigeria. *Proceedings of the Prehistoric Society,* 53, 445-455.

Okpoko, P.U, Okonkwo, E. E, and Eyisi, A. P. (2016). Preliminary Study of Affia Cave, Waterfall and Natural Bridge in Okpatu, Enugu State. *Journal of Tourism and Heritage Studies,* 5 (1 & 2), 50 – 63.

Shaw, T. (1970). *Igbo-Ukwu: An Account of Archeological Discoveries,* (I & II). London: Faber and Faber.

Shaw, T. (1975). Those Igbo-Ukwu Radiocarbon Dates: Facts, Fictions and Probabilities. *The Journal of African History,* 16 (4), 503 – 517. Retrieved from http://www.jstor.org/stable/180494

The Telegraph (2013). *Professor Thurstan Shaw,* 31 March. https://www.telegraph.co.uk/news/obitu aries/culture-obituaries/9964085/Professor-Thurstan-Shaw.html

# CHAPTER 2

ONWUKA N. NJOKU

# Igbo Land In The Modern Era: 1900-1970

## CHAPTER OVERVIEW

## Summary

*The 20th century dawned on the Igbo with the British colonization of their fatherland, by armed conquest. That event marked the process of bringing Igbo land to the threshold of modernity. It introduced many fundamental changes, some positive; others, negative, in the way the Igbo had lived their lives and conducted their affairs culturally, socially, economically and politically, over several millennia. However, although the changes have turned out to be pervasive and in most instances far reaching, they have not obliterated the core of traditional Igbo way of life. Rather, Igbo political, social, cultural and economic systems have demonstrated remarkable resilience.*

## 1. Introduction

**W**ITH THE FORCEFUL ADVENT OF COLONIAL RULE, the Igbo people's pre-colonial system of doing things could no longer hold intact; a fact embodied in Chinua Achebe's *Things Fall Apart* and *No Longer at Ease*. Nevertheless, the Igbo have been able to blend some aspects of their culture with imported vogues that began with British colonial rule, up to this era of globalization. The rest of this chapter discusses this by first giving a brief overview of the Pre-Modern Era of Igbo land. This is followed by a discussion of the Modern Era and the Independence Era up to the Civil War.  ⌐

## 2. The Pre-Modern Backdrop

The pre-modern Igbo society was essentially rural and agrarian, and every Igbo household engaged in farming, if not full time, at least part-time. Children acquired knowledge and skills from their parents, older relations and the wider society. Moonlight tales relayed instructive historical, ethical and motivational homilies to the young ones. In the process, they became educated and rooted in the 'dos' and 'don'ts' of their community, and participated in various aspects of community affairs, from childhood to old age. The threads that held this traditional society together was personal hard work that was beneficial to the community.

The Igbo did not have large centralized kingdoms in which power and authority resided in a powerful individual, as was the case in Benin, Igala and Yoruba kingdoms, for instance. Rather, Igbo polities were essentially village democracies or republics; the highest level of effective administrative and political arrangement being the village or the village group, composed of people with or claiming a common paternal ancestry. Rulership resided in a council of elders who made administrative and policy decisions based on consensus; the head of the council being virtually, first among equals. Even in the few kingships, such as Onitsha, Nri and Arochukwu, the king was never an autocrat, as Chieka Ifemesia

(1979) has emphasized. He ruled with his council of elders, each of whom represented a section of the village. However, although governance was in their hands, the elders brought matters of grave public concern before the general assembly of the village, where every freeborn citizen had the right to speak out their minds. Final decisions on such matters were based on the balance of popular opinion. Thus, the system combined gerontocracy (leadership by elders) with popular democratic participation of younger citizens.

Traditional Igbo were, as they still are, an achieving society, in which a person's standing in his community derived from material achievement, made according to socially approved norms. Such achievement enabled a person to buy membership of leading title societies in his community, such as *ozo* (*nze*) and *ogbu enyinya*. Achievers became *ogaranya* and sometimes, *ọnụ na-ekwuruọha;*'the mouth(piece) of the community', too. The titleholder enjoyed social respect far beyond the dreams of ordinary citizens. For this reason, society emphasized hard work among men, women, and even children; indolence attracted derogatory comments and taunts. Olaudah Equiano (1969:8) pointed out in the 18th century that his people were so habituated to work, "we have no beggars". Thus, *Ikenga*, the Igbo god of enterprise, was one of the most highly revered deities.

Although the society was male dominated, women had their own areas of political and economic authority, distinct from that of the men. Enterprising women, like *Omu Okwei: the Merchant Queen of Ossomari* (Ekejiuba,1967:366-643), achieved *ogaranya* status and recognition, appropriate to their achievements. Hardworking women and girls were the targets of suitors; indolent ones had difficulty attracting suitors, except the dreg among men. Thus, although people were assumed to be born equal, in reality they died unequal through hard work or indolence.

The central point in the foregoing prefatory presentation is that Igbo philosophy abhors inherited social ascription; rather, it emphasizes personal striving and achievement. However, individual person's achievements had to have beneficial effects on society as a whole.

## 3. The Modern Era

From around 1900 to September 30, 1960, Igboland was under British colonial rule, imposed by force of arms or threat of its use, in some instances. Igbo communities' resistance against the invaders failed because the latter had superior military weaponry. The military conquest of Nigeria by Britain had a purely economic motive: to make the territory a source of raw materials for British industries and an assured market for the sale of their industrial products. The center-periphery theory underlay the colonizers' development policies and projects; in other words, British interest came first in official development calculations; those of the colonized were peripheral (Njoku, 2001:190-194). To achieve this principal objective of colonizing Igbo land, the colonial rulers needed to introduce fundamental changes in Igbo land. These included an effective administrative system and essential infrastructure, and Western

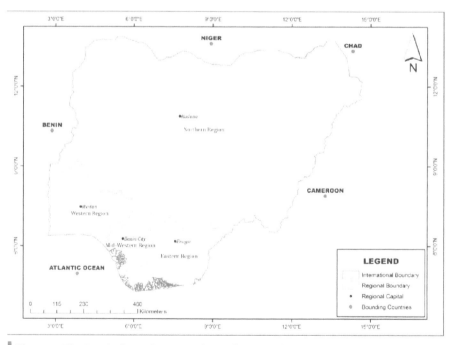

*Figure 1. The Pre-Independence Regions of Nigeria in 1954*

education. In the process of undergoing these changes, the traditional Igbo society was affected in many profound and, in some cases, permanent ways. I shall sketch the above infrastructure and thereafter consider their overall impact on modern day Igbo people up to the end of the Nigeria-Biafra War in January 1970.

## 3.1 Colonial Infrastructure

### 3.1.1 Colonial Administration:

An immediate priority of the colonial rulers was to introduce British system of administration, law and order. To this end, they established instruments with which to command the submission and obedience of the people, namely; an army, a police force, a prisons department and a judiciary.

The colonial army emerged from the British West Africa Frontier Force, formed during the period of the European powers' scramble for African territories. The colonial army, using sophisticated weaponry, subdued resistant Igbo communities; the police arrested law offenders; the courts sentenced convicts to prison and the police enforced the colonial system of law and order. In fact, during the early years of colonial rule, the army was busy subduing resisting communities, patrolling uneasy districts; with the police quelling disturbances intermittently here and there.

Shortage of work force and finance made the colonial authorities use, at the local level, some existing traditional institutions and persons to consolidate their control of Igbo land. This system has gone down in history as "indirect rule", especially after Lord Frederick Lugard became the Governor of the entire colony of Nigeria in 1914. Ruling the people through their own traditional institutions and agencies aimed to serve two principal purposes. First, it would mellow the people's opposition to foreign rule, as the local office holders would mediate relations between their people and the foreign rulers. Second, it would save cost because emoluments of local personnel, such as chiefs and other low-level local employees were far lower than were those of European staff.

Against this backdrop, the administration established a local administrative system anchored on Native Courts (NCs). By the Native Court Proclamations of 1900 and 1901, the administration grouped contiguous communities, it perceived to have historical and cultural affinities, into administrative units known as Native Court Areas (NCAs). It appointed some indigenes into each NC and gave them authority ('warrant', hence 'Warrant Chiefs') to perform, on its behalf, legislative, judicial and executive functions, over their given areas of jurisdiction. The powers of the NCs over such areas went beyond what the Igbo had ever experienced in their remembered history. The Warrant Chiefs (WCs) were accountable to the White District Officers; not to their communities. As long as the WCs remained in the good books of the D.O., their position was secure. To be in the good books of the colonial authorities invariably translated to being in the bad books of the local community. This was the case because the WCs ruled in disregard of the traditional institutions of governance, such as the village council of elders and the village assembly.

Interestingly, the appointments of the WCs followed no rational order. Most communities pushed forward for appointment as WCs people considered as expendable; some were of inferior status. Some were appointed WCs because of their commanding physical appearance or because they welcomed the British invaders while the traditional dignitaries were in hiding. When an appointee returned to his community with a piece of paper (warrant/authoity) to rule over his traditional superiors, in complete disregard of the centuries-old democratic participatory system, there was general outrage.

The WCs flagrantly abused and exploited their people and enriched themselves through extortions, bribery and use of public labor for their personal works. NC clerks and court messengers added to the misery of the locals; they too used their positions to exploit their helpless people.

Thus, in carrying out the orders of their colonial masters, the WCs became ready instruments that assaulted their own people's cherished collective heritage, such as sacred places, which tradition expected them to defend and preserve. Not surprisingly, the people saw and loathed the NCs and the WCs, as instruments and symbols of foreign oppression and exploitation.

The people's accumulated hatred blew up in the open in the Aba Women's Rebellion of 1929-1930. In 1926, had government conducted a census of men and followed this up with the introduction of direct taxation on men in 1927. In 1928, the administration embarked on another census, conducted under the supervision of WCs, which included the counting of women. Rumors went viral that government was preparing to tax women. The upshot was the Women's Rebellion, which targeted Native Court buildings, WCs and expatriate trading stores for attacks. The Great Depression of the late 1920s-30s, which was marked by continuing drop in the prices of exports (palm oil and palm kernel) against escalating prices of imports, contributed to the tension.

The administration responded by modifying the WC system in the hope of making it acceptable to local conditions. However, attempts to fish out and use elders of appropriate traditional standing failed because such elders were often too old to perform the roles the colonial authorities required of them. Besides, the system sidelined swelling ranks of educated elite, who were clamoring for radical administrative change. As Kirk-Greene (1965:xii) states, accumulated experience had shown that Lugard's indirect rule model was wholly unsuited to African conditions, outside Hausa land.

### 3.1.2 Transport Revolution

The colonial government was aware of the inadequacies of the existing modes of transportation based on human carriage and paddled canoes, in some riverine areas. For the army, the police and the administration in general to operate effectively, modern transportation was a prime necessity. Troops needed to move quickly to areas of turbulence. It was also necessary to link administrative centers together for effective monitoring and control of many communities, which were still restive. This need had become glaring during the conquest period, when the colonial troops had to trudge from one village to the next, in the effort to subdue each one of them. Modern transportation was equally critical in stimulating the production and evacuation of export produce and importation of foreign goods; the principal rationale for colonizing the territory.

The administration started by clearing snags to traffic on navigable waterways that linked the coast to riverine communities inland; for instance, the River Niger, Imo River and Ossomari River. On these rivers, government and some expatriate trading firms, such as the United Africa Company (UAC) and the Elder Dempster Shipping Company, introduced launches to ferry passengers and haul both imports and exports. European firms that had stagnated on the coast, started moving inland and establishing trading depots at Onitsha, Oguta, Asaba and Unwana beaches. Gradually, the stations developed into centers of commerce between the expatriate trading firms and the communities and their neighborhoods. However, the catchment areas of the rivers did not extend to many distant inland areas, where the bulk of Igbo population lived. Introducing rail and vehicular transportation became an absolute necessity.

The first significant effort to modernize transportation in Igbo land came by way of railway construction along with the introduction of train service. Locomotive railway transportation ("the iron horse") had already demonstrated its capacity to transform rural and intermediate economies in the Americas, Australia and parts of Asia. The first railway in Nigeria started construction in 1898, from Iddo, in Lagos, through Yoruba land and got to Kano in 1912. The Lagos-Kano rail transportation stimulated massive burst of groundnuts and cocoa exports from Northern

Nigeria and Yoruba land, respectively. The administration expected a similar export burst in the East. The justification for constructing a railway in the East became most compelling with the discovery of coal in 1909 at Udi, in the northern part of Igboland. Coal was, at the time, the primary source of power generation, especially important because the Udi coal deposit was the only source of such power generation in British West Africa. Coal for running the locomotives and other power plants in Nigeria came from Britain, at exorbitant costs and risks. With the possibility of a World War growing fast, the strategic importance of the local source became increasingly compelling. How to access the resource, which lay far away from the coast, was a knotty problem. The answer lay in accessing the deposits by rail from the coast. This problem impelled a search for a deep-sea harbor where ocean liners could berth. The search discovered Diobu (Port Harcourt) to have a suitable deep-sea harbor. This discovery triggered frantic construction in 1909 of what became the Port Harcourt - Enugu railway, which got to the coal mines in1914, the year WW1 commenced. The line was extended after that war to the North where it linked up with the Western line in Kaduna.

Many European trading firms quickly followed the railway from the coast inland and established trading beaches at Aba, Umuahia, Uzuakoli, Agbani and Enugu. The beaches in time became focal points of European-Igbo commercial intercourse and nuclei of incipient urbanization. However, the single-track rail line left many areas of Igbo land outside the emerging Igbo-European trade nexus. The advent of motor vehicular transportation from the 1920s, made up for this deficiency. Road building was far less costly and required much less technical expertise than railway construction did. Unlike rail transportation, which was rigid, road transportation was flexible and connected disparate and remote communities all over Igbo land. The Public Works Department built the roads on the cheap; by merely widening existing footpaths. The early roads at first aimed to connect the headquarters of the various levels of the administrative structure. District Officers and Provincial Commissioners were eager to link with motor roads their administrative headquarters to the major communities under their charge.

Competition between provinces and divisions in this endeavor resulted in fast increase in the number and mileage of roads pliable by motor vehicles, though most of the roads were very bumpy and hardly pliable during the rains. True to Igbo communal competitive character, once a village was linked up with a motor road, their neighbors responded by constructing their own to link up with others, so as not to be put in the shade. With time, many areas became accessible by motorized road transportation. By the end of the colonial era, a substantial number of communities were accessible by road transportation.

It is instructive that Igbo entrepreneurs pioneered commercial motor transportation in Igbo land. In those early days, expatriate firms believed that commercial road transportation had little future because of the poor quality of the roads and because the vehicles that plied them were very heavy and frequently broke down. Igbo entrepreneurs proved their thinking wrong. Many Igbo pioneer commercial motor transporters were hugely successful; for instance, Sir Louis Odumegwu Ojukwu, Chidi Ebere, Ekene Dili Chukwu and P.N.C. Emera, among others.

To ease commercial activities, the administration introduced a portable currency of different denominations, based on the British pound sterling, and made it legal tender. Pre-existing heavy commodity currencies, such as manilas, copper rods and cowries, prevalent in various parts of Igbo land, were demonetized. Modern banking was also introduced to promote economic activity. The first of them was the Bank of British West Africa in 1894 (now First Bank of Nigeria), followed by Barclays Bank (1926). The early banks were all European-owned, and discriminated against African businesses in their loan policy. In response, some African entrepreneurs established their own banks in the 1920s - 30s. Most of the banks collapsed, in part, because of the severe global economic depression of the period. With returning prosperity and increasing nationalist movements after WW11; many indigenous banks appeared, among them, the African Continental Bank, founded by Dr. Nnamdi Azikiwe (1948).

### 3.1.3 Colonial Education: Church and School.

The colonial rulers saw western education as the most effective and lasting instrument to entrench their rule in Nigeria, particularly by fostering modern local elite. It was important that the colonized learned to speak the language of their 'masters' and serve in various administrative positions, like the judiciary, prisons, railways, customs and as clerks in commercial firms and teachers in Christian mission schools. Christian missions pioneered western education in Igbo land. Accordingly, during the colonial years, church and school were one, Siamese-like. Every person that went to a Christian mission school became inevitably a Christian. Thus, the Christian missions served as the spiritual wing of British imperialism. Mission schools aimed principally to produce people literate enough to read the Scriptures and perform clerkly jobs in government and commercial firms. Pupils were taught British history by rote but not their own society and environment. Thus, the system was externalist in orientation and trained pupils away from, rather than into, their community and culture.

In fact, the Christian missions came to Igbo land with a fixed notion of the superiority of their religion and culture to that of the Igbo. They perceived Igbo society as drenched in paganism and ignorance, and assumed that it was their manifest responsibility to rescue the presumed benighted people from their supposed ignorance. Thus, they condemned, without reservations, most Igbo traditional practices, and sought to replace them with their own. In a couple of cases, such as the mistreatment of twin babies and mothers, their concern and actions were in order and commendable. In most other cases, they over-reached in their snobbish attitude and actions towards Igbo social and cultural practices, such as polygamy, ancestor worship, title and secret societies and new yam festivals.

As would be expected, initially, the cream of traditional elite, such as titled men and culture custodians, strongly opposed the Christian missions and western education. However, after the initial resistance and rebuff, Igbo people in general embraced Western schooling with characteristic competitive zeal. This was for rational reasons. In the emerging colonial dispensation, western education was becoming the gateway to the future. Igbo youth, who had acquired some modicum of western literacy, were getting respectable jobs, as mission schoolteachers, court clerks, produce inspectors and employees of expatriate firms. They were getting generally richer, more influential and knowledgeable of the world beyond Igbo land than the traditional elite who had not acquired the mystery of writing and speaking the white man's language.

## 3.2 The Impact of the Colonial Infrastructure

The foregoing developments produced important economic, social and political spin-offs, most of which are still with the Igbo until date. These spin-offs are examined below.

### 3.2.1 Economic and Social Spin-offs

The Port Harcourt-Enugu railway crossed parts of the richest oil palm belt in Nigeria and triggered massive export of palm produce almost instantly. The growth of trade at Umuahia station typifies the general trend of what was happening in the other towns on the railway. Before the railway went through Umuahia and its vicinity, the area had not exported palm produce. Within two years of the arrival of the railway, no less than eight European firms had established trading depots there. In the first half of 1918, the firms had bought a total of 5,240 casks of palm oil and 2,169 tons of palm kernels (Njoku,1983/84:36-53). The motor roads and the railway inter-linked and drew many communities into the widening areas of import-export commerce. Within two decades, the Eastern Region became one of the leading exporters of palm produce in the world. However, colonial government's emphasis on export crop production in time started the process of undermining domestic food security of Nigeria, which became troubling from the 1970s.

The railway and the Colliery at Enugu intertwined, too. The construction of the railway drew many Igbo young men into the labor sector of the emerging colonial economy. The coal mining industry had a similar effect of drawing many young Igbo men from the rural areas to the mines. Soon Enugu would emerge as the capital of the Eastern Provinces of Nigeria, with a fast growing urban population. Over time, more roads continued building and bringing more remote communities into the widening frontiers of business.

The new modes of transportation facilitated free movement of passengers, increased the volumes of traded goods and intensified social and commercial engagements not only within Igbo land but also in other parts of Nigeria. The first urban centers were sprouting up at railway-road intersections and waterfronts at Aba, Enugu ('the Coal City'), Onitsha, Port Harcourt and Umuahia. The emerging urban centers, in turn, were transforming into melting pots of cultures (Igbo and non-Igbo), ideas and skills as well as the frontier of economic opportunities. Expectedly, they started to attract droves of young people from the rural farming communities, in various parts of Igbo land and beyond.

Rural-urban migrant Igbo, some of them proficient metal artisans from Awka, Abiriba and Nkwere, went far beyond Igbo land to the other regions of Nigeria, as modern means of transportation expanded. By the late 1930s-40s, a substantial population of Igbo migrants had emerged in every urban center of some size in Nigeria, including Jos, Lagos, Ibadan, Warri, Kano, Maiduguri and Sokoto, to mention only these few. In 1936, Governor Bourdillon (NAE,1939) observed that

> *...the Ibo seems to have a special aptitude for handicraft. Wherever I go, whether next-door into the Ibibio country or west to Ondo or north to the tin mines, I find the Ibo artisans holding the majority of the skilled artisan jobs...*

After WW II, the tempo of Igbo migration to various towns in Nigeria increased markedly. In 1950, the Igbo constituted 12% of the total population of Lagos; and the city had eight times more Igbo policemen than Yoruba (Lloyd, 1972:111). Not all Igbo migrants took to cities. Some went to export crop-producing areas in Ondo, Benin, Tivland, Ikom and Ogoja.

The urban immigrants, particularly to the big cities, faced the problem of adjusting to life in a multi-cultural and multi-ethnic setting. This problem led to the birth of Igbo village, town and clan unions, for solidarity, for which Igbo people are well known today. Diaspora Igbo initiated town and divisional development unions through which they introduced in their natal communities social amenities and infrastructure available in the cities. Thanks to such unions, many communities in Igbo land today enjoy paved roads, schools, health centers, community halls, potable water and electricity; provided through self-help efforts. In addition, through mingling with other Nigerian nationalities of different backgrounds, Igbo city dwellers adjusted their own traditional social and cultural dispositions, to blend with the norms and values of urban life. Because of their tradition of self-actualization through hard work, many Igbo in Diasporas, often from inauspicious beginnings, were hugely successful in various areas of endeavor (Ajaegbo, 2013:162-174). Unfortunately, their successes sometimes made them targets of ethnic hate attacks by some other less enterprising Nigerian ethnic groups.

The fore-going emerging socioeconomic scenario had its negative aftermath, among the Igbo, especially early in the colonial years. While western education and Christianity brought the Igbo to the threshold of the modern world, they also created intense socio-cultural tension between the Christian converts and adherents of the religion of their fathers. Often, the new converts over-reached in their zeal for their new faith and flagrantly desecrated sacred places and disrupted traditional events that had nothing fetish about them. In 1915, some Christian fanatics rampaged through many parts of Igbo land destroying many excellent traditional works of art, including such precious murals as *mbari* art. In the evolving contests, the traditionalists were on the losing side because the missionaries had the tacit support of the colonial authorities. The upshot of the emerging scenario was the unrelenting erosion of some core aspects of Igbo culture and worldview; for instance, acquisition of material wealth through questionable means and declining ability of many a' modern' Igbo to speak Igbo, their ancestral language.

A good part of the problem emanated from the colonial education system, which was clerical and mimetic, and created no links with traditional skills and modern occupations. Rather, it trained its recipients essentially for clerkly jobs in government, foreign firms and Christian mission establishments. Thus, the system tended to set the recipients against their roots. Many dropped their indigenous names, loaded with meanings and rich in history, in favor of English or Biblical names, whose meanings they did not know. Not surprisingly, colonial education neglected completely Igbo history and culture studies. Rev. G.T. Basden (1921:90) observed, "Many an Igbo modern youth knows more English history than that of his own country". Anne Leith-Ross (1939:54), some years later lamented, though with some exaggeration, that "Igbo youths are prepared to have no past as long as they can have a future". The outcome of this trend was unpalatable. Some products of the mission schools began to see their own society from the European perspective; believing that to be modern, one had to abandon one's native roots and embrace the western way of life. However, those who attempted to do so, became persons of two worlds, none of which they truly belonged (Okafor-Omali, 1965:87).

Of course, many other products of the system dissented from the White attitude towards indigenous Igbo cultural and social practices. As Simon Ottenberg thoughtfully observed, although the Igbo may seem to have changed the most, among Nigerian ethnic nationalities; they have changed the least in many particulars (in Russell and Herskovits, 1959). Alvan Ikoku dissented from the religious fixation of the missionaries and established Aggrey Memorial College at Arochukwu. Kenneth O. Dike, an eminent Igbo historian of world renown, pioneered the writing and teaching of Nigerian history from the internal, rather than the external perspective. He set the pace for succeeding Nigerian historians (Igbo and others), to teach and write Nigerian as well as Igbo history from the perspective of the people in focus. Indeed, Dike's school of historiography serves as the holy grail of the discipline, not just in Nigeria but also all through Africa and the Western world. The products of his endeavor are countless and include the best minds in Nigerian history in universities across the globe. Among them, we may mention only a handful: Professors Abdullahi Smith, Ade Ajayi, Adiele Afigbo, Ebiegberi Alagoa, Emmanuel Ayandele, Geoffrey Nwaka, Okon Uya, Toyin Falola, Victor Uchendu and Walter Ofonagoro.

In the import-export trade, European firms were the dominant players. This was because, unlike their Igbo counterparts, they had the advantages of a strong capital base, being limited liability companies with international connections, and tacit collusion among themselves. For these reasons, they were able to dictate the prices of imports as well as exports to their own advantage. All the same, Igbo intermediaries played a central role, which the expatriate companies could not, in the import-export trade arrangement. On the one hand, the intermediaries combed remote communities where they purchased export produce in tiny quantities from peasant farmers. They bulked the produce in sizable quantities, and sold them to the expatriate firms, stationed at the major trading stations. On the other hand, expatriate firms imported manufactured goods in bulks and broke them down into sizable amounts for sale to the intermediate local traders. The intermediaries purchased the goods from expatriate firms and further broke them down into tiny bits, to meet the low purchasing power of the average consumer.

In time, though, some very enterprising Igbo businesspersons broke through the European cartels and became major importers and exporters. Thus, while colonial rule subverted indigenous Igbo economy in some significant respects, it also opened up to the Igbo, commercial opportunities that they quickly seized. Their culture of competitive entrepreneurship equipped them to exploit the commercial opportunities which colonial economy offered. In the area of modern business, Sir Louis Odumegwu Ojukwu, father of Odumegwu Ojukwu, IkembaNnewi, provides a shining example. He started commercial vehicle business (Ojukwu Transport), with a used vehicle. He subsequently established Ojukwu Stores and Ojukwu Textiles in the 1930s. By the close of colonial rule, he was already a multi-millionaire and the richest Nigerian at the time. At his death in 1966, he was the first Nigerian billionaire. Women have left their own imprints on the commercial arena. For instance, Omu Okwei of Osomari (born in 1872) started petty trading in export produce and imported goods on the Niger in the closing years of the 19th century. In the 1920s, she was diversifying investment in lorries and canoes, cash advances to other traders and landed property. At her death in 1943, she left a substantial fortune which included lorries and canoes, 24 houses in Onitsha and a substantial amount of money in the bank.(Hopkins,1973;205)

The same Igbo drive for achievement, manifested in their quest for western education. Although the Igbo were somewhat late comers to Western literacy, compared to the Efik and the Yoruba, for instance, they rapidly measured up. By the close of colonial rule, they had produced a glittering array of erudite scholars and education administrators. Only a handful of them may be listed here: Akanu Ibiam, Medical practitioner and first African Principal of the prestigious *Hope Waddell Training Institution*, Calabar; Alvan Ikoku, founder, *Aggrey Memorial College*, Arochukwu; Chinua Achebe, African literature guru and novelist; Eni Njoku, first African Vice Chancellor of both *University of Lagos* (1962-9165) and *University of Nigeria*, Nsukka(UNN) (1966-1970); Kenneth Onwuka Dike, first African Vice Chancellor of *University of Ibadan* and pioneer of the *Ibadan School of History*; James Ezeilo, Vice Chancellor,

UNN., Nnamdi Azikiwe, founder of UNN; the first autonomous degree awarding institution in Nigeria.

## 3.2.2 Political Impact

Colonialism presented the Igbo with a new political experience. The emerging system had little scope for the traditional elite with mostly native wisdom. The demarcation of Igbo land into administrative districts, divisions and provinces, was an entirely new experience and challenged the Igbo to adjust to the evolving administrative and political reality. For the first time in their known history, traditionally autonomous communities had been merged into administrative and political units. The Igbo responded to the colonial administrative arrangement by forming District and Provincial Improvement or Development Unions; such as Mbano, Mbaise and Mbaitolu (federated) Unions. In the 1930s, two all-Igbo unions had emerged; one at Port Harcourt and the other, Lagos. Later, the federated unions would become platforms for political and social mobilization of Igbo people. Educated Igbo elite began to develop political consciousness and co-operation that transcended traditional village arrangements. Marginalized by the indirect rule system, these elite began to criticize political, economic and social injustices inherent in colonial rule. They played frontline roles in national agitations for independence, with the *National Council of Nigeria and the Cameroons* (NCNC) as their favored party and Dr. Azikiwe, the party's leader, after the demise of Albert Macaulay. Zik, as he was fondly known, used his newspaper media to attack relentlessly the colonial government's exploitative policies. Unlike the Action Group (AG) and the Northern People's Congress (NPC), which were essentially regional parties, the NCNC had national spread. The party won the Western regional election of 1951. However, carpet crossing to AG by Yoruba members of the NCNC ensured the AG, not the NCNC, formed the regional government. That action solidly enthroned ethnicity as a manipulative tool in Nigerian politics. ∎

## 4. The Independence Era to 1970

On October 01, 1960, Nigeria became an independent country. Her prospects of becoming a strong economic and political power appeared bright. Sadly, barely five years on, she was in political chaos, resulting from a chain of events rooted in ethnic and regional politics. These included manipulated national census figures in favor of the North, massive nationwide election rigging and wanton destruction of lives and property in Western Nigeria, which led the federal government to impose a state of emergency there. To salvage the country from imminent collapse, on 15 January 1966, a group of young army officers, led by Chukwuma Kaduna Nzeogu, fired by patriotic zeal, toppled the government of AlhajiTafawa Balewa. The coup was welcomed all over Nigeria as very timely. Shortly after the euphoria, Northern political leaders started branding it as an Igbo coup. They contrived a 'revenge' coup, which toppled the Aguiyi Ironsi military government in July 1966. Since then, northern military officers have staged all the nine military coups in the country from July 1966 to 1993. Nobody has called any of them Northern Nigeria or Hausa-Fulani coup.

The July 1966 coup generated rounds of horrible massacres of thousands of innocent civilians of Eastern Nigeria origin, especially the Igbo, in the North. The atrocities happened with seeming connivance of the Federal Military Government (FMG) headed by General Yakubu Gowon. The Igbo had no choice but to flee for safety to their Eastern Nigeria homeland, where Lt. Col. Odumegwu Ojukwu was military Governor. The FMG hastily divided Nigeria into 12 states, three of them in Eastern Nigeria; namely, East Central, Southeast and Rivers States. The aim was to create division among Easterners.

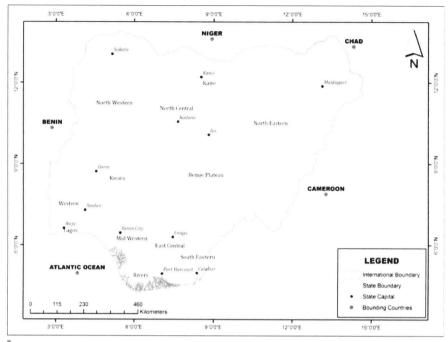

| Figure 2. The Twelve States of Nigeria in 1967

The President of Ghana stepped into the brawl and at Aburi, Ghana, brokered a peace agreement between the FMG and the Government of Eastern Nigeria. Surprisingly, Gowon later repudiated the Aburi agreement to which he had put his signature. Fearing for their safety in the Nigerian federation, where they had been mercilessly slaughtered in large numbers without FMG intervention, Eastern Nigerians decided to secede from Nigeria, declaring their region as the Republic of Biafra (ROB) in May 1967. The FMG responded by declaring was on nascent ROB. In July the Nigeria–Biafra war began.

The odds against ROB were awesome: Nigeria, with a huge population and landmass, a long-standing military force, had the full backing of Britain, Russia and the USA. On the other hand, the ROB army was very poorly equipped. Not surprisingly, Gowon boasted that Nigeria would run over ROB in a few short months. He was grossly mistaken.

The President of Ghana stepped into the brawl and at Aburi, Ghana, brokered a peace agreement between the FMG and the Government of Eastern Nigeria. Surprisingly, Gowon later repudiated the Aburi agreement to which he had put his signature. Fearing for their safety in the Nigerian federation, where they had been mercilessly slaughtered in large numbers without FMG intervention, Eastern Nigerians decided to secede from Nigeria, declaring their region as the Republic of Biafra (ROB) in May 1967. The FMG responded by declaring was on nascent ROB. In July the Nigeria–Biafra war began.

The odds against ROB were awesome: Nigeria, with a huge population and landmass, a long-standing military force, had the full backing of Britain, Russia and the USA. On the other hand, the ROB army was very poorly equipped. Not surprisingly, Gowon boasted that Nigeria would run over ROB in a few short months. He was grossly mistaken.

What ROB lacked in population, territorial size, weaponry and foreign power backing, she made up in the Biafran spirit. By this is meant the determination of the Igbo to fight to the last, the commitment of the military leadership to the war and, most importantly, in the marvel of their scientific and technological ingenuity. Cordoned off by Nigeria from external contacts, Biafra recoiled to herself and marveled the world in startling technological inventions; such as command detonators, rocket propelled missiles (*ogbunigwe*), armored vehicles and shore batteries; crude oil refining and construction of airplane runways. In all these respects, Nigeria was no match to ROB. The ROB military scored telling victories against Nigerian forces that sent shivers down the spines of their military and political leadership.

Nigeria resorted to indiscriminate tactics that ignored the Geneva Convention on military engagement. Her warplanes bombed obvious civilian targets, such as markets, churches, hospitals, refugee camps and farms. She barred international humanitarian organizations from giving relief materials in aid of millions of starving Biafrans. In the heat of the war, Chief Obafemi Awolowo, civilian Deputy to Gowon's military council, justified hunger as a legitimate weapon of war. Towards late 1969, the situation was desperate. Biafra was losing more lives to diseases, hunger and starvation than to the shooting war. It made absolute sense to end the war, bearing in mind that one who fights and tactically pulls back, lives to fight another time, when conditions are favorable. Accordingly, the Biafran leader, General Ojukwu, flew out of ROB, making way for the cessation of war. Thus, on 15 January 1970, General Philip Effiong, Biafra's Chief of General Staff, presented to General Gowon, ROB's document of surrender. That ended the war, after 30 months of bitter fighting and carnage. Igbo land was a pathetic wreck from material and human perspectives. Over two million Igbo lives had been lost to the war; hundreds of thousands were homeless; many were maimed.

On accepting the document of BOF's surrender from General Effiong, General Gowon announced that the war produced 'No Victor, No Vanquished'. He assured the world that there would be no retribution against former secessionists; and that all Nigerians could live and work freely wherever they chose in the country, as equal citizens under the law. Before then, the FMG had already constituted the National Committee on Reconstruction, Rehabilitation and Reintegration (the 3Rs), with the aim of bringing back the former secessionists to the mainstream of Nigeria's economic, social and political life, and thereby erase the scars of the war. Gowon's reassuring pronouncements received popular endorsements from many quarters. A news media likened him to Abraham Lincoln, the 16th President of the USA, who led his nation through her civil war, 1861-1865 (Njoku in Uzoigwe, 2000).

Sadly, Gowon's policies and actions soon showed that his seeming candor was mere window dressing. As it has turned out, all post-war Nigerian governments – civilian and military - not least of them the current one, seem to have forgotten nothing about the war and learned nothing from it. Rather pre-war and wartime prejudices against the Igbo have increasingly stiffened. The wounds of the war, rather than healing, are putrefying with the passage of time and infesting Nigeria with inflammable canisters.

# References

Ajaegbo, D.I; "Road Transport Entrepreneurs and Road Transport Revolution in Igbo land, 1920-1999". *African Research Review*; vol.7(4); Sept;2013:162-173

Basden, G.T. *Among the Ibos of Nigeria*.Philadelphia:J.B.Lippincott,1921: 90

Bourdillon, H.B. (Governor), "Industrial Education in Nigeria, 1936". National Archives Enugu, 30 April, 1936. Rivprof. 9/1/416.

Ekejiuba, F. I., "Omu Okwei, The Merchant Queen of Ossomari: A Biographical Sketch". *Journal of the Historical Society of Nigeria,*111, 4(1967)

Edward, Paul (ed.), *Equiano's Travels*. London: Heinemann Books (2$^{nd}$ impression), 1969:8

Hopkins, A.G., *An Economic History of West Africa*. London: Longman Group Ltd;1973:205
Ifemesia, C.C; *Traditional Humane Living Among the Igbo*. Enugu: Fourth Dimension Publishers (1979).
Kirk-Green, A.H.M., *The Principles of Native Administration in Nigeria: Selected Documents,1900-1947.*London:Oxford University Press,1965.:xii

Leith-Ross, Sylvia, *African Women: A Study of Ibo Women of Nigeria*. London: Routledge and Kegan Paul.1939.

Lloyd, P.C; *Africa in Social Change: Changing Traditional Societies in the Modern World*. Harmondsworth: Penguin Books Ltd;(1972):111

Njoku, O. N., "Development of Roads and Road Transportation in Southeastern Nigeria,1903-1939".*Journal of African Studies*[UCLA] vol5,No4(1978).

Njoku, "*Pattern of Moving Traders' Frontier in Eastern Nigeria, 1901-1939"*. *The African Historian*, vol.x (1983/84) 36-53

Njoku, "Era of Misguided Good Feeling: Yakubu Gowon and the Birth of a New Nigeria". In L.A. Nwachukwu and G.N.Uzoigwe (eds.), *Troubled Journey: Nigeria Since the Civil War*. Dallas: University Press of America (2000): Chapter 2.

Njoku, *Economic History of Nigeria, 19$^{th}$-21 Centuries*. Nsukka: Great AP Express Publishers, (2014):90-94.
Okafor-Omali,Dilim, *A Nigerian Villager in Two Worlds*. London: Faber and Faber (1965)
Ottenberg, Simon, "Ibo Receptivity to Change." In Bascom W.Russell & Melville I. Herskovits (eds), *Continuity & Change in African Cultures*. Chicago: The University of Chicago Press,1959.

# CHAPTER 3

AUSTINE UCHECHUKWU IGWE & ABUOMA AGAJELU

## The Igbo In Present Day Nigeria: In Historical Perspective

### CHAPTER OVERVIEW

1. INTRODUCTION
2. POST-CIVIL WAR RECONSTRUCTION IN IGBO LAND TILL 1975
3. THE POLITICAL STRUCTURE OF IGBO LAND SINCE 1975
4. ECONOMIC AND SOCIAL STRUCTURE OF IGBO LAND SINCE 1976
5. CONTRIBUTIONS OF THE IGBO TO NIGERIA'S POLITICAL, ECONOMIC AND SOCIAL LIFE SINCE 1970
6. CONCLUSION

## Summary

In modern Nigeria, the Igbo occupy the Southeast geo-political zone of the country, made up of five states: Abia, Anambra, Ebonyi, Enugu and Imo. Nonetheless, Igbo-speaking people also form the major ethnic groups in Delta and Rivers states (although some of these claim they are non Igbo). However, for purpose of analysis, the Igbo as used in this chapter denote the group that speaks Igbo language (in diverse dialects) in the five Southeast states of Nigeria. Similarly, the Igbo as put to use in this chapter share a lot of things in common, particularly their cultural outlook, a common sense of Igboness, synonymous with migration, especially the penchant to live in other parts of Nigeria, which made Ozigbo (1999, p. 117) to describe the Igbo as "a migrant race". There is also a general consensus among the Igbo that they are marginalized in the political economy of the Nigerian state. It is no mean feat that they were able to dust off the rubbles of war within a short time after they were forced into what could be described as a war of attrition. As could be seen in the study, the federal government's post-war policies did not help to ameliorate the plight of the people; instead, in some instances it appeared to have exacerbated it. Even though the Igbo lost some admirable traits, which they were known for in the pre-civil war years, (Ota, 2016: 520) they went on to develop a culture of self-help, which could be said to be responsible for their speedy growth since the mid-1970s.

## 1. Introduction

**T**HE IGBO IN THIS DISCOURSE WAS A MAJOR PART OF THE EASTERN REGION OF NIGERIA that seceded from Nigeria and declared an independent state of Biafra. This secession of the Igbo and the whole of the old Eastern Region of Nigeria led to the outbreak of the Nigerian civil War in July 1967. The war lasted for thirty months, but ended with the defeat of Biafra and its official surrender to the Federal Government of Nigeria on 15 January, 1970. The civil war was fought mostly on the Biafran soil, due mainly to the Federal Government of Nigeria's war policy, which was characterized by the economic blockade of Biafra. Thus, the end of the war saw the total devastation of Igbo land, the main theatre of war. The Igbo lost virtually everything at the end of war, their loved ones and properties across Nigeria. They were dehumanized. But one thing the Igbo did not lose at the end of the civil war in January 1970, was the "resilient spirit of survival in any situation".

The southeast is endowed with a lot of human and natural resources. The discovery of petroleum resource in southern Nigeria in the late 1950s opened Igbo land up to the petroleum economy. Today, two Igbo states; Imo and Abia are recognised oil producing states in the country. Within the land mass of Imo and Abia States, there are crude oil, phosphate, zinc, salt, lignite, gypsum, marquisate, limestone, and gold among others (Nenge, 2019). Petroleum resources have also been discovered in the Agulu-Eri, Anambra East area of Anambra State. This development prompted the establishment of an indigenous oil refinery, Orient Petroleum Refinery (OPR) (Enyim, Oritse and Ujumadu, 2012). Nonetheless, the lands where the resources were discovered is still under contention between three states; Enugu, Kogi and Anambra States.

It is against this backdrop that this chapter examines the Igbo in present day Nigeria from 1970 till date (2020). Thus for the purpose of analysis and clarity, other than this introduction, this chapter is divided into the following subheadings: post-civil war reconstruction in Igbo land till 1975, political structure of Igbo land since 1976; economic and social structure of Igbo land since 1976; contributions of the Igbo to Nigerian political and socio-economic life since 1970; and a conclusion.

## 2. Post-Civil War Reconstruction in Igbo land till 1975

After thirty months of intense fighting, the last shots of the Nigerian civil war were fired and the short-lived republic of Biafra capitulated. Igbo land of course had no option but to accept to be known as East Central state, which was created shortly before the war with eleven other states by General Gowon on 27 May 1967. Dr Ukpabi Asika, whom General Gowon had appointed its administrator in 1967, retained this position as the post-civil war governor of the state. There were devastations of various sorts during the war, both human and economic, to be followed by the so-called three Rs of Reconstruction, Rehabilitation and Reconciliation.

*Human Devastation*

It has been difficult to name a definite figure with regard to those who died during the war, especially that of the Igbo. Madiebo (1980, p. xi) affirmed that at the end, the whole exercise of splitting and re-uniting Nigeria cost the nation over three million lives. Ojiakor (2014, p. 2) believes that over five million lives were lost in the war on both sides, with the Eastern Region, particularly the Igbo, accounting for 90 percent of whatever figure that was reached. According to Achebe (2012, p. 227), the Igbo head count at the end of the war was perhaps three million dead, which was approximately 20 percent of the entire population. Apart from the dead, many others were wounded and permanent physical deformity among the Igbo became common.

*Economic Devastation*

There was massive destruction of properties, looting, arson and other forms of aggression that were meted out on the Igbo. These acts of aggression led to other heinous social conditions that included permanent dislocation of family ties as some members migrated to unknown places where they sought refuge and never came back. What is more, the war led to a distasteful situation of massive unemployment among the Igbo people. Both the private and public sectors of the Eastern Region's economy grossly suffered. Major industries were either destroyed or closed down. Essential infrastructures were not spared in the carnage. Hospitals, communication facilities, transportation infrastructure, educational facilities, oil refineries among others were laid to waste. Notable markets across Igbo land were destroyed. The Onitsha Main Market, which grew to be acclaimed the largest market in the West African sub-region, was reduced to rubble during the war.

*Reconstruction, Rehabilitation and Reconciliation*

It was in the light of the foregoing that the Federal Military Government (FMG) of General Yakubu Gowon, immediately after the civil war, set out to attempt a reconstruction of the war-battered Igbo land based on the spirit of "no victor no vanquished". General Gowon introduced a policy of *Reconstruction, Rehabilitation and Reconciliation* (the 3Rs). As explicated by Ojeleye (2010, p. 76), the thrust of the 3Rs was to create an atmosphere conducive for resettling those displaced and others who had fled their homes; reunite families and friends; rebuild physical facilities which had suffered some damage during the civil war; and place demobilised armed forces personnel in gainful employment in civilian life. Ojeleye further observes that in contrast to other post-civil war policies on the African continent, the 3Rs was multifaceted rather than being explicitly demobilisation, disarmament and reintegration focused. It is claimed that the need for an over arching post-civil war policy in Nigeria, in contrast to an explicitly disarmament, demobilisation and reintegration-focused policy, was informed by the difficulty the federal government had in differentiating between a Biafran combatant and a Biafran civilian.

The bedrock of the 3Rs policy was the Second National Development Plan 1970–74 (SNDP) for post-war reconstruction which had been under discussion during 1969. In a nationwide broadcast on 11 November 1970, Gowon stated that the plan was "another decisive step in the nation's forward march to progress and stability" and the choice of a four-year period was anchored on the need to "enable the economy to recover fully from the strains and stresses of the war [whilst] at the same time ... short enough to remind us of the challenge of post-war reconstruction". About 40 per cent of the total net public sector programme of £780 million was devoted to the reconstruction element of the SNDP (Ojeleye, 2010, p. 76)

In reality, the 3Rs came into existence with the formation and empowerment of a Commission mandated to fulfill the objectives of the initiative. The Commission was established by the Decree No. 41 of 1968 and was named the National Rehabilitation Commission (NRC). Appointed to head the Commission at the national level was Timothy Omo-Bare, while Ukpabi Asika (the Administrator of East Central State, 1967-1975) was empowered to prosecute the programme in the zone where it was needed most, which was the East-Central State. The NRC in partnership with relief agencies, notably the Nigerian Red Cross Society, provided basic needs for the Igbo people. In a collaborative endeavour, the federal and state governments, donor agencies and individuals donated essentials such as food items, healthcare, clothing, money and so on to the Commission (Ojiakor, 2014, p. 6-7).

*Appraisal of the Reconstruction, Rehabilitation and Reconciliation (3Rs)*

The federal government's attempt to reconstruct Igbo land after the war has been variously appraised with mixed reactions. Paul Obi-Ani (1998: 11) believes that the effort did not yield the desired results. This situation may partly be blamed on the insincerity of the government of Gowon and the lack of empathy on the side of the Igbo leaders charged with executing the reconstruction programmes. As Paul Obi-Ani explicates:

> **❝** *...feeling of insecurity and despair prevailed among the Igbo. All of Igbo land was studded with innumerable road blocks mounted by the victorious Nigerian Army. The people's plight was confounded by a variety of other factors. First, the Administrator of East Central State, Mr. Ukpabi Asika, a Federal loyalist and General Gowon's appointee, did not seem to appreciate the enormity of the plight of the Igbo people.* **❞**

Generally, most Igbo share the view that full integration of the Igbo was not achieved, contrary to Gowon's pledges, as the Igbo were discriminated against in all the sectors of the economy such as employment, appointments, capital investment and so on. Worst of all was the implementation of the Banking Obligation (Eastern States) Decree of 1970. Ahazuem (2008, p. 212) opines that the decree was a form of demonetization of the Igbo; as the decree nullified all pre-civil war savings of the Igbo. In its implementation, a paltry sum of twenty Nigerian pounds was paid to each Igbo depositor regardless of the amount of his pre war deposit balance. It was with this paltry sum of money that the average post-civil war Igbo family began a fresh life in a re-united Nigeria. Thus, Gowon's sincerity at reconstruction of the country is questioned as his objective of separating the military from the politics of the country could not be met. In fact, the transitional programme to civilian rule initiated by him evaporated with him and his administration as he and his junta were deposed in a military coup that saw General Murtala Muhammad's ascendance to power in July 1975. ∎

## 3. The Political Structure of Igbo land since 1976

The year 1976 marked a new dawn in the political structure of Igbo land, after the ousting of the military government of General Yakubu Gowon and his replacement with General Murtala Muhammad. The political structure from this period witnessed the continuous splitting of Igbo land into smaller and smaller administrative units in the name of seeking for national stability through state creation and local government creation, but with the states witnessing a continually changing administrative system over the years, from military administrators to elected governors.

With the new military regime of General Murtala Muhammad, Colonel Anthony Aboki Ochefu was appointed as the new Military Governor of East Central State to replace Dr. Ukpabi Asika. The new military regime also created seven new states, bringing the total to nineteen states in Nigeria.

*Figure 1. The 19 States in 1976 (https://commons.wikimedia.org/wiki/File: Nigeria states-1976-1987.png)*

The creation of new states on 3 February 1976 led to the division of the former Igbo state, - East Central State into two: Anambra and Imo states. Recall that few days into his administration, the new military Head of State appointed a Committee on state creation under the chairmanship of Justice Ayo Irikefe of the Supreme Court. Before then, the country comprised of twelve states. The Committee on state creation submitted its Report recommended that the creation of more states would guarantee political stability in Nigeria. General Mohammad's Supreme Military Council accepted the recommendations from the Committee and announced the creation of seven more states in the country.

By the state creation exercise, Anambra state retained Enugu (former capital of Eastern Region and East Central state) as capital; while Owerri was named the capital of Imo state. The bulk of Anambra state was derived from old Onitsha Province, which included Enugu; including groups from the old Abakaliki and Nsukka Divisions. Imo state was derived from the old Owerri Province, which included old Orlu and Okigwe divisions; and the former Afikpo division. The military administration also appointed new governors for the two states in Igbo land. Colonel John Atom Kpera served as military Governor of Anambra state from March 1976 till November 1978. On the other hand, Navy Commander Ndubuisi Kanu was appointed the first military governor of Imo state; and served from March 1976 up till 1977. By the time General Olusegun Obasanjo succeeded General Muhammad as military Head of state in February 1976, he introduced reforms in local government structure in Nigeria. The reforms led to uniformity in local government administration in Nigeria. The outcome of this was the creation of Local Government Areas (LGAs) in all states in Nigeria in 1976. While Anambra state was divided into 23, Imo state was divided into 21 Local Government Areas (Okeke, 2010, p. 201).

Before the enthronement of democracy in Nigeria in 1979, which ushered in the Second Republic, Igbo land had only two states. However, other than the military governors mentioned above, other military governors /administrators were appointed for the two Igbo states before the civilian dispensation of 1979 (these will be highlighted in tables later). General Olusegun Obasanjo kept faith with the transition to civil rule programme, which was initiated by the late General Murttala Muhammad. The Igbo participated in the formation of political parties across Nigeria; the five major ones were the National Party of Nigeria (NPN), the Unity Party of Nigeria (UPN), Nigerian Peoples Party (NPP), Peoples Redemption Party (PRP) and Great Nigeria Peoples Party (GNPP). Specifically, an Igbo, Dr. Nnamdi Azikiwe was the Presidential candidate of the Nigerian Peoples Party in the 1979 elections. Although, Alhaji Shehu Shagari of the National Party of Nigeria won the Presidential elections held in 1979, the NPP led by Dr. Azikiwe entered into a political alliance with the NPN to form the government at the centre in 1979. With the alliance, an Igbo, Chief Edwin Ume-Ezeoke was elected the Speaker of the Federal House of Representatives in 1979. The Igbo held prominent positions during the Second Republic (October 1, 1979-December 31, 1983). During this period, an Igbo man, Dr. Alex Ekwueme, was the Vice President of Nigeria.

Many other persons of Igbo extraction were appointed Federal Ministers, such as Chief Emeka Anyaoku, Foreign Affairs Minister from October 1983 till December 31 1983, when the military ousted the democratically elected government of President Shagari. In the elections at the state level, the NPP won the gubernatorial election of 1979 in both Anambra and Imo, with Chief Jim Nwobodo and Chief Sam Mbakwe who emerged as Governors in both states. However, in the election conducted in 1983, Chief Christian Onoh of the NPN emerged victorious as governor of Anambra state, while Chief Sam Mbakwe defeated Chief Collins Obi of NPN to emerge in his second term as governor of Imo state; a position he held till December 31, 1983 when the military brought the second Republic to a sudden end via a coup d'état.

From January 1984 till December 1992, the whole of Nigeria was under full military rule. General Muhammad Buhari who ousted the civilian administration of President Shehu Shagari was officially in power from January 1984 till August 1985, when General Ibrahim Babangida ousted him in a palace coup. General Babangida was in power as Nigeria's head of state from August 1985 up till August 1993, when "he stepped aside". However, before stepping aside, earlier in August 1991, General Babangida had created additional nine states, which included Abia and Enugu states in Igbo land. Recall that General Babangida had in September 1987 created two additional states in Nigeria, Akwa-Ibom and Katsina states, which then brought states in Nigeria to twenty-one, although the Igbo did not benefit from that exercise.

The creation of Abia and Enugu states in August 1991 brought the number of states in Igbo land to four. Abia state was carved out from the then old Imo state, while Enugu state was created from the old Anambra state. The new Enugu state retained Enugu, the capital/ administrative capital of old Anambra state as its capital; while Umuahia was named the capital of Abia state. It should be stressed here that most often, people from current Anambra state argue that what was created in 1991 by General Babangida was the "new Anambra state" not Enugu state and vice-versa. Whatever side of argument you may agree with, the fact is that state creation exercise led to two additional states for the Igbo. As part of General Babangida's transition to civil rule programme, elections at the states and national assembly levels preparatory for hand- over to a civilian government were conducted in 1991. This led to the emergence of new civilian governors, who were sworn into office in January 1992 in the four states of the Igbo (names of these governors and their states will be highlighted in tables later). At the time General Babangida stepped aside in August 1993, he handed over to an Interim National Government (ING), having cancelled the June 12 1993 Presidential election. However, the tenure of these governors was cut short in November 1993 by a successful coup led by by General Sanni Abacha, which brought the Chief

Ernest Shonekan-led Interim National Government to a sudden end.
The military regime of General Sanni Abacha lasted from November 1993 till his death in June 1998. Like previous military regimes before his, he promised a transition to civil rule programme; he first convoked a National Constitutional Conference, which met from late 1994 to 1995. A major outcome of the Conference, which had representatives of diverse groups in Nigeria was the division of the country into six geopolitical zones: north-west, north-east, north-central, south-west, south-east, and south-south zones. One remarkable feat of the Sanni Abacha administration was the creation of six new states in October 1996, one for each geopolitical zone of the country. It was then that the fifth state in Igbo land, Ebonyi was created, some sections of Enugu state: old Abakaliki division and some sections of Abia state: old Afikpo division formed the nucleus of the new state, with Walter Feghabo as its first Military Administrator. General Abacha's transition to civil rule programme was cut short by the mysterious death of its initiator in June 1998.

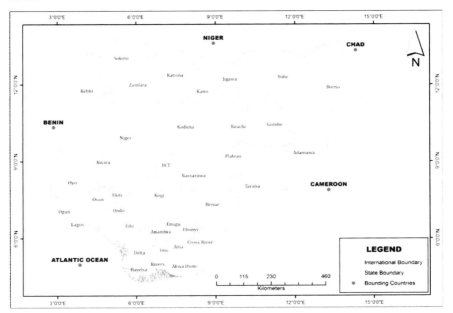

*Figure 2. The 36 States of Nigeria with the Federal Capital Territory, Abuja*

After the death of Sanni Abacha on 8 June 1998, General Abdulsalam Abubakar who took over as Head of State promised a speedy return to civil rule. He put in motion a transition programme, which included the formation of political associations, and the registration of political parties. Some political parties, which included Peoples Democratic Party (PDP), All Peoples Party, later All Nigerian Peoples Party (ANPP) among others were registered and contested the 1999 elections at all levels that led to the enthronement of democratic rule and birth of Nigeria's Fourth Republic on 29 May 1999. The Igbo played key roles in the politics that ushered the Fourth Republic. Specifically, Dr. Alex Ekwueme, an Igbo from Anambra state contested the first Presidential Primary election of the PDP; although, he lost to Chief Olusegun Obasanjo, but he received some support from his allies in the old NPN, and he later worked towards the unity of his party. Other than this, Chief Evan Enwerem, another Igbo from Imo state was elected the first Senate President of Nigeria's Fourth Republic.

The democratic process in Nigeria has been sustained from 1999 till date. Many Igbo have played roles at the national level, as ministers, special advisers or special assistants to successive presidents. Other than Evan Enwerem, the following Igbo were elected as Senate President in the last twenty-one years: Dr Chuba Okadigbo, 1999-2000, Chief Anyim Pius Anyim, 2000-2003, Chief Adolphus Wabara, 2003-2005, Chief Ken Nnamani, 2005-2007; while Dr. Ike Ekweremadu served as Deputy Senate President for twelve years, 2007-2019. Similarly, Chief Emeka Ihedioha from Imo state was former Deputy Speaker of Nigeria's House of Representatives from 2011 to 2015. Other Igbo were appointed ministers in the last twenty-one years; they included late Chief Ojo Maduekwe, former Minister of Foreign Affairs during Alhaji Umaru Yar'Adua's administration, 2007-2010; Dr Chris Ngige, who has been Minister of Labour and Employment from 2015 till date; among many others.

In the same vein, many persons were elected as state governors in the five states in Igbo land since 1999. The tables below show the lists of governors in each state in Igbo land since their creation, starting in their order of seniority: Anambra, Imo, Enugu, Abia and Ebonyi.

| No | Name | Title | Took Office | Left Office | Party |
|----|------|-------|-------------|-------------|-------|
| 1 | John Atom Kpera | Governor | March 1976 | July 1978 | Military |
| 2 | Col. Datti Sadiq Abubakar | Governor | July 1978 | October 1979 | Military |
| 3 | Jim Nwobodo | Governor | October 1979 | October 1983 | NPP |
| 4 | Christian Onoh | Governor | October 1983 | December 1983 | NPN |
| 5 | Allison Madueke | Governor | January 1984 | August 1985 | Military |
| 6 | Samson Omeruah | Governor | August 1985 | December 1987 | Military |
| 7 | Robert Akonobi | Governor | December 1987 | August 1990 | Military |
| 8 | Herbert Eze | Governor | August 1990 | January 1992 | Military |
| 9 | Joseph Abulu | Administrator | 27 August 1991 | January 1992 | Military |
| 10 | Chukwuemeka Ezeife | Governor | 2 January 1992 | 17 Nov. 1993 | SDP |
| 11 | Dabo Aliyu | Acting Administrator | November 1993 | December 1993 | Police |
| 12 | Mike Attah | Administrator | 9 December 1993 | 21 August 1996 | Military |
| 13 | Rufai Garba | Administrator | 21 August 1996 | 6 August 1998 | Military |
| 14 | Emmanuel Ukaegbu | Administrator | 6 August 1998 | 29 May 1999 | Military |
| 15 | Chinwoke Mbadinuju | Governor | 29 May 1999 | 29 May 2003 | PDP |
| 16 | Chris Ngige | Governor | 29 May 2003 | 17 March 2006 | PDP |
| 17 | Peter Obi | Governor | 17 March 2006 | 3 November 2006 | APGA |
| 18 | Virginia Etiaba | Governor | 3 November 2006 | 9 February 2007 | APGA |
| 19 | Peter Obi | Governor | 9 February 2007 | 17 March 2014 | APGA |
| 20 | Willie Obiano | Governor | 17 March 2014 | 9 November 2021 | APGA |
| 21 | Charles Soludo | Governor | 9 November 2021 | Present | APGA |

*Table 1. List of Administrators and Governors of Anambra State (Source: www.wikipedia.org)*

| Name | Title | Took Office | Left Office | Party |
|------|-------|-------------|-------------|-------|
| Ndubuisi Kanu | Governor | Mar 1976 | 1977 | Military |
| Adekunle Lawal | Governor | 1977 | Jul 1978 | Military |
| Sunday Ajibade Adenihun | Governor | Jul 1978 | Oct 1979 | Military |
| Samuel Onunaka Mbakwe | Governor | 1 Oct 1979 | 31 Dec 1983 | NPP |
| Ike Nwachukwu | Governor | Jan 1984 | Aug 1985 | Military |
| Allison Amakoduna Madueke | Governor | Aug 1985 | 1986 | Military |
| Amadi Ikwechegh | Governor | 1986 | 1990 | Military |
| Anthony E. Oguguo | Governor | Aug 1990 | Jan 1992 | Military |
| Evan Enwerem | Governor | Jan 1992 | Nov 1993 | NRC |
| James N.J. Aneke | Administrator | 9 Dec 1993 | 22 Aug 1996 | Military |
| Tanko Zubairu | Administrator | 22 Aug 1996 | May 1999 | Military |
| Achike Udenwa | Governor | 29 May 1999 | 29 May 2007 | PDP |
| Ikedi G. Ohakim | Governor | 29 May 2007 | 29 May 2011 | PPA / PDP |
| Owelle Rochas Anayo Okorocha | Governor | 29 May 2011 | 29 May 2019 | APC |
| Emeka Ihedioha | Governor | 29 May 2019 | 15 Jan. 2020 | PDP |
| Hope Uzodinma | Governor | 15 January 2020 | Incumbent | APC |

*Table 2. List of administrators and Governors of Imo State (Source: www.wikipedia.org)*

As can be seen from the tables above, southeast Nigeria consists of just five states; other zones consist of six states, with northwest, which consists of seven states. This anomaly has made scholars and commentators to argue that south-east vis-à-vis the other geo-political zones of the federation is marginalized in all ramifications (Amanchukwu et al 2018, p. 166). The structural anomaly in state creation against the Igbo in Nigeria has serious financial implications. In this regard, since the states have been operationalised as the basis for the sharing material and political resources through the federal character principle since 1979, the region with lesser number of states must necessarily lose out in the distribution of resources. It therefore appears to be an act of injustice to deny a major ethnic nationality in the country equality in state creation.

Similarly, with respect to local government creation, the southeast zone (Igbo land) has the least, just 94, out of 774 local government areas in Nigeria, 12.27% of the lot; whereas the northwest zone with seven states has 181 local government areas or 23.69% (Ohaneze, 1999, p. 6). This shows that the Igbo are generally marginalized in the political economy of the Nigerian state. With few local government areas, the Igbo have the least of federal constituencies among the geopolitical zones, and with few local government areas, the southeast zone receives the least annual

| Name | Title | Took Office | Left Office | Party |
|------|-------|-------------|-------------|-------|
| Frank Ajobena | Administrator* | August 28, 1991 | January, 1992 | None |
| Ogbonnaya Onu | Executive Governor | January, 1992 | November, 1993 | NRC |
| Chinyere Ike Nwosu | Administrator | December 9, 1993 | September 14, 1994 | None |
| Temi Ejoor | Administrator | September 14, 1994 | August 22, 1996 | None |
| Moses Fasanya | Administrator | August 22, 1996 | August, 1998 | None |
| Anthony Obi | Administrator | August, 1998 | May 29, 1999 | None |
| Orji Uzor Kalu | Executive Governor | May 29, 1999 | May 29, 2007 | PDP, PPA |
| Theodore A. Orji | Executive Governor | May 29, 2007 | May 29, 2015 | PPA |
| Okezie Ikpeazu | Executive Governor | May 29, 2015 | Incumbent | PDP |

Table 4. List of the Administrators and Governors of Abia State (Source: www.wikipedia.org)

| Name | Title | Took Office | Left Office | Party |
|------|-------|-------------|-------------|-------|
| Walter Feghabo | Administrator | 7 October 1996 | August 1998 | Military |
| Simeon Oduoye | Administrator | August 1998 | May 1999 | Military |
| Sam Egwu | Governor | 29 May 1999 | 29 May 2007 | PDP |
| Martin Elechi | Governor | 29 May 2007 | 29 May 2015 | PDP |
| Dave Umahi | Governor | 29 May 2015 | Incumbent | PDP |

Table 5. List of Administrators and Governors of Ebonyi State (Source: www.wikipedia.org)

revenue from the Federation account, as other than monthly allocation of revenue to states, there is also monthly allocation of revenue to the local government areas from the federation account. The Igbo through the auspices of the pan-Igbo socio-cultural group, Ohanaeze Ndigbo presented series of marginalization of the Igbo to the Human Rights Violation Investigation Commission of Nigeria (Oputa Panel), which was constituted by President Olusegun Obasanjo in 1999. Nonetheless, till date the marginalization of the Igbo in Nigeria's political economy remains.

Below is the list of number and names of local government areas in the states of the southeast zone, arranged alphabetically:

### Abia State

The state was created in 1991 from part of *Imo State*. It comprises of seventeen local government areas. They are:Aba North, Aba South, Arochukwu, Bende, Ikwuano, Isiala Ngwa North, Isiala Ngwa South, Isuikwuato, Obi Ngwa, Ohafia, Osisioma Ngwa, Ugwunagbo, Ukwa East, Ukwa West, Umuahia North, Umuahia South, and Umunneochi.

### Anambra State

The *Old Anambra State* was part of the *East Central State* that had its capital in Enugu. Later in 1991, *Old Anambra State* was divided into *Anambra State* (with capital in Awka) and *Enugu State* with the capital in Enugu. The present Anambra State, which is the product of the 1991 division, comprises of twenty-one local government areas. They are Aguata, Awka North, Awka South, Anambra East, Anambra West, Anaocha, Ayamelum, Dunukofia, Ekwusigo, Idemili North, Idemili South, Ihiala, Njikoka, Nnewi North, Nnewi South, Ogbaru, Onitsha North, Onitsha South, Orumba North, Orumba South and Oyi.

### Ebonyi State

Was created from part of both Enugu State and Abia State in 1996. It comprises of the following thirteen local government areas: Abakaliki, Afikpo North, Afikpo South (Edda), Ebonyi, Ezza North, Ezza South, Ikwo, Ishielu, Ivo, Izzi, Ohaozara, Ohaukwu, and Onicha.

**Enugu State**

The State part of the *Old Anambra State*, a major part of the *East Central State* that had its capital in Enugu. The division of the *Old Anambra State* in 1991, led to the mergence of *Anambra State* (with capital in Awka) and *Enugu State* with the capital in Enugu. The new *Enugu State* comprises of the following seventeen local government areas: Aninri, Awgu, Enugu East, Enugu North, Enugu South, Ezeagu, Igbo Etiti, Igbo Eze North, Igbo Eze South, Isi Uzo, Nkanu East, Nkanu West, Nsukka, Oji River, Udenu, Udi, and Uzo-Uwani.

**Imo State**

Previously part of the *East-Central States*, the state was created in 1976 under the Military leadership of Murtala Mohammed. It comprises of the following twenty-seven local government areas: Aboh Mbaise, Ahiazu Mbaise, Ehime Mbano, Ezinihitte Mbaise, Ideato North, Ideato South, Ihitte/Uboma, Ikeduru, Isiala Mbano, Isu, Mbaitoli, Ngor Okpala, Njaba, Nkwerre, Nwangele, Obowo, Oguta, Ohaji/Egbema, Okigwe, Onuimo, Orlu, Orsu, Oru East, Oru West, Owerri Municipal, Owerri North, and Owerri West.(Olawale, 2018)

## 4. Economic and Social Structure of Igbo land since 1976

When the civil war ended in 1970, Igbo land, as earlier noted was devastated. Nonetheless, the people had to resort to various means to help themselves. These included traditional agriculture, small and medium enterprises, industry, trade, transport, infrastructure, community health, education, health, social change and religion.

## Agriculture

The people had to fall back on their traditional agricultural practice (which sustained them to some extent during the war) for survival. The principal food crops produced were yams, cassava, coco-yam, three-leaved yam and varieties of vegetables; among others in most Igbo communities. Some communities in the old Abakaliki division engaged in rice faming at subsistence level, many household engaged in animal husbandry, poultry at subsistence level for the protein needs of the people. Some people in communities located very close to rivers and lakes engaged in fishing both for subsistence and for commercial purposes. Specifically, people of Ogbaru, located very close to an arm of the River Niger were professional fishermen who took some of their catches to the popular Onitsha market, sold these and purchased their other needs with profit realized therefrom.

Generally, the overt importance the Igbo attached to agriculture is probably borne out of the uncertainty that surrounded trade and manufacturing. While trade and manufacturing were directly influenced by the market forces, agricultural production and the insurance against starvation were largely determined by the people's willingness to cultivate the land. Victor Uchendu (1965) has this to say of the Igbo as regards their prioritization of agriculture over other sectors of the economy:

 *To remind an Igbo that he is ori mgbe ahia loro, 'one who eats only when the market holds' is to humiliate him. This does not imply that traders are not respected: all it means is that the Igbo see farming as their chief occupation and trading as subsidiary not a substitute for it.* **99**

This shows that throughout history, the Igbo hardly trust another means of livelihood other than that which they directly provide for themselves through the cultivation of the soil. This does not however mean that the Igbo abhorred trading but it explicitly portrays the self-sufficiency of the Igboman. This trait obviously informs the contemporary attitude of the average Igboman towards working for another person for wages. The belief is that no one should determine when they "eat" or not. With this mindset, the people are prone to struggle for their own business enterprise where they will be able to determine the flow of their wealth. The foregoing development may have informed the contemporary Igbo's inclination for trade, manufacturing and services, as Nigeria's economy kept de-emphasizing agricultural productivity. That is why in the Igbo states one finds a great number of small and medium enterprises (SMEs) as well as appreciable number of large-scale enterprises (LSEs) owned by the indigenous people of the states.

*Small and Medium Enterprises (SME)*

The small and medium enterprises that emerged in Igbo land after the war were witnessed in the cities of Aba, Nnewi, Onitsha; and some other areas, where local artisans through indigenous raw materials and metal wastes fabricated categories of personal and household needs. Specifically, artisans in Aba have perfected shoe making to the extent that shoes and other products made in Aba became popular in many parts of Nigeria. It is due to the dexterity of these artisans who manufactured diverse products that are even exported to other countries in West Africa, that the acronym "made in Aba" became popular. In recent times, especially since the 1990s when the craze for foreign products became high in Nigeria, some products like shoes and hand bags manufactured in Aba were labeled with foreign countries as their places of production.

*Industry*

Generally, the industrial sector in Igbo land is mostly private sector driven. Though, in the 1980s and the 1990s, state governments in the southeast established few industries, such as the attempted reactivation of the Nkalagu Cement Industry, attempted reactivation of Aba textile industry, the attempted reactivation of the Golden Guinea and Premier breweries; all collapsed due to the human factor. Consequently, in present day southeast Nigeria, the private sector controls virtually all thriving industries, whether small, medium or large scale industries. Among these are: Innoson Automobile Manufacturing (IVM) located at Nnewi, manufacturers of vehicles, with 70% of vehicle parts locally sourced, Intafact Beverages Limited, owned by SabMiller, a multinational brewery and beverage conglomerate, producers of Hero Larger beer, Budweiser, Castle milk stout and Beta malt located in Onitsha. There are also many plastic fabrication firms such as Millennium Industries limited, Awka and Gincol Group limited, Owerri, among others. Other private sector controlled industries in Igbo land include those engaged in pharmaceutical manufacturing such as Juhel (Nig.) limited based in Awka; chemical industries like Intercolor Industries limited, Enugu; aluminum and roofing sheet manufacturing, food processing industries, and firms that manufacture household products and toiletries, etc.

*Trade*

With regards to trade, this has been a major economic activity of the Igbo since the 1970s. Other than the traders within Igbo land, migrant wage earners, that includes itinerant Igbo traders abound throughout the thirty-six states of the Nigerian federation and the Federal Capital Territory, Abuja. In many cities across Nigeria, Igbo entrepreneurs dominate the import of vehicle spare parts and accessories, as well as import of pharmaceutical products. To date, Nnewi is popular as "the Mecca" of automobile parts; not just for the Igbo, but for the entire nation (Igwe, 2010:124). Igbo traders are known to be the major distributors of goods and services to different states in Nigeria. The post-civil war survival instinct of the Igbo, and with the introduction of "luxurious buses" on Nigerian roads as from the mid-1970s made it possible for Igbo traders to convey diverse goods via the buses, even on night trips to areas those goods were needed in Nigeria. This trend continues till date, and the introduction of electronic monetary transfer has facilitated the movement of goods by these Igbo traders.

## Transport

In the service sector, the Igbo have not been found wanting. Igbo have also contributed to the development of motor transport industry in Nigeria since 1970 (Njoku, 2001, p. 145). A notable post- civil war transport magnet was Chief Augustine Ilodibe (1932-2007), founder, Ekene Dili Chukwu Nigeria Limited; whose passion for and unwavering commitment to the success of road transport business contributed to the emergence of other transport companies in Igbo land. He was the pioneer of modern "luxurious buses" on Nigerian roads. In later years, other inter-state luxurious bus transport companies emerged in Igbo land. In this category are Izuchukwu Transport Company, Chidiebere Transport Company, New Tarzan Transport Company, The Young Shall Grow Transport Company; among many others (Iweze, 2013). It was from the late 1990s that the state governments in Igbo land became involved in road transport business; although, in recent times Mini-buses are common in inter-state travels from Igbo land to other parts of the country.

## Infrastructure

Social and infrastructural development in Igbo land since 1970 has been a mixed grill; because most Igbo communities have imbibed the philosophy of "self help" to provide for their needs with minimal contribution from the government. Most communities in Igbo land during the period under review adopted the "community development method" in the provision of their basic infrastructure. Thus, Nwabughuogu (1993, pp. 302-303) opines that the community development method not only utilizes traditional means to achieve modern result, but also economizes on scarce resources and strengthens the ties joining members of the community. Specifically, "the community development spirit" is in vogue throughout Igbo land, as it common to see visible signs of projects in every Igbo community initiated and completed by the people, coordinated by their Town Unions, which became popular and was embraced by each Igbo community as from the 1970s.

*Community Help*

Till date, in many parts of Igbo land, there are Community Secondary Schools, Community health Centre/ Maternity Homes, and markets constructed in communities through self-help efforts in the guise of community development. During the early 1980s, the governor of Imo state initiated the construction of an airport in Owerri, the state capital through self-help efforts via fund raising and donations by the indigenes of the old Imo state.. In recent times in some communities across Igbo land (especially Anambra state), individuals have tarred roads that led to their villages, and even to their homes. Other than this, many communities in Igbo land provided their own energy supply; they contributed money and liaised with the former Power Holding Company, and current energy Distribution Company to provide the vital electricity for their communities. This self-help/ community development trait of the Igbo has to some extent enhanced socio-economic activities in the communities.

*Education*

With respect to education and health sub-sectors, since 1970, there has been remarkable improvement in the number of educational and health institutions in Igbo land. In the education subsector, the numbers of primary and secondary schools have tripled, for there are now primary and secondary schools in almost every Igbo community. This has made virtually all southeast states (apart from Ebonyi) to be in the league of educationally advantaged states in Nigeria. Similarly, the number of tertiary institutions in Igbo land has risen tremendously. For instance, before 1970, there was just University of Nigeria as the only university in Igbo land; but today (2020), there are officially five functional federal and five functional state universities and about eight private recognized universities in the southeast zone of Nigeria.

*Health*

In the health sub-sector, other than the community health centres mentioned earlier, in recent times, especially as from 1999, state governments have boosted the health care delivery system in their respective states by building and equipping General Hospitals at the headquarters of the local government areas. There are also some Teaching Hospitals, Federal Medical/ Specialist hospitals in Igbo land. No doubt, the provision of these health facilities by states and the federal government has brought health care delivery system closer to the people.

*Religion and Social Change*

There has also been some social changes in Igbo land since 1970. With respect to religion and belief for example, indigenous/traditional religion was the centre of Igbo belief and worship up to the 1950s, but by the 1960s many Igbo have embraced Christianity as their religion. Though Christianity had made inroad into Igbo land before 1970, the orthodox core denominations of Roman Catholic, Anglican Communion, Methodist, and to some extent Presbyterian were the visible ones at the end of the civil war. However, from the 1970s, the Pentecostal Movement swept over Igbo land from the United States. Today, the Pentecostal Churches in diverse forms are a force to be reckoned with in Igbo land.

Another social change was facilitated through the advent of the Global System for Mobile (GSM). Before the GSM incursion, communication was mostly run by the government. However, by early 2000s, with the Federal Government's liberalization of the communication sector, some Igbo entrepreneurs effectively invested in the new telecommunication trend, the GSM. Pascal Dozie, a renowned Igbo investor owns enormous shares in the giant multinational GSM company MTN. He was at one time also the Chairman of the company in Nigeria. Generally, some of the changes have positively affected the Igbo in the form of high number of educated Igbo, both in Nigeria and in the Diaspora. To date, Igbo professionals in North America, Western Europe and Middle East (which includes Dr. Philip Emeagwali, the computer expert) are a force to be reckoned with if accurate data is obtained. In like manner, financial reparations of the Igbo in the Diaspora have contributed immensely to the socio economic growth of many Igbo communities. ■

## 5. Contributions of the Igbo to Nigeria's Political, Economic and Social Life since 1970

The preceding sections of this chapter presented series of political, economic, socio-structural developments in Igbo land from 1970 till present. All these point to the fact that the Igbo (in spite of their defeat in the Nigerian civil war) have made immense contributions to national political, economic and social life of Nigeria since 1970.

*Politics*

Without doubt, notable contributions of the Igbo in Nigerian political life include their involvement in political activities and governance of Nigeria at all levels since 1970. Specifically, two Igbo persons – Dr. Alex Ekwueme and Commodore Ebitu Ukiwe were Vice Presidents of Nigeria, while five Igbo indigenes - Chuba Okadigbo, Evan Enwerem, Anyim Pius Anyim, Adolphus Nwabara and Ken Nnamani - were Senate president, one person, Ike Ekweremadu, was deputy Senate president for eight years; while another, Emeka Ihedioha, was deputy speaker of the House of Representatives for four years. As also observed in the course of analysis, the Igbo have participated fully in all elections conducted in Nigeria since 1979.

*Economy*

In the economy, the ingenuity of Igbo traders in Onitsha and Nnewi markets in Igbo land, the Alaba International market in Lagos and across other cities in Nigeria has revolutionalised the import trade with Asian countries such as China, Pakistan, India and Taiwan. Some of these Igbo traders have received trademarks of some firms in Asia, and commenced the replication of similar products in Nigeria (a sort of transfer of technology), while some had through their experiences established small/medium scale industries, thereby contributing to the nation's quest for industrialization Many Igbo entrepreneurs have also invested in various sectors of Nigerian economy that have had positive impact on the nation.

*Social*

Without doubt, some aspects of the social contributions of the Igbo manifest in their propensity as a migrant race that have settled among other ethnic groups in Nigeria, and as well contributed to the socio-economic growth and development of such areas. For instance, it has been noticed that some of the valued properties (real estate) in Abuja belong belong to the Igbo (Igwe, 2010, p.129). Many Igbo also own "choice" properties in many state capitals and cities across Nigeria. It is not in doubt that this Igbo attitude of investing all over Nigeria has facilitated national cohesion and socio-cultural integration.

*Education*

Similarly, in the field of education, the Igbo produced first indigenous Vice Chancellor of the University of Ibadan, Professor Kenneth Onwuka Dike, Professoe Eni Njoku, probably among the earliest Vice Chancellor of the University of Lagos, was of Igbo extraction. These were men who rose to their enviable positions on merit through hard work (a trademark of the Igbo). Eminent Igbo academicians such as Professors Chinua Achebe, Anya O. Anya, Adiele Afigbo, and Dr. Pius Okigbo; among many others excelled in their chosen fields, which had positive impact on Nigeria,

*Sports*

In sports, Chioma Ajunwa, an Igbo athlete won the first Olympic gold medal for Nigeria in long jump, a field event at the 1996 Atlanta Olympics in the United States. Similarly, the Enyimba Football Club of Aba became the first and only Nigerian club to win the African Champions League in 2003 and 2004 respectively. There also abound many sports persons of Igbo extraction, both in Nigeria and in the Diaspora, whose contributions have had proactive effects on Nigeria

## Entertainment

In the field of entertainment, the Igbo contributed to launching the Nigerian movie industry on the global landscape, and played a pivotal role in the development of the brand, Nollywood. The roles of renowned film makers such as Amaka Igwe and Kenneth Nnebue ensured the establishment and popularity of Nollywood across the globe. Musical acts such as P-Square, Phyno, and Flavour effectively make their mark in the Nigerian music scene.

## 6. Conclusion

In spite of the fact that Federal Government presence is conspicuously lacking in the South-East geopolitical zone of Nigeria, the Igbo seem not to be obscured in almost all aspect of the Nigerian national life even after they were virtually subdued after the civil war. The Igbo have conspicuously contributed to the socio-economic growth and development of the country. This could be seen in the number of Igbo people in the private sector of the country's economy, where the people have shown themselves to be creative and innovative, which also goes on to enhance the industrial economy of the country. The people's penchant for western education has also ensured qualitative population and a relative high index in human development and capacity building. Many Igbo people have also contributed in the political development of the country through initiating ideas that strengthened the political fabrics of the rather fragile federation, for example the idea of dividing the country into six geopolitical zones in an effort to ensure broad representation of the people especially the minority ethnic groups.

Finally, although the Igbo have contributed immensely to Nigeria's political, economic and social development, much still needs to be done by the Igbo in Igbo land, especially in the provision of infrastructure. There is the urgent need for the government and the private sector in the Igbo-speaking states to cooperate in the provision of adequate functional infrastructure that could help to reinvigorate productivity in the rural areas, so as to enhance the socio-economic growth and development of the region. The Igbo should not remain "good ambassadors abroad" while minimal signs of development persist at home. Similarly, the Igbo should reexamine their mindsets, put a stop to the idea of their being marginalized and utilize their quality human resources to assert themselves as major stakeholders in Nigeria. ◾

### References

Achebe, C. (2012). *There Was a Country: A Personal History of Biafra*, New York: Penguin Books.
Ahazuem, J.O. (2008). "Post War Economic Development: the Case of Ndigbo and Nigeria", Onwuka Njoku and Obi Iwuagwu (eds.)*Topics in Igbo Economic History*, Lagos: First Academic Publishers

Amanchukwu, I.A., Ezedinachi, I.E., and Orizu, O.N., (2018). "State Creation, Federal Character and the Igbo Question: A Comment," *Renaissance University Journal of Management & Social Sciences (RUJMASS)*, Vol. 4 (1).

Enyim, Oritse and Ujumadu (2012). "Jonathan Commissions Orient Petroleum Refinery in Anambra," *Vanguard*.
Igwe, U. (2010). "Economic and Social Development of Ndi-Igbo in Time Perspective", U.D.

Anyanwu (ed.) *Themes on Igbo Culture, History and Development*, Lagos: Ubaond and Associates
Iweze, D.O. (2013). Biographies of Selected Igbo Transport Entrepreneurs in Nigeria," *Igbo Studies Review*, Vol. 1
Madiebo, A.A. (1980). *The Nigerian Revolution and the Biafran War*, Enugu: Fourth Dimension Publishing Co., Ltd.
Nenge, K. (2019). Top 10 Oil Producing States in Nigeria, http://www.legit.com/ accessed on 09/11/2020.

Njoku, O.N. (2001). "*Economic History of*

*Nigeria in the 19th and 20th Centuries*, Enugu: Magnet Business Enterprises
Njoku, R. (2013). "Chinua Achebe and the Development of Igbo/African Studies," Chuku, Gloria (ed), *The Igbo Intellectual Tradition: Creative Conflict in African and African Diaspotic Thought*, New York: Palgrave Macmillan.

Nwabughuogu, A.I. (1993). *The Dynamics of Change in Eastern Nigeria, 1900-1980, Indigenous factor in Colonial Development*, Owerri: Esther Thompson
Obi-Ani, P. (1998). *Post-Civil War Social and Economic Reconstruction of Igbo land: 1970-1983*, Anambra: Mikon Press.

Ohaneze N. (1999). *The Violations of Human and Civil Rights of Ndigbo in the Federation of Nigeria (1966-1999)*, Enugu: Snaap Press Ltd.

Ojeleye, O. (2010). *The Politics of Post-War Demobilisation and Reintegration in Nigeria*, Farnham: Ashgate Publishing Limited.

Ojiakor, N. (2014). *Social and Political History of Nigeria 1979-2006*, Enugu: EWANS Press.
Okeke, O.E. (2010). "Igbo Politics since 1975", U.D. Anyanwu (ed.), Themes *on Igbo culture, history and development*, Lagos: Ubaond
Ozigbo, I.R.A. (1999). *A History of Igbo land since the 20th Century*, Enugu: Snaap Press Ltd
Uchendu, V.C. (1965). *The Igbo of Southeast Nigeria*, New York: Holt Rinehart and Winston. ◾

# Part Two

# Igbo Language

# Chapter 4

MBANEFO CHUKWUOGOR

## How Many Dialects Does The Igbo Language Have?

### CHAPTER OVERVIEW

1. INTRODUCTION

2. LANGUAGES, DIALECTS AND STANDARDS

3. THE IGBO LANGUAGE

   3.1 STANDARD IGBO AND CENTRAL IGBO

   3.2 IGBO DIALECTS AND THEIR FEATURES

   3.3 MUTUAL INTELLIGIBILITY AND THE UNIFORMITY OF TONE ACROSS DIALECTS

   3.4 OTHER ISSUES IN IGBO DIALECTOLOGY

4. SUMMARY AND CONCLUSION

## Summary

Whenever 'Igbo dialects' are mentioned there always arises the thought of a multiplicity of dialects, lack of mutual understanding, and ultimately a lack of unity amongst the Igbo people as a whole. All such thoughts have accumulated from the early assumptions of colonial linguists who even saw some of the Igbo dialects as entirely different languages. Therefore, the concept 'Igbo dialects' has an accretion of some negative associations that have contributed to questions like: How many dialects does the Igbo language have? Can the speakers of the various dialects understand each other? Do speakers of the various dialects regard themselves as Ndɩ Igbo? This chapter gives an overview of the different Igbo dialects and their features; It also shows what holds them together, despite their diversity.

## 1. Introduction

PEOPLE HAVE ALWAYS SAID THAT THE Igbo LANGUAGE has many dialects. The colonial and other foreign linguists, in addition to native Igbo-speaker linguists, made this statement. What do they mean? Starting with the somewhat problematic distinction between the labels 'language' and 'dialect', this chapter also highlights the criteria used by linguists to draw the distinction between the two. Subsequently, the chapter gives an overview of the different dialects of the language and their features. Additionally, some observations are made about the cross-dialectal uniformity of tone in Igbo, and issues surrounding other speech forms considered by some as Igbo dialects are highlighted, in addition to the confusion between Standard Igbo and Central Igbo, as well as how the Igbo orthography affects the growth and research on many of its dialects.

## 2. Languages, Dialects and Standards

The terms language, dialect and standard, in that sequence shall first be briefly explained in this section before going into the issue of the Igbo language and the dialects of the language.

The term *language* is usually understood as a system of communication used by a group of people of a particular nationality, race, or region. People then speak in this sense of 'the ... language', as in 'the English language', 'the French language', 'the Yoruba language', 'the Ibibio language', 'the Igbo language', and so on. Such designations give the impression of a one, uniform language, and consequently underplay the fact that each of these languages has a number of dialects, and it is one of such dialects that is given the status of *language*, because of its prominence in education, business, and government. This naïve view of 'the ... language' also applies to the understanding of the term *dialect*, which is often seen as a substandard, low-status, or rustic form of a particular language, generally associated with the peasantry, the working class, or other groups lacking in prestige. The term is also used to refer to languages spoken in isolated parts of the world, or to erroneous deviations from the norm (Chambers & Trudgill, 2004:, p. 3). In this chapter, we shall not be adopting any of the above points of view. The primary reason behind dropping these views is a purely linguistic one of egalitarianism (equality). In linguistics (the field concerned with the scientific study of language), all languages are regarded as equal. In the same vein, no dialect or variety of a language is in any way linguistically superior to any other. Hence, we will continue the discussion with the assumption that all and anyone who speaks a language is a speaker of at least one dialect of the same language.

At another and higher level of discussion, is the issue of the level of intelligibility between the dialects, otherwise called 'level of mutual intelligibility'. According to Chambers and Trudgill, (2004, p. 3) 'a language is a collection of mutually intelligible dialects', while dialects on the other hand are regarded as the forms or varieties of a language spoken in a particular geographical location or region. In this way, we may talk of the Bavarian dialect of German, the Ife dialect of Yoruba, the Onicha dialect of Igbo, and so on. However, this distinction between a language and a dialect is not usually so straightforward. This is because there is no generally accepted measure for differentiating and isolating two unique languages from two dialects of the same language. But one major criterion that is often used to differentiate between dialects of the same language and two different languages is 'the mutual intelligibility test'. In line with this criterion, two dialects are said to be dialects of the same language if speakers of one of them can understand and be understood by speakers of the other. Otherwise, they are said to be different languages. Unfortunately, this mutual test is unable to successfully distinguish between a language and a dialect in some instances. An example is the case of the Scandinavian languages: Norwegian, Swedish, and Danish, which are usually considered to be different languages. However, they are mutually intelligible. Speakers of these three languages can easily understand and communicate with one another. Chinese, on the other hand, presents a different picture. For example, while we would normally consider Chinese to be a single language and as a result speak of 'the Chinese language', there are some dialects of Chinese that are not intelligible to speakers of other dialects. Another point is that mutual intelligibility is a matter of degree, and it may not be equal in both directions. For instance, many Swedes can easily understand the Norwegians, while the Norwegians do not understand the Swedes so well. Similarly, whereas it is often said that Danes understand Norwegians better than Norwegians understand Danes. It can be seen from the foregoing that the distinction between the labels 'language' or 'dialect' cannot easily be decided on purely linguistic terms. For this reason, most scholars prefer to use the more or less neutral term "variety" in similar discussions.

Finally, it is prudent to mention two vital notions: the notion of "dialect continuum" and the notion of a "standard dialect". The first is best illustrated by the quotation below:

> If we travel from village to village, in a particular direction, we notice linguistic differences which distinguish one village from another. Sometimes these differences will be larger, sometimes smaller, but they will be cumulative. The further we get from our starting point, the larger the differences will become. The effect of this may therefore be, if the distance involved is large enough, that (if we arrange villages along our route in geographical order) while speakers from village A understand people from village B very well and those from village F quite well, they may understand village M speech only with considerable difficulty, and that of village Z not at all. Villagers from M, on the other hand, will probably understand village F speech quite well, and villagers from A and Z only with difficulty (Chambers & Trudgill, 2004, p.5).

Drawing from the above, dialects at the extreme geographical areas may not be mutually intelligible, but they are connected by a chain of shared intelligibility.

A standard dialect is also known as a standardized dialect or standard language. It is the dialect that is supported by the government and used formally for education, in literary works like grammars, dictionaries, and in everyday usage. Usually, it is presented as the "correct" form of a particular language. Having introduced a few of these terminological differences, we now turn to the Igbo language. **L**

## 3. The Igbo language

The Igbo language is one of the prominent languages in modern-day Nigeria. It is one of the four largest languages of West Africa with a total of about 18-25 million people or roughly 16.6% of the Nigerian population as native speakers, especially in the eastern part of the country and about 29 million speakers globally (Ethnologue, 2020). It is the De facto provincial language in south-eastern region and the language of wider communication (LWC) of Abia, Anambra, Ebonyi, Enugu, and Imo states. Emenanjo (2015, p. 4) reveals that Igbo is also spoken as a major language in Delta and Rivers states in the South-South geo-political zone of Nigeria. Pockets of Igbo-speaking communities are also to be found in Benue, Cross River and Akwa Ibom states. Igbo is one of Nigeria's 'major' languages, and is taught as a second, additive language in Nigerian secondary schools in keeping with the language provisions of the *National Policy on Education* (2004). It is classified as a Kwa language of the Benue-Congo sub-family of the Volta-Congo and Atlantic Congo branches of the Niger-Congo language family (Bendor-Samuel, 1989) or the West Benue-Congo subfamily of the Niger-Congo language family (Williamson & Blench 2000).

Ubahakwe (2002, 255), following Armstrong (1967), opines that Igbo began to separate as a distinct language from the proto- Kwa sub family about 4000 to 6000 years ago. That process of linguistic differentiation is continuing: first yielding accent variations, then dialects and, if time and other conditions permit, further languages. Before delving into the discussion of Igbo dialects, we shall first shed some light on the somewhat related terms ('standard' or 'central') associated with the Igbo language in the next section.

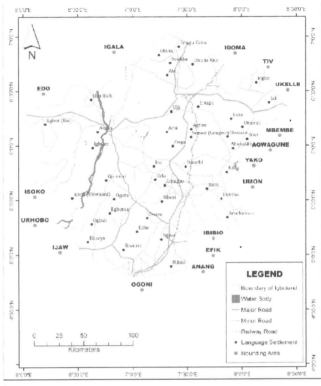

Figure 1. Igbo Speaking Region and Neighbouring Languages

## 3.1 Standard Igbo and Central Igbo

Many a times normal speakers of Igbo confuse or mix up the labels 'Standard Igbo' and 'Central Igbo'. In truth, these two terms, although closely related, do not mean the same thing. Standard Igbo like the name implies, is a form of Igbo generally agreed upon to be used in the teaching and learning of the language. Hence, it is the variety of the language used in Igbo texts, schools, and examinations. Ubahakwe (1984, p. 140) notes that formal education in Igbo language began about one hundred years ago. Since then, at least three successive dialects (Isuama, Onitsha and Union Igbo) have been tried as standard with outright failure, and a fourth - the much-diffused Central Igbo - is in use on ad hoc consensus. The absence of a clearly acceptable standard literary dialect of Igbo has, therefore, hampered the development of a formal education in the language. Similarly, Emenanjo (2015, p. 12) reveals that over the years, two standard Igbo varieties have developed in the Igbo culture area: a spoken standard, and a written standard. Some of the factors that have made these possible include improved communication, greater and easier mobility, Christian missionary activities, and the colonial enterprise and agencies of globalization and social media communication. He goes further to point out that for historical reasons, the spoken Standard Igbo has a northern Igbo texture, while the written Standard Igbo has a southern Igbo one. Anyanwu (2010, p. 51) explains that amidst the various dialects of Igbo is a 'standard' variety (known in the Igbo language as *Igbo Izugbe*), which is more or less imagined than real, because it is practically impossible to locate/trace this 'standard' variety to a particular geographical setting within the Igbo speaking communities.

Central Igbo, on the other hand, covers mainly the Owerri and Umuahia areas including Ohuhu (in Umuahia district) (Onumajuru, 2016, p. 226). It gradually established itself as the accepted form by writers, publishers and education authorities for use in schools and for many years has been used as the medium of written Igbo. The Central Igbo does not represent any particular dialect of Igbo. It appears to be a compromise between the extremely nasalized Owere group of dialects and totally denasalized Ọnịcha group. One can even infer that the Central Igbo and Ọnịcha Igbo are similar to some extent since both are written and spoken with neither nasalization nor aspiration. Herein lies the confusion that needs to be resolved. The Onwu orthography (the one currently in use) is based on Central Igbo. However, as seen above, the term 'Standard Igbo', in the strictest sense, refers to the written (literary) form of Central Igbo. One may ask "Are there native speakers of Standard Igbo". The answer is No. this is because the Standard dialect or variety of Igbo is not restricted to a particular area. Rather, it is an amalgamation of the features of the variety of Igbo spoken around the central Igbo area. In the words of Emenanjo (2015, p. 13), "Standard Igbo (SI) is a neo-language with inbuilt features for language growth and development."

The next section looks at the way the dialects or varieties of Igbo have been grouped or classified by different scholars.

## 3.2   Igbo dialects and Their Features

This section first summarizes the history of the study of Igbo dialects, before going fully into the features of the identified dialects.

Over the years, the study of Igbo dialects has been carried out by different linguists. Nwaozuzu (2008), for example, opines that the study of Igbo dialects received its first attention from Koelle's (1854) *Polyglotta Africana*. Most of such early works were not usually thorough and extensive, considering the enormity of requirements involved in carrying out a dialectological survey of the language. Later on, some studies were carried on some dialects after the settlement of the Igbo orthography controversy in the 60's. Armstrong's work (1967), for example, was on five Igbo dialects that stretched from the west to the eastern end of the River Niger (cf. Nwaozuzu, 2008), while Armstrong (1967) was on the consonantal and vocalic segments of some dialects. Welmers (1970) worked on Central Igbo and concluded that Central Igbo comprises the variety of Igbo spoken in Umuahia and Owerri areas, while Meier and Bendor-Samuel (1975) concentrated on the phonology and syntax of the Izii dialects. Ubahakwe (1981), cited in Nwaozuzu (2008), studied the widespread usage of a number of lexical items across some Igbo dialects. Building on earlier studies, Ikekeonwu (1985) studies the consonantal and vocalic phonemes of Otu Onitsha Dialect (OOD) and Enyimba Central Igbo (ECI), both of which were drawn from Onitsha Igbo and Central Igbo dialect groups respectively.

In addition to the above efforts, some studies have attempted to establish the exact number of Igbo dialects and to classify them. Such studies include: Grimes (1974), who identifies 30 dialects; Ward (1941) 47 dialects; Talbot (1926) lists 59 clans of Igbo which many believe correspond more or less to the dialects of the language. Recent studies (Williamson, 1973; Emenanjo, 1981; Manfredi, 1991; Ikekeonwu, 2001; Nwaozuzu, 2008; Ohiri-Aniche, 2013) have also provided different classifications of the Igbo dialects. Nwaozuzu (2008, p. 10), using a phonologically-based approached in her analysis of the dialects, geographically classifies them into the following eight (8) major dialect groups. The groups are as follows:

- West Niger Group of Dialects (WNGD)
- East Niger Group of Dialects (ENGD)
- East Central Group of Dialects (ECGD)
- Cross River Group of Dialects (CRGD)
- South Eastern Group of Dialects (SEGD)
- North Eastern Group of Dialects (NEGD)
- South Western Group of Dialects (SWGD)
- Northern Group of Dialects (NGD)

Nwaozuzu (2008) also discusses the phonology, morphology and syntax of these different dialect groups. However, it should be noted that the dialectal differences shown in her work are mostly at the phonological level. Nwaozuzu's eight major dialect groups are summarised in the table overleaf.

In a similar vein, Ikekeonwu (2001) also uses a phonological criteria in dividing the Igbo language into the following six dialect clusters:

- Niger Igbo (NI) Cluster
- Inland West Igbo (IWI) Cluster
- Inland East (IEI) Cluster
- Riverian Igbo (RI) Cluster
- Waawa/ Northern Igbo (W/NI) Cluster
- Arọ Igbo (AI) Cluster

| Dialect Group | Members | Features |
|---|---|---|
| WNGD | Agbor, Asaba, Ogwashiukwu, Isele Uku, Ukwuani, Ibusa Akoko, Kwale, etc | - Most WNGD dialects have 28 consonants like the standard, Asaba has 26, while Ika has 27 including /v/ e.g: *evele* (plate)<br>- In Ika, the negative marker is *ele* e,g:<br>*Elē nedi e* (It is not his father); the future marker is *be* e.g:<br>*Be we je Aba* (They will go to Aba) |
| ENGD | Onitsha, Obosi, Awka, Amawbia, Ogidi, Alor, Abatete, Enugwuukwu, igbo Ukwu, Nibo, Nimo, Nri, Ihiala, Oba, etc | - ENGD has sounds ranging from 25 consonants (Umunya/Nteje) to 38 consonants (Amaiyi).<br>- The past tense marker is the usual *-rV/-lv* harmonising high vowel/-lu (consistent) form e.g:<br>*O siri nri* (She cooked food)<br>*Ọ sụlụ akwa* (She washed clothes)<br>*Ọ lịlị enu* (He climbed up)<br>- The perfective is *-la/-gwo/-go/-wo/-cho/-sho* e.g:<br>*O nyela m ego* (He has given me money)<br>*Ha ejego afịa/avịa*, etc |
| ECGD | Owerri, Uratta, Okpuala, Mbaitoli, Ikeduru, Mbaise, Awomama, Orlu, Umuahia, Okigwe, Mbano, etc | - Most of the consonant sounds found here do not exist in standard Igbo e.g the ingressive alveolar plosive /ɗ/ and the glottal stop /ʔ/ in Mbaise, Mbiere, Owerri, etc.<br>- Palatalization is a feature of ECGD.<br>- The perfective is *-na/-ne or -le/-la*, e.g:<br>*Ọ gaana ahia* (He has gone to market)<br>*O shiene nri* (She has cooked food)<br>*O shiele nri* (She has cooked food)<br>- The negative form is *-hụ/-hi/-dị/-ghị*<br>- The progressive form is *ga/ge* or *-gha/-ghe* |
| CRGD | Abiriba, Ohafia, Afikpo, Abam, Bende, Omasiri, Arochukwu, etc | - Most dialects of this group operate a nine-vowel system (this includes a schwa /ə/ e.g:<br>/əka/ (hand), /əbʊɔ/ (two)<br>- The negative marker is *-gị/baa/mbe/maa*, e.g:<br>*O baa ri* (He will not eat.)<br>*O wu mbe ji* (He has not cooked yam.)<br>*Ọ gagị eri* (He will not eat)<br>*Ọ maa chu mmiri* (He will not fetch water)<br>- The future is marked with "*ba*" instead of *ga* e.g:<br>*Wa ba je ubi* (They will go to farm.) |

*Table 1: The Igbo Dialect Groups (Nwaozuzu, 2008)*

On the other hand, Manfredi (1991) uses an approach that is both anthropological and linguistic, sometimes more diachronic (comparing different points in the history of a language) than synchronic (focusing on a particular time without recourse to the history of a language). He breaks

| SWGD | Ikwere, Ohaji, Egbema, Mgbichiri, Umuagwo, Etche, Okirika, Bonny etc | - In some of the dialects, nasalisation is phonemic<br>- Have as many as 42 consonants<br>- The negative marker is *lam/lem* e.g:<br>*O kwulem* (he did not speak.) |
|------|------|------|
| NEGD | Abakaliki, Izzi, Ezza, Ikwo, Ohaozara, Ezangbo, Uburo, Okposi, etc | - Phonemes (sounds) peculiar to this dialect group include: /dz, pt, bv, s$^w$ b$^y$, ts, l$^w$, h$^w$/<br>- The negative marker is *-du/-nu* e.g:<br>*Mụ te eridu nri* (I am not eating)<br>*Mi ejenu* (I will not go)<br>- In Izzi, the future and progressive constructions are similar. E.g:<br>*Anyị abya* (We will come)<br>*Anyị èje as$^w$a* (We are going to the market) |
| SEGD | Ngwa, Azumili, Obo ohia, Asa, Akwete, Ohambele, etc | - Has a system of 8 vowels and not less than 40-46 consonant sounds.<br>- Aspiration and nasalization are phonemic (influence change in the meaning of a word)<br>- the negative marker is *-ghị/fughị/ghụ* e.g:<br>*O nweghi akwụkwọ* (He doesn't have a book)<br>*I richafughụ ri* (You didn't eat the food all up at the time.)<br>- the perfective marker is *-la* e.g:<br>*Ọ zaala ụlọ* (He has swept the house.)<br>- in most dialects here, the past marker is the -rV form<br>- the progressive marker is *-dị* e.g:<br>*Ọ dị-ịwụ ahụ* (He is taking his bath.) |
| NGD | Nsukka, Enugu Ezike, Udi, Obolo Afor, Ikem, Ngwo, etc | - Most of the communities have at least a nine-vowel system with the schwa /ə/. Others have ten vowels with the schwa /ə/ and the half open, spread vowel /ɛ/<br>- the negative marker is *kọgə* e.g:<br>*Ọ tekọgə egwu* (She will not dance)<br>- the past marker is *-rə* e.g:<br>*O shirə nka* (She fetched firewood,)<br>-the perfective marker is *-wo/-wọ* or "*-gwome/-gwo*" e.g:<br>*Emeka anụwọ* (Emeka has heard)<br>*Ugwu ejegwome* (ugwu has gone)<br>*Ọ tagwo* (He has chewed.)<br>- the progrssive marker is *na-/ne-, -kọ*, or *le-* e.g<br>*Ọ ne-eri ji* (He is eating yam.)<br>*Ọzọ rikọ ihnye* (Ọzọ is eating something.)<br>*O le-eri nri* (He is eating food.) |

Igbo into nine dialect clusters:

- Èhwuda (Ẹkpẹyẹ)
- Ọ̃gbàkìrì (S. Ìkwere)
- Eleèlè (N. Ikwerre)
- Ọmọ̀kụ̀ (Ọgbà)
- Àbò (Ụkwụ̀ànì)
- Ọ̀nịchà (N. Ìgbò)
- Ọ̀maahyā (S. Igbo)
- Ãbankelēke (Ìzii)        (Manfredi, 1991: 59)

Using an essentially diachronic classification, he goes further to divide Igbo into two major clusters, the Northern and Southern. This is shown in Figure 1 below.

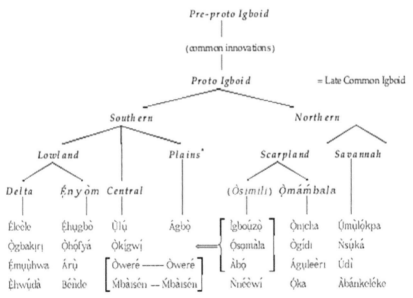

| Figure 1: Dialects of Igbo (cf. Manfredi, 1991: 32)

Another classification is Ubahakwe (2002), who uses the Lexico-Semantic Technique for his classification. Central to his technique are the notions of 'intelligibility and 'acceptability'. Through these, he is able to isolate dialects with a greater precision than has been done in previous attempts at classifying Igbo dialects. His study is restricted to the parts of

Igbo land stretching West to East from Onicha on the bank of the River Niger to Ogwu, and diagonally North-West to South-East from Igboariam to Ovum. He is able to identify more than twenty-four (24) dialects within the area. Fifteen dialects identified in his work are presented in Table 2 below.

| S/No | Dialect | Constituent members | Sample expressions |
|---|---|---|---|
| 1 | Abatete | Abagana, Abatete, Aba, Abacha, Adazi, Alo, Eziowele, Ideani, Mkpoo, Neni, Nnewi, Nnobi, Oba, Obosi, Ogbunike, Ojoto, Oraukwu, Ufuma, Uke, Ukpo, Umudioka, Umunnachi, Umuoji | *ogu* (twenty), *asato* (eight), *akpu-Otula* (buttocks), *rie* (eat), *miri* (water), *echiele* (tomorrow), *uno-gbamgbam* (zinc house), *nnedi* (one's husband's mother) |
| 2 | Aguleri | Aguleri, Otuocha, Okuzu, Umunya, Igboariam, Umuleri | *isi* (head), *isato* (eight), *mili* (water) *nwaobala* (cat), *teghete* (nine) |
| 3 | Enugwu-Ukwu | Agulu, Enugwu-Agidi, Enugwu-Ukwu, Isu-Aniocha, Nnofia, Nri | *afou* (belly), *itenani* (nine),*oku* (fire), *enu*-igwe (sky), *owhu* (twenty), *anyanwu* (sun), *nwamba* (cat) |
| 4 | Isiagu | Amobia, Amansea, Isiagu, Oka, Mbaukwu, Nibo, Nise, Umuawulu | *mili* (water), *okpa* (leg), *teghete* (nine), *akpu-otula* (buttocks), *nwamba* (cat), *anyanwu* (sun) |
| 5 | Ekwulobia | Ogbu, Ekwulobia, Ezinifte, Igboukwu, Ikenga, Isuofia, Nanka, Ndiokolo, Ndiokpaleke, Umuona | *afou* (belly), *nnaa* (one), *akpu-otula* (buttocks), *ishi* (head), *ogige* (fence), *nkita* (dog) |
| 6 | Ogboji | Akpu, Aguluezechukwu, Mpkologwu, Ogboji, Oko | *nnaa* (one), *ohu* (twenty), *miri* (water), *oku* (fire), *nwunye* (wife), *ogige* (fence) |
| 7 | Achina | Achina, Agbudu, Akpo, Am aesi, Enugwu-Umuonyiba, One, Umuchu, Umuomaku | *teghete* (nine), *utu-ohu* (buttocks), *afou* (belly), *isi* (head), *nkita* (dog), *oku* (fire) |
| 8 | Ndiowu | Ndiowu, Ndikelionwu, Ndiokpalaeke, Ndiukwuenu, Omogho | *akpu-otula* (buttocks), *okpa* (leg), *miri* (water), *kpakpando* (stars), *nkita* (dog), *anyanwu* (sun) |
| 9 | Umunze | Ajali, Akawa, Akpugo, Amaokpala, Awa, Eziagu, Eziama, Ezira, Ihite, Isulo, Nofija, Nkerefi, Ogbunka, Owere-Ezukala, Ubahu (Isuochi), Ufuma, Umunze | *okpa* (leg), *ishi* (head), *nnaa* (one), *isi* (head), *alopuotula* (buttocks), *nnedi* (one's husband's father) |
| 10 | Okigwe | Amadi, Egbake, Ezinachi, Okigwe, Obiohia, Odu, Ubahu Okigwe, Uturu | *afou* (belly), *nnaa* (one), *otu* (one), *ogige* (fence), *ok(h)a* (corn) |
| 11 | Ngodo | Amorie Ngodo, Amuda, Ezi Ngodo, Mbala, Ohara Obingu, Ubahu, Umuaku, Umuelem | *otu* (one), *uho* (fence), *uwamba* (cat), *okpa* (leg), *ogu* (twenty), *nwunye* (wife) |
| 12 | Ihube | Aku, Ihube, Ubahu-Okigwe, Okannachi, Umuawa-Ibu, Umulolo | *ukwu* (leg), *nnaa* (one), *otu* (one), *nnekwu* (hen), *anyanwu* (sun) |
| 13 | Ovum | Imenyi (Ahaba, Ezere, Ovum), Isuamawa (Umuobiala, Umualum), Oguduasa (Amaiyi, Umunekwu, Acha), Amaigbo (Amaokwe, Nonya, Otampa) | *egho* (belly), *otila* (buttocks), *nge* (one), *ishi* (head), *teghete* (nine), *ohu* (twenty) |
| 14 | Lekwesi | Isiama, Lekwesi, Lokpa-Ukwu, Leru, Ukomi | *asato* (eight), *owhu* (twenty), *miri* (water), *afuu* (belly), *teghete* (nine), *kpakpando* (stars) |

*Table 2: The dialects of Igbo (adapted from Ubahakwe, 2002)*

Based on the views presented so far, one can safely say there are approximately thirty Igbo dialects which vary considerably with respect to degree of intelligibility with the standard dialect (Grimes, 1974; Chukwuogor, 2017; Ethnologue, 2020). This variation is mostly lexical and phonological. The standard form is based on the Umuahia and Owerri dialects (omitting the nasality and aspiration found in those dialects) and is still being developed. Agbo (2010) notes that the current trend in Igbo linguistics is to classify Igbo dialects based on the common features associated with the states within which the dialects located. Hence, there exist the Anambra, Ebonyi, Enugu, Imo and Rivers dialects. He deems this classification to be more realistic and practical because speakers of Igbo dialects are associated with features common to their states. In the next section, we highlight a common feature of the dialects of Igbo.

3.3  Mutual Intelligibility and The Uniformity of Tone

To what extent are the Igbo dialects mutually intelligible? This question has arisen now and again amongst Igbo language scholars. This section presents some of the contributions to answering the question.

Emenanjo (2015, p. 6) holds the view that all Igbo dialects derive from one proto-Igbo language. That is why they share many grammatical, lexical and phonological features. However, Ubahakwe (2002, p. 267) notes that given the many instances of variability among the Igbo dialects, it should be obvious that dialects of a language do not constitute an entity whose members are only just marginally different from one another. The question that immediately arises is: how then do speakers of the different dialects of a language manage to engage in effective communication, if indeed there are as much variations as the data indicate. Ubahakwe offers three possible reasons for this:

- The notion of intelligibility and communication act are not a matter of absolutes (as speakers of the same dialect may often have difficulties understanding one another).

· Also, the role of linguistic accommodation at dialect boundaries should be emphasized. He notes that the level of effective communication between speakers of different dialects is largely dependent upon how willing the speakers are to adjust and to understand each other.

· Finally, looking at a dialect map, it would normally be the case that the intelligibility between one dialect and another adjacent to it would be higher than the intelligibility between that dialect and any other farther away from it.

The last point that Ubahakwe raises is related to the concept of a dialect continuum. In the Igbo dialect continuum, at no point is there a complete break such that geographically adjacent dialects are not mutually intelligible, but the cumulative effect of the linguistic differences will be such that the greater the geographical separation, the greater the difficulty of comprehension.

In a similar vein, Emenanjo (2015) agrees that the differences between dialects of Igbo do not inhibit effective communication as mutual intelligibility is possible between 'after some adjustments'. Emenanjo (2015, p. 8) also observes that "in terms of consonants: Onicha has 28, Ọlụ, 64; Ọwère, 60, and Ọfụfụ 55." Yet, if one asks how Igbos manage to communicate across boundaries, the answers are that:

· They may speak English
· They may actually learn a more widely used or more prestigeful dialect,
· They may take some form of pidgin Igbo, or
· They may take advantage of the common vocabulary and of the systemic sound shifts which these word lists show to exist.

Armstrong (1967: 4-5) observes that "...common vocabulary, ... sytematic sound shifts (and)... the extraordinary stability of tone through the whole range of dialects studied... contribute to mutual intelligibility across Igbo dialects. Igbo who speak or understand other dialects than their own are relying to a great extent on tones. Tones (are) one of the principal means to mutual intelligibility (across Igbo dialects)". Emenanjo (2015, p. 133) notes that "one very important, significant and interesting feature of lexical and grammatical tones in Igbo is that, by and large, they are regular, systematic and, indeed, systemic across all Igbo dialects". Furthermore, he asserts that the word lists available in Ward (1941), Ubahakwe (1981), Armstrong (1967), Emenanjo and Ogbonna (2013) contain words which show isoglossic differences in consonants, vowels, syllabic nasal and sometimes, tones. He affirms nevertheless, that typical noun phrases (like the associative and the specific), clauses (like the stative, factative, perfective and serial constructions) have identical if not same tonal patterns which cut across Igbo dialects (Emenanjo, 1981). He therefore maintains that the uniformity of tone in Igbo is the main basis for mutual intelligibility. Based on this, Chukwuogor (2017: 17) argues for the inclusion of tone in any cross-dialectal study of Igbo. This is because, the assumption that there is little or no difference of tone to show in the dialects of Igbo underplays the importance of tone in Igbo studies generally. In the next section we briefly mention a few issues that have often featured in the study of Igbo dialects.

## 3.4 Other issues in Igbo dialectology

Some issues that have always featured in the study of Igbo dialects include the problem of a cross dialectal orthography for the many dialects, and the issue of varieties of those varieties of Igbo whose speakers claim not to be Igbo. We make a few comments on them in the following paragraphs.

One of the criticisms levelled against the official (Ọnwụ) orthography of 1961 is that it does not represent some important sounds in many Igbo speech varieties or dialects. This is actually the case in respect to aspiration and nasalization which are distinctive in the speech of some

Igbo communities. However, Ohiri-Anichee (2007, p. 429ff) points out that no orthography of any language is perfect. She also goes on to note that the official Igbo orthography has, over the years, been criticized on some of the following points:

(a)   The use of diacritic marks makes it difficult to reproduce Igbo mechanically and electronically.

(b)   Even in manual writing, many people find the sub dots of /ị, ọ, ụ/ and the supra dot of /ṅ/ tedious to write, leading to their often being left out.

(c)   The official tone-marking convention, which marks a low tone with a grave (`), down stepped tone with a macron (-), and leaves a high tone unmarked is seen as not capturing the reality of Igbo. This is because the inherent tone of lexical items may change in certain syntactical and phonological environments. The difficulty this raises causes many writers to avoid the tone-marking of Igbo texts altogether.

(d)   Many Igbo dialect groups complain that the official orthography does not represent some important sounds in their dialects. This is especially so with regard to aspiration and nasalization which are distinctive in Ọhụhụ (Ụmụahịa) area dialect. For example, aspiration and nasalization, represented here by (h) and (˜) respectively, distinguish the following pairs of words:

/ba/ 'be rich'   and   /bha/ 'peel'
/re/ 'sell'   and   /rẽ/ 'burn'

A sample of speech sounds in different dialects not found in the official orthography are presented in the table below:

| Dialect | Sound | Word | Standard | English |
|---------|-------|------|----------|---------|
| Owere | [ t˂ ] | [at˂ ɔ] | [atɔ] | three |
| Awka | [ β ] | [oβe] | [ofe] | soup |
| Ogidi | [ ts ] | [ itsi] | [isi] | head |
| Agbani | [ c ] | [ɔca] | [ɔʧa] | white |

| Dialect | Sound | Word | Standard | English |
|---------|-------|------|----------|---------|
| Arondizuogu | [ hʷ] | [ahʷɔ] | [afɔ] | stomach |
| Orlu | [ ŋᵐ] | [ɔŋma] | [ɔma] | good |
| Udi | [ɛ] | [ɛka] | [aka] | hand |
| Nsukka | [ə] | [anə] | [anʊ] | meat |
| Mbieri | [ʒ] | [oʒi] | [ozi] | message |

|Table 3: Some Dialectal Igbo Sounds and Words (cf. Ohiri-Aniche, 2007, p. 430)

Ohiri-Aniche also states that the issue of dialectal sounds can adequately be addressed through the production of a Pan-Igbo Orthography. It is important to note here that some efforts have been made in this regard. Examples include the publication by the *Igbo Archival Dictionary Project* titled the *Unified Standard Orthography for the Igbo Language (Cluster)* 2011, funded by the *Centre for Black and African Arts and Civilization (CBAAC)* and the *Centre for Advanced Study of African Societies (CASAS)*.

Another issue in the study of Igbo dialects lies in the inconclusive argument about which varieties are Igbo and those that are not. One of the most recent and comprehensive works on Igbo dialectology, Ohiri-Aniche (2013), addresses this issue by way of making statements about which languages are Igbo or not (in the case of Ekpeye, Ikwere and Ogba). In doing so, she not only provides general information on the Igbo language and its speech forms, but also carries out detailed synchronic description of the sound systems of Standard Igbo and of some Igbo speech varieties. With the use of lexicostatistics and reconstruction rules, she analyzes how the sound systems had changed from one variety to the other. She also attempts to reconstruct what the original or ancestral Igbo language (which she referred to as 'Proto-Igbo') sounded like. Using the lexicostatistical scores, Ohiri-Aniche concludes that with scores above 80, Ikwere, Owere, Onicha, Izhii and Ukwuani are members of *Igbo Dialects*, while Ekpeye's score of between 71% - 75% places it under the *Igbo Language Cluster* as shown in Figure 2.

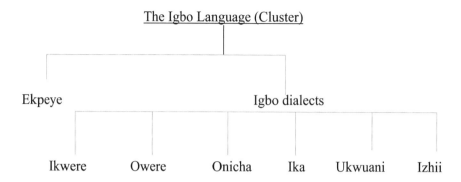

As glaring as the results shown with linguistic methods may be, one valid point that remains is that linguistics alone cannot resolve the issue of whether a group of people are assumed to speak the same language or separate language. Instead, historical and socio-political factors could contribute to resolving the issue or even aggravating it. For example, Ohiri-Aniche (2013, p. 61) confirms that since the Nigerian civil war of 1967-1970, many areas that used to be part of Igbo land (like some parts of Rivers and Delta states) have now been declared non-Igbo areas. Similarly, erstwhile Igbo populations in such areas now assume separate identities from Igbo such as Ikwere, Ekpeye, Ukwuani, Ika, etc.

## 4. Summary and Conclusion

This chapter has looked at some of the issues associated with the Igbo language and the question of Igbo dialects. These are issues that could take a quite complicated turn. Nevertheless, an objective review of the state of things was the aim. There are indications of variety, disagreements, and even 'disavowing' being an Igbo, all of which are concrete facts that cannot be dismissed through linguistic arguments. The conclusion is that the points of convergence and similarity is like an invisible template holding together all the seemingly incompatible dialects together.

# References

Armstrong, R.C. (1967). *A comparative wordlist of five Igbo dialects*. Ibadan: Institute of African Studies.

Bendor–Samuel, J. & Meier, P. (1974). 'Izi' in: *Ten Nigerian tone systems. Studies in Nigerian Languages* No. 4. Jos: Institute of Linguistics and the Centre for the study of Nigerian Languages, Kano.

Chambers, J. K., & Trudgill, P. (2004). *Dialectology*. Cambridge: Cambridge University Press.

Chukwuogor, M. C. (2017). Underscoring the cross-dialectal uniformity of tone in Igbo. *Igbo Language Studies*. Vol 2. 11-18

Clark, M. (1988). *A dynamic treatment of tone with special attention to the tonal system of Igbo*. Ph. D Dissertation University of Massachusetts at Amherst.

Cysouw, M. and Good, J. (2013). "Languoid, Doculect, and Glossonym: Formalizing the Notion 'Language'." *Language Documentation and Conservation*. 7. 331–359. hdl:10125/4606.

Emenanjo, E. (2015). *A grammar of contemporary Igbo: Constituents, Features and Processes*. Port Harcourt: M & J Grand Orbit Communications Ltd.

Emenanjo, E. N. et al. (2011). *A unified standard orthography for the Igbo language cliuster (Nigeria)*. Center for Advanced Studies of African Society (CASAS), South Africa and Center for Black and African Arts and Civilization (CBAAC), Nigeria.

Ezenwafor, C. (2014). Contour tones in Igbo: 'where they come from'. In *Theory and Practice in Language Studies*, Vol. 4, No. 4, pp.661-667. Finland: Academy Publisher.

Goldsmith, J. (1979). *Autosegmental phonology*. M.I.T/New York: Garland.

Grimes, B. F., & Wycliffe Bible translators. (1974). *Ethnologue*. Huntington Beach, Calif: Wycliffe Bible Translators.

Ikekeonwu, C. (1985). Aspects of Igbo dialectology: A comparative phonological study of Onitsha and Central Igbo dialect. *JWAL* XV.

Kamuselle, T. (2016). The History of the Normative Opposition of 'Language versus Dialect:' From Its Graeco-Latin Origin to Central Europe's Ethnolinguistic Nation-States. *Colloquia Humanistica*. Vol 5. 189-198.

Manfredi, V. (1991). *Agbo and Ehugho: Igbo linguistic consciousness: Its origins and limits*. Ph.D Dissertation, Harvard University

Nwachukwu, P. (1995). *Tone in Igbo syntax*. Studies in Igbo linguistics 2, Nsukka.

Nwadike, U.I. (1981). *The Development of written Igbo as a school Subject. 1766 – 1980. A Historical Approach*. Masters' Degree Thesis submitted to the Faculty of Graduate Studies of the State University of New York, Buffalo.

Nwaozuzu, G. (2008). *Dialects of Igbo language*. Nsukka: University of Nigeria Press.

Ohiri-Aniche, C. (2007). Stemming the tide of centrifugal forces in Igbo orthography. *Dialect Anthropoloy 31: 423-436*

Ohiri-Aniche, C. (2007). Stemming the tide of centrifugal forces in Igbo orthography. *Dialectical Anthropology, 31*(4), 423-436.

Retrieved January 17, 2021, from http://www.jstor.org/stable/29790801

Ohiri-Aniche, C. (2013). *Igbo speech varieties.* Abuja: Centre for Igbo Arts and Culture.

Onumajuru, V. C. (2016). A Contrastive Study of Two Varieties of Onicha and the Central Igbo Language. *International Journal of Arts and Humanities (IJAH)* Vol 5(2) No. 17, 225-240

Stephen, R. A. (1978). Tone features. In V. Fromkin (ed.), *Tone: a linguistic survey.* New York: Academic Press Limited

Talbot, P. A. (1926). *The peoples of southern Nigeria: Vol. 2.*

Ubahakwe, E. (1981). *Lexical and syntactic variations in Igbo dialects.* Unpublished Ph.D Thesis: University of Ibadan, Ibadan.

Ubahakwe, E. (1982). Towards a Standard Literary Dialect of Igbo. In Leben, W.E. (ed.)

*Studies in African Linguistics* Supplement 8. University of California, Los Angeles

Ubahakwe, E. (2002). The language and dialects of Igbo. In G.E.K. Ofomata (ed.), *A Survey of the Igbo Nation.* Onitsha: AFP. 252-271.

Ward, I.C. (1941). *Ibo dialects and the development of a common language.* Cambridge: Heffer

Williamson, K. (1972). The Igbo associative and specific constructions. In K. Bogers, H, Vander Hulst and M, Maar ten, *The phonological representation of suprasegmentals.* Dordretch, USA: Forris Publications. 195-208.

Williamson, K. & Blench, R. (2000). Niger Congo. In Heine, B and D. Nurse (eds.). *African Languages: An Introduction.* Cambridge: CUP.

Yip, M. (2002). *Tone.* Cambridge: Cambridge University Press. **L**

# CHAPTER 5

CHINEDU UCHECHUKWU & PURITY UCHECHUKWU

## Is The Igbo Language Dying?

1. Introduction

2. The Signs of the Death of the Igbo Language

   2.1 The Signs within the Igbo Community

   2.2 The Signs within the Igbo Family

3. The Signs of Resistance to Death

4. Summary and Conclusion

## Summary

Many people, including many Igbo native speakers, believe that the Igbo language is dying. From the perspective of change as an inevitable part of life, the death of the Igbo language would not be different from the death of any other language in the history of mankind; after all, languages die and new languages arise. The indicators of this downward trend for the Igbo language are the growth in the use of a mixture of English and Igbo, Ingiligbo, and a consequent decrease in the number of competent speakers of the language over the years. This decrease in competence seems to apply at the community level, at the family level, and at the level of the individual speaker of the language. But from the perspective of the well-known adaptive nature of the Igbo people, it should be surprising that their language could be dying without any adaptive reaction on their part. In fact, such adaptive reactions can actually be confirmed. In other words, this chapter examines how the well-acclaimed adaptation of the Igbo speaker to change, which has been noted to negatively impact on his language, is presently impacting on his language in a positive manner, leading to a form of renewal that can also be interpreted as the signs of resistance to the death of the language.

## 1. Introduction

JUST LIKE THE HUMAN BEING IS NOT A STATIC ENTITY, so also is his instrument of communication, the human language, non-static. In its functions as a means of communication, the human language is constantly adapting to a world that is in constant change and fluctuation. And in this state of flux many languages come into existence and disappear without a trace, some fully give rise to other languages before dying, while others simply provide the genetic materials for the birth of new languages before dying. The Igbo language, like any other living language before it, is faced with all of these possibilities; it is subject to the same state of flux, struggle and adaptation to the ever changing world. It has no choice; neither do the speakers of the language. That is why, right from the colonial period to the present, the short history of the Igbo language can be described as a struggle with adapting to the changes and fluctuations of the times.

One of the major issues the language and its speakers had to struggle with during the colonial period was the colonial administrator's communication of his decisions in English, in addition to the Christian Missionaries' endeavor to Christianize the natives also in English. The convergence of purpose on the part of the colonial authority and the Christian missionaries confronted the natives with the option of both adapting and moving forward within the colonial context by learning the English language, or not adapting and being left out in the course of events. Also, the language of the colonial masters brought with them a lot of foreign terms for foreign things into the Igbo speaking area, and for which the Igbo language lacked the equivalents. The struggle for survival through learning the colonial master's language therefore became paramount. And within such a state of affairs, it is obvious that any effort at the development of the Igbo language could not originate from the native speakers themselves. They had not learnt enough of the colonial master's language to go into the study, description and teaching of their own mother tongue.

The next struggle was with the Church politics of the colonial period, which set the native speakers against each other for about 30 years, with the native speaker Catholics and Protestants fighting over whose orthography should be used for writing the Igbo language. Chinua Achebe lamented over the negative impact of this 'orthography war' on the development of the Igbo language, because the creative impulse that would have led to the production of a lot of creative writings in the Igbo language was suddenly diverted into the issue of allegiance to a particular denomination. Achebe skillfully adapted to the situation by deciding not to write his creative works in the Igbo language.

With the settlement of the orthography issues in the 60's, the language once more stood before another opportunity to move forward, but then came the Nigeria-Biafra civil war. This caused a devastation of immense human resources, especially through the untimely death of millions who would have contributed to the growth and further development of the language. A good example is Christopher Okigbo, the world class Igbo poet, who died at the warfront during the war. His death has always raised many unanswered questions in the minds of some Igbo intellectuals who either personally knew him or also got to know of him and his creative works (Okigbo 1971): What could have become of Okigbo, if he had survived the war? What could he have done if he had witnessed the revival of the Igbo language within the first decade after the war? Would he have started writing in Igbo? And what would he have contributed to the development of Igbo literature? Would he have written the first major epic poem of the Igbo language? These are sorrowful questions that no generation after him has been able to answer, as the language continues with the struggle to adapt to the changing state of things even after the war.

The major adaptation to the state of things after the war was pioneered by *Chief F.C. Ogbalu*, who used his personal resources to spear-head the development of the Igbo language through founding and funding the *Society for the Promotion of Igbo Language and Culture (SPILC)*. Through this effort, the materially and psychologically devastating effects of the war were transformed into the *creative and productive 70's and 80's*, the period of great impulse in the development of the Igbo language. For example, the Igbo equivalents for the parts of speech (like *noun, verb, adjective,* etc) and literary expressions (like *metaphor, metonymy, etc.*), which did not exist before then, were developed within this period. The further effect was that, for the first time, Igbo grammar books could be written in the Igbo language. In fact, even the Igbo term for the word 'grammar', which is *Ụtọasụsụ*, was established within the period. Before then, Igbo grammar books were written in English, like the Igbo grammar books of the colonial linguists, and native speaker students of the Igbo language in secondary schools had to study the grammar of their language in English. The 80's therefore marked a new phase in the development of the Igbo language. It was a victorious adaptation to the destructions and devastations of the Civil war. The main product of the efforts of this period, *Igbo Meta Language*, continues up to date to serve as a strong reference point in igniting incursions into the development of more Igbo terms and the writing of Igbo dictionaries.

Towards the end of the last century came the *Internet and Communication Technology* and its *linguistic globalization* effects. ICT gave rise to a deluge of terminologies (far beyond the initial encounter of the Igbo language with the English language during the colonial period), in addition to exposing the lack of the appropriate means for typing the Igbo language. This was further aggravated through linguistic globalization, which is associated with the spread and dominance of English as a means for global communication (Phillipson, 1992). That is why globalization for African languages is seen as an additional "harsh linguistic environment" to the struggle of indigenous languages to survive in a situation where "in every African country a non-indigenous language serves as the official language for public interaction" (Ndimele 2005, p. 68). The Igbo language is not an exception to this fact. And to this old colonial inheritance has now been added the struggle to hold one's head above water in the new media, and to adapt through *UNICODE*, *YouTube, FaceBook, WhatsApp, Google* and other internet resources to the realities of the 21$^{st}$ century.

Finally, the path of the Igbo language over the years can be described as a path of adaptation to both natural and man-made phenomena. The 'natural' is the phenomenon of change which is unavoidable, while the 'man-made' include the colonial experience, the orthography war, the Nigerian Civil War, and globalization and its devastating effects on some languages. And now comes the corona pandemic, whose effects on the language is yet to be determined. In spite of all these, the struggle continues ... as one says. But one factor that cannot easily be categorized as 'natural' or 'man-made' is the well-known Igbo person's disposition for 'the new and the practical', which has often led to the abandonment of anything that is perceived as old and not practical, including sometimes his language, so long as it is somewhat felt at that moment to be a hindrance to a certain goal. All these have in one way or the other contributed to the intermittent outcry within Igbo land that the Igbo language is dying. And from outside Igbo land comes UNESCO and its invitation to various language communities to watch out on the endangerment of their language.

The rest of this chapter goes into these issues as follows. Section 2 revisits UNESCO's (2003) parameters and uses it to give an impressionistic evaluation of how the Igbo language could be dying within the Igbo speaking community, while section 3 applies the same parameters to an average Igbo family and the individual speaker of the language. Section 4 presents the new and emerging trends in the adaptation of the Igbo language to the realities of the 21$^{st}$ century, while section 5 forms the summary and conclusion.

## 2. The Signs of the Death of the Igbo Language

Having drawn the attention of the world to the problem of language death, UNESCO (2003) has additionally provided some factors with which a language community can assess the vitality and/or endangerment of its language. They are nine factors, out of which six are to be used for evaluating the vitality and level of endangerment of a language, two for the assessment of language attitude, and the last for the evaluation of the urgency to document the language. They are summarized in the table below.

Without going into the later developments, improvements, adjustments and even statistical implementation of the above named UNESCO factors by various authors, the rest of this section simply relates these factors to the Igbo language community and to the average Igbo family and the individual Igbo speaker. The approach is simply impressionistic (subjective), and no serious effort is made at any form of statistical analysis.

### 2.1 The Signs within the Igbo Community

#### 2.1.1 Intergenerational Language Transmission

This factor involves the extent to which a language is transmitted from one generation to the next, and there is evidence of intergenerational

| Language Vitality and Endangerment | Language Attitudes | Urgency of Documentation |
|---|---|---|
| 1. Intergenerational Language Transmission<br>2. Absolute Number of Speakers<br>3. Proportion of Speakers within the Total Population<br>4. Trends in Existing Language Domains<br>5. Response to New Dimensions and Media<br>6. Materials for Language Education and Literacy | 7. Government and Institutional Language Attitudes<br><br>8. Community Members Attitude towards Their Own Language | 9. Amount and Quality of Documentation |

|Table 1. UNESCO's (2003) Language Vitality Assessment Factors

transmission of the language when the members of the older generation fully speak the language to the next generation. As a means for measuring how efficiently and effectively this is achieved, the language could be categorized as follows:

*Safe*: the language can be spoken by all generations; no sign of threat, and intergenerational transmission is not affected

***Stable yet threatened***: The language is spoken in most contexts by all generations with unbroken intergenerational transmission, yet multilingualism in the native language and one or more dominant language(s) has usurped certain important communication contexts.

***Unsafe:*** Most but not all children or families of a particular community speak their language as their first language, but it may be restricted to specific social domains (such as at home where children interact with their parents and grandparents).

***Definitively endangered***: The language is no longer being learned as the mother tongue by children in the home. The youngest speakers are thus of the *parental generation*. At this stage, parents may still speak their language to their children, but their children do not typically respond in the language.

***Severely endangered***: The language is *spoken* only by *grandparents and older generations*; while the parent generation may still *understand* the language, they typically do not speak it to their children.

***Critically endangered:*** The youngest speakers are in the *great-grandparental generation*, and the language is not used for everyday interactions. These older people often *remember* only part of the language but *do not use* it, since there may not be anyone to speak with.

***Extinct:*** There is no one who can speak or remember the language.

How does the Igbo language fare with regard to all these? First, the language is not fully spoken by all generations. Both at home and at the place of work, the average adult Igbo person does not consistently use the Igbo language without adding some English words. At the place of work, whether in the private or the public sector within the Igbo speaking states or region, he/she is not required to communicate with his/her colleagues in Igbo, neither is he/she required to transmit official communications in Igbo. A similar lack of compulsion also exists at the home front, where the communication with the children is more through the English language than in Igbo, or at best, in a mixture of English and Igbo: *Ingiligbo.*

What then could be transmitted to the children if not the same mixture? Therefore an intergenerational transmission of the language within the Igbo speaking communities is very weak, except in some village settings, where the people who cannot make it to the towns have no other means of communication but their local village dialects that they also transmit to their next generation. One of the memorable incidents resulting from this scenario is the often amusing encounter between the 'village child' and the 'town/city child', when the city children visit the village with their parents. Of course the 'city child' can only communicate with his mixture of Igbo and English, just like its parents. The village child cannot help having a good laugh thereafter, ending it with statements like *Ọ na-asụrụ m oyibo.* 'He is speaking English to

| Category | State of the Igbo Language |
|---|---|
| 1  Safe | NOT *Safe*, because: (a) it is not spoken by all generations; (b) intergenerational transmission is weak because of *Ingiligbo* |
| 2  Stable Yet Threatened | (a) NOT    *Stable*   because the smooth intergenerational transmission to bring about the stability is poor <br><br> (b)    *Threatened*   because another language (English) has seriously encroached on its areas of usage |
| 3  Unsafe | *Unsafe* because many children or families do not <u>fully</u> speak Igbo as their first language, except with few grandparents |

| 4 | Definitely Endangered | *Definitely Endangered*, because (a) the children do not fully learn Igbo as their mother tongue, and (b) the parents speak to their children in Igbo, but many children do not typically respond in Igbo |
|---|---|---|
| 5 | Severely Endangered | *Onset of Becoming Severely Endangered* because (a) a lot (i.e. almost the majority) of present generation of parents speak Igbo with their own parents (i.e. their children's grandparents), but do not speak Igbo to their own children |
| 6 | Critically Endangered | *Not Critically Endangered* because it is not the grandparents alone that speak it, and the language is still being used for everyday interaction |
| 7 | Extinct | Does not yet apply. |

From the above assessment, the state of the Igbo language with regard to *Intergenerational Transmission* cannot definitely be described as *extinct* or *critically endangered*. Instead, the language is presently *not safe, unstable*, and *threatened*; it has entered the threshold of the onset of *severe endangerment*, though not yet critically endangered.

### 2.1.2 Absolute Number of Speakers

UNESCO (2003) points out that a small population is vulnerable to any form of decimation through disease, warfare or natural disaster. Crystal (2014: 16) formulates this in a more poignant manner: "any language which has a very small number of speakers is bound to be in trouble, and commonsense tells us that this should usually be the case". The Igbo language does not seem to fall within this group, because the population of the Igbo speakers in Nigeria runs into several millions. Nevertheless it is also a fact that it is actually the number of the 'mixers' that runs into several millions, and their number would continue to increase as the number of the older generation of fully competent speakers decreases over the years. In other words, the number of competent Igbo speakers has been decreasing over the years, in spite of the immense growth in the population of the speakers. Hence, in terms of the *Absolute Number of Speakers* of the language, the Igbo language can also be described as *unstable, threatened,* and *definitely endangered,* though not yet *severely endangered.*

### 2.1.3 Proportion of Speakers within the Total Population

The Igbo ethnic group constitutes the third majority ethnic group within Nigeria. However, a situation where millions of the speakers of the language communicate by code-mixing cannot lead to the sustenance of the language; instead, it would only gradually lead to the emergence of a Creole language sometime in the future. Hence, an increase in the total population of code-mixing Igbo speakers within Nigeria does not amount to an increase in the total number of competent speakers of the language within the whole country. Instead, it actually indicates a progressive reduction. Another relevant point is the fact that the Igbo speaking group are surrounded by other language minorities who would rather protect their languages from being eroded by the Igbo language. This gives a false impression of the Igbo language being dominant. But in real terms, it is the code-mixing speakers of the language that are becoming more and more dominant, not the fully competent speakers of the language.

### 2.1.4 Trends in Existing Language Domains

What range of topics can be discussed with the Igbo language? Where? And with whom? These are pertinent questions which UNESCO sees as useful for examining and establishing the extent of the domains that a language can cover. More concretely, the points to be examined with regard to the available language domains are: (1) universality in the use of the language, (2) multilingual parity with one or two other languages, (3) dwindling domains of use, (4) limited or formal domains, (5) highly limited domain, and (6) extinct.

In terms of universality of usage, Igbo is not used in all domains. It is code-mixed in interactions and other discourse domains like entertainment and creativity. It is exclusively in radio and TV news broadcasts that we have almost 100% transmission in Igbo. But even in this domain, the English language dominates, because the greater portion of broadcast time by most radio stations within the Igbo speaking states is in English. English dominates in almost all domains, because it is seen as the language of social, economic, and political opportunity. However, one domain that has been resistant to the encroachment of the English language is the traditional *Kolanut Ceremony*, which is a core part of Igbo tradition and culture. The ceremony is executed only in Igbo, and it is an unspoken law that *Ọji anaghị anụ oyibo* "the Kolanut does not understand a foreign language." Therefore, whoever is to say the kolanut toast must endeavor to say it in Igbo. A mistake in the form of code-switching during the process is not to the favour of the speaker. This domain is like one of the last bastions yet to be encroached upon through code-mixing. One can therefore speak of a narrowing down or a *dwindling* in the number of domains involving the exclusive use of the Igbo language, because looking out for a competent Igbo speaker when breaking the kolanut is already an indication of a limited number of fluent speakers.

### 2.1.5 Response to New Domains and Media

The manner in which a language responds to new domains is described as follows. It is dynamic if the language is used in all new domains; robust/active if it is used in most new domains; receptive if it is used in many domains; coping if it is used in some new domains; minimal if used only in a few new domains, and inactive if not used in any new domain. How does the Igbo language respond to new domains?

The Igbo language is not used to express all existing domains, neither has there been the quick response to express all new domains in the langauge. The language can therefore not be described as dynamic with regard to the nature of its response to new domains. Instead, it is still struggling with the deluge of terms from all the already existing domains. This struggle most often ends up as code-switching or outright use of already existing English terms. Therefore, its manner of response to new domains can also not be described as robust/active. It is also not receptive because it is not used in many new domains; neither is it coping, because it is not used on <u>some</u> new domains. Instead, it can be described as minimal, because it is used in only a few new domains (like mobile phone and internet). Although its response to new domains cannot be described as inactive, the position of the language on this scale is still precarious, because it needs more effort to move up the scale from coping, to receptive, to robust/active, up to dynamic, but less effort for it to move down from minimal to inactive.

## 2.1.6 Materials for Language Education and Literacy

UNESCO's (2003, p. 12) position that "education in the language is essential for language vitality" is a point the Igbo language is still struggling with. Written Igbo is not used in official government communication, although there is an existing standard orthography, with some dictionaries and literary works. There is actually no explicit dedication to the promotion of literacy in the language on the part of the governments of the Igbo speaking states. Hence, the quantity of written educational material in Igbo is low, and the many individual efforts to translate and write various types of books in Igbo, cannot be compared with the enormous amount of books being produced in the English language by speakers of the Igbo language in Igbo land. In addition, the available books in Igbo are limited in terms of domain of coverage and target audience. For example, children's literature in Igbo is not only not widely available, but it is also limited in scope, compared with the more readily available children's literature in English that has a wide scope of coverage in terms of topics and age range of the children. Most of what can be considered children's literature in Igbo are, for now, mainly the compulsory books used in the primary and secondary schools but not in the homes; contrary to the great number of children's books in English that many Igbo parents regularly buy for their children. The conclusion is that written material in Igbo is available to only a minority of the population of Igbo speakers.

### 2.1.7 Governmental and Institutional Language Attitudes and Policies

Governmental attitude revolves around the nature of the support it provides the languages and the language groups, as well as the extent to which it encourages or discourages the assimilation of minority language groups. For the Igbo language, two main factors highlight the governmental and institutional language attitudes in Nigeria, one at the federal level and the other at the level of the Igbo speaking states.

At the federal level stands Nigeria's National Policy on Education, with its stipulation that the medium of instruction in the first three years of primary education should be in the child's mother tongue, starting with the three major Nigerian languages, Hausa, Igbo and Yoruba. This policy was made with a view to encouraging the growth and development of Nigeria's three major languages as a national asset. At the state level is the constitutional right of the various state governments, including the Igbo speaking states, to fashion out and implement language policies that address the linguistic peculiarities of their states.

The conclusion from this scenario is that the Igbo language has both federal and state level constitutional rights, support and protection. However, this institutionally favourable environment is contradicted by the simple fact that the activities of the government and other institutions in the Igbo speaking states of Nigeria are not compulsorily executed and documented in Igbo. Hence, English remains the official language for all government activities, while the code-mixed Engiligbo remains the language of everyday interaction, with the Igbo language being gradually assimilated.

### 2.1.8 Community Members' Attitudes toward Their Own Language

The core points here are (1) does one value one's language? and, (2) does one wish it to be protected?

Over the years a lot of effort has gone into drawing attention to how the

Igbo people have gradually been abandoning their language, either as a result of the effect of the colonial educational system or also as a result of the desire to 'move forward' through adaptation to the modern world by using the English language. This situation has not escaped many Igbo language promoters and enthusiasts, whose clamour for the promotion of the language has not been without some effects, especially on some parents who wish to see their children speak Igbo. For example, some parents now deliberately register their children in those primary or secondary schools where they hope their children would learn Igbo. There are also cases where the Parents-Teachers Association of some schools deliberately get the schools to engage an Igbo teacher for their children. Such developments are indeed very good and noteworthy, but need not be one-sided. For example, the late Prof. Ohiri-Aniche once narrated to me the case of a mother who berated the administrative authority of a primary school for not teaching Igbo to her child. Having made clear her 'strong feelings' to the proprietor of the school, the same parent turns to her child with the words: "Juniour, come. Enter the car let's go". She forgot to speak Igbo to her child! There is no doubt here that this particular parent has recognized the need for the child to learn Igbo; but she does not yet see any role in it for herself; instead, she sees it as the responsibility of the school. It should also be pointed out that it might not be obvious to her that she would actually contribute a lot to revitalizing the language if she were to start re-learning the language with her child, and the effort of the school would only supplement the initiative at the home front. This example is not an exception, because many Igbo speakers are not different.

### 2.1.9 Amount and Quality of Documentation

The urgency for documenting a language is dependent on the type and quality of existing materials. According to UNESCO, a language can be graded in this regard as excellent, good, fair, fragmentary, inadequate, and undocumented.

A language is to be graded as excellent if the following conditions are met:

> **There are comprehensive grammars and dictionaries, extensive texts; constant flow of language materials. Abundant annotated high-quality audio and video recordings exist.**

The Igbo language does not seem to meet these conditions for the following reasons. First, it does not yet have comprehensive grammars and dictionaries. There are definitely some old, well-known grammar books of the language like Green and Igwe's (1961) A Descriptive Grammar of Igbo Igbo, Welmers and Welmers (1968) Igbo: A Learner's Manual, and Williamson's (1973) Igbo English Dictionary, which is a combination of a grammar book and a dictionary (later repackaged in 2012 by Roger Blench: www.rogerblench.info). These are all bilingual, and the later grammar books by native speakers are also bilingual, for example Ọgbalụ's (1972) School Certificate/G.C.E. Igbo and Okonkwo's (1974) A Complete Course in Igbo Grammar, both of which for many years served as the grammar books for those who wished to take Igbo at the G.C.E. level. Thereafter followed the years of gradual recovery from the civil war, which of course delayed a lot of material and intellectual developments in the South East and neighbouring South-South. That is why the next grammar books of the language took years to come. For example, Emenanjo's Elements of Modern Igbo Grammar: A Descriptive Approach was published in 1978, to be followed by a lull of about thirty years, after which he published his most comprehensive Grammar of Contemporary Igbo (Emenanjo 2015) before his demise in 2016. But all these works, whether before or immediately after the Nigerian civil war, are all bilingual. None is monolingual, and a comprehensive, monolingual grammar book of the language is yet to be written.

There are nevertheless genuine efforts at writing monolingual grammar books of the language. These had their origin in the terminological developments of the already mentioned Society for the Promotion of Igbo Language and Culture (SPILC). With the availability of the needed Igbo grammatical terms in the late seventies, Igbo scholars of the period started writing monolingual grammar books of the language, especially for secondary schools and colleges of education. Some of the monolingual grammar books of this period include Ume, Ugoji and Dike's (1989) Ụmị Nkọwa Ụtọaụsụ Igbo, Osuagwu's (1989) Igbo Maka Ndi Sekondiri Nta, Ezikeojiakụ's (1989) Fọnọlọji na Ụtọasụsụ Igbo, Ngọesi's (1989) Nchịkọta Ọmụmụ Nke Asụsụ Igbo, and Emenanjo's (1983) Fonọlọji na Mọfọlọji n'Igbo. It is not a coincedence that these grammar books were published within the same period by this set of authors, because most of them were also members of SPILC. Hence, their works marked the immediate application of the Igbo grammatical terms formulated by SPILC. Thereafter followed other minor monolingual secondary school grammar books by many other authors, most of who were their students.

However, the fact that the majority of the monolingual grammar books of the language are mainly for primary/secondary schools and colleges of education has not escaped some Igbo language scholars who, now as university lecturers and professors, feel the need to go beyond the terminological needs of the 70s and 80s that were fully satisfied by the achievements of SPILC at the time. This desire has gradually led to the production of different forms of monolingual Igbo grammar and language books for higher levels of education. Both Ikekonwu, Ezikeojiaku, Ubani and Ugoji's (1999) Fonọlọji na Gramma Igbo, and Ụba-Mgbemena's (2006) Ntọala Usoro Asụsụ Igbo, and many others fall within this group.

The dictionaries of the language are in a comparable state. Welmers and Welmers' (1968) Igbo: A Learner's Dictionary and Williamson's (1971) Igbo English Dictionary served as the two main dictionaries of the language for many years after the Nigerian civil war, until the achievements of SPILC in the area of grammar books of the language impelled some to attempt something similar for the dictionaries of the language. A good example is Nnaji's (1978) Modern English Igbo Dictionary (with Illustrations). Some years later came Echeruo's (1998) Igbo-English Dictionary (With an English-Igbo index) and Igwe's (1999) Igbo-English Dictionary, to be followed by Eke (2001) Igbo-English Dictionary (Ọkọwa Okwu), Emenako (2005) Nkọwaokwu Igbo n'Okwu Bekee (Igbo-English Dictionary), and Akponye's Bi-Lingual Dictionary of the Igbo and English Languages. Of all these, Igwe's dictionary is the most comprehensive in terms of dialect coverage and the number of headwords. Nevertheless, they are all bilingual (Igbo-English or English-Igbo) dictionaries. This move towards bilingual lexicography, which had its origin in the colonial dictionaries, has been countered by the specialized dictionary, Igbo Adị, by Mbah, Mbah, Ikeokwu, Okeke et al (2013), which adopts Igbo as the language of explanation. In addition, a new Igbo monolingual dictionary titled Osanye Okwu Igbo na Nkowa Ya by Mbah is expected to be published before the end of the year 2021. All these efforts to produce various materials in Igbo can definitely not be described as excellent or superlative; nevertheless, they indicate a positive development.

The second condition of excellence with regard to the Amount and Quality of Documentation of a language is the existence of extensive texts in the language. This is yet to be achieved for Igbo, because written Igbo texts are not extensive in quantity and scope of domain coverage. There is also no constant flow of Igbo language materials arising from an enduring research and continuous effort to improve on existing materials. Presently, annotated high quality audio and video recordings are gradually being facilitated through the internet and ICT technology.

In the light of all these points, Igbo cannot be regarded as excellent with regard to the amount and quality of its documentation, although from the presently available materials it can also not be described as undocumented, inadequate (with few grammatical sketches) or fragmentary (with some grammatical sketches for linguistic investigation). Its present state cannot be described as other than fair, which, in line with the UNESCO explanation, involves the existence of sufficient amount of grammars, dictionaries, and texts. One would add here, 'sufficient only for a while, with the danger of being outdated if not continued'

Finally, according to Moseley, of all the factors discussed, the most decisive is the intergenerational transmission, i.e. "the likelihood of a language being passed on to the next generation" (Moseley 2007 p. xi). However, at the center of the intergenerational interaction is the individual family. Hence, the family should serve as the springboard for any effort at a language revival. That is why the next section examines the average Igbo family with regard to the intergenerational transmission of the Igbo language.

## 2.2  The Signs within the Igbo Family

UNESCO factor of Intergenerational Language Transmission need not be seen as a rigid factor that is strictly restricted to only the language community, but can also be applied to a family as well as to an individual human being. In other words, the state of the Igbo language within an Igbo family shall be examined with regard to the parameters of intergenerational transmission: safe, vulnerable, definitely endangered, severely endangered, critically endangered, or extinct.

### 2.2.1  How _Safe_ is the Igbo Language within the Family?

A language is safe within a family when it is fully spoken by all generations within the family, and fully transmitted from one generation to the next. The Igbo language is presently not fully spoken by all generations within an average Igbo family. The older members of the family speak it better than the younger ones, but still with a lot of code-mixing. One cannot therefore speak of an 'uninterrupted' transmission of the Igbo language from one generation to the next, because the code-mixing in itself is indeed the interruption of the flow of one language by another. Therefore, with the present situation of things, the Igbo language is not safe within an average Igbo family.

### 2.2.2  How _Vulnerable_ is the Igbo Language within the Family?

A language is vulnerable in a family when most children speak it, but it is restricted to certain areas/domains, like for example only 'at home'. This does not seem to apply to the Igbo language, because most Igbo children generally do not fully speak the language, not to talk of their fully speaking it 'at home', where the mixing of English and Igbo reigns supreme. Hence, the language is not just vulnerable, but actually 'below' the scale of being vulnerable.

### 2.2.3  How _Definitely Endangered_ is the Igbo Language within the Family

A language is definitely endangered within the family, if the children no longer learn it as their mother tongue at home. This seems to apply to a lot of Igbo speaking (i.e. Igbo-mixing) families, where Ingiligbo is the language that is spoken to the children from the very first day. In such families, the Igbo language is definitely endangered, because the children cannot learn the language as their mother tongue,

### 2.2.4 How Severely Endangered is the Igbo Language within the Family?

Where a language is severely endangered within the family, it is spoken mainly by the grandparents and the older generations; the members of the parent generation may understand it, but do not speak it to their children or among themselves. This scenario partly applies to many Igbo families, where the grandparents speak the language and the parent generation understands it but does not speak it fully to their children, except through code-mixing. Therefore, as this already happens within many families, though not within the majority of Igbo families, the conclusion is that the Igbo language is on the entry point of being severely endangered within the family.

### 2.2.5 How Critically Endangered/Extinct is the Igbo Language within the Family?

For a langauge to be *critically endangered* within a family, the youngest speakers of the language must be the grandparents, who speak it partially and infrequently. And for it to become *extinct*, there must be no speakers left. Both conditions do not 'yet' apply to the Igbo language, because in the majority of families the grandparents still speak the language.

Finally, the state of the Igbo language with the average Igbo family can be described as not only *definitely endangered*, but also at the onset of *severe endangerment*. But what about the level of the individual speaker of the language? The individual can apply the same parameters to himself. For, if he/she cannot hold a conversation in the Igbo language without code-mixing, and can also not fully speak it to a child without code-mixing with English, then the langauge is *definitely endangered* in him/her, because he/she cannot fully transmit it to the next generation. Furthemore, if such an individual understands the language, but is not able to speak it to his/her children, then the language is *severely endangered* in him/her. It suffices to draw attention to these levels of endangerment, so that the individual speaker can use them to examine himself/herself for, as UNESCO (2003, p. 4) puts it, "In the end, it is the speakers, not outsiders, who maintain or abandon languages."

## 3. The Signs of Resistance to Death

All the parameters examined point towards a downward trend for the Igbo language, and many Igbo scholars have been documenting and commenting on this downward trend over the years. Asonye (2013) for example, gives several examples of the negative attitudes of many Igbo parents and some instances where the parents forbid their children from speaking Igbo because of a hoped-for advantage in speaking English. Others that have strongly raised their voices against the downward trend include Nwadike (2014), Onwudiwe (2016), *Otu Subakwa Igbo,* and many others. Some of the comments on this downward trend have been so negative that one could not see any way out for the Igbo language. But

| | Category | State of the Igbo Language |
|---|---|---|
| 1 | Safe | NOT *Safe*, because: (a) it is not spoken by all generations; (b) intergenerational transmission is weak because of *Ingiligbo* |
| 2 | Stable Yet Threatened | (a) NOT *Stable* because the smooth intergenerational transmission to bring about the stability is poor<br><br>(b) *Threatened* because another language (English) has seriously encroached on its areas of usage |
| 3 | Unsafe | *Unsafe* because many children or families do not <u>fully</u> speak Igbo as their first language, except with few grandparents |
| 4 | Definitely Endangered | *Definitely Endangered*, because (a) the children do not fully learn Igbo as their mother tongue, and (b) the parents speak to their children in Igbo, but many children do n ot typically respond in Igbo |
| 5 | Severely Endangered | *Onset of Becoming Severely Endangered* because (a) a lot (i.e. almost the majority) of present generation of parents speak Igbo with their own parents (i.e. their children's grandparents), but do not speak Igbo to their own children |
| 6 | Critically Endangered | *Not Critically Endangered* because it is not the grandparents alone that speak it, and the language is still being used for everyday interaction |
| 7 | Extinct | Does not yet apply. |

surprisingly, there has also been another trend which seems to go against the downward trend, and which can be described as "a resistance to the death of the Igbo language". This new trend is not powered or sponsored by any individual or organisation; instead, it can be described as the gradual emergence of various efforts that never existed before, but whose origin lies in the general feeling that the Igbo language should be promoted. The trend has been facilitated by the new media, especially the social media and the Internet. This section is a summary of the efforts at utilizing the new technology for the promotion of the Igbo language.

The first huddle that has been overcome here is the development of the appropriate fonts and keyboard for the language. The font problem has been taken care of through UNICODE, and many fonts are now available for the realization of the script of the language. With regard to keyboard, a list of available keyboards for the Igbo language is available here: https://scriptsource.org/cms/scripts/page.php?item_id=entry_detail&uid=6g48c96422. The first is the Igbo Basic keyboard (https://keyman.com/keyboards/basic_kbdibo), which can serve the simple purpose of writing Igbo, while the second keyboard, Naija NFD (https://keyman.com/keyboards/el_naija), has the capacity to meet higher demands like tone marking for Igbo and some other Nigerian languages. The other keyboards are: *Nailangs, Nigeria Dot (SIL), Pan Africa Mnemonic (SIL),* and *Pan Africa Positional (SIL).* With these developments some Nigerians have also started developing additional keyboards for various Nigerian languages, like the efforts by Nnenna Nwosu and Adebunmi Adeniran. With these developments one can conclude that the Igbo language can now avail itself of these facilities to navigate the $21^{st}$ century and adequately address the fears that "systems and application software are not available by default for Igbo" (Iloene et al 2013, p.)

This section presents some of the efforts that can be described as 'resistance to the death' of the Igbo language. They can be divided into purely academic and research oriented websites, Igbo language learning websites, Igbo language and culture websites, and Igbo *YouTube*

| | Name | Goals/Objectives | Web Address |
|---|---|---|---|
| 1 | About the Igbo Language | A collection of valuable, materials on Igbo compiled by the late Mrs. Frances W. Pritchett (1922-2012) | http://www.columbia.edu/itc/mealac/pritchett/00fwp/igbo_index.html |
| 2 | Ókwú Ìgbò | A support to Research on the Igbo Language through:<br><br>✓ Igbo Language Symposium<br>✓ Igbo Language Studies Series [a monograph series]<br>✓ Igbo Language Studies [a journal] | http://okwuigbo.org/ |
| 3 | Language Learning: Igbo | A Research Guide | https://library.bu.edu/igbo |

# Some Igbo Language Websites
## (A) For Academic and General Research

| | Name | Goals/Objectives | Web Address |
|---|---|---|---|
| 1 | MANGO | Learn Igbo and embark on a journey through Nigeria's Igboland. | https://mangolanguages.com/available-languages/learn-igbo/ |
| 2 | Ezinaụlọ | The push adults need to teach themselves Igbo . | https://ezinaulo.com/ |
| 3 | Learn101 | to help you learn Igbo, by going step by step. | http://learn101.org/igbo.php |
| 4 | Nwadaigbo | ✓ Complete Igbo Language Course<br>✓ Translation and Transcription<br>✓ Teach Your Children Igbo<br>✓ Conversation Classes in Igbo | https://nwaadaigbo.com/ |
| 5 | Learn Igbo Now | ✓ To help both adults and children speak Igbo language fluently whilst learning about Igbo culture and heritage. | https://www.learnigbonow.com/?r_done=1<br><br>[A highly creative way of teaching Igbo to children] |
| 6 | Igbo School | offers Igbo language courses from beginner to intermediate stages | https://www.igboteacher.com/ |
| 7 | Learn Igbo | to teach you and help you learn Igbo for free | http://ilanguages.org/igbo.php |
| 8 | IgboStudy | A collection of Igbo books for Children and adults | https://www.igbostudy.com/igbo -books |

*(B) Igbo Language Learning Website*

---

[1]https://guardian.ng/technology/scientist-develops-keyboards-in-nigerian-languages/
[2]https://venturesafrica.com/this-nigerian-linguist-is-changing-the-face-of-technology-with-the-invention-of-a-multilingual-keyboard/

| | Name | Goals/Objectives | Web Address |
|---|---|---|---|
| 1 | Ụwa Ndị Igbo | ✓ Promotion of Igbo Tradition and Culture<br>✓ Making Igbo known to the World at large<br>✓ Teaching Igbo to Diaspora Children<br><br>https://uwandiigbo.org/services/ | https://uwandiigbo.org |
| 2 | Igbo Guide | ✓ provides simple and easy-to-read insights in Igbo language and Igbo culture.<br>✓ contains a complete guide on Igbo language, highlighted in sample conversations including native audio clips, includes an Igbo English dictionary and explains the basic Igbo grammar structure. | https://www.igboguide.org/ |
| 3 | Ọkpara House | To produce  Igbo Cultural content elevated and made relev ant to contemporary lifestyles. | https://www.okparahouse.com/ |
| 4 | Ikenga Nation | Through the use of puppets (like on Sesame Street): to educate young Igbo children (in Igbo land, Nigeria) about academic concepts and steer them away from superstitious beliefs, and give them life skills to grow and prosper in life. | https://ikenganation.com/ |

*(C) Igbo Language and Culture*

| | |
|---|---|
| 1 | *Mmuta Di Uto - Igbo Children's Show*<br>https://www.youtube.com/channel/UCsYsgOrQUbmbP5RRRZ3Btjg |
| 2 | *Learn Igbo - Aha m efula*<br>*https://www.youtube.com/channel/UCnLGeT3u_K4AOYk2xtSpCRg* |
| 3 | *Learn Igbo – A Channel for Learning Igbo*<br>*https://www.youtube.com/c/LearnIgbo/featured* |
| 4 | *Made  in Igbo*<br>*https://www.youtube.com/channel/UCyA-4K1kSpo0VcxmKhV5cvw* |
| 5 | *Learn Igbo with Ugbo Oyibo*<br>*https://www.youtube.com/channel/UCmkhA2TSUcJp-i9236WKEZA* |
| 6 | *Learn Igbo – Aha m Efula*<br>*https://www.youtube.com/channel/UCnLGeT3u_K4AOYk2xtSpCRq* |
| 7 | *Ness-ana TV - Igbo Language for Preschool*<br>*https://www.youtube.com/watch?v=1sajihaGB3M&list=PLXsOc2mvOruDNPL9Q12XCcIS9FomINYDx&index=6* |
| 8 | *Bino Fino – An Igbo Cartoon for Children*<br>*https://www.youtube.com/watch?v=NPmtxkDnf7A* |
| 9 | *The Story of Jesus in Igbo*<br>*https://www.youtube.com/watch?v=1RV9fTTtgBA* |

*(D) Igbo YouTube Channels and Resources*

Finally, these new developments are indeed highly encouraging, and seem to indicate that all hope is not lost for the Igbo language. It is indeed noteworthy that the most creative of these efforts are concentrated on the children and the family, which are the very core of the intergenerational transmission of any human language. One can therefore hope that the present upswing is maintained so that the already existing gap in the *intergenerational transmission* of the Igbo language would be permanently closed as the Igbo language gradually covers more domains in the 21$^{st}$ century. ᴸ

## 5. Conclusion

*Ndị Igbo* have been known for always welcoming and adapting to change with bursts of creative impulse in various directions, but most often to the neglect their language. That is why the history of the Igbo language can be described on the one hand, as an internal struggle of the language to survive this strong drive of *Ndị Igbo* towards change and adaptation; and on the other hand as an external struggle with the limited and limiting technological possibilities of the 20th century. Now in the 21$^{st}$ century the external struggle has been overcome, because all the possibilities for the realization of the Igbo language in all forms of the new media are now available, much more than has ever been athe case since the origin of the language and the existence of *Ndị Igbo*. One thing needful is *the internal struggle*, within the family as well as within the individual, to not only adapt to the peculiarities of the new media in the use of the language, but to also adapt the new media to the peculiarities and needs of the Igbo language. The few websites and the efforts therein are indications in this direction, as we look forward to going beyond these bursts of creative impulse to sustained growth within this and other domains. ᴸ

## References

Akponye, O. (2009). *Bi-lingual dictionary of the Igbo and English languages.* Owerri: Totan Publishers.

Asonye, E. (2013). UNESCO prediction of the Igbo language death: Facts and Fable. *Journal of the Linguistic Association of Nigeria,* 16 (1-2), 91-98.

Crystal, D. (2000). *Language death.* Cambridge: Cambridge University Press Echeruo, M. J. C. 1998. *Igbo-English dictionary.* New Haven/London: Yale University Press.

Eke, J. G. (2001) *Igbo-English dictionary (Okowa Okwu).* Enugu: New Generation Books.

Emenako, G.E. (2005). *Nkowaokwu Igbo n'okwu bekee (Igbo-English Dictionary).* Owerri: Pearl Marble Nigeria Limited.

Emenanjo, N.E. (1978). *Elements of modern Igbo grammar: A descriptive approach.* Ibadan : Oxford University Press

Emenanjo, N.E. (1983). *Fonoloji na mofoloji n'Igbo.* Onitsha: Varsity Publishing Company.

Emenanjo, N.E. (2015). *A Grammar of contemporary Igbo: Constituents, features and processes.* Port Harcourt: M & J Grand Orbit

Ezikeojiaku, P. A. (1989). *Fonoloji na utoasusu Igbo.* Yaba: Macmillan Nigeria. Green, M. M. & Igwe, G. E. (1963). *A descriptive grammar of Igbo.* Berlin: Akademie-Verlag.

Igwe, E. G. (1999). *Igbo-English dictionary.* Ibadan: University Press Plc. Ikekeonwu, C., Ezikeojiaku, P. A., Ubani, A. &

Ugoji, J. (1999). *Fonoloji na grama Igbo.* Ibadan: University Press Plc

Iloene, M. I., Iloene, G. O., Mbah, E. E., & Mbah, B. M. (2013). The use of new technologies for the teaching of the Igbo language in schools: Challenges and prospects. In L. Bradley & S. Thouësny (Eds.), *20 Years of EUROCALL: Learning from the Past, Looking to the Future. Proceedings of the 2013 EUROCALL Conference, Évora, Portugal* (pp. 117-122). Dublin/Voillans: Research-publishing.net

Moseley, C. (Ed.) (2007). *Encyclopedia of the world's endangered languages.* London: Routledge.

Ndimele, O. (2005). Globalization and the vanishing voices of Africa: Any glimmer of hope at this turbulent seas. In O. M. Ndimele (Ed.), *Globalisation and the study of languages in Africa.* Port Harcourt Nigeria: Grand Orbit Communication.

Ngoesi, M.C. (2000). *Nchikota omumu nke asusu Igbo.* Nkpor (Nigeria): Optimal Press.

Nnaji, H.I. (1985). *Modern English Igbo dictionary.* Onitsha: Gonaj Books.

Nwadike, I.U. (2014). *Igbo language in education: An historical study.* Obosi: Pacific Publishers.

Nwanze, R. E. (1991). *Mua Igbo. Igbo grammar for language students.* Ibadan: Claverianum Press.

Ogbalu, F. C. (1972). *School certificate Igbo.* Onitsha: University Publishing.

Okigbo, C. (1971). *Labyrinths with path of thunder.* London: Holmes & Meier Publication.

M. CHIBU ONUKAWA

# How To Count In Igbo

## Summary

*Counting is an ancient activity in human society as there has always been the need to count. As applicable to other activities, societies has old system of counting which became modernized as people encountered complexities in counting. This situation is applicable to the Igbo society. In Igbo there existed the old system of counting, popularly referred to as the traditional counting system. Various short comings and deficits were experienced in the traditional counting system over the years: and thus there was serious need for improvement. This led to the evolvement/development of a modern counting system that is currently in use in the Igbo language.*

## 1. Introduction

Counting is the individual isolation of items, occurrences or events in terms of tokens that follow one another (Maduka-Durunze 1997). From time immemorial man has always had the need to count. Counting was just to take inventory of stock or to keep track of events. The need for counting increases as societies become more complex with the increase in transactions and other activities that need to be assessed in terms of counting.

Counting co-exists with more-than-one. In other words, from ancient times counting, as an exercise, has been connected to plurality. Plurality itself begins with doubling (of an item etc) and any concept represented by the number 'two' must, of course, be of greater significance than what is known of it. Counting is also based on number systems. The need for elaborate counting necessitates a number system. Some issues are involved in the development of a number system: the concepts for numbers are given names, and radical numbers (landmark numbers) are developed. Radical numbers are bases upon which lengthy counting could be anchored. A radical number is called a radix (Maduka-Durunze 1997). It is likely that the number 2 was the earliest radix in all cultures, but the numbers, 5,10, 20 etc. displaced it following the increase in complexity of entities in the society. These examples are also applicable to the Igbo traditional counting system that was later replaced with a modern counting system.

## 2. The Traditional Counting System

The traditional counting system is an essentially analogue system. It is a complex system which (in theory) cannot count beyond 400 (*nnụ*). The system is old-fashioned and cannot operate in a computer-driven world where many radices and digitalization are involved. The traditional counting system has only four radices (landmarks): one (*otu*), ten (*iri*), twenty (*ọgụ*), four hundred (*nnụ*). It does not have a place for zero (*ziro/efu*), and it is non-decimal. It is partly additive, partly subtractive and partly multiplicative. It also has a poorly developed paradigm for numbers. It is only through an intricate manipulation of the numbers (one, ten, twenty and four hundred) that some other high numbers are generated and expressed (Emenanjo 1978). For instance a number like *160, 103* is expressed as *"Nnụ nnụ na ọgụ iri na atọ"*. The involvements here are highly demanding and replete with ambiguities and inadequacies, and the average adult of the present day generation can hardly make sense of them.  L

## 3. The Modern Counting System

In 1978 The Society for *Promoting Igbo Language and Culture (SPILC)* in conjunction with the *National Language Centre* painstakingly designed a modern counting system for Igbo to replace the old system (Emenanjo 2015). This was a matter of necessity given the shortcomings and deficits of the traditional counting system. Precisely, the modern counting system was designed to resolve the ambiguities inherent in the traditional system, to broaden the scope of the traditional system in line with the demands of modern technology, and to decimalize the counting system.

The modern counting system has many advantages over the traditional system: it has seven radices (landmarks): 0 (*ziro, efu*), 1 (*otu*), 10 (*iri*), 100 (*narị*), 1,000 (*puku*), 1,000,000 (*nde*), 1,000,000,000 (*ijeri*). It is digital, multiplicative and additive. With the seven radices the new counting system can handle very high numbers which the traditional system (with highest place value of 400) cannot handle. The new system has names for tens and powers of ten up to a billion. It also has names for zero, and for the place values: unit, tens, hundreds, thousands, millions, billions.

It is however necessary to point out that the modern counting system was enriched through the dialects. For example, the names of some numbers were drawn from some dialects of Igbo. *Narị* (Nsukka dialect), *Puku* and *Nde* (Orlu dialect), *Ijeri* (Igbo Uzọ/Ibusa dialect). The tables below show samples of *one* to *ten* of the modern counting system with their dialect:

| ENGLISH | IGBO |
|---------|------|
| One | otu, nnaa, ofu |
| Two | abụọ, abụa, ịbụa, ịbụọ, |
| Three | atọ, ịtọ, ẹtọ |
| Four | annọ, anọ, ịnọ, ẹnọ |
| Five | ise, iso |
| Six | isii, ishii |
| Seven | asaa, ịsaa, ẹsaa |
| Eight asatọ | ịsatọ, ẹsatọ |
| Nine | itoolu, itoghoolu, iteghete, itenaanị |
| Ten | iri, ili |

In spite of such dialect variations, we shall be presenting the modern counting system in the tables below in standard Igbo (*Igbo izugbe*).Most of the examples here are drawn from Emenanjo, 91978, 2015), and Okaasusu Igbo, publication of the Society for Promoting Igbo Language and Culture (SPILC).


## 3.1 One to One Hundred

In the table below, 'one to one hundred' involves the use of one word expression, while all the numbers above ten involve a combination of other numbers with the particular radix through the use of the conjunction *na* 'and'. Hence, *iri na otu* means 'ten and one' (eleven), *iri na anọ* 'ten and four' (fourteen), *iri na itoolu* 'ten and nine' (nineteen). The same method is used to form higher numbers, by adding the first ten numbers to the next radix. For example, *iri abụọ* 'two tens' (twenty), *iri abụọ na otu* 'two tens and one' (twenty one). The follow the other higher numbers: *iri atọ* 'three tens' (thirty), *iri anọ* 'four tens' (forty), *iri ise* 'five tens' (fifty), *iri isii* 'six tens' (sixty), *iri asaa* 'seven tens' (seventy), *iri asatọ* 'eight tens' (eighty), and *iri itoolu* 'nine tens' (ninety). Hundred is *narị* which marks the onset of a new combination of the basic 'one to ten' but at a higher level.

| NUMBER | ENGLISH TRANSLATION | IGBO TRANSLATION |
|---|---|---|
| 0 | Zero | Efu/Ziro |
| 1 | One | Otu |
| 2 | Two | Abụọ |
| 3 | Three | Atọ |
| 4 | Four | Anọ |
| 5 | Five | Ise |
| 6 | Six | Isii |
| 7 | Seven | Asaa |
| 8 | Eight | Asatọ |
| 9 | Nine | Itoolu |
| 10 | Ten | Iri |
| 11 | Eleven | Iri na otu |
| 12 | Twelve | Iri na abụọ |
| 13 | Thirteen | Iri na atọ |
| 14 | Fourteen | Iri na anọ |
| 15 | Fifteen | Iri na ise |
| 16 | Sixteen | Iri na isii |
| 17 | Seventeen | Iri na asaa |
| 18 | Eighteen | Iri na asatọ |
| 19 | Nineteen | Iri na itoolu |
| 20 | Twenty | Iri abụọ |
| 21 | Twenty one | Iri abụọ na otu |
| 22 | Twenty two | Iri abụọ na abụọ |
| 23 | Twenty three | Iri abụọ na atọ |
| 24 | Twenty four | Iri abụọ na anọ |
| 25 | Twenty five | Iri abụọ na ise |
| 26 | Twenty six | Iri abụọ na isii |
| 27 | Twenty seven | Iri abụọ na asaa |
| 28 | Twenty eight | Iri abụọ na asatọ |
| 29 | Twenty nine | Iri abụọ na itoolu |
| 30 | Thirty | Iri atọ |
| 31 | Thirty one | Iri atọ na otu |
| 32 | Thirty two | Iri atọ na abụọ |

*Table 1 - One to Thirty Two*

| NUMBER | ENGLISH TRANSLATION | IGBO TRANSLATION |
|---|---|---|
| 33 | Thirty three | Iri atọ na atọ |
| 34 | Thirty four | Iri atọ na anọ |
| 35 | Thirty five | Iri atọ na ise |
| 36 | Thirty six | Iri atọ na isii |
| 37 | Thirty seven | Iri atọ na asaa |
| 38 | Thirty eight | Iri atọ na asatọ |
| 39 | Thirty nine | Iri atọ na itoolu |
| 40 | Forty | Iri anọ |
| 41 | Forty one | Iri anọ na otu |
| 42 | Forty two | Iri anọ na abụọ |
| 43 | Forty three | Iri anọ na atọ |
| 44 | Forty four | Iri anọ na anọ |
| 45 | Forty five | Iri anọ na ise |

| 46 | Forty six | Iri anọ na isii |
| 47 | Forty seven | Iri anọ na asaa |
| 48 | Forty eight | Iri anọ na asatọ |
| 49 | Forty nine | Iri anọ na itoolu |
| 50 | Fifty | Iri ise |
| 51 | Fifty one | Iri ise na otu |
| 52 | Fifty two | Iri ise na abụọ |
| 53 | Fifty three | Iri ise na atọ |
| 54 | Fifty four | Iri ise na anọ |
| 55 | Fifty five | Iri ise na ise |
| 56 | Fifty six | Iri ise na isii |
| 57 | Fifty seven | Iri ise na asaa |
| 58 | Fifty eight | Iri ise na asatọ |
| 59 | Fifty nine | Iri ise na itoolu |
| 60 | Sixty | Iri isii |
| 61 | Sixty one | Iri isii na otu |
| 62 | Sixty two | Iri isii na abụọ |
| 63 | Sixty three | Iri isii na atọ |
| 64 | Sixty four | Iri isii na anọ |
| 65 | Sixty five | Iri isii na ise |
| 66 | Sixty six | Iri isii na isii |
| 67 | Sixty seven | Iri isii na asaa |
| 68 | Sixty eight | Iri isii na asatọ |
| 69 | Sixty nine | Iri isii na itoolu |
| 70 | Seventy | Iri asaa |
| 71 | Seventy one | Iri asaa na otu |
| 72 | Seventy two | Iri asaa na abụọ |
| 73 | Seventy three | Iri asaa na atọ |
| 74 | Seventy four | Iri asaa na anọ |
| 75 | Seventy five | Iri asaa na ise |
| 76 | Seventy six | Iri asaa na isii |
| 77 | Seventy seven | Iri asaa na asaa |
| 78 | Seventy eight | Iri asaa na asatọ |
| 79 | Seventy nine | Iri asaa na itoolu |
| 80 | Eighty | Iri asatọ |
| 81 | Eighty one | Iri asatọ na otu |
| 82 | Eighty two | Iri asatọ na abụọ |
| 83 | Eighty three | Iri asatọ na atọ |
| 84 | Eighty four | Iri asatọ na anọ |
| 85 | Eighty five | Iri asatọ na ise |
| 86 | Eighty six | Iri asatọ na isii |
| 87 | Eighty seven | Iri asatọ na asaa |
| 88 | Eighty eight | Iri asatọ na asatọ |
| 89 | Eighty nine | Iri asatọ na itoolu |
| 90 | Ninety | Iri itoolu |

*Table 2 - Forty Six to Ninety*

| NUMBER | ENGLISH TRANSLATION | IGBO TRANSLATION |
|--------|---------------------|------------------|
| 91 | Ninety one | Iri itoolu na otu |
| 92 | Ninety two | Iri itoolu na abụọ |
| 93 | Ninety three | Iri itoolu na atọ |
| 94 | Ninety four | Iri itoolu na anọ |
| 95 | Ninety five | Iri itoolu na ise |
| 96 | Ninety six | Iri itoolu na isii |
| 97 | Ninety seven | Iri itoolu na asaa |
| 98 | Ninety eight | Iri itoolu na asatọ |
| 99 | Ninety nine | Iri itoolu na itoolu |

*Table 3 - Ninety One to Ninety Nine*

## 3.2 One Hundred to Two Hundred

The numbers from one hundred upwards involve a progressive and recursive recruitment of the smaller numbers. For example, 101 is *narị na otu* 'one hundred and one'. This sounds of course like the English expression, but watch out for the others! *Narị na iri na otu* 'one hundred AND ten AND one' (one hundred and eleven); *narị na iri na abụọ* 'one hundred AND ten AND two' (one hundred and twelve); *narị na iri abụọ* 'one hundred AND two tens' (one hundred and twenty); *narị na iri abụọ na abụọ* 'one hundred AND two tens AND two' (one hundred and twenty two); *narị na iri ise na atọ* 'one hundred AND five tens AND three' (one hundred and fifty three), and so on, up to two hundred, which is realized as *narị abụọ* 'two hundreds' (i.e. hundred in two places).

| NUMBER | ENGLISH TRANSLATION | IGBO TRANSLATION |
|--------|---------------------|------------------|
| 100 | Hundred | Narị |
| 101 | Hundred and one | Narị na otu |
| 102 | Hundred and two | Narị na abụọ |
| 103 | Hundred and three | Narị na atọ |
| 104 | Hundred and four | Narị na anọ |
| 105 | Hundred and five | Narị na ise |
| 106 | Hundred and six | Narị na isii |
| 107 | Hundred and seven | Narị na asaa |
| 108 | Hundred and eight | Narị na asatọ |

| 109 | Hundred and nine | Narị na itoolu |
| 110 | Hundred and ten | Narị na iri |
| 111 | Hundred and eleven | Narị na iri na otu |
| 112 | Hundred and twelve | Narị na iri na abụọ |
| 113 | Hundred and thirteen | Narị na iri na atọ |
| 114 | Hundred and fourteen | Narị na iri na anọ |
| 115 | Hundred and fifteen | Narị na iri na ise |
| 116 | Hundred and sixteen | Narị na iri na isii |
| 117 | Hundred and seventeen | Narị na iri na asaa |
| 118 | Hundred and eighteen | Narị na iri na asatọ |
| 119 | Hundred and nineteen | Narị na iri na itoolu |
| 120 | Hundred and twenty | Narị na iri abụọ |
| 121 | Hundred and twenty one | Narị na iri abụọ na otu |
| 122 | Hundred and twenty two | Narị na iri abụọ na abụọ |
| 123 | Hundred and twenty three | Narị na iri abụọ na atọ |
| 124 | Hundred and twenty four | Narị na iri abụọ na anọ |
| 125 | Hundred and twenty five | Narị na iri abụọ na ise |
| 126 | Hundred and twenty six | Narị na iri abụọ na isii |
| 127 | Hundred and twenty seven | Narị na iri abụọ na asaa |
| 128 | Hundred and twenty eight | Narị na iri abụọ na asatọ |
| 129 | Hundred and twenty nine | Narị na iri abụọ na itoolu |
| 130 | Hundred and thirty | Narị na iri atọ |
| 131 | Hundred and thirty one | Narị na iri atọ na otu |

*Table 4 - One Hundred to One Hundred and Thirty One*

| 132 | Hundred and thirty two | Narị na iri atọ na abụọ |
| 133 | Hundred and thirty three | Narị na iri atọ na atọ |
| 134 | Hundred and thirty four | Narị na iri atọ na anọ |
| 135 | Hundred and thirty five | Narị na iri atọ na ise |
| 136 | Hundred and thirty six | Narị na iri atọ na isii |
| 137 | Hundred and thirty seven | Narị na iri atọ na asaa |
| 138 | Hundred and thirty eight | Narị na iri atọ na asatọ |
| 139 | Hundred and thirty nine | Narị na iri atọ na itoolu |
| 140 | Hundred and forty | Narị na iri anọ |

| 141 | Hundred and forty one | Narị na iri anọ na otu |
| 142 | Hundred and forty two | Narị na iri anọ na abụọ |
| 143 | Hundred and forty three | Narị na iri anọ na atọ |
| 144 | Hundred and forty four | Narị na iri anọ na anọ |
| 145 | Hundred and forty five | Narị na iri anọ na ise |
| 146 | Hundred and forty six | Narị na iri anọ na isii |
| 147 | Hundred and forty seven | Narị na iri anọ na asaa |
| 148 | Hundred and forty eight | Narị na iri anọ na asatọ |
| 149 | Hundred and forty nine | Narị na iri anọ na itoolu |
| 150 | Hundred and fifty | Narị na iri ise |
| 151 | Hundred and fifty one | Narị na iri ise na otu |
| 152 | Hundred and fifty two | Narị na iri ise na abụọ |
| 153 | Hundred and fifty three | Narị na iri ise na atọ |
| 154 | Hundred and fifty four | Narị na iri ise na anọ |
| 155 | Hundred and fifty five | Narị na iri ise na ise |
| 156 | Hundred and fifty six | Narị na iri ise na isii |
| 157 | Hundred and fifty seven | Narị na iri ise na asaa |
| 158 | Hundred and fifty eight | Narị na iri ise na asatọ |
| 159 | Hundred and fifty nine | Narị na iri ise na itoolu |
| 160 | Hundred and sixty | Narị na iri isii |
| 161 | Hundred and sixty one | Narị na iri isii na otu |
| 162 | Hundred and sixty two | Narị na iri isii na abụọ |
| 163 | Hundred and sixty three | Narị na iri isii na atọ |
| 164 | Hundred and sixty four | Narị na iri isii na anọ |
| 165 | Hundred and sixty five | Narị na iri isii na ise |

*Table 5 - One Hundred and Thirty Two to One Hundred and Sixty Five*

| 166 | Hundred and sixty six | Narị na iri isii na isii |
| 167 | Hundred and sixty seven | Narị na iri isii na asaa |
| 168 | Hundred and sixty eight | Narị na iri isii na asatọ |
| 169 | Hundred and sixty nine | Narị na iri isii na itoolu |
| 170 | Hundred and seventy | Narị na iri asaa |
| 171 | Hundred and seventy one | Narị na iri asaa na otu |
| 172 | Hundred and seventy two | Narị na iri asaa na abụọ |

| 173 | Hundred and seventy three | Narị na iri asaa na atọ |
|------|---------------------------|------------------------|
| 174 | Hundred and seventy four | Narị na iri asaa na anọ |
| 175 | Hundred and seventy five | Narị na iri asaa na ise |
| 176 | Hundred and seventy six | Narị na iri asaa na isii |
| 177 | Hundred and seventy seven | Narị na iri asaa na asaa |
| 178 | Hundred and seventy eight | Narị na iri asaa na asatọ |
| 179 | Hundred and seventy nine | Narị na iri asaa na itoolu |
| 180 | Hundred and eighty | Narị na iri asatọ |
| 181 | Hundred and eighty one | Narị na iri asatọ na otu |
| 182 | Hundred and eighty two | Narị na iri asatọ na abụọ |
| 183 | Hundred and eighty three | Narị na iri asatọ na atọ |
| 184 | Hundred and eighty four | Narị na iri asatọ na anọ |
| 185 | Hundred and eighty five | Narị na iri asatọ na ise |
| 186 | Hundred and eighty six | Narị na iri asatọ na isii |
| 187 | Hundred and eighty seven | Narị na iri asatọ na asaa |
| 188 | Hundred and eighty eight | Narị na iri asatọ na asatọ |
| 189 | Hundred and eighty nine | Narị na iri asatọ na itoolu |
| 190 | Hundred and ninety | Narị na iri itoolu |
| 191 | Hundred and ninety one | Narị na iri itoolu na otu |
| 192 | Hundred and ninety two | Narị na iri itoolu na abụọ |
| 193 | Hundred and ninety three | Narị na iri itoolu na atọ |
| 194 | Hundred and ninety four | Narị na iri itoolu na anọ |
| 195 | Hundred and ninety five | Narị na iri itoolu na ise |
| 196 | Hundred and ninety six | Narị na iri itoolu na isii |
| 197 | Hundred and ninety seven | Narị na iri itoolu na asaa |
| 198 | Hundred and ninety eight | Narị na iri itoolu na asatọ |
| 199 | Hundred and ninety nine | Narị na iri itoolu na itoolu |
| 200 | Two Hundred | Narị abụọ |

*Table 6 - One Hundred and Sixty Six to Two Hundred*

## 3.3 One Hundred to One Thousand

The recursive progression continues at the level of hundreds, but this time involving mainly the multiplication of a hundred by the number attached to it. Thus, while *narị* or *otu narị* means 'hundred' or 'one hundred', *narị abụọ* means 'two hundreds', *narị atọ* 'three hundreds' and so on, up to *narị itoolu* 'nine hundreds', (i.e. hundred into nine places), and so on. All these are in line with the word formation process of the Igbo language, whereby explicit plural markers (like the English *s*, are not used. For example *otu mmadụ* means 'one person', while *mmadụ abụọ* means 'two persons', *mmadụ atọ* 'three persons' *mmadụ ise* 'five persons', *mmadụ iri* 'ten persons' and so on. So do the numbers beside *narị* 'hundred' indicate <u>how many hundreds</u> are meant: *narị asaa* 'seven hundreds', and so on.

| NUMBER | ENGLISH TRANSLATION | IGBO TRANSLATION |
| --- | --- | --- |
| 100 | Hundred | Otu narị |
| 200 | Two hundred | Narị abụọ |
| 300 | Three hundred | Narị atọ |
| 400 | Four hundred | Narị anọ |
| 500 | Five hundred | Narị ise |
| 600 | Six hundred | Narị isii |
| 700 | Seven hundred | Narị asaa |
| 800 | Eight hundred | Narị asatọ |
| 900 | Nine hundred | Narị itoolu |
| 1000 | One thousand | Otu puku |

|Table 7 – One Hundred to One Thousand

## 3.4 One Thousand to One Million

Here the recursive progression continues at the level of thousands. Hence, while *puku* is 'one thousand', which can also be realized as *otu puku*, the rest, from two to nine thousand, are realized through the multiplication of 'one thousand' with the number attached to it. For example, *puku ise* is 'five hundreds' i.e. 'hundred into five places'.

| NUMBER | ENGLISH TRANSLATION | IGBO TRANSLATION |
|---|---|---|
| 1000 | One thousand | Otu puku |
| 2000 | Two thousand | Puku abụọ |
| 3000 | Three thousand | Puku atọ |
| 4000 | Four thousand | Puku anọ |
| 5000 | Five thousand | Puku ise |
| 6000 | Six thousand | Puku isii |
| 7000 | Seven thousand | Puku asaa |
| 8000 | Eight thousand | Puku asatọ |
| 9000 | Nine thousand | Puku itoolu |
| 1,000,000 | One million | Otu nde |

I *Table 8 – One Thousand to One Million*

## 3.5 One Million to One Billion

The recursive progression continues here but at the level of millions. Hence, while *otu nde* is 'one million', *nde abụọ* is 'two millions', *nde ise* 'five miilions', up to *nde itoolu* 'nine million', and finally *ijeri* 'one billion'.

| NUMBER | ENGLISH TRANSLATION | IGBO TRANSLATION |
|---|---|---|
| 1, 000, 000 | One million | Otu nde |
| 2, 000, 000 | Two million | Nde abụọ |
| 3,000,000 | Three million | Nde atọ |
| 4,000,000 | Four million | Nde anọ |
| 5,000,000 | Five million | Nde ise |
| 6,000,000 | Six million | Nde isii |
| 7,000,000 | Seven million | Nde asaa |
| 8,000,000 | Eight million | Nde asatọ |
| 9,000,000 | Nine million | Nde itoolu |
| 1,000,000,000 | One billion | Otu ijeri |

I *Table 9 – One Million to One Billion*

## 4. Some Counting Exercises

In this section, we shall try to count in the Igbo modern counting system. As part of the fun, try not to look at the answers at the end of this chapter. First try to write the numbers in Igbo drawing from all the tables above. Thereafter, compare your work with the answers at the end of this chapter.

| NUMBER | IGBO NAMES |
|--------|------------|
| 0 | |
| 1 | |
| 2 | |
| 3 | |
| 4 | |
| 5 | |

*(A) Exercise One*

| NUMBER | IGBO NAMES |
|--------|------------|
| 6 | |
| 7 | |
| 8 | |
| 9 | |
| 10 | |

*(A) Exercise Two*

| NUMBER | IGBO WORDS | NUMBER | IGBO WORDS |
|--------|------------|--------|------------|
| 11 | | 136 | |
| 12 | | 137 | |
| 13 | | 138 | |
| 14 | | 139 | |
| 15 | | 140 | |
| 16 | | 136 | |
| 17 | | 137 | |
| 18 | | 138 | |
| 19 | | 139 | |
| 20 | | 187 | |
| 30 | | 188 | |
| 31 | | 189 | |
| 32 | | 190 | |
| 37 | | 191 | |
| 38 | | 100 | |
| 39 | | 200 | |
| 40 | | 300 | |
| 50 | | 400 | |
| 59 | | 500 | |
| 60 | | 1000 | |
| 70 | | 2000 | |
| 80 | | 3000 | |
| 90 | | 1, 000, 000 | |
| 100 | | 2, 000, 000 | |

*(B) Exercise One*

## 5. Conclusion

For a very long time the Igbo language had a traditional counting system that was deficient in many ways. The basic-scale of counting in Igbo was twenty, and four hundred was the highest single number. This and other issues of this system made enumeration in Igbo ineffective and generally problematic.

The shortcomings and deficits of the traditional counting system were of concern to the *Society for Promoting Igbo Language and Culture (SPILC)*, and other groups and individuals who were interested in the development of the Igbo language. Efforts of the SPILC (in conjunction with the *National Language Centre*) at erasing the traditional system, gave rise to the Igbo modern counting system, with significant landmarks among other advantages. The Igbo modern counting system is a spectacular improvement on the traditional counting system. However, like every other human creation, the Igbo modern counting system is not devoid of some ambiguities and complexities. For instance it is not quite clear on how to distinguish between numbers like 20, 005 and 25, 000 in Igbo. Each of the numbers is expressed as: *puku iri abụọ na ise*. For now, this can only be disambiguated when the counted item is involved, as in: *puku iri naira abụọ na naira ise* (N20,005), and *puku iri naira abụọ na ise* (N25, 000)   We believe that with more efforts in language engineering on the Igbo language such issues will be rectified.   ▙

### References

Emenanjo, E.N. (1978) *Elements of modern Igbo grammar*. Ibadan: OUP Ltd

Emenanjo, E.N. (2015) *A grammar of contemporary Igbo: constituents, features and processes*. Port Harcourt: M&J Orbit Communication Ltd

Maduka-Durunze (1997) "counting and the Igbo number system: a diachronic perspective' *Studies in terminology* (SIT) vol. 1

*Okaasusu Igbo (Igbo metalanguage)* published by the *Society for Promoting Igbo Language and Culture (SPILC)*.   ▙

# Part Three

# IGBO CULTURE, RELIGION AND TRADITION

# The Idea Of Igbo Philosophy

1. Introduction: Philosophy

2. Igbo Philosophy of Life

3. Chinua Achebe's Philosophy of Leadership

4. Theophilus Okere: The Hermeneutics of *Egbe Bere Ugo*

5. Conclusion

## Summary

*The paper starts with the exposition of the difficulty inherent in looking for an understanding of philosophy that will be unanimously acceptable. The reason for this is that each philosophical current or trend defines philosophy in a way that suits its project. However, taking philosophy as hermeneutics is the closest thing to a generally acceptable conception of philosophy. Hermeneutics is interpretation mediated by the totality of factors that impinge on the subject of philosophy. It thus emphasizes the importance of culture and its symbols which are seen as raw materials for the individual interpretation that gives rise to philosophy. Philosophy is also understood in terms of culture and its symbols, and this gives rise to traditional philosophy or other genre like world-view, religion, folktales, etc. On account of the importance of the context of philosophy or non-philosophy, or first order activity that undergirds philosophy, we explore here what we call Igbo philosophy of life through the Igbo world view, with a view to seeing how the character of the Igbo is marked by what we can call their philosophy of life. The paper next explores the leadership philosophy of Chinua Achebe, linking his thought on leadership to his Igbo culture or philosophy of life. The paper finally reviews Theophilus Okere's hermeneutics of Egbe bere ugo bere as the ideal of peace and justice in Igbo ethics, and arrives at the conclusion that, quite contrary to the Western attempt to justify the chaos of war for their self-interest, Igbo ethics totally abhors war, and when one must fight, it is not for individual gain, nor even for self-defense, but on account of innocence. It is clear from all of the above that in line with Igbo anthropomorphism, Igbo philosophy is strongly anchored in the existential condition of its subjects.*

## 1. Introduction: Philosophy

THE WORD PHILOSOPHY ORIGINATES FROM TWO GREEK WORDS: philos (lover) and sofia (wisdom). So etymologically philosophy stands for lover of wisdom. From etymological derivation, it is clear that philosophy is primarily hinged on the human ability to know and to think, because, however one understands wisdom, it is not concerned directly with the physical activities of the human person. Hence, the elementary *Michael West Dictionary* defines the philosopher as "a thinker."

That definition of philosophy in a sense underlines the reality that it is a very natural activity of the human being. The human being is generally defined as a rational animal. Being rational includes the ability to know and to think. The ancient Greek philosopher Aristotle says that all human beings by nature desire to know (Aristotle: 1984, p. 1553). He confirms this assertion by the interest that humans have in sense knowledge, especially the sense of sight. But from there Aristotle goes on to present a gradation of human knowledge, from sense to memory, experience, art, knowledge of causes and principles (science). For him the greatest sign of wisdom is universal knowledge, since only at that level can one be a teacher; being in position to command other human beings with more practical knowledge who are less wise and thus must obey the man of wisdom. Thus for Aristotle, wisdom is not meant for practical or utilitarian ends. That explains why in his view the quest for knowledge of causes and principles first began where humans had leisure, where they had satisfied their elementary needs, in ancient Egypt, "for there the priest caste was allowed to be at leisure" (1554).

The natural desire for knowledge also leads the human being to inquire about the origin and end of life. It is regarded as the quest for meaning and for causes of reality. But this quest is primarily anchored on the quest for the meaning of life:

*The question (What is the meaning of life?) is put in many different ways. What is the meaning of it all? What is the meaning of everything? What is it all in aid of? Why is there anything at all and why just what there is and not something quite different? (Britton, 1969, p. 1-2)*

Despite its strong base on the nature of human beings, philosophy is almost impossible to define in a manner that will be unanimously acceptable by its practitioners. Philosophy can be seen as the quest for meaning; as the analysis of language in use; it can be seen as phenomenology; and as hermeneutics, as well as the quest for the ultimate cause. What is peculiar to what can be called professional philosophy is that each definition arises from a particular understanding or current of the discipline. It means that each current of philosophy has definitions that are suitable to their specific understanding of the discipline, or its conception of what philosophy should be.

On a broader plain, there is a distinction between philosophy in a very general sense and philosophy as an academic discipline. The former is often generally referred to as philosophy of life. The Ghanaian philosopher Kwasi Wiredu introduced this distinction as the difference between a first order and a second order activity of the human being:

*Implied here is a contrast between two senses of the word "philosophy," one narrow and the other broad. In the first sense, philosophy is a technical discipline in which our (i.e., the human) world-out-look is subjected to systematic scrutiny by rigorous ratiocinative methods (ideally that is). In the second sense, philosophy is that way of viewing man and the world which results in a world-outlook in the first*

*place. It might be said, then, that philosophy in the first sense is a second order enterprise for it is a reflection on philosophy in the second sense. If so, philosophy in the first sense is of a doubly second-order character, for that on which it reflects – namely, our world-out-look – is itself a reflection on the more particularistic, more episodic, judgements of ordinary, day-to-day living, (1991, p. 153).* **”**

African philosophic workers have very divergent views on the distinction that Wiredu makes in the above passage. Joseph Omeregbe for example regards philosophy in the Michael West meaning of thinking. For him, there is no distinction between philosophy as a way of life or general tradition and philosophy in the sense of strict academic discipline. For Omeregbe, the human being is generally a thinker. Those who are acclaimed philosophers are those who devote more time to thinking than others, and not necessarily those who are engaged in any special specialized academic activity. Every tradition has had its thinkers or philosophers, even though some traditions did not properly document the results of their thinking due to absence of writing. But then the "fragments" of the thought of these philosophers are left behind in "mythologies, formulas of wise-sayings, traditional proverbs, stories, and especially religion", (Omeregbe, 1985, p. 6-7).

One understanding of philosophy that is very close to encompassing all the divergent conceptions of philosophy is that philosophy is hermeneutics. Hermeneutics is in a very general sense interpretation. It is bringing to the fore of the hidden meaning in reality. Etymologically, hermeneutics refers to the Greek god Hermes, the notable god of cunning and the messenger of the Olympian gods. Philosophy as hermeneutics is an attempt at explanation, at seeing meaning in reality as a whole. In this attempt all the factors that impinge on being in general are taken into serious consideration. That is why proper hermeneutics is akin to comprehensive understanding of reality. In doing this, it necessarily takes proper account of the whole context in which reality is embedded or rooted, including primarily the existential context of the subject of philosophizing. The context speaks of the cultural ambience of the subject. That is why the French philosopher, Paul Ricoeur, sees hermeneutics as traversing several stages: the phenomenological stage; the hermeneutical stage and the reflexive stage. For Ricoeur, one can only philosophize from culture, or at least from those elements of culture that are symbols: *le symbole donne are penser* (symbols are pregnant with meaning).

"Philosophical discourse is, therefore, a hermeneutical development of the symbols, these enigmas which precede and nourish it," (Okere, 1983, p. 18).

The thoughts of Ricoeur underline the importance of culture. Philosophy and culture are intimately intertwined. Hermeneutics is seen as the mediator between them. For as much as hermeneutics seen as a method in social science can be extricated from philosophy, it is viewed as the methodical mediator between philosophy and culture: "Hermeneutics, that is, interpretation is the mediating factor between the two poles." (Okere, 1983, p. 18). This relationship between culture and philosophy points to the fact that culture is not in itself philosophy. Philosophy is an individual or hermeneutical interpretation of culture or of its symbols. It means that philosophy and culture are not the same realities: "There is no art whereby one can automatically deduce a philosophical system from a culture" (Okere, 1983, p. 8). Philosophy is an individual enterprise, and it is frequently "a mis-en-cause, and a radical questioning of the collective image" (Okere, 1983, p. 7).

Still philosophy as hermeneutics is rooted in culture. Theophilus Okere sees the relationship between philosophy and culture as a dialectical relationship. The cultural base of philosophy is what Okere broadly terms non-philosophy and affirms as follows:

*Philosophy and non-philosophy have a dialectical relationship with each other. Philosophy reflects on experience, experience contradicts the resulting system; a new philosophy arises taking into account what the former ignored; and this is the pattern of development in the history of philosophy, (Okere, 1983, p. 83).*

Non-philosophy here must be very broadly understood as the presuppositions and the presumptions of the new philosophy. Without those presuppositions, reflection itself cannot take place. It is what Henri Bergson refers to when he states that the normal human agent assumes innumerable presuppositions in his thinking and behavior. *Il faut pasque il faut* - You must because you must (1988, p. 19). Some of these presuppositions or non-philosophies of the new philosophy are also the results of previous philosophies which with the passage of history is assumed by the current society without question. Kwasi Wiredu obliquely affirms this philosophy/non-philosophy relationship in discussing Henri Odera Oruka's sage philosophy:

*There is an intimate relationship between the thought of the individual, traditional sage-philosophers and the communal world-outlook of their people. It is the communal philosophy which provides the point of departure for the sage-philosopher. It provides, in fact, the philosophical education and must, in many ways, determine his theoretical options. On the other hand, a little reflection must show that the communal thought itself is the pooling together of these elements of the thought of the individual philosophers of the community that remain stuck in the common imagination, (Wiredu, 1991, p. 159-160).*

Thus, even though according to Okere, philosophy is very different from one individual to the other, it is nevertheless rooted in the common patrimony of a culture, or a tradition. Its results, to a greater or lesser extent, eventually become assimilated into the wider society and also become assumed as non-philosophy which becomes the raw material of a new philosophy. This dialectical relationship between philosophy and culture or between philosophy and non-philosophy speaks of the contextualization of all philosophies. Nobody speaks from nowhere, and nobody speaks without the load imposed by the context of his life and being. It means that philosophy while aiming at universalism is burdened by its particularity. A universal philosophy is not better than a chimera. For long Western philosophy live with the hubris of universal philosophy or philosophy as such. But in recent times, this age-long pretension has been abandoned in theory as uninformed. Today for instance, hardly anybody writes a history of philosophy, but rather a history of Western, African, Arab, Jewish, and American philosophy. Philosophy may aim at universal conclusions but it must do so through contextual presuppositions. How realistic this aim of universalism is will always remain an enigma for the enterprise of philosophy. But it shows that while the universal aim remains very oblique, we can comfortably speak of Igbo philosophy or the philosophy of any other group of people or of any culture. Thus, the rest of this paper will dwell on Igbo philosophy of life; Chinua Achebe's philosophy of leadership and Theophilus Okere's hermeneutics of *Egbe bere ugo bere*.

## 2. Igbo Philosophy of Life

We have seen the divergence in the understanding of philosophy. Kwasi Wiredu speaks of philosophy of a people as first order activity while methodic academic philosophy is a second order activity. Omeregbe would not subscribe to that distinction based on his conviction that philosophers exist in all human communities and that those whose thoughts were not recorded in formal writings filtered into the different literary genre and the religion of the society. Okere takes philosophy as hermeneutics, discounting communal philosophy while emphasizing that hermeneutics or philosophical interpretation is strongly rooted in culture and its symbols or in the non-philosophy that serves as the fulcrum of any new philosophy. Here, we shall dwell on the cultural symbols of Igbo culture by dwelling briefly on their world view which undergirds their philosophy of life.

Igbo philosophy of life is here understood as the ensemble of qualities which several writers on the Igbo people have pinpointed as prevalent among them. These qualities indicate general tendencies which can be channeled by individuals or groups of individuals to noble or sometimes despicable objectives. According to Okigbo, "you can tell the spirit of a people by the qualities they admire." (Okigbo, 1986, p. 18) Among the Igbo this spirit can be viewed positively and sometimes negatively. The Igbo have been described variously as stubborn, troublesome, headstrong, and ambitious (Echeruo, 1979, p. 23). They have also been seen as aggressive, arrogant and clannish (Achebe, 1983: 45). They have been praised as hard working (Equiano, 1979, p. 7). Their hard work is linked with competitiveness and their desire for achievement (Odumegwu-Ojukwu, 1989, p. 95). They are community conscious (Nworga, 1984: 52), but also egalitarian and individualistic (Okigbo, 1986, p. 14; Leith-Ross, 1937, p. 357) and hence ultra-democratic in their political and social organizations (Odumegwu-Ojukwu, 1989, p. 87; Leith-Ross, p. 67; Ejiofor, 1982, p. 337). They are also marked by their adaptability and receptivity to change (Davidson, 1969, p. 96; Ottenberg, 1959, p. 135). Our effort here is to see how these qualities are reflected in Igbo world view.

The central point of Igbo world view is that it is very strongly anthropocentric. This means that the human being is squarely at the center of Igbo universe. The Igbo people believe in very many spiritual beings, but these are taken into account in so far as they affect human beings either positively or negatively. Nature is also taken into account but its relevance is measured according to its influence on *mmadụ* 'the human being'.

There have been attempts to etymologically derive the meaning of *mmadụ* from its possible etymological derivation. Thus the Igbo word *mma* 'beauty' and *di* 'be' is taken to be its root and so *Mmadụ* would mean 'let goodness be'. Another attempt seeks to add the personal pronoun first person singular *mụ*. *Mmadụ* in this interpretation would then mean *Mma mụ dị* 'the goodness or beauty in me'. These interpretations are very close to the Christian idea where God the creator is viewed as endowing the human being with goodness; or where the creator is viewed as all good. But quite contrary to the Graeco-Roman conception, *Mmadụ* is not viewed as a composite. Not that he/she is a completely material being. Apart from the visible, material body, there are other principles, but "these do not detract from his basic unity" (Uzukwu, 1983: 9). *Mmadụ* has *obi* 'heart' and *mmụọ* 'spirit'. But these are not really thought of as separate entities inhabiting the body in the Platonic sense.

Another principle associated with *Mmadụ* is the *Chi*. *Chi* is described as "personal genius" (Meek, 1937, p. 55); as a "spiritual double" (Forde and Jones, 1950, p. 50). Igbo concept of *Chi* is very fluid. Metuh sees *Chi* as a co-worker with God in the creation of the individual. Chukwu (God) creates the individual and assigns him/her a *Chi* (and *Eke*). It is the *Chi* who chooses from many possible alternatives the destiny of the person (Metuh, 1981: 68). Generally the idea of destiny is associated with Igbo conception of *Chi* and *Eke*. A person's *Chi* may be that of ill-luck, and nothing can change the situation (*Chi ketalụ ụbịam nyịrị ụla agụ*). *Chi* is regarded in some parts of Igboland as an *alụsị* 'god', but in some vague way equal in power to the person whose *Chi* it is. Thus the Igbo say that one who is more powerful than another person is also more powerful than his/her *Chi* (*onye karịrị onye karịrị chi ya*). Perhaps Anderson is right in saying that "Chi is life (*ndụ*) conceived as animate self and guides the course of existence (1972, p. 101). A person's *Chi* or destiny is signed in his palm as *akalaka* or *akala Chi*. It is *Chi* that controls the life and death of the individual *ebe onye dalụ bụ Chi ya kwatulu ya,* 'where a person falls is where his *Chi* has pushed him down.' Again the Igbo say *Chi onye adịghị n'izu ma ọnwụ egbu egbuna ya* 'if a person's *Chi* is not part of the bargain, he will not die.' But the Igbo are far from being deterministic as the concept of *Chi* might suggest. Hence, ironically they say *onye kwe Chi ya ekwe* 'if a person agrees, his *Chi* will do the same.'

*Mmadụ* is good, but his goodness is unconditionally linked with factors that are extrinsic to his being. The Igbo view these factors as bound together with *Mmadụ's* goodness. Some abnormal conditions affecting the human being are viewed as connected with the moral order and constitute major detraction from the goodness of the human. Leprosy, small pox, and abnormal birth (e.g. of twins) were tabooed. A child growing first the upper teeth and swelling of the tommy from cirrhosis were viewed as abomination. "When a man was afflicted with swelling," says Achebe, "he was not allowed to die in the house. He was carried to the evil forest and left there to die", (1988, p. 28). Survival in a tolerable way is a major concern to the Igbo, and this in a large measure determines their attitude to life.

Survival in a tolerable way greatly affects Igbo conception of the destiny of the human being. The Igbo believe in the continued existence of the human being, *post mortem.* For them the afterlife is a replica of life on earth even though it is *ana mmụọ* 'the spirit world', believed to be situated somewhere below the earth. This underlines the importance of the earth goddess, the guardian of morality; and the controller of all fertility and the owner of all human beings, *ana nwe mmadu nine* 'the earth owns every human being'. It is the spirit world that is encompassed by Ala that the human being returns to through burial, after sojourn on earth. The dead is believed to rejoin the ancestors and await reincarnation. "The wish of every Igbo man or woman," says Basden, "is to rest among the souls of their ancestors, and it is a very real and poignant hope," (1966, p. 278).

Admittance into the land of the ancestors is based on certain conditions. The individual must live a morally upright life; he must also be a successful person, and his success is shown in the possession of wife (or wives) and children, especially male offspring as well as enough material possession. To merit to live with the ancestors, a person must also live a considerably long life and die a good death; not death from accident or abominable illness. All these conditions must be sealed by a befitting burial since for the Igbo, a person who is not given a decent burial cannot be admitted into the land of the ancestors. The spirit world is viewed to be much like the terrestrial. There is no idea of endless and blissful existence akin to the Christian heaven. The ancestors depend on the living for their wellbeing. They are fed by the sacrifices offered to them by their offspring. While they await reincarnation, and are fed by the living, they are also duty bound to protect their living offspring and prosper their activities. Reincarnation is the destiny of Igbo traditionalist. It is a source of inspiration for a good life, moral and economic. It is a dear hope of Igbo traditionalist, and the "greatest evil is to be thrown out of the life cycle through the denial of reincarnation," (Basden, 1966, p. 278).

The stringent conditions for admittance into the afterlife can explain the attitude of the Igbo for earthly success. It is not just a vain glorious quest. It has telling implication for their destiny, *post mortem*. There is really no excuse for failure. G. T. Basden observed this attitude among Igbo immigrants in other parts of Nigeria when he writes: "Whatever the conditions, the Ibo immigrants adapt themselves to meet them, and it is not long before they make their presence felt in the localities where they settle," (1966, p. XI). Given the dependence of powerful ancestors on the living for their welfare, and that the ultimate reward is the ability to reincarnate, it could be said in a certain sense that this imperfect world is a sort of *summum bonum* 'highest good' (Oguejiofor, 2005) for the traditional Igbo. The importance given to this good in human destiny goes to explain the seriousness with which the traditional Igbo takes his/her activities in life. A residue of such attitude to life can also explain the perceived tendency among the Igbo to succeed in life by tenacity of purpose.

In addition to the pragmatic relationship with the ancestors whereby they are dependent on the living and are expected to protect them and prosper their engagement, the traditional Igbo have also a very pragmatic relationship with their spiritual beings. There are innumerable deities in the Igbo pantheon, the Supreme God, the cosmic potentates (Ala, Igwe, etc), and the *alụsị* 'uncountable spirits'. For the Igbo, these spirits are there for their wellbeing. They are acquired to solve specific problems and are responsible for certain departments of life. Failure to prove their mettle incites the anger of the Igbo. The spirits can be neglected as a consequence or their shrine can be destroyed, and the spirits expelled. But the Igbo respect and reverence and sometimes fear their *alụsị*, but "What is specific in Igbo relationship with their alusi is that they insist that the alusi must deserve the respect, reverence, and cult offered to them." (Oguejiofor, 1996, p. 76). Echeruo puts this more succinctly:

 *We (Igbos) respect the gods, but as the proverb says, we also expect the gods to respect us humans. We acknowledge the power of gods, and cultivate that power; but when these gods consistently fail to prove themselves, we reserve the right to discard them and seek out new gods (1979, p. 19).*

The beliefs, practices and attitudes explained above have undergone far-reaching changes. Igbo philosophy of life, especially its receptivity to change and its pragmatism ensured the massive conversion of Igbo people to Christianity with consequences in terms of changing some of the convictions mentioned above and embracing disparate ones. But there is no doubt that much still remains of the attitudes for which the Igbo were known in their more traditional settings. What has almost been forgotten are the beliefs and practices that initially gave rise to some of these enduring philosophies of life.

## 3. Chinua Achebe's Philosophy of Leadership

In hermeneutics such genre as worldview and philosophy of life are the raw material for interpretation, which always emerges as personal reflections on actual life situations. This is again what Kwasi Wiredu called a first order activity, while for him the second order, rooted in the first, is philosophy in the strict sense. Chinua Achebe's thought on leadership in Nigeria can be considered as the result of reflection on a situation of concern for the whole nation even though hermeneutically one can still see the influence of his ambience as a product of the Igbo culture which we have described in the foregoing. Achebe a renowned novelist is one of the most influential literary figures that have bestrode the African continent. He is very often described as the father of modern African literature. His best known books are *Things Fall Apart, Arrow of God* and *No Longer at Ease*. Achebe did not study philosophy as a discipline, but his reflections on the problems of Nigeria including the Igbo people; his independent convictions and his moral stance bring him out as an eminent philosophical thinker. For two times, Achebe rejected the Nigerian national honour because of his belief that the mismanagement of Nigerian affairs that he called government's attention to had not been tackled.

In 1983 Achebe penned a slim book *The Trouble with Nigeria* in an attempt to discuss the most fundamental issue the country was facing. By 1983, Nigeria had gone from rancorous civilian governments at independence to military rule, and had experienced a very bloody civil war. It was obvious that the country was not moving in the right direction; that it was performing below its capacity and sliding into economic, social and political disorder. Not taking the easy part of blaming either civilian or military rule as such, Achebe clearly states that the real and fundamental problem of Nigeria is the problem of leadership and starts the first chapter with a statement which has become one of the most widely known statements on Nigeria:

*The trouble with Nigeria is simply and squarely a failure of leadership. There is nothing basically wrong with the Nigerian character. There is nothing wrong with the Nigerian land or climate or water or air or anything else. The Nigerian problem is the unwillingness or inability of its leaders to rise to the responsibility, to the challenge of personal example which are the hallmarks of true leadership (1983, p. 1).*

Achebe goes on to elaborate on other problems bedeviling the Nigerian socio-political and economic spheres. He discourses tribalism, patriotism, social justice and the cult of mediocrity, indiscipline and corruption. However the question of leadership is the basic problem that either creates or nurtures these ills of the Nigerian society. It is therefore appropriate that he zeroes in on what he calls the Nigerian leadership style. In doing this, Achebe pinpoints the "absence of intellectual rigour in the political thought of our founding fathers." He singles out the most prominent of Nigerian political giants, Nnamdi Azikiwe and Obafemi Awolowo and graphically exposes how they were merely motivated by the allure of wealth. Azikiwe decided early in his career "to secure my enjoyment of a high standard of living" and Awolowo on his part vowed "to make all the money that is possible for a man with my brains and brawn to make in Nigeria" (1983, p. 11). For Achebe thoughts as these can only produce aggressive and corrupt millionaires than selfless leaders of the people. It is thus not surprising that the political terrain in which these titans operated is one that is today infested with massive corruption and abuse of office while selfless leadership appears far removed from the typical Nigerian psyche.

One weighty point of concern for Achebe is the question of social justice and the cult of mediocrity. He paints the picture of two nationals *A* and *B* who apply to fill "a very important and strategic position." *A* has the right qualification, competence and character, but the job is given to *B* because he belongs to the "right tribe." *A* goes off embittered while *B* throws a party and messes up the job. The greatest loser is the nation which has to battle with the legitimate grievance of an embittered citizen; and endure the decline of morale and subversion of efficiency. So for him social injustice is not just a question of morality but also of the negative impact on the developmental possibilities of a nation. He quotes a minister who said "we will buy, hire or steal technology," and reacts as follows:

> *It probably never occurred to him that the people from whom he proposed to steal got where they are because they will never hire a man to perform an important task unless he is the best they can find. Nigeria, on the other hand, is a country where it would be difficult to point to one important job held by the most competent person we have. I stand to be corrected! (1983: 19)*

It means that as far back as 1983 Nigeria has become so accustomed to tribalism and the cult of mediocrity that competence or merit is no longer the criterion for appointments in important jobs. For Achebe it is like playing with our third and fourth eleven while dumping the first eleven on grounds of tribalism. The result is very predictable. Our nation cannot "make it to the world league. Until, that is, we put merit back on the national agenda" (1983, p. 20).

It is exactly 37 years ago that Achebe highlighted these fundamentally misguided habits of our national life. Today it can confidently be said that the situation has gotten much worse than it was at the time. While Achebe was writing about important positions in his discussion of social injustice and the cult of mediocrity, it is today almost unimaginable that even lower jobs in the public service are given out on merit. Virtually all positions in our public service are filled with slots distributed to the so-called stake holders and men and women of influence who just forward their list of those to be appointed. Sometimes aptitude tests and interviews are conducted but with the clear understanding that in today's Nigeria, they do not mean anything anymore.

Again, it is not only injustice on grounds of tribalism; the situation has evolved to be much worse than tribalism. Even though Achebe spoke of "prejudice of whatever origin," it is clear that the situation has so deteriorated that what plays out now is survival of the fittest. Corrupt officials sell jobs at prices that are up to two year salaries of young employees. From the national level and for important positions, Nigerians have come to face themselves at their state and local government administrations where there is no longer difference of tribe but difference of interest. But the habit that dominates and has been internalized is that of social injustice and the cult of mediocrity. Nigerians must go through somebody to apply for a job, and very often these "somebodies" offer their "service" at high prices.

Still the foundation of poor leadership has been penciled as absence of intellectual rigour and poverty of thought exhibited by the greatest political figures of our nation. This intellectual wooliness is seen more glaringly in the Nigerian coat-of-arms. Unity and Faith is the motto boldly inscribed in the coat. But for Achebe these two concepts are like double aged swords. They do not specify what they are meant for. What is the nation uniting to do? Unity is the most commonly enunciated ideal but not much is heard about the purpose of this almighty unity. "Unity can only be as good as the purpose for which it is desired." Uniting to achieve a positive end is surely desirable, but uniting to rob a bank or to burn down the house of perceived enemies is certainly not commendable. Nigeria talks of unity, and our current president is quick to affirm that Nigerian unity is non-negotiable. That is a society where injustice on grounds of tribal and sectional considerations is taken for granted as the norm, and where one's state or local government of origin is always in question. The existence of these practices and the proclamation of unity also point to absence of intellectual rigour. The same consideration goes for faith "which is as good as the object on which it reposes."

Achebe returns to the issue of leadership in 1986 at a lecture at the University of Nigeria. He used the occasion to affirm his position, to answer his critiques and to enjoin the university to stand up to the challenge of leadership. On the issue of system, he argues against those who rather uphold the importance of the operative system over leadership. While system has its importance, "the basic problem with efforts to bestow pre-eminence on system is, however, their inability to explain how an abstract concept can bring itself into being autonomously. Would the system drop from the sky and operate itself?" This entails that whatever weight accorded to any system, the system must first be thought out, operated and internalized, and to do all these requires efficient leadership.

Again in discussing followership Achebe defends himself against the accusation of elitism in emphasizing the importance of leadership. "Leadership is a sacred trust like the priesthood in civilized, humane religions." It is not everybody who can be a leader, and so it is not correct to quip that followers get the leader they deserve. To insist on leadership is viewed as elitist, but for Achebe "a word is more likely to become abused when the concept it represents becomes corrupted." So for him the real issue about the elite is not the issue of its necessity but rather whether it is "genuine or counterfeit." Achebe opines that very often genuine leaders emerge "in diverse places from every conceivable system." But the emergence of leaders in so to say unplanned circumstance does not excuse us from making them responsible: "if we cannot compel greatness in our leaders we can at least demand basic competence." (1986, p. 19)

For Achebe, the real problem posed by leadership is the problem of recruitment. Every age, including our traditional societies, has battled with the problem. The example of monarchical traditional societies is instructive. Kingmakers were schooled in the history and tradition of the kingdom and were themselves not eligible for the kingship. They were thus reasonably disinterested. Achebe sees the universities as similar to the kingmakers in the following words:

> " *The universities and other elite centers with deep knowledge of national and world issues can play a role somewhat analogous to that undertaken by kingmakers of the past, not in selecting the king themselves but by spreading, in advance, general enlightenment and a desire for excellence in the entire constituency of the nation including those who will aspire to national leadership. (1986, p. 20)* "

Achebe's discourse on leadership is aimed from all intent and purposes at Nigeria as a country. Still it is not too farfetched to observe how Igbo idea of leadership as it is decipherable from their world view finds expression in Achebe's reflection on leadership. In the first place, it is obvious that his description of Nigerian leadership bespeak of a person imbued with the value of egalitarianism where the leader is not just reverenced and adored but is regarded as not greater than the society that he serves as a leader. It is not surprising that given Igbo republicanism, the trenchant critique of Nigerian leadership should be coming from someone who is so thoroughly bred in Igbo socio-political ethos.

Another point that hacks back to Igbo philosophy of life is Achebe's insistence that leadership must be judged by the good it can purvey for human beings. Here we see Igbo anthropocentrism. The society and all its institutions are there for the wellbeing of all the members of the society. Leaders must therefore be tasked like every facet of the society to work for the welfare of its members. The critique of Nigerian leadership style would be strange to a thinker who internalizes the idea of divine mandate of rulers and who regards the citizens as mere subjects with virtually no right vis-à-vis their divinely ordained leaders. Again Igbo strong anthropocentricism enjoins that even the gods who were mostly acquired to fulfill certain roles in the human community must prove themselves to deserve the respect and worship they receive from humans. In the same way, for Achebe leaders are there for a purpose and that purpose is not personal to them. They must fulfill their expected role as leaders if the society is to function optimally. That is a direct derivation from Igbo world views, the centrality it places on the human being, its egalitarian ethos and its attitude of confidence even before their divinities.

## 4. Theophilus Okere: The Hermeneutics of *Egbe Bere Ugo Bere*

Another well-known Igbo philosopher is late Catholic priest, Msgr. Theophilus Okere. Okere is the founder of the now widely practiced hermeneutical method in contemporary African philosophy. In the midst of the English colonial dominance of analytic philosophy in African departments of philosophy, Okere penned a thesis with the title: "Can there be an African Philosophy?" part of which was later published with the title: *African Philosophy: A Historico-Hermeneutical Investigation into the Conditions of its Possibility.* In these works Okere argued that philosophy is hermeneutics and that African philosophy must be a hermeneutics of the African reality, African culture and its symbols (1983: 114). These works have become seminal in contemporary African philosophy, and it goes without saying that hermeneutics is today the most widely applied philosophical methodology in contemporary African philosophy. Okere himself applied this method in his numerous reflections on the conditions of the Igbo people and Nigeria in general. Let us present in a brief summary Okere's interpretation of a very popular saying in Igbo language which epitomizes the Igbo idea of peace and justice: *Egbe bere ugo bere, nke si ibe ya ebela nku kwaa ya* 'Let the kite perch, let the eagle perch; whichever would not let the other perch, let its wings be broken'.

Okere begins his interpretation by first inveighing against the presumptions of colonialism and Western culture which are today relentlessly spread by unstoppable globalization. He notes that "Africa and its own ideas and institutions have always been quietly ignored and notably absent from the debate, no matter how decisive the outcome may be for the destinies of millions." Departing from the Igbo of Nigeria, he affirms that Africa does have values, conceptual equipment "useful if not completely adequate to confront and manage its problems of war and peace, if only the intrinsic omnipresence of alien values and solutions would let it try." For Okere history and indigenous philosophies of the

African people clearly show that they have mechanisms for peaceful resolution of conflict; cultures that are more disposed and aligned for peace than for war; as well as religious reverence for life that imposes an aversion for total war. They show a people with down to earth concept of peace; peace founded on justice, straight dealing and mutual understanding instead of one imposed by force of arm.

Contrary to these historic and philosophic realities the history of Western Christianity and civilization has presented itself as the history of destructive wars. That is why the dominance of the rest of the world by the West is largely owed to the fruits of war and violence:

> *The West has succeeded only too well in demonstrating to the world how to win and succeed without being in the right and in glorifying violence as the principal way for a people to get on in the world (Okere, 2005, p. 13).*

History is littered with the West's glorification of violence: in the Old Testament; the Trojan wars; Alexander and Caesar; Constantine; the Germanic war hordes; the Barbarian invasion; the Crusade; the long wars, hundred and thirty years; the wars of successions and those of revolution; the Trans-Atlantic slave trade; colonial genocide in the Americas and other climes; Hitler's genocide and the murderous bombs at Hiroshima and Nagasaki. The list is almost endless. Christian thinkers like Augustine, Aquinas, Grotius and Suarez developed the theory of the just war which turned into "a credo for all Christian war mongers and the laundering mechanism for all the excuses for war making" (Okere, 2005: 16). This is why to Okere, a scourge as terrible as war has become accepted and rationalized with little or no burden on the conscience. However, if peace is the ultimate rational goal, war must be adjudged as certainly wrong, and thus the old Roman saying *si vis pacem para bellum* 'if you want peace, prepare for war' is deadly wrong.

The Igbo option that Okere interprets looks for peace, not in war, but rather in "patient search for justice and fairness which is reached by agreement and by means of dialogue" (2005, p. 16). Okere first explores etymologically Igbo concepts of peace and justice. Peace is translated as *udo* or *ndokwa* which originates from *ido*, meaning 'to place/put properly'. This sense is also realized in the activity of block laying where the Igbo block layer describes his activity as *ido block* 'to properly lay/place blocks'. *Ndokwa* implies to harmonize together everything that have been previously properly laid. Its root has to do with measurement and alignment and thus the word has geometric implications. But it goes from geometric to esthetic, the psychological and the ethical concepts of peace. An alignment of all these generates a sense of pleasure, of harmony and of beauty. Such a harmony will be what constitutes social peace which arises from arranging from situations of chaos a mosaic that is both meaningful and helpful:

> *When the vital interests of one group are reconciled with those of another and these with those of yet others, each in its place, the result is peace, the peace of order and harmony. What makes this peace possible is the element of placing things, each in its due place (Okere, 2005, p. 19).*

The idea of placing things in their due place links peace directly with justice. The controlling elements of justice are traceable in the most quoted aphorisms of Igbo ethics. They are as follows:

(i) *Egbe bere ugo bere, nke siri ibe ya ebela nku kwaa ya.*

'Let the kite perch, let the eagle perch; whichever would not let the other perch, let its wings be broken'.

(ii) *Onye anwula, ma ibe ya efula.*
'Let no one die, but let one's neighbour not also get missing.'

**(iii) *Ya bara onye bara onye.***

'Let there be profit for one, and let there be profit for the other.'

**(iv) *E mee nwanyị etu emere ibe ya, obi adị ya mma.***

'If a woman is treated as her fellow women are treated, then will she be happy.'

The philosophy that is enunciated in these sayings is that of total fairness, which is the only sure guarantee for peace. If justice is fairness (cf John Rawls) the following is the direct implication: "It is justice that creates peace or perhaps better, peace is not something that happens but rather a situation that arises when justice happens. It is happy state of things that happen when the state of things is just" (Okere, 2005, p. 20).
Like peace, justice has geometric and esthetic dimensions. A just thing is translated as *ihe ziri ezi,* something that is right and straight. *Ezi Okwu* 'truth' is literally a straight word. *Mmezi* is to do the right thing, to be straight and truthful.

> *The just is the straight thing, not crooked, meandering dealings. The just thing is the right thing, the honest thing to do. The just is the truthful. The just is the ihe ahaziri ahazi literally something that is arranged in proper order, like something arranged in a straight line. Thus the just is where true and the beautiful and the good meet (Okere, 2005, p. 20).*

These etymological considerations lead Okere to see coalescence between peace and justice; the two are in fact one and the same thing. *Ihe ziri ezi* is one and the same as *Ihe ahaziri ahazi,* thus "it is not only that peace is based on justice, rather, peace is justice and justice is peace" (2005, p. 21). It is therefore antithetical to speak of a just war since war strikes at the very root of both justice and peace. War is the wrong "attempt to use force to violate the will of the unwilling." Its cost in terms of human life makes it irretrievably evil. Life is the ultimate good of human life here on earth; any conceivable assault on it represents the greatest evil which cannot be justified in any circumstance. War represents the substitution of force for argument and that is why it remains in a class of its own as an unjustifiable aberration. For Okere, legitimization of such chaos as war makes it the most evil invention that has ever been inflicted on the human society (2005, p. 23).

It is in order to avoid the absurdity inherent in war that Igbo peace ethics has no room for war. It is not acceptable even though one must fight if one has to. But the justification for fighting in Igbo ethics raises another distinction

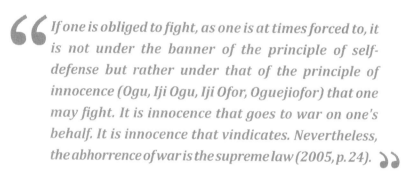

*If one is obliged to fight, as one is at times forced to, it is not under the banner of the principle of self-defense but rather under that of the principle of innocence (Ogu, Iji Ogu, Iji Ofor, Oguejiofor) that one may fight. It is innocence that goes to war on one's behalf. It is innocence that vindicates. Nevertheless, the abhorrence of war is the supreme law (2005, p. 24).*

Thus through the hermeneutics of the ethics of *Egbe bere ugo bere*, Okere arrives at the conclusion that war is inherently abhorrent in Igbo ethics. Contrary to Christian Medieval thinkers who sought conditions to make war a just engagement, Okere's interpretation of Igbo concept of peace and justice makes the two to be one and the same thing. It is conceivable that one is obliged to fight in spite of the abhorrence of Igbo ethics for war, but even then, it is not self-defense or one sided justice that is at play. It is rather innocence that goes to war on behalf of the fighters.

EDITOR'S NOTE:
There is a connection with the Igbo verb *izi* 'to show' => *izi ezi* 'to actually show'=> *Ihe ziri ezi* 'something that actually/clearly shows (itself)'. This is also related to the Igbo word for truth: *Ezi Okwu* 'clear word'. Just like *ihe ziri ezi* means 'something that actually/clearly shows itself', so does *Okwu ziri ezi* mean 'word/speech that clearly shows itself' i.e. 'true word' => 'the truth' *Ezi Okwu*.

## 5. Conclusion

We have tried to present very brief expose of Igbo philosophy. We departed from the realization that philosophy as a discipline is almost impossible to define in a manner that will be acceptable to all currents of the discipline. Still it is our view that the most generally acceptable understanding of philosophy is that it is hermeneutics, an interpretation that reveals the hidden meaning from the apparent. Hermeneutics highlights the importance of culture and its symbols which are like raw materials for the enunciation of philosophy which for some thinkers must be personal and divergent from generally accepted genres of a society. This makes cultural symbols and traditional genre of utmost importance in the enterprise of philosophy. As an ode to this importance we explored what we called Igbo philosophy of life by analyzing its world view, seeing the general characteristic attributable to the Igbo as direct consequence of their spirit as outlined in the world view. Chinua Achebe's philosophy of leadership is reviewed as an example of how such modern or contemporary reflection can also be seen as having a deep foot in Igbo philosophy of life. Okere's hermeneutics of peace and justice through the aphorism *Egbe bere ugo bere* is presented as an example of full-blown engagement of an Igbo philosopher in highlighting the hidden implications of Igbo ethics especially with reference to peace and justice. Peace is synonymous with justice in Igbo ethics and this realization leaves no room for such chaos as war. The abiding link in these stages of Igbo philosophy is their focus on solving real problems of life and thus making life more livable, more fulfilling and more attuned to its positive and ultimate goal. ∎

---

**EDITOR'S NOTE:**
When *izi* 'to show' is combined with the verb *ime* 'to do', we have *imezi* which means 'to do clearly' i.e. 'to do the right thing', which can also be used to refer to correcting something that was wrongly done. Another related expression is formed from the verb *kwụ ọtọ* 'to stand (erect/straight)'. With regard to human speech, one could refer to someone's speech as *okwu kwụ ọtọ* which means 'a word that stands straight' i.e. 'a forthright, straight speech'.

# References

Achebe, C. (1983). *The Trouble with Nigeria*. Enugu: Fourth Dimension Publishers.

Achebe, C. (1988). *Things Fall Apart.* London: Picador

Achebe, C. (2006). *The University and the Leadership Factor in Nigerian Politics.* Enugu: ABIC.

Anderson, R. (1972). *The King in Every Man.* New Haven: Yale University Press.

Aristotle (1984). *The Complete Works of Aristotle.* Edited by Jonathan Barness, vol 2. Princeton: Princeton University Press.

Basden, G. (1966). *Niger Ibos.* London: Frank Cass

Bergson, H. (1988). *Les deux sources de la morale et de la religion.* Paris: Quadrige.

Britton, K. (1969). *Philosophy and the Meaning of Life.* London: Cambrige University Press.

Davidson, B. (1969). *African Genius.* Boston: Little Brown.

Echeruo, M. (1979). *A Matter of Identity.* Owerri: Ministry of Information.

Equiano, O. (1967). *Equiano's Travel.* P. Edwards (ed.), London: Heineman.

Ejiofor, L. (1982). *Igbo Kingdoms.* Africana: Onitsha.

Forde and Jones. (1950). *The Igbo and the Ibibio Speaking People of Southern Nigeria.* London: International African Institute.

Kwasi W. (1991). "On Defining African Philosophy," in C. Neugebauer (ed.), *Philosophie, Ideologie und Gesellschaft in Afrika:* Wien 1989, Frankfurt a.M: Peter Lang, p. 153 -171.

Leith-Ross, S. (1937). *Igbo Women.* London: Routledge and Kegan Paul.

Meek, C. K. (1937). *Law and Authority in a Nigerian Tribe.* London Heineman.

Metuh, E. (1981). *God and Man in African Religion.* London: Geoffrey Chapman.

Nwoga, D. (1984). *Focus on Igbo World View.* Owerri: Ministry of Information.

Odumegwu-Ojukwu, E. (1989). *Because I am Involved.* Ibadan: Spectrum.

Oguejiofor, J. (1996). *The Influence of Igbo Traditional Religion on the Socio-political Character of the Igbo.* Nsukka: Fulladu.

Oguejiofor, J. (2005). The World as Summum Bonum: Impact of African Idea of Ultimate Reality on Christian Spirituality. In M.S. Nweachukwu & A. Oburota (Ed.), *Spirituality and Pietyin Nigeria.* Enugu: Victojo Productions.

Okere, T. (1983). *African Philosophy: A Historico-Hermeneutical Investigation of the Conditions of its Possibility.* Lanham: University Press of America.

Okere, T. (2005). *Philosophy, Culture and Society in Africa: Essays.* Nsukka: Afro-Orbis Publications.

Okigbo, P. (1986). *Towards a Reconstruction of the Political Economy of Igbo Civilization.* Owerri: Ministry of Information.

Omeregbe, J. (1985). "African Philosophy: Yesterday and Today," in P. Bodunrin (ed.), *Philosophy in Africa: Trends and Perspectives.* Ile-Ife: University of Ife Press, p. 1 – 14.

Ottenberg, S. (1959). "Igbo Receptivity to Change," in W. Bascom and Herskovit (eds), *Continuity and Change in African Culture.* Chicago: University of Chicago Press.

Uzukwu, E. (1983). "Igbo World and Ultimate Reality and Meaning" *Lucerna* 4 (1).   🔲

# CHAPTER 8

George C. Odoh

## Art In Igbo Culture: Reflections On The Creative Spirit Of Igbo People Of Southeastern Nigeria

1. Introduction

2. Living Life, Living Art: The Igbo Experience

3. Manifestations of Art in Igbo Culture
   3.1 Textile
   3.2 Pottery
   3.3 Body and Wall Decorations
   3.4 Sculpture

4. Conclusion

## Summary

*This essay provides an easy to understand view of art in Igbo culture. It discusses manifestations of art in Igbo society under four major art genres (textile, pottery, body and wall decoration and sculpture) that represent the dominant forms of visual art practice in traditional Igbo society. Effort has been made to discuss selected artforms that are representative of each category and whose formal attributes, symbolic value and aesthetic qualities provide insightful snapshots of the centrality of art in Igbo culture. Where necessary, conceptual and contextual frameworks guiding the production of these works as well as production processes, techniques and iconography are discussed so as to enable a deeper understanding of how these artforms embody Igbo identity and culture. Also, the essay looks at the impact of acculturation agencies like colonization, modernization, Christian evangelization and globalization on Igbo art. Looking at the bigger picture, the range of works discussed in the essay highlights the scope, expansiveness and multi-stylistic attributes of Igbo art. They equally reveal how art plays a significant role in projecting Igbo identity.*

## 1. Introduction

IGBO PEOPLE OF SOUTHEASTERN NIGERIA LIKE MANY OTHER indigenous African tribes are known for their rich art traditions which form an important basis for understanding their cultural identity. Art holds a unique position in Igbo culture and touches on almost every aspect of Igbo life. It functions as a form of entertainment; a spiritual act that activates and also renews the bonds between the living and the dead; a way of expressing personal beauty and aesthetic ideals and also, a way of gaining access into the world of the gods and spirits. Over time, Igbo culture, including its art tradition, has undergone a lot of changes as a result of contact with acculturation agencies like colonization, modernization, Christian evangelization and globalization.

With regard to contact with the colonial rule, the colonialists viewed the colonial subjects as savages who needed to be emancipated from their primitive state. In their quest to achieve total control of the natives, they waged a relentless war on their customs and traditions which they perceived as exerting a strong influence on the social, political and cultural aspects of their lives. To counter this influence, various traditional institutions and cultural/religious practices were strongly condemned and vigorously attacked. They were labelled as primitive, devilish and a stumbling block in the transformation of the natives into civilized subjects. Consequently, most of these cultural practices and institutions were outlawed. The colonial government introduced their own systems of governance and social control which was done "to overshadow or pre-empt the local authority of their secret societies, their mask organizations, and the ancestral cult" (Kasfir, 2007). By presenting themselves as belonging to a superior race and civilization, the colonialists pushed the narrative that to become modern, refined or civilized, the natives must turn their backs on their respective cultures and traditions and embrace the civilizing culture of the West. This view had a significant impact on the psyche of the African people and greatly affected their lives socially, politically and culturally. For example, it created a situation where many Africans were neither at home with their own culture nor having firm grasp of the alien culture. This caused the neglect and in some cases, abandonment of many indigenous cultural practices and value systems.

Christian evangelisation is one factor that has significantly affected Igbo culture. The eminent Nigerian historian, Adiele Afigbo observes that early experience of Christianity in Igbo land was "marked by waves and waves of iconoclasm in which invaluable works of art and culture were destroyed" (Afigbo, 1981 as cited in Ikwuemesi, 2016). Ikwuemesi (2016) is of the view that "if earlier colonial Christian evangelisation dealt a blow to Igbo autochthonous traditions, Pentecostalism, since the last decade of the twentieth century has driven more nails into the coffin."

Globalization is another existential factor that has significantly impacted on the indigenous culture of various African societies. Advancements in technology have turned the world into a global village. Access to the internet and social media networks like Facebook, Twitter, WhatsAp, Instagram, Tik Tok among others, have facilitated cross-cultural encounters. Obviously, this has socio-political and cultural implications. For example, there is a noticeable tendency particularly among the youth to express a global identity rather than ethnic, regional or national ones. Being modern in today's environment is measured on the scale of one's familiarity and level of participation in what is trending globally. The youth seem to be more at home with pop culture than they are with their respective indigenous cultures. This is clearly reflected in their mode of dressing and the type of music they listen to. As long as this trend persists, sustenance of indigenous cultural practices and values will continue to suffer. Also, appreciation and understanding of indigenous art traditions will be affected given that in most cases, they carry the cultural weight of the identity and ideals of various African societies.

It is in the light of the above background that this essay seeks to provide a panoramic view of art in Igbo culture. It employs both narrative and descriptive approaches in its appraisal of various art forms produced by Igbo artists. It looks at the history, philosophy, production process, technique, formal attributes, aesthetics and symbolism embedded in the works. Art in Igbo culture is discussed under four broad categories namely: pottery, body and wall decorations, textiles and sculpture. These four categories represent the dominant forms of visual art practice in traditional Igbo society, and each category contains a broad range of art forms that highlight the expansiveness, scale and scope of Igbo art tradition.                                                                            ∎

## 2.0 Living life, living art: The Igbo Experience

The accidental discovery of bronze artifacts in Igbo Ukwu in 1938 by Isaiah Anozie while digging a cistern in his compound provided earliest clues to the existence of a rich art tradition in ancient Igbo civilisation. Subsequent archaeological excavations carried out by Thurstan Shaw in 1959 and 1964 in the Igbo Ukwu area reaffirmed this and further revealed the artistic ingenuity and sophistication of Igbo art.

Dating to 9th century AD, long before the earliest contact with Europe, Igbo Ukwu art is regarded as the earliest bronze using culture in Nigeria and admired for the sophistication of the technical skill employed in creating the works (Willet, 1973). Some of the artifacts (Figure 1) excavated at the Igbo Ukwu sites include elaborately decorated objects/vessels, mace-heads, a belt, and other items for ceremonial wear comprising a crown, a pectoral, a fan, a fly-whisk, beaded metal armlets, together with more than 100,000 beads. These findings not only reveal how important art was in ancient Igbo societies in terms of religious and social usage, but also show the diversity and range of materials and techniques employed by ancient Igbo artists. According to Cole and Aniakor (1984, p.18):

> " The remarkable discoveries at Igbo Ukwu are highly significant not only for the history and art of the Igbo but for all of Nigeria and West Africa...Among Igbo Ukwu finds are the earliest known African bronze castings, the earliest complicated 'shrine' assemblage, the earliest elaborate set of regalia for a leader, and the first Nigerian textiles. Even by contemporary standards Igbo Ukwu remains among the most technically advanced, virtuosic, and delicate art styles south of the Sahara. "

Art plays a significant role in the life of Igbo people. Simply put, in Igbo society, art and life are intertwined and thus one cannot exist without the other. Creativity in Igbo land is commonly associated with the term, *nka* which encompasses a wide range of creative experiences. In this regard, any person who creates art or craft is usually referred to as *omenka* while the act of producing art/craft is known as *ịkwa nka*. It has been noted that in Igbo land, art "expresses and celebrates various aspects and estates of the human person and condition" and finds strong expression in the belief that "life/living in its entirety is art *ịno ndụ bụ ịkwa nka*" (Ikwuemesi, 2016). In Igbo art, various aspects of Igbo worldview are symbolically expressed through the use of iconographical elements that embody these beliefs. This fundamental attribute of Igbo art is re-echoed in the statement that "man's religious beliefs and rituals have always been a source for his artistic creations from the ancient cave cultures to the present day" (Obichere & Cole, 1973, p.86). In Igbo society, art is consumed at individual, family and community levels where it serves social, political and religious purposes. Igbo art encompasses various creative activities that include the production of textile, sculptures (either in wood or clay), metal work, pottery and painting in the form of body and wall decorations. Masking/masquerading is another critical component of Igbo art that straddles both the visual and performing arts. It serves entertainment purposes and also plays an important role in establishing and cementing bonds between the living and the dead. As a medium for honouring the dead ancestors, masquerades are perceived as the "incarnate dead" (Henderson as cited in Cole & Aniakor, 1984).

Prior to the colonial encounter and contact with Christian missionaries, art production in Igbo land, particularly statuaries made in either wood or clay, were strongly influenced by how the people understood and interpreted natural or supernatural phenomena as well as physical or metaphysical elements. Two levels of earthly reality, *ala mmadụ* 'land of human beings' and *ala mmụọ* 'land of spirits' are identified in Igbo cosmology. These two entities are in close proximity, complementary and frequently intersect. Art plays a vital role in the visualisation and

consecration of this relationship as seen for example in the image and concept of the *Ikenga*. It is also manifested in masking traditions where various art forms are used to activate and also dramatize its culturally

*Figure 1:*

*9th century bronze*

*ceremonial pot found*

*in Igbo-Ukwu, Anambra State*

Attribution: Ochiwar at Wikipedia

Source: https://commons.wikimedia.org/
wiki/File:9th_century_bronze_ceremonial_pot._
Igbo-Ukwu,_Nigeria.JPG

assigned role as reincarnations of dead ancestors. Igbo philosophy of balance and complimentary duality which embodies the concept of *ife dị abụọ abụọ* 'things occur in twos' or *ife kwụlụ, ife akwụdebe ya* 'when one thing stands, another thing stands beside it' is another aspect of Igbo worldview that plays a major role in Igbo creativity. This is very common in Igbo statuaries which strongly reflect the concept of male and female as well as masculine and feminine forces. Igbo aesthetics also expresses this duality as embodied in the concept of physical and inner beauty.

Motifs derived from animals, plants, man-made objects, experiences of daily life and the cosmic world are widespread in Igbo art and constitute a significant aspect of iconographical elements which Igbo people use to explain the world and their understanding of its beauty and mysteries. In essence, the use of motifs is a defining attribute of both the three-dimensional and two-dimensional arts of the Igbo. Some of the animal motifs found in Igbo arts are representative of the leopard, python, lizard, eagle, elephant, tortoise, owl, crocodile, toad, guinea fowl, monitor lizard, wall gecko, snail and fish among others. Plant motifs include those derived from cassava leaf, tendrils of water plant, head of kolanut, kola pods, flowers, banana, plantain shoot, oil bean leaf, tender shoot of oil palm tree, etc. The sun, star and moon motifs are representative of celestial bodies. Through these motifs, Igbo ideals and existential realities are given visual form as a way of recording observations and discoveries from physical and transcendental phenomena. Motifs also project the formal and ethno-aesthetic attributes of Igbo art.

In Igbo culture, aesthetic value and judgement recognise both external and internal qualities of the object under consideration. Igbo aesthetic experience is not linear but occurs at physical, spiritual and abstract levels. It is also not a monolithic concept but finds interpretation and application in diverse contexts that impact on aesthetic value and judgement. For instance, it is not uncommon to find Igbo people appreciating someone based on the qualities of certain parts of the body. Hence, expressions like *mma iru* 'beauty of the face', *mma arụ* 'beauty of the body', *mma obi* 'beauty of the heart', *ọmalịcha imi* 'beautiful nose', among other expressions. It is equally common among the Igbo to use ideas borrowed from nature to reference beauty. This is found in expressions like *akwa nwa* 'beauty that is as delicate as an egg', *achala ugo* 'beauty associated with the majesty and splendour of the eagle', *oji ugo* 'beauty referencing the rarity of the eagle kola nut', among others.

As pointed out earlier, individuals, families and communities can commission and own art works in Igbo land. This "emphasizes the importance, in Igbo life, of personal needs and responsibilities and those that concern one's family and the community at large" (Cole & Aniakor, 1984, p. 24). In the light of this, art in Igbo land plays an important role in ascribing both personal and communal identities. Although Igbo belief systems govern every aspect of Igbo life including the production of art, different Igbo communities interpret and express these beliefs in ways that reflect the peculiarities of their respective socio-political and cultural environment. Cultural borrowings arising from contact with communities outside Igbo land also contribute to the stylistic variations inherent in Igbo art. *Ikenga* images found in the northcentral, northwest, southern and western areas of Igbo land provide a good example of such stylistic differences.

## 3.0 Manifestations of art in Igbo culture

Art manifests in diverse forms in Igbo culture. This is understandable because art constitutes a major medium through which Igbo people express their beliefs and life experiences. Thus, art permeates every aspect of Igbo life. Whether as a utilitarian tool, a way of expressing Igbo aesthetics or a symbolic medium for interpreting and visualizing metaphysical concepts, art constructs the Igbo identity and differentiates Igbo people from other ethnic groups. Therefore, knowledge of Igbo arts is very crucial to the meaningful understanding and appreciation of Igbo culture. Manifestation of art in Igbo society is examined under the following creative areas: textile, pottery, body and wall decoration and sculpture. Due to space constraints, the broad spectrum of works that characterize Igbo art cannot be exhaustively presented in the panoramic view of this chapter. However, the areas covered in this essay provide useful insights into the rich art culture of the Igbo people. Where necessary, the art forms are examined within the context of the philosophy that guides its production, the processes involved in creating the works, mode of representation as well as stylistic changes that have occurred over time.

### 3.1 Textile

Before the appearance and use of machine printed fabrics for textile wears in Igbo land, Igbo people wore locally woven clothes which point to the existence of a weaving tradition. A number of textile fragments excavated along with other artifacts in Igbo Ukwu validate the presence of locally woven textile materials in ancient Igbo society. Various scholars have contributed to our understanding of weaving in Igbo land. Pereira's account of first Europeans purchasing pepper, ivory and locally made textile, is the earliest description of weaving in Igbo land (Isichei as cited in Cole & Aniakor, 1984, p. 56). Igbo weaving in Igalaland was also positively identified by Balkie in 1854 (Cole & Aniakor, 1984). Tree bark, raffia and cotton were the major materials used in cloth production in pre-colonial Igbo societies. Igbo cloth produced from these materials was used for various purposes such as garments, towels, chair slings, mask costumes and sacrificial offerings. Various weaving centres existed in Igbo land. From the pre-1950 colonial record, weaving flourished in several communities in the old Nsukka Division. These include Aku, Ibagwa-Ani, Edem Ani, Enugu-Ezike, Okpuje, Nsukka and Obukpa (Afigbo & Okeke, 1985). Other areas are Ezzamgbo village in Ishielu, Asaba, and some villages of the southeastern Ndoki Igbo including Akwete whose woven fabric that goes by the same name is very famous.

Cloth weaving is generally undertaken by women who usually work with vertical looms that produce cloth widths varying from about 25 centimetres to over 150 centimetres with the latter size common in Akwete examples (Cole & Aniakor, 1984). Young girls learn weaving techniques informally under the guidance of established women weavers. In Akwete for example, a toddler is brought close to the loom and at the age of seven, is taught the weaving art when the horizontal called *agada-ekwa* in Abakiliki, *Nsu* in Aniocha, *nkwe* in Ndoki area and

*Figure 2: African woman weaving Akwete cloth*
Copyright: Ekekeh Ubadire Obioma
Source: https://commons.wikimedia.org/w/index.php?title=User:OBankz&action=edit&redlink=1

*Ogwere* in Nsukka (Afigbo & Okeke, 1985). Weaving on the loom (Figure 2) involves the interplay of vertical (warp) and horizontal (weft) network of threads. The weft thread is passed side to side over and under the warp threads. This can be passed over more than one warp thread at a time to produce variations of thread colours and patterns in the woven cloth.

Various colours and designs are used by Igbo weavers. The coloration of the woven cloth is dependent on the colour of dyed threads used. Undyed off-white cotton threads as well as indigo and brown dyed threads are predominantly used by women weavers in Nsukka and Abakiliki areas. In Nsukka, woven cloth produced with undyed white or off-white cotton thread is called *akpoto* and is characterized by its gauze like perforations. *Akpoto* is generally used for producing masquerade clothing and also in certain religious rituals or ceremonies. In *Akwete* weaving, earth colours seem to predominate. However, due to the availability of imported chemical dyes and yarn and eclectic taste of an expanding market, Akwete weaving has witnessed the introduction of other interesting colours like reds, rusts, browns, purples, black and white (Davies, 1974,

*Figure 3: An example of ukara cloth*
*Author: Ukabia*
*Source: https://commons.wikimedia.org/wiki/File:Ukara_cloth.jpg*

p. 22). Different motifs and designs are incorporated into the locally woven materials. This is more prevalent in Asaba and Akwete weavings. In Akwete, the motifs appear on one side or both sides of the woven cloth and are usually named according to their appearance. Some of these include *ebe* 'yam beetle', *ikaki* 'tortoise motif', *nna dede* and *nnụnnụ* 'bird motif', Most of the motifs are derived from already existing motifs. Akwete weavers seldom use more than three or four motifs in a cloth even though some weavers claim to know over one hundred different motifs (Davis, 1974, 25). While some of these motifs reflect the Akwete weavers' innovativeness and openness to foreign influence and change, others also represent traditional legends and practices, beliefs and household items. In Asaba weaving which is predominantly carried out in the Aniocha/Oshimili zones, the weavers, like those in Akwete, also derive patterns from local motifs as well as from other influences. These patterns which often appear in colour are inlaid into a predominantly white background. There are no coloured decorations in many traditional cloths called *aguba*. Instead, "designs and textures occur with considerable subtlety as white-on-white patterns" (Cole & Aniakor, 1984, p.58). Taking into consideration the different roles that locally woven cloth plays in the socio-political, cultural and religious life of Igbo people, they constitute an important component of their tangible cultural heritage.

## 3.2 Pottery

In the Igbo Ukwu archaeological finds, we find strong evidence of a vibrant ancient pottery tradition. Similarly, it has been revealed that Afikpo women in Igbo land as far back as 1902 before the time of British colonial rule relied on the production and sale of native pots as an important source of income (Ottenberg, 1959 as cited in Ali, 2014). The roles that pottery plays in the socio-economic and cultural life of Igbo people, either as household items or as ritual objects, foreground its importance in Igbo culture. Various pottery centres exist in Igbo land. Some of the centres include Aguleri and Owerre-Ezukala in Anambra State, Inyi and Nrobo in Enugu State as well as Afikpo and Ishiagu in Ebonyi State. In recent times, some of these pottery centres are no longer as vibrant as they used to be in the past. Major factors that have affected pottery making in Igbo land include the introduction of alternative storage materials like plastic, glass and enamel wares. Also, the influx of cheap foreign ceramics wares in the market has drastically reduced the demand and use of locally made ceramic wares. Access to other sources of income generation considered less tedious and demanding has equally affected interest in pottery making. For instance, the exploitation of gravel for house construction in Owerre-Ezukala which is considered to be more financially rewarding has reduced the number of potters in the town (Okpoko, 1987, p. 447). A similar experience is also observed in Ishiagu where mining and crushed rock industries have diverted attention of women potters away from pottery practice (Ali, 2014).

Pottery making in traditional Igbo society is essentially a female profession (Figure 4). Young girls in a potting family learn the art at an

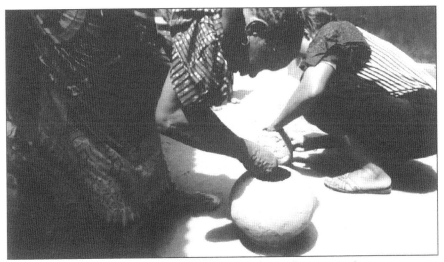

*Figure 4: Pottery production by women potters in Nrobo community.*
Copyright: Ozioma Onuzulike

early age. By the time they are fifteen to seventeen years, they too have become experienced potters. Distribution of pottery centres in Igbo land is largely dependent on the availability of clay which is the major raw material in pottery production. Cultural and economic considerations also play crucial roles in pottery practice. In the different pottery sites in Igbo land, the process involved in pottery production is basically the same although clay type, innovativeness and technical proficiency of the potter, as well as the use of different decorative techniques account for variation in styles at individual and regional levels. Pottery manufacture usually passes through five main stages which include: procurement of raw material (clay), preparation of clay, forming and decoration, drying/smoking and firing. To manufacture a pot, a lump of clay is kneaded with the palm. From this lump, the base of the pot is formed. This is subsequently placed on an inverted neck and shoulder of a pot (*onu ite*) which acts as a stand. *Onu ite* comes in different sizes and a particular size is used depending on the size of pot to be produced. Subsequent processes involved in pottery making are illustrated thus:

> *Clay is made into different rolls. These clay rolls are then worked in, one on top of the other by hand. While supporting the clay ring with the left palm, the potter uses the forefinger of the right hand to stick it onto the one before. She tries to maintain a uniform thickness first by the hands and secondly by using a scraping tool, for example, a piece of bamboo or calabash which generally smoothens the pot on the inside. This process continues until the required shape of pot is produced. The pot is then dried in the shade or in direct sunlight, depending on the intensity of the sun. After some six hours neck and rim are then added to the pot. Since rim and neck are introduced during the leather hard stage, it becomes necessary to use just the right amount of water that will help in this attachment. Also during this leather hard stage the potter uses a smooth pebble, a piece of calabash or a coconut shell to smoothen the body of the pot. The pot is then left to dry before it is polished. (Okpoko, 1987, p. 448)*

After the pot has been polished (this is not mandatory), it is decorated and further left to dry before firing. In the traditional setting, firing is done in the open and is predominantly a collective effort involving different potters. This process involves arranging dry pots (large pots are placed below and smaller ones on top) on sticks carefully arranged over baked clay or stones. Subsequently, dry grasses, green leaves and light firewood are used to cover the pots and then set on fire which lasts for a few hours. After the fire must have died down, the pots are removed and allowed to cool (Figure 5).

Pottery decoration in Igbo land has aesthetic and symbolic value. This is reflected in the use of various techniques and decorative elements that not only take into consideration the principles and elements of design but also incorporate motifs that embody various aspects of Igbo cosmology and beliefs. For instance motifs like *agwọlagwọ* 'snake coil', *anyanwụ* 'sun'. *ọnwa* 'moon', *kpakpando* 'star', *abụba* 'leaves', *mbe* 'tortoise', *ngwele* 'lizard', *aghụ* 'alligator' and *ebe* 'yam beetle' are frequently used as decorative elements by Igbo potters. Naturalism, stylization and abstraction are usually employed in representing these motifs. Given their symbolic significance in Igbo culture, these motifs go

*Figure 5: Earthenware firing by women potters in Nrobo community.*
Copyright: Ozioma Onuzulike

beyond their ethnoaesthetic appeal to infuse the pots with transcendental awe and historical value. Decorative techniques that are common in Igbo pottery tradition include grooving, burnishing, relief decoration, incision, perforation, rouletting and impression. From available ethnographic evidence, the types of decoration used in most cases are dependent on the functions of pots (Okpoko, 1987, p. 450).

In Igbo land, pottery is generally classified based on the presence or absence of a neck. While *ite* (pot) refers to pottery with neck, *oku* (bowl) is used to describe the ones without neck. *Ite* is further divided into two sub-categories based on the shape of the neck. While *ite* is characterized by a wide mouth opening and short neck, *udu* is known for its long neck and narrow mouth. Often times, the forms of *ite* and *udu* are related. According to Okpoko (1987, pp. 450-451):

> " *...a small (necked) pot with a rim diameter of 3-5 cm, used for getting water from a well or used in taking water to the farm or market, is called either ite mmili or udummili (water pot). A pot of such a size and shape when used as an infant water fetching pot is called ite mmili, but when found in shrines or when it is of ritual significance it is called udu alusi or ite alusi.* "

There are also perceivable differences between *ite ofe* (soup pot) and *ite mmili* (water pot). The two pot types are differentiated based on the height as well as the diameter of the mouth opening (Okpoko, 1987, p. 451). It is important to point out here that there are pots that do not fit into the two categories. These are usually used for ritual purposes. There defining characteristic include having stirrup handle, double-spouted with one false spout, and possessing relief forms that infuse them with sculptural attributes. In terms of decoration, "ceremonial vessels found in shrines are more elaborate than strictly practical wares, in keeping with the Igbo notion that the best and finest of everything should serve the gods and ancestor" (Cole & Aniakor, 1984, p. 78). An example is *udu nono*,

Figure 6: Pot showing
influences of indigenous
Igbo pottery forms,
techniques and
decoration on
contemporary ceramics

Artist: Vincent Ali

a ritual pot with a neck and many spouts. Pottery forms that belong to the
ọkụ family are typically of three types based on the functions they
performed. They include hemispherical bowls with upturned, in turned

and everted rims. While the first is mainly used for bathing and washing of clothes, the second is used for preparing food such as yam pottage and in certain occasions for serving food. The third is used primarily for serving food and called ọkụ ọma 'beautiful bowl' because it is usually profusely decorated (Okpoko, 1987).

Modernity has had a huge impact on traditional pottery practice in Igbo land. It has been reported that although modern influence began to be felt in the 1950s, its effects was gradual and thus allowed the pottery tradition to reach its peak in 1970s (Ali, 2014, pp. 123-124). Tourist and expatriate markets which developed during the colonial period played a huge role in boosting the local pottery industry. This also engendered the culture of appropriating new forms and techniques in pottery production. Pressed by the urge to confront the threat posed by the influx

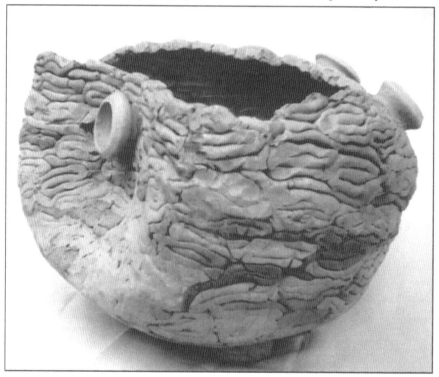

*Figure 7: Bowl showing influences of indigenous Igbo pottery forms and decorations on contemporary ceramics*
*Artist: Vincent Ali*

of western alternatives, Igbo potters had to modify their pottery practice by adding certain features that were hitherto absent in their pottery forms. These include handles, spouts, nubs, covers etc. Thus, hybridization of forms became a discernable characteristic of traditional Igbo pottery designs. Beyond its utilitarian and ritualistic functions, pots began to acquire the status of fine art and were purchased as decorative pieces based on its aesthetic value. Academically trained ceramics artists have played significant roles in infusing conventional pottery with modernist sensibilities. Drawing inspiration from Igbo traditional pottery forms and decorative techniques, some of these artists have produced works (Figures 6 and 7) which show how cross-cultural influences can give new life to old forms and thus ensure the promotion, sustainability and viability of the local pottery tradition.

## 3.3    Body and Wall Decorations

Body decoration is well embedded in Igbo culture. The politics of decorating one's body in traditional Igbo societies is basically geared towards the need for beautification as well as to communicate certain values. In using the body as a canvas to express these ideals, the body is physically and symbolically transformed. In the physical sense, the body is altered and becomes a carrier of Igbo aesthetics. At the symbolic level, it embodies and communicates messages "about sex, age, rank, wealth, as well as political and spiritual ties. Of the many forms of body decorations practiced by Igbo people including body painting, coiffure, wearing of beads and anklets, *ichi* markings and *uli* body art are its finest examples. *Ichi* marking is a form of facial scarification that permanently alters the features of the wearer's face. This involves creating low relief designs by incising the layers of the skin (Figure 8). *Ichi* practice is widespread in areas where both Nri influence and the *Ozo* institution are strong. *Ichi* patterns in most cases comprise "small crescent shapes on the forehead or sets of parallel intersecting lines on the forehead and temples" (Cole & Aniakor, 1984, p. 35). These patterns are equally found in several Igbo masks, statuaries and carved doors/panels and thus

*Figure 8: Facial scarification (Ichi markings) in Igbo land*
*Photograph of a man identified as Dofe taken by the British Government Anthropologist.*
*N. W. Thomas. in Nise (present day Anambra State) in 1911. Museum of Archaeology & Anthropology,*
*University of Cambridge P.31920.* **https://re-entanglements.net**

Traditional *uli* art encapsulates the artistic sensibilities of women in Igbo communities. This indigenous design system that was practiced in various communities across Igbo land encompasses both the decorating of the human body as well as the walls of shrines and family compounds. In *uli* body decoration, the women artists use *mma nwuli* (a rather thin and slender drawing tool made from wood) dipped into a clear brownish which turns dark blue upon drying to draw delicate and beautiful patterns on various parts of the body of their subjects. These patterns are outcomes of the freehand rendition of curvilinear designs involving open and closed spirals as well as circles, meanders, curves and angular outlines held in asymmetrical balance. In the traditional context, *uli* body decoration is not an everyday affair. Rather, it was done during special ceremonies/festivals like female rites of passage when young women reach the age of betrothal or marriage or during the naming ceremony of a newborn or at the untimely death of a young woman. It has been suggested that in addition to its primary function of enhancing and expressing beauty, *uli* body art may have also functioned as a form of self protection through the use of certain animal motifs. Therefore,

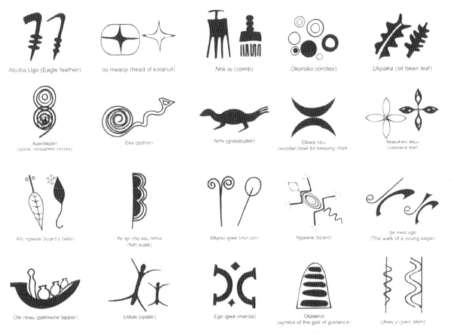

*Figure 9: Examples of uli motifs after Elizabeth Willis, 1987*
*Illustration: George Odoh*

"modifying the skin in this fashion may have created an effective barrier to potentially destructive forces permeating the human environment (Neaher, 1981, p. 54).

Irrespective of the surface (human body or wall) on which it is executed, traditional *uli* art possesses peculiar formal attributes that include linearity, spontaneity in execution and brevity of statement, space management that emphasizes asymmetrical balance as well as dramatic interplay of positive and negative spaces. *Uli* art employs patterns and motifs derived from nature (various plant types as well as domestic and forest animals), man-made objects, celestial bodies and ideas from Igbo cosmology. Some examples are shown in Figure 9. Unlike the dark blue tone that characterizes *uli* body painting, *uli* paintings executed on walls make use of an austere colour palette made up of earth tones. The basic colours are *nzu* 'white', *ufie* 'red', *edo* 'yellow' and *oji* 'black'. Blue colour derived from washing blue was a later addition to the *uli* palette. Although wall paintings, particularly in the decoration of walls of shrines, are products of group activity (Figure 10), individual stylistic traits shine through in the finished work. *Uli* art practice is almost extinct. Contributing factors to this include changes in cultural/aesthetic values engendered by modernization, preference for foreign cosmetic products and tattooing techniques as well as the proliferation of modern architectural designs and materials. In the 1970s at the Department of Fine and Applied Arts, University of Nigeria, Nsukka, studio experimentation of the design attributes of traditional *uli* art led to the development of a modernist art language that drew attention to *uli* art nationally and internationally. The Nsukka experiment highlighted the potency of using indigenous design systems as a viable tool for negotiating artistic and ethnic identities in the global art space. Beyond this modernist approach, *uli* art can still be made relevant in today's contemporary society by using its design attributes and aesthetics in producing various crafts and other items that can be mass produced.

## 3.4 Sculpture

It is in the sculpture tradition that one finds the finest, most engaging, and most enduring examples of Igbo art. This is also true for most indigenous tribes in sub-Sahara Africa. Sculptures (either in wood or clay) provide access points for understanding the socio-political, cultural and religious dynamics of Igbo society. Every aspect of Igbo life finds concrete manifestation in the diverse range of sculptures that highlight the bonds between the individual, the family unit and the community on one hand, and that between the individual, the family unit, the community and the dead ancestors on the other hand. Sculpture exists as relief works (as observed in carved doors and panels) and as three dimensional works comprising masks and free standing statuaries. Naturalism, stylization and abstraction are extensively used as modes of representation in Igbo sculpture tradition. Irrespective of the mode of representation,

*Figure 10: Uli women artists at work*
*Copyright: Chuu Krydz Ikwuemesi*

conceptualization and production of these sculptures is usually guided by Igbo worldview which also shapes aesthetic value and judgement in Igbo society.

Sculptures perform various roles in Igbo society. They function as a symbol of identity, status and authority. They equally play major roles in religious and ritual practices as well as in masking traditions where they are used to animate the bond between the living and the dead. The *Ikenga* is a very common and popular sculpture in Igbo land. In male cults where it is primarily used, it encapsulates the powers, successes and failures of an individual. According to Cole and Aniakor (1984, p. 24), *"Ikenga*, as shrine, symbol, and idea, incorporates a person's *chi*, his ancestors, his right arm or hand, *aka ikenga*, his power, *ike*, as well as spiritual activation through prayer and sacrifice." In this context, the *Ikenga* sculpture underlines the social, political, cultural and religious dimensions of sculpture in Igbo land. At its most simplified state, *ikenga* is depicted as an abstract image of a human head with horns set on a base.

Larger versions of *ikenga* (Figure 11) show a male figure seated on a stool. In most cases, he is shown with either a complex or not too complex headdress amplified in part by the presence of horns. The figure is also shown holding and wearing various symbols as well as the incorporation of several other motifs (Cole & Aniakor, 1984, p. 24). Stylistic variations occur in *ikenga* sculptures.

These highlight artistic and technical subjectivities on the part of local carvers (Figure 12) as well as the taste of clients who commissioned the work. However, the underlying Igbo philosophy that anchors this practice provides a common ground for understanding and appreciating the differences in formal language and iconography.

Iconographical evaluation of *ikenga* sculptures sheds light on various Igbo beliefs and how these are expressed symbolically through metaphors embedded in the *ikenga* image. The horn on the *ikenga* are often identified as those of a ram; an animal known for going to battle with the head/horns. Rams are also known for their aggression, perseverance and persistence.

These are attributes associated with 'real' men. According to Cole and Aniakor (1984, p. 30), "in ritual contexts, rams are not meant to show any pain, thus the strong man must also be stoic." The image of the *ikenga* figure holding a knife in his right hand and a severed trophy head in the left hand symbolically expresses acts of valour, superiority and success in warfare which are critical components of male ethos in traditional Igbo societies. The knife/head metaphor in *ikenga* is described thus:

 *The knife is a means; the head is the end, the trophy which is a symbol of accomplishment. Only the naive would strictly equate the heads on ikenga with trophies and head-hunting, though some Igbo were head hunters and did take them as trophies. Rather the head is achievement, the result of hard-fought effort. Bravery is explicit, but beyond that and more*

*Figure 11: Ikenga*
Copyright: Krydz Ikwuemesi
Source:https://commons.wikimedia.org/wiki/
File:Statuette_masculine_ikenga,_Nigeria,_
Mus%C3%A9e_du_quai_Branly.jpg

*Figure 12: Local wood carver at work*
Copyright: Krydz Ikwuemesi

*implicit is the courage to respond to whatever challenge one meets and with the help of one's chi, ancestors, and the alusi, to succeed. (Cole & Aniakor, 1985, p. 30)* **,,**

Apart from personal *ikenga* which are commonplace, community owned *ikenga* also exists. This is usually larger and incorporates more iconographic elements comprising figural and animal forms that reflect a much more expansive use of formal elements, imagery and aesthetics to amplify as well as express communal ideals and identity.

In many Igbo communities, carved stools, doors and panels are visual markers through which an individual's rank in the society as well as level of affluence is projected and affirmed. Although these sculptural forms appear widespread in Igbo land, it is in the north-central region where *Ozo* institution and other title societies hold sway that we find revelatory contexts that highlight their socio-cultural significance in Igbo culture. In the *Ozo* institution, every titled man was mandated to own a carved stool as they were forbidden from sitting on the ground (Cole & Aniakor, 1984). Awka carvers are renowned in the art of stool carving. Their virtuosity and expertise in wood carving also extend to carved doors and panels. Traditional Igbo carved stools are generally three or four legged although other leg formats do exist. In terms of style, leg supports either occur as simple forms or as complex structures characterized by the intersection of dynamic curvilinear forms that emphasize movement and also dramatize the relationship between positive and negative spaces. In some cases, the stools incorporate figural and animal forms which act as the legs of the stool and also function as decorative and symbolic devices.

Locally carved doors and panels offer deep insights into how sculpture and architecture intersect in Igbo art tradition. Like the carved stools, they are produced from male woods particularly the *iroko* which is associated with power and certain mysteries. Before the iroko tree is felled, the spirit believed to reside in the tree is placated. Carved doors serve as entrance portals to the *obi* (male meeting house). In other words, they act as gateway into and out of the inner space of a typical traditional Igbo compound. Beyond this literal context, Neaher (1981, p. 44) views them as boundaries between inside and outside, what is known and what is not known, the world within and the outside world. She also notes that because they belong "neither to the inside nor to the outside, they form boundaries that universally signify a special point of transition, both hallowed and threatening". She goes further to assert that their visibility and their location on the boundary not only "permit them to serve as both a warning and an invitation to the viewer" but also given their role as status symbols within the *Ozo* society, "the carvings act as visual representations of the status and privileges of the household."

Igbo carved doors are intricately decorated with the chip carving technique which creates V-shaped grooves on the wood. Adze and chisels are the major tools used by local carvers. Although animals, human figures and valued artifacts sometimes feature in carved doors, the designs consists primarily of geometric abstract designs that call to mind the Igbo tradition of facial scarification *(Ichi)* as well as the design attributes of traditional *uli* art. Neaher (1981) views the fusion of these two artistic modes as s symbolic representation of strength and human fertility. In contemporary Igbo societies, changing socio-cultural values as well as the influence of modern architectural sensibilities have negatively affected the production and use of locally carved doors and panels as entrance portal in Igbo households. Metal gates have virtually taken over this function.

Igbo masks and statuaries offer interesting contexts for understanding and appreciating the dynamism and aesthetic richness of Igbo arts. The broad range of iconographical elements appropriated in the production of these sculptural forms underscore their symbolic value as visual containers that embody Igbo worldview and philosophy. In performing this role, they act as socio-political, cultural and religious signifiers of Igbo culture. Masks and figural sculptures occur in diverse forms and contexts across various communities in Igbo land. One outstanding characteristic of Igbo masks and statuaries is the strong recognition and reflection of the Igbo philosophy of duality. As such, their morphological attributes are frequently structured around diametrically opposed entities like male and female, masculinity and femininity, good and bad, beautiful and ugly, among others. Figural sculptures are predominantly found in shrines where they are used to represent various tutelary deities. These wood carvings are "conceived of and materialized on the human family model, wives, husbands, children, *ikenga*, messengers and other helpers" (Cole & Aniakor, 1984, p. 89). During festivals or ceremonies that celebrate the deity, the statuaries are lined up in front of the shrine or paraded around the largest market in the community. In the northcentral region of Igbo land, wooden figural sculptures, irrespective of whether it is female or male, show a homogenous stylistic approach in their rendition. They express a frontal orientation with the body parts symmetrically balanced. They are depicted in a standing position with the legs slightly apart. Also, the hands which cut free from the sides are shown with open palms as a way of denoting open handedness or generosity of the deities (Cole & Aniakor, 1984, p. 92). In most cases, the female figures are depicted with the single-crest hairstyle. Elongation of the neck region is also a common attribute of these figural sculptures. Some equally bear facial markings reminiscent of *ichi* markings.

Masking tradition in Igbo land serves various purposes which include acting as agents of socio-political control, means of entertainment and more importantly, as representations of the dead ancestors who have

*Figure 10: Agbogho mmu 'maiden mask' in performance.* Photo: George Odoh

*Figure 11: Agbeje a masquerade of the Omabe cult.* Photo: George Odoh

come to commune with the living. The diversity and range of masks spread across the length and breadth of Igbo land attest to the cultural dynamism of Igbo people. Some popular masks in Igbo land include *Ijele* (considered the mother of masquerades), *Mgbedike* 'Time of the brave', *Ekwe* (similar to *Ijele* and common in the Nsukka area), *Agaba, Odo, Ọmabe, Ogbodo Enyi, Ọyawa, Ụlaga, Ogolo, Ojiọnụ* and *Agbọghọ Mmụọ* 'maiden masks' among many others. From the giant and elaborately constructed *Ijele* to the pseudo-masks worn by small children, the preponderance of masked forms in Igbo communities affirms its central role to Igbo art and culture. Several factors are responsible for the diversity and range of Igbo masks. Technical proficiency, innovativeness as well as artistic virtuosity on the part of the mask carver is one contributing factor. Again, rivalry and competition between groups and communities also factor in influencing stylistic traits. Generally, morphological attributes of Igbo masks draws from the symbolic as well as conceptual representation of an idea or ideal. For example, feminine masks like the *Agbọghọ Mmụọ* (Figure 10) expresses and exaggerates Igbo concept of feminine beauty which recognizes the intrinsic worth of both its physical and moral components. From another perspective, *Mgbedike* masks project masculine attributes like valour, strength, bravery, aggression and fearlessness. They usually have a large head structure surmounted by horns with bold and exaggerated facial features such as bulging eyes, flared nostrils and open mouths with large menacing teeth. In masks dedicated to tutelary deities like *Ọmabe* (Figure 11) and *Odo*, wooden mask heads are almost non-existent. The *Ọmabe* headpiece is primarily configured with locally woven cloth with white thread radiating from the eye area. The head is also decorated with a rich plume of coloured feathers which radiate outwards to create what looks like a vegetal canopy over the body of the masquerade. Body costume usually features hundreds of shiny buttons that are sewn unto its surface to simulate leopard spots.

Production of masks is usually carried out in a secluded area. The process of roughening out the features is undertaken in the bush where the wood used for its production is cut. The mask carver may then relocate to a private enclosure at the back of his compound where the mask is eventually finished. Keeping the production process secret not only prevents rival groups or competitors from stealing the design and improving on it, it also helps to maximize the awe and excitement which the mask generates during the time of its unveiling to the public. In terms of decoration, headdresses of Igbo masks can be simple, moderate or elaborate. Anthropomorphic forms, figural and animal forms, abstract forms and motifs as well as items from everyday life are used extensively to decorate masks. The super-structural configuration of *Ijele* and *Ekwe* headdresses deserves mention. The headdress of these two masquerades is replete with decorative elements rich in iconographic symbolism. Viewed holistically, the masquerades embody the very essence of Igbo life and arts and thus are seen as a compendium of Igbo cultural history as well as storehouse of Igbo knowledge and wisdom. Masking tradition in Igbo land is not static but continues to evolve in response to existential realities. The appropriation and incorporation of foreign elements into the iconography of masks underscores the dynamism of this all important cultural phenomenon. Although masking is still an intrinsic aspect of Igbo culture, the strong influence which it wielded in the lives of Igbo people has weakened considerably due to the experiences of colonization, modernity and Christian evangelization. Despite these challenges, it still remains a potent signifier of the cultural identity of Igbo people.

Another interesting context for appraising Igbo sculpture tradition is the *mbarị* house, an art-based architectural installation dedicated to Igbo deities particularly *Ala*, the earth goddess. The *mbarị* complex which encompasses the fields of architecture, sculpture and painting is constructed as a sacrificial offering in response to disasters or problems that befall a community. In describing *mbari* as a communal religious obligation that demonstrates allegiance and dedication to the gods, Obichere and Cole (1973, p.86) equally notes that it is "an act of supplication as well as an expression of thanksgiving" Some *mbari* houses are known to contain over a hundred figural sculptures made entirely in clay. Images of animals and artifacts also play secular and symbolic roles in the assemblage. Construction of *mbari* house is an expensive undertaking. In the Owerri-Igbo area where *mbari* art is a key aspect of the religious life of the people, the process of erecting an *mbari* house is initiated by the chief priest after consultations with diviners and oracles. The selection of individuals charged with the physical construction of the *mbari* house also involves acts of divination initiated by priests and elders of the community. This group of individuals known as *Nde Mgbe* in the Owerri-Igbo area "are supposed to represent not only the most beautiful people in the community, but also the most creative and artistic. A few professional and itinerant artists are added to these people, selected from the community over whom the deity has sway, for the creation of the Mbari experience" (Obichere & Cole, 1973, 86-87). *Nde Mgbe* is not subjected to secular control. Rather, their status as agents of the supernatural within the *mbari* enclosure engenders a new lifestyle moderated by taboos and religious licence that allows them to behave and express themselves in ways that transcend secular norms. After the unveiling of the *mbari* which is a joyous event marked by singing, music making and dancing, *Nde Mgbe* undergo a purification process involving rituals and sacrifices which psychologically rehabilitates them as they return to secular life and communal social control (Obichere & Cole, 1973). After the unveiling and its associated rituals, *mbari* house is not preserved or maintained but left at the mercy of the elements to decay. This act, as Achebe (1984, ix) explains, underscores the aesthetic value of Igbo people which places emphasis on process rather than product. The belief is that the impulse to recreate a process is compromised when the product is preserved or venerated.　∎

## 4.0　Conclusion

In its embodiment of Igbo world view, Igbo aesthetics and existential experiences, Igbo art acts as a carrier of Igbo identity. Art in Igbo society accommodates a broad range of creative activities in the areas of textile, pottery, body and wall decorations, metal works and sculpture. Consumption of art occurs at individual, family and community levels and is informed by the need for beautification as reflected in the art of body decoration. It is also used as a way of expressing one's rank, status, wealth and political authority as embodied in *ichi* markings and the use of *ukara* cloth, carved stools, carved doors and panels. Again, art is utilized in rituals/ceremonies that honour tutelary deities and the dead ancestors. Statuaries, ritual pots and bowls, *mbari* house and masks play key roles in this regard. The multiplicity of styles that characterize Igbo art reflects the creative virtuosity, innovativeness, and artistic sensibilities of Igbo artists as well as the differences in aesthetic tastes and judgement on the part of individuals, families and communities who commission the works.

In today's contemporary Igbo society, factors like urbanization, Christian evangelization, advancements in digital technology, access to internet and use of social media among other acculturation forces have significantly affected the dynamism of Igbo art and by extension, Igbo culture. These factors in many ways have overrun the socio-political and cultural spaces in which Igbo art once flourished. It is also important to note that Igbo art has equally drawn from these experiences to reinvent new forms and aesthetics that communicate how Igbo people adapt to their changing environment. With respect to the changing fields of society, it is advocated that Igbo artists and cultural producers should "use the past as a datum for confronting and coming to terms with the present to make the future more meaningful" (Ikwuemesi, 2016). To effectively do this, it is important to generate and document information that facilitates understanding and appreciation of Igbo art and culture. It is perhaps this context that one finds the relevance and significance of this essay.

## References

Achebe, C. (1984). Foreword. *Igbo arts, community and cosmos,* Cole, H. & Aniakor, C. (ix-xii) Los Angeles: Museum of Cultural History, University of California

Afigbo, A. E. & Okeke, C. S. (1985). *Weaving tradition in Igbo land.* Lagos: Nigeria Magazine

Bentor, E. (2015). A historical understanding of ukara cloth. *Ukara: Ritual Cloth of the Ekpe Society* (exhibition catalogue). Available from https://hoodmuseum.dartmouth.edu/new s/2015/03/ukara-ritual-cloth-ekpe-secret-society

Cole, H. & Aniakor, C. (1984). *Igbo arts, community and cosmos.* Los Angeles: Museum of Cultural History, University of California

Davis, M. (1974). Akwete cloth and its motifs. *African Arts, 7*(3), pp. 22-25. http://www.jstor.org/stable/3334858

Ikwuemesi, C. K. (2016). Art as a tool for cross-cultural conversation: A personal dialogue with Igbo and Ainu art. *Cogent Arts & Humanities. 3*(1). https://doi.org/10.1080/23311983.2016.1262997

Kasfir, L. S. (2007). *African art and colonial encounter: Inventing a global commodity.* Indiana University Press.
Neaher, N. C. (1981). Igbo Carved Doors. *African Arts, 15*(1), pp. 49-55+88. doi:10.2307/3336006

Nzewi, U. C. & Watters, E. (2015).

Introduction. *Ukara: Ritual Cloth of the Ekpe Society.* Available from https://hoodmuseum.dartmouth.edu/new s/2015/03/ukara-ritual-cloth-ekpe-secret-society

Obichere, B. I., & Cole, H. M. (1973). Mbari: Art and Religion among the Owerri Igbo. *African Arts, 7*(1), pp. 86-87. doi:10.2307/3334765

Okagu, G. O. (n.d.). Indigenous knowledge system on traditional textile weaving technology among the people of Aku in Igbo-Etiti LGA. of Enugu State. *Ikenga International Journal of Institute of African Studies, 12*(2), pp. 1-28. http://www.unn.edu.ng/publications/files /11898_INDIGENOUS_KNOWLEDGE_SYST EM_ON_TRADITIONAL_TEXTILE_WEAVING _TECHNOLOGY_AMONG_THE_PEOPLE_OF_ AKU_IN_IGBO-ETITI_L_G_A_OF_ENUGU-STATE.pdf

Okpoko, I. (1987). Pottery-making in Igbo land, Eastern Nigeria: An ethnoarchaeological study. *Proceedings of the Prehistoric Society, 53,* pp. 445-455. DOI: 10.1017/S0079497X00006332

Otosirieze, O. (2020). The women weavers of Akwete. Available from https://folio.ng/the-women-weavers-of-akwete/

Willett, F. (1973). Igbo-Ukwu: An Account of archaeological discoveries in Eastern Nigeria by Thurstan Shaw. *Africa: Journal of the International African Institute, 43*(1), p. 88. DOI: https://doi.org/10.2307/1158558 ∎

# Igbo Traditional Religion And Institutions

1. Introduction

2. Features of Igbo Traditional Religion
   2.1 Belief in *Chiukwu*
   2.2 Belief in Divinities
   2.3 Belief in the Practice of Medicine

3. Worship in Igbo Traditional Religion
   3.2 Private Worship
   3.2 Public Worship

4. Igbo Institutional Patterns and Customs:
   *Ụmụnna, Ogbe, Obodo, Ụmụ Ada, Otu Ọgbọ, Mmanwụ, Omenanị*

5. Rites of Passage in Igbo Traditional Religion:
   *Pregnancy Rites, Birth Rites, Puberty Rites, Marriage Rites, Rites for the Dead*

6. Summary and Conclusion

## *Summary*

*Igbo Traditional Religion and institutions are the results of answer seeking reflections of Igbo ancestors over the mysteries surrounding the existence of man and the universe. Igbo Traditional Religion is the original religion of the Igbo people before the coming of Christianity and Islam. The chief characteristics of Igbo religious life are three according to Ilogu (1974) namely: variety, communality and utility. Variety exists in the number of deities, places where they are worshipped and the methods and manner of worship. Communality is the essence of the deities. They are the common possessions and guardians of all. Religion among the Igbo is a group affair. Chukwu and other minor deities have jurisdiction over the whole group. Therefore, there are common celebrations and common religious practices covering a large area. Utility is the most important reason the Igbo man can give for the existence of the deities. Hence all of his life activities of planting food crops, or in the upbringing of his children, or in the more individual incidence of being born, being married and being buried are understood from the point of view of his relationship with the divinities. The social organization and the social structure of the Igbo constitute the formal political forum in which people live much of their political lives. It is a systemized setting that enables people to express themselves in terms of power, influence and authority, and know on what platform they expect to get what, how and when.*

## 1. Introduction

**T**HE LIFE AND THOUGHT OF THE PRE-LITERATE PERIOD OF A PEOPLE is best studied through their religious practices and traditional institutions, because the two are like the strong threads that run through the fabric that hold the traditional society together. Hence the rest of the chapter rightly concentrates on the different features of, and the elements that make up, Igbo traditional religion and institutions. ⌐

## 2. Features of Igbo Traditional Religion

Igbo Traditional Religion is notable for certain characteristics which include, but are not restricted to, the following:

### 2.1 Belief in God (the Supreme Being)

The belief in the Supreme Being or God is a cardinal element of Igbo Traditional Religion. The Supreme Being is the cohesive or unifying supernatural ultimate reality that holds the religion together. He is believed to be the absolute controller of the universe. According to Basden (1985) amongst the Igbo people there is a distinct recognition of a supreme being - beneficent in character - which is above every other spirit, good or evil. He is believed to control all things in heaven and earth, dispenses rewards and punishments according to merit. Anything that occurs, for which no visible explanation is forth-coming, is attributed to either Him or His eternal enemy, *ajonmuo* (the devil).

The central association in the concept of the principal God is belief in a beneficent source of creation. The great God is believed to be the author of heaven and earth who makes animal and plant life grow. As the source of human life, He gives to every man at the time of his birth that man's particular portion of being, called Chi, which becomes the spiritual double of the man throughout his life. Whatever abilities, good or bad fortunes, success, failures or weaknesses possessed by the man are often attributed to his *Chi*. It is this idea which also leads to the world *Chi Ukwu* which, as the name for the great God, explains that the individual Chi, which each person possesses derives from the great Chi who is the creator of all that has life and being. A man does not exist without his *Chi*. The magnanimity or ignominy of his actions, as well as his success and failure, are due to his *Chi*. The Igbo have a proverb: *Ebe onye daalu ka Chi ya kwaturu ya* 'The place where one falls is where his *Chi* pushes him down'. Another proverb is: *Onye Chi ya na-egbughi, e nweghi ihe ga-eme ya* 'one does not die before one's *Chi* has consented to such death' (adapted from Ilogu, 1985).

## 2.2 Belief in Divinities

Igbo Traditional Religion is evidently dominated by the belief in minor divinities that are subject to the Supreme Being. Some authors refer to these divinities as sons and daughters of the Supreme Being or representative of God. According to Achebe (1986), "*Chukwu* is so great that He works through the agency of many lesser deities to fulfill His purpose. The lesser deities are autonomous, yet function interdependently" (p. 15). Idowu (1973) points out that "they are brought into being as the functionaries in the theocratic government of the universe, that they are ministers each with its own definite portfolio in the monarchical government of the universe" (p. 165). According to Ugwu and Ugwueye (2004), "The divinities are also intermediaries between God and man, and frequently worshipped through them and they receive day- to-day sacrifices" (p. 38). They have temples, shrines, priests, priestesses and devotees. They can be described as constituting

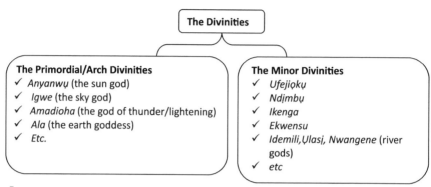

*Figure 1. Some Igbo Divinities*

Anyanwu (The Sun god), is sometimes addressed in prayer as if he were the same as Chineke. At other time he is regarded as a messenger of the creator God. Through whom sacrifices tied on the top of a long bamboo pole should reach Chineke. A popular way of offering sacrifice to the sun god is to address him as the companion of the king of the heavens (Anyanwu na eze elu 'the Sun and the King of the Heavens'. Sacrifices are offered to the sun god mostly on the order of the diviner for a specific purpose. For example, during a severe illness in which the sick person's breath is feared to be high and fast, the sun god is prayed to make the heartbeat normal. The sun god, by and large, can be beneficent.

Igwe (the sky god). Igwe is the husband of Ala who sends rain to moisten Ala so as to be productive. Just as husband fertilizes his wife, so does Igwe fertilizes Ala through rainfall. Through his intercession, Chukwu nourishes the green vegetation of the earth and sees to the health of the living. Not much prayer is offered to this god as he is often known through his "wife", the earth goddess, who happens to be the most important of these four gods of Igbo religion and life after Chineke.

Amadioha (The god of thunder and Lightning). Amadioha is the wrathful messenger of the Supreme God, Chukwu, who sends Amadioha in the form of thunder to punish evildoers. Hence oaths are sworn by him and priest can curse suspected persons by him. He is not a beneficent god to whom various sacrifices are offered; rather occasional public appeasements are ordered by diviners so as to ward off impending doom from his wrath. Amadịọha expresses his power in thunderbolts and lightening. He is an agent of Chukwu against undetected crimes. He lightens up the world and gathers evidences as well as bears witness for good deeds and against evil deeds of people. He ensures that the natural order as set by Chukwu is not upset. His principle is simple, "an eye goes for an eye and a tooth goes for a tooth". Whatever one sows, one will reap.

Ala (The earth goddess). Ala is the most important deity in Igbo social and religious life after the Supreme God. She is the guardian of morality, the controller of the minor divinities of fortune and economic life. It is she who works in conjunction with the spirits of the dead ancestors to order prohibitions and ritual avoidances. Many social offenses become alụ or pollution or abominations because they infringe on the laws of Ala. Because of her importance in ensuring health, agricultural fortune and hunting successes, she is well known all over Igboland. Most public worships of various communities are offered to Chukwu through Ala as well as seasonal celebrations which relate to the various seasons of the year. Her shrine is found in most homes and public squares of any village.

There are also other minor divinities which are sometimes personifications of the facts and features of nature and of daily life. Prominent among these minor deities are Ufejiọkụ, the god of farm work; Agwụ (the god of divination and healing). He is the chief messenger of God. He is charged with the responsibility of providing man with tools of existence. He holds the key to those secrets of creation which man is expected to know and reveal such secrets as are necessary for advancement of mankind. In the study of science, religion, philosophy, mysticism and occultism, he is the first port of call. Ndịmbu, the edified spirits of the dead ancestors; Ikenga, god of adventure in h u n t i n g   a n d business enterprise; Ekwensu (god of warriors). Christian missionaries have wrongly identified Ekwensu with the Christian concept of devil. Ekwensu is in fact, the spirit of violence and patron of warriors and not the Christian devil. Among some communities in Anịọma, Delta state, there is a festival called Ekwensu festival, and it constitutes their major annual feast, during which they display their military prowess as well as how Chukwu intervened in precarious war experiences of their ancestors and gave them victory that eventually settled them in their present communities. There are also river gods like Idemili, Ụlasị or Nwangene etc. These divinities have their cult symbols in public squares as well as in private homes but some like Ufejiọkụ, receive much public sacrifices and community worship with big celebrations at seed planting time and harvest time.

The prominent spirit in the group of spirit-gods is Ndịmbụ, the deified spirits of the dead ancestors. What makes Ndịmbụ a prominent feature of Igbo religious life is the belief that the dead ancestors are invisible members of the community. There is a belief in life after death as well as in reincarnation among the Igbo. One of the most striking doctrines of the Igbo is that every human being has, associated with his personality, a genius or spiritual double known as his Chi. This Chi is given by Chineke at the time when the child is formed in its mother's womb. It is also believed that the Chi is sometimes part of the soul of a noble ancestor, who has chosen to be reincarnated in order to be a special influence for the good of the child. Not every dead ancestor is so reincarnated. It is the good and wise who could easily do so in order that they may continue the good work that they have started in their previous life. But Chineke is Almighty, and if it pleases Him, He may give the Chi of a poor man to one who in previous life was rich, so that his experience may be enriched by the knowledge of these two possible human conditions (Ilogu, 1985).

The role of the ancestors in the afterlife is important, for in some undefined way they influence Chineke in respect of the well-being or punishment of their offspring. They are therefore invested with divine qualities, and among the Igbo no concept of God is complete without them. It is they who, in one form or another, become the link between the living and the supernatural world. They are propitiated with sacrifices and symbolically represented by divine images and objects, notably the Ofo stick. It is a calamity to both the living and the dead if no sons remain to offer daily payers, libations of wine, and sacrifices of kola nuts or pieces of food to the ancestors.

The ancestors work conjointly with Ala in protecting the community from harm in the form of famine or epidemics like small pox or abominations. The very important feature of Igbo social structure described as the lineage or Umunna is religiously upheld by the ancestor cult. People who trace their origin to a common ancestor must keep together and help one another or else incur the displeasure of these ancestor spirits. This is the foundation of Igbo communalism. The spirits of the departed ancestors are of tremendous significance in this concept of Igbo communalism. At death the ancestors are believed to have entered the spirit world, and as spirits they share in the ordering of the community. They are always happy to plead with the deities for the well-being of their offspring. Contravention of the people's laws and customs, which the ancestors had either established or upheld in their lifetime, grieves and displeases them. When this is discovered, propitiation must be made at once, or evil would befall the village concerned.

Prayers are always offered to the Almighty God (Chukwu) through the minor deity directly concerned, and nearly always through the ancestors. The most frequent subject of prayer is protection from harm and danger, and this includes prosperity, long life and abundance of children and crops. Prayer request are preceded by a historical account of the clan's origin, emphasizing the assistance that the ancestors had received from

God. The chief priest, who may also be the head of the clan, leads the prayer, holding his Ofo stick in his hand. At the end of each significant section, all the Ozo-tittled men strike the ground with their own Ofo and say isee-amen, so be it.

There are also sacred days among the Igbo. These are days which are holy to the deities and to most adults in Igboland. There are four market days running in two parallel thereby forming one complete native week of eight days made up as follows: Eke nta; Orie nta; Afo nta; Nkwo nta, Eke ukwu; Orie ukwu; Afo ukwu and Nkwo ukwu. (Nta means small while Ukwu means great). Certain deities must be worshipped on their holy days.

## 2.3 Belief in the Practice of Medicine

Medicine is used by man to conquer his environment. It is used to procure what cannot be obtained in the ordinary way. By medicine the Igbo mean any substance or substances that are used in treating or preventing disease or illness; in other words, medicine is a recipe of herbal mixtures and some ritual formulae designed to generate some powers which are built into nature by God, which can be tapped and applied with help of God and other spiritual beings to meet various human needs (Chidili, 2012). For Metuh (1987), medicine also means any power that has greater influence over other powers. It is best, therefore, to understand Igbo medicine in the sense of efficacious substance or force in substance. It can also mean forces contained in, and can be extracted from, the properties of some plants and herbs and applied to the solution of a variety of human problems. Medicine is based on the belief that there are vital forces or supernatural powers in the universe that can be tapped and controlled by man for the maintenance of balance in the system. Awolalu and Dopamu (1979) define medicine as "the act of using the available forces of nature to prevent diseases and to restore and preserve health" (p. 24). It is both prophylactic and therapeutic (preventive and curative).

Specialists in Igbo medicine are known as the Dibịa or herbalists, with the knowledge of herbs, roots, or even fruits with the power to prevent or cure diseases or other afflictions. However, the herbalist can also make some other medicines from herbs mixed with some other miraculous or benign effects, and consequently can affect man and human conditions. As such, medicine can act for anyone who observes the proper ceremonies for becoming the owner of it, and indeed observes the taboos surrounding the medicine carefully. This category of Igbo medicine men are referred to Dibịa Ọgwụ. Dibịa Afa (Diviners) on the other hand consists of men and women specialists who frequently rely on divination for their practices. In this case then, the diviner diagnosis the cause of illness and recommends adequate treatment which may come in the way of herbs, twigs, roots or animal parts, separately or their mixture. Herbalists who specialize in the bone setting are Dibịa Ọkpụkpụ. They specialize in the treatment of fractures, operations and suturing wounds. The bone setters deal with fractured bones with equal perfection of western surgeons. There is also Dibia Aja, whose primary expertise is to perform necessary and adequate sacrifices either to ward off evil spirits or to curry favour from the divinities. In some cases the sacrifices are prescribed by the diviner. In other cases too, Dibia Aja can also be a diviner. The important thing is that the Dibia in this category has the knowledge, either by inheritance, natural endowment or through rigorous apprenticeship programme, to interact with spiritual entities for the purposes of relating the spiritual atmosphere to humanity.

Igbo medicine, therefore, goes beyond mere scientific findings of the healing ingredients. Rather, it targets holistic healing through the effective mobilization of all affordable resources (physical, spiritual, economic and even political) in preventing or curing a person's illness. This is so since the human person is a composite of the physical, the psyche, the social, the moral and the spiritual, any of the parts could be afflicted either in part or as a whole at any time. This is why Adibe (cited by Chidili, 2012) notes that "any medicine man or woman worth his/her name must have an unflinching alliance with mystical powers" (p. 218). He explains these mystical powers as the spiritual beings whose potency attracts reverence and homage. According to Onuwa (2005), "The traditional religion is indeed society itself and there is no clear demarcation between the sacred and the profane" (p. 80). Both the spiritual and the physical realms of the universe are believed to work in a consistent harmony and are subject to an ordered system and rhythm. Any breach in the system causes a disaster and the whole system is disrupted. The whole essence of man's religious rituals is to keep the system in a consistent harmony (to maintain the balance). Medicine is part of that whole complex religious attempt to keep the system in consistent harmony.

In Igbo traditional societies, sickness, disease and misfortune are generally believed to be caused by the ill will or ill action of one person against another. The medicine man is thus consulted to diagnose the type of sickness and trace the cause of it. The satisfactory answer that people seemed to need at a time when the question of the cause is sought is that someone caused it. Even if it is a mosquito bite, someone must have sent the mosquito. As a solution to the problem in question, the cause must be found, counteracted and punished. It is also the duty of the medical practitioner to provide countermeasures that can counteract future inflictions. They are the doctor and pastor of the sick.

## 3. Worship in Igbo Traditional Religion

*Chukwu* in Igbo religion is sometimes spoken of as *Amama Amacha Amacha* 'He who is known but not completely known'. It is a name which among other things indicates the mysterious nature of God. Yet Igbo spirituality generated the practice of trying to penetrate into the being of this mysterious God through prayers, invocations, incantations, sacrifices and annual celebrations in the pleasing of the constituents of the mysterious God head. It is all these put together that Ilogu (1985) speaks of as worship in Igbo religious life. There are private and public worships.

## 3.1 Private Worship

This is divided into two. The first is the routine private worship which includes the daily offerings made by the head of a household to the ancestors for the protection, prosperity and well-being of the family while holding up the *Ọfọ* stick. The second is the routine private worship offered once in a year by the head of the family when the *Ọfọ* stick is ceremoniously cleansed with blood of a chicken sacrificed to the ancestors. Occasional private worship is done when ordered by the diviner as a result of his being consulted by the individual concerned or on his behalf. There are also cases of a diviner conveying a message from the divinities to an individual requiring him to offer some sacrifices. The special intention of such private worship is usually one or more of such needs as:

* *To seek favour from ancestral spirits.*
* *To seek protection from evil spirits like those of witches or evil minded persons.*
* *To seek healing from an illness or cleansing from defilement in eating forbidden animal or entry into bush or contact with menstruating woman.*
* *To propitiate neglected ancestral spirits or angered deities.*
* *To seek the gift of children.*

## 3.2  Public Worship

This is also divided into two kinds: the family or extended family worship and the clan worship. Both kinds involve annual or biannual celebrations bringing people together to enact aspects of the history of the family, clan or tribe; but more so to celebrate aspects of natural and agricultural manifestations of the local and family deities.

Occasional public worship includes the sacrifice of atonement. After epidemics of any kind the diviners are consulted to know what had defied the land. If no particular individual is accused as being responsible, the entire village then becomes guilty. Sacrificial animal is brought with money collected from adult men. The priest of the clan or a priest of a particular deity mentioned by the diviner will tie the four legs of the animal, drag it around some public places and sacrifice the animal at the shrine of the clan earth goddess. The meat is not eaten but rather given to the *Osu*-people, who are people dedicated to the deity. There is also public worship for the propitiation of *Ufejioku* deity (the god of farming) before the new yam is eaten. This sacrifice has metamorphosed into new yam festival celebrated annually in most Igbo societies. The climax of public worship is the annual propitiation of clan deity. Each clan has its own public shrine dedicated to its own clan protector.

The picture of Igbo worship is incomplete without some discussion about the priests. The Igbo believe in the priesthood of all heads of households, extended families and clans. Also *Ozo* title men are priests in so far as they offer sacrifices and perform ritual functions including praying to *Chukwu* and the ancestors. In addition to this there is a class of special priests made up of two categories. One class comes from the *Osu* (people dedicated to special deities). One of them is always chosen to be the special priest of a particular deity and must live near the deity's shrine. The other class of priests consists of men who become priests through appointment by the ancestral spirit. Such men behave queerly and are noticed by those already priests who take them in and train them. Such people do sometimes combine three functions: those of medicine men with knowledge of healing herbs, secondly divination and thirdly sacrificing priests. They also have power at times to exorcise, prepare medicine for warding off evil, for protection from harm and bringing good fortune in trade or hunting. Such medicines are what people sometimes referred to as charms. In each village a priest is known to be specifically related to one or more deities. When a diviner prescribes sacrifice he also names the proper priest that should perform the function. In this way priests exercise leadership among the people. Strictly speaking, a priest is a person specially trained to mediate between a god and his worshippers, especially in sacrificial and allied matters. They are always ready to give consultations and spiritual advice and to do all in their power to tie down evil spirits. The Igbo call him *Eze mmụọ* (king of the spirits). They help to preserve oral tradition, the myths and the body of religious concepts and ideas which constitute the people's heritage.

It is also pertinent to note that *Ọfọ* is a major ritual symbol and instrument of worship in Igbo Traditional Religion. According to Ejizu (1986) the term *Ọfọ* is a proper name of two related objects. It immediately designates a particular plant species which grows in the Igbo area. And then in a derived sense, it identifies the twig or bracelet from the wood of the tree. Both the plant and its sticks are equally referred to as *Ọfọ*.

One of the special features of *Ọfọ* tree is that the branches fall off from the parent trunk when they are fully grown. No cutting of the *Ọfọ* branch is done. It is believed that *Chukwu* purposely created this tree to be sacred, and by the manner its branches fall off unbroken, *Chukwu* symbolizes the way families grow up and establish new extended families and lineages. Therefore the *Ọfọ* made out of these branches is regarded as the abode of the spirit of the dead ancestors, hence the authority and sacredness of the *Ọfọ*, as well as the special place given to it as the emblem of unity, truth and indestructibility for the individual or the group possessing the *Ọfọ*.

The *Ọfọ* of the lineage is the outward symbol of the presence of the dead ancestors of the lineage or the clan, and therefore must be displayed when all the living are assembled for important family discussions and because the head of each level of the lineage is charged with holding the *Ọfọ* of that group, he becomes not only the political social leader, but also the family priest and uses the *Ofo* in blessing the people at all public worships. *Ọfọ* is a means of prayers to the divinities. It is also used by the *Ala* priest to remove all the evil effects of abominations after the proper sacrifices have been performed. When any *Ọzọ* person speaks and kisses his *Ọfọ* stick, it is a sign of a most solemn protestation as to the gravity of the truthfulness of what he is saying The diviner uses the *Ọfọ* as one of the apparatus of divination, as it is generally believed that the ancestors, whose spirits the *Ọfọ* represents, are always helpful in determining a successful result of the particular subject for which the divination is carried out.

## 4. Igbo Institutional Patterns and Customs

The cultural pattern that emerges through looking at the traditional social structure of Igboland as well as the institutions of family, religion and economic pursuits could be termed communalistic. Emphasis is placed on the commune rather than the individual, and moral obligations are regulated more by the moral codes, tradition and custom than by the exercise of individual moral judgment and conscience. Yet the individual's responsibility to the commune is clear and never shirked because social expectations as well as shared values are commonly observed and the social ethos of the village is jealously guarded and upheld both by religion as well as by the accepted practices and prohibitions of the community. The socio-cultural and socio-political institutions in Igboland vary from village to village and from town to town. However, there are areas where they more or less remain quite similar, especially when one looks at the major segments of the institutional patterns and customs presented below.

## 1. Ụmụnna (Lineage)

*Ụmụnna* literally means 'the children of the father', whereby the concept of 'father' need not be seen as the immediate father or grand father, Instead, *Ụmụnna* is made up of descendants, in the male line, of a founder ancestor by whose name the lineage is sometimes called. At the bottom of the lineage are families of men, their wives and children living in homesteads surrounded by mud wall. *Ụmụnna* is a unit found in all Igbo communities and as such has a separate social entity. It provides a better chance of engaging in more varied economic pursuit and interaction. It also fulfills a broad enough social and economic objective in the traditional Igbo setting. Ejiofor (1982) while speaking of *Ụmụnna* posits that each unit in the social formation serves as a comprehensive insurance against the vicissitudes of life. The *Ụmụnna* is approached for help as of right in the event of major losses in trade. Conversely, the well-being of an individual is reflected in those units as a concentric extension of self. Owing to this level of network of relations within the *Ụmụnna* a man is always certain of "belonging". He has responsibilities and claims according to his status, age or ability. For example the work of building of a new house for any member of the *Ụmụnna* is shared by his kinsmen. Equally so the farm works of the senior members of the unit is the responsibility of all the women and young men at least once in a while. This is a type of corporate personality shared by all the members of a given lineage. Births, deaths, and memorials, or any of such occasions, are the concern, in some instances, of all the members of the lineage. There is even the practice which is dying out now, where debt owed by a member of such *Ụmụnna* can be forcibly settled by the initiative of the creditor in seizing a goat, or any other such property, as may belong to any member of the debtor's *Ụmụnna* or lineage.

*Ụmụnna* has a head called *diọkpa* or *ọkpala*. He is both a coordinator and the manager of the group. He presides over meetings of the constituent families and takes care of the common shrine of his lineage. Each household has its head and each *Ụmụnna* has its own. Most, if not all of such heads are elderly senior titled men. When there is a dispute to be adjudicated publicly in the interest of the village made up of various *Ụmụnna*, all the elders and heads of all the *Ụmụnna* concerned would assemble at the senior *ọkpara's iba/obi* (the nobleman's public meeting and ceremonial house) with their *Ọfọ* sticks (emblem of being representatives of dead ancestors and of religious authority) and listen to the two sides of the quarrel and judgment delivered according to custom. According to Ogbukagu (2008), "*Ụmụnna* constitutes the strongest and the most effective means of managing and controlling excesses in the village democracy and also an essential vehicle for maintenance of law and order" (p. 86). The sort of things that are publicly judged include abominations which are against the earth goddess, believed to be capable of bringing disintegration to the *Ụmụnna*, village or town, such as murder of a fellow town's man, incest, stealing of yam especially by an *Ọzọ* titled person. Where the suspect pleads innocent of the offence, the council of elders may direct that he swears by *Ala* (the earth goddess).

2. Umuada (Women Genealogical Lineage)

Unlike the *Ụmụnna* that literally means 'the children of father' and refers to a male genealogical lineage, *Ụmụada* does not mean 'children of mother' (which is the meaning of *Ụmụnne*). Also because the name *Ada*, which means 'first borne female in the family' is also the name usually given to such first children, the designation *Ụmụada* does not mean 'children of Ada, i.e. Ada's children'. Instead, it refers to groups of women born into a particular family or families with essentially the same outlook to life. Women who are married to other towns are all *bona fide* members of their respective *Ụmụada* groups in their parent's villages, but not in their husband's viallage.

*Ụmụada* is an important organ for maintenance of peace, tranquility and good democratic government in Igboland. Senior married women also enforce their own laws about markets, their cleaning and the cleaning of the springs from where water is collected. Different women age sets do different community duties depending on their seniority, for example, the ten to twenty years group sweeps the village square and newly married wives clean the springs.

## 3. Ogbe (The Village)

*Ogbe* is an Igbo word that is used to designate a group of *Ụmụnna* or the lands and homesteads along a given path. The village consists of a number of quarters which are generally located in a defined area in the town. The village is understood here as a segment of a community. The village is a unit of planning and policy implementation. The deliberative bodies of the village are the *Izu Ogbe* (village deliberative body) and the *Izu ọra* (the people's assembly). Membership of the *Izu Ogbe* principally includes but not restricted to *Diọkpa Ogbe* of the constituent *Ụmụnna*. Village assemblies are held on particular market days in honour of the local deities of the respective market of village communities. According to Ilogu (1974), there are two types of villages: one is a village made up of various homesteads or compounds whose owners are members that claim ultimate common descent. The other type is a cluster of hamlets made up of homesteads or compounds whose occupants are members of various lineages, all of which do not claim ultimate common descent, and therefore can intermarry. The village in this later instance is mainly a geographical unit providing some considerable solidarity based on neighborhood rather than immediate blood relation. According to Basden (1985), every village has its own market-place, shrine and public meeting ground. The markets are designated by names of the day on which they are held. Viz *Eke, Oye, Afọ, Nkwọ*.

## 4. Obodo (Town)

Various villages or sub-clans group to form what the Igbo call *Obodo* (town). Ilogo (1974) prefers the term "village groups" to "town" because Igboland is predominantly agricultural, and various homesteads are separated by farms and gardens, making it difficult for the term "town" to be applied to such a unit. But because such people share a market place, possibly one ruler and an assumption of common ancestry and possibly a common *Ọzọ* title rank, they regard themselves as a unit or a town for the purpose of modern development. The *Obodo* is in most cases the highest political unit and centre of the modern form of development and cooperative activities.

*Obodo* is a social unit which comprises a number of villages knit together by kinship bonds and whose inhabitants consider themselves distinct and autonomous from other such units under one traditional political system. The highest institution of government is the *Izu Obodo,* which is the assembly of all the village officials, the heads of *Ụmụnna* and other administrative functionaries.

Various other groups apart from the council of heads of lineages perform one form of political activity or the other. Although the elders have some judicial powers, Igbo society does not know anything like an oligarchy and the society was a republic in the true sense of the term because the government was a cooperation in which decisions were the responsibilities of all concerned. However, in modern times, the *Igwe* institution (Kingship) has become a very prominent feature of Igbo political structure. Each Igbo town selects or elects their own *Igwe, Obi* or *Eze* as the case may be, according to the given provisions made available by the constitution, consensus or custom of the town. The king is the supreme political authority who reigns from his palace either provided by the efforts of the entire town or by the king himself. However, the king does not rule the town alone, but rather in conjunction with the *Igwe* in council (palace chiefs) selected in such a way that will reflect the political spread of the constituent villages in the town and headed by an *Onowu* (the traditional prime minister). Nevertheless the council of elders is an important arm in the political administration of the Igbo town that assembles in the palace when the need arises. The king is powerful enough to rule over extensive areas, exercise both priestly and social leadership through the heads of families, lineages and clans rather than through his own staff.

The Ọzọ titled men also form part of the governing body of any Igbo society. This constitutes a well-structured and highly esteemed stratum, which recognizes and places a member belonging to the group at a status much higher than the social level of his age or other mates in the society (Ogbukagu, 2008). They are supreme in matters affecting the progress and well-being of the community. Title-taking elevates one into this class of the Ọzọ society. Members of this group are drawn from all works of life across the villages in the town. The important criteria are that an aspirant to this group must be a person of integrity who must have distinguished self through hard work and palpable achievements in the community. Members of this group are obliged to always say and stand by the truth in any social issues in the village no matter whose ox is gored. Ilogu (1974) argues that the most important reason for the Ọzọ title is that the continuity of the lineage; clan or village depends on the existence of God-fearing men who share in the spirit of the land through their relationship with the earth goddess and also know how to placate the spirit of the dead ancestors and uphold the ordinances of the land. The Ọzọ title is said to be the religious means of achieving these ends. Therefore the person who has taken the Ọzọ title must live a holy life, uphold publicly and privately the morality of the land and observe all taboos, religious ceremonies and rituals of all the deities of his community.

## 5. Otu Ọgbọ (The Age Grade System)

The age grade system is a group of men and women born within a given span of time with a range in age of members varying from three to six years. Age groups participate in matters affecting the social, economic and political development of the Igbo communities. Apart from serving as an instrument or vehicle for identifying men and women born within a specific period of time, the age grade system creates an awareness of love and good togetherness among men and women belonging to the same age span. Basden (1985) notes that the age grade system constitutes an indispensible tool of good governance and hence forming a vital component of administrative machinery for sustaining the well-being of many Igbo societies. The age grade system also serves as the task force of the communities. They organize themselves into groups for community labour and they also help in enforcing policies originating from the palace. The age grade in most cases forms the local vigilante of most pre-colonial Igbo societies.

6. Mmanwu (Masquerade Institution)

Masquerade institution in Igboland is organized for general entertainment, social reformation and maintenance of peace and order. In pre-colonial Igbo setting, the masquerade institution is the police of the community of a sort. The Igbo believe that masquerades represent images and spirits of the dead ancestors coming from the world of the spirits for the maintenance of peace and order in the communities. They also appear in the communities during festivals for the purposes of entertainment as well as to dine and wine with their living relatives. The masquerade institution is highly respected and regarded in Igboland. *Otu Muo*, as the masquerade society is sometimes referred to, also performs some political duties: they guard the village against thieves, collect fines from people pronounced guilty of offences, and help in seeing that abominations are not hidden. Membership of the masquerade society is not open to everybody. In most cases, it is restricted to the male adults in the community. However, some women who have attained their menopause are in some cases allowed to join the masquerade society.

To complete the picture of the traditional Igbo institutions, mention must be made of the laws of the land, which, by and large are in the form of prohibitions, said to have been sanctioned by *Ala* (the earth goddess). These are the codes that regulate community life and yet they bear much religious significance, hence the leadership and the significance of *Ala* priests and the diviners who say what customs or codes have been broken and what social, political and religious steps are to be taken to secure justice for God and man.

## 7. Omenaanị

The Igbo word used in describing custom is *omenaanị*, which literally means 'that which happens on the ground'. This word is sometimes interpreted as tradition. There are two kinds of custom: customs that pertain to morality and those that are purely social and cultural. All the codes of morality are nearly always in the form of prohibitions sanctioned by the earth goddess and communicated from her by the dead ancestors to the community. Social and cultural traditional practices are detailed for each activity that makes up the institutions of society. There are various *omenaanị* governing, for example, marriage, and burial, offering of kola nuts, drumming or style of speaking. This means that Igbo traditional custom ranges from very serious subject, like methods of social control, to the more minute demand of etiquette and polite behaviour. It is against *omenani*, for instance for a young man to look an elderly man in the eyes while talking to him or for a young person to talk back at an elder while reproaching him no matter how right the young person thinks he is. It is against *omenaanị* to mourn loudly on *Eke ukwu*, it is against *omemanị* for a man who is not an *Osu* (persons dedicated to deities) to marry an *Osu*. No breach of *omenaanị* goes unpunished.

Another type of *omenaanị* is what is commonly called taboo or ritual avoidances. There are ritual avoidances which custom prescribes for persons holding specific offices or positions. *Ala* priest for instance or *Ozo* title men or minstrels do observe taboos peculiar to their callings. Certain sacred bushes, groves and streams are not to be entered into by any other person than the priests or initiated persons. Fish in sacred streams are regarded to be sacred and not be caught or eaten. Because *omenaanị* is derived from the earth goddess and sanctioned by the ancestors, it is religious in nature, although it fulfils social, moral and cultural functions. In the absence of writing and formal school education *omenaanị* becomes the means of summarizing the social philosophy and religious doctrine of the Igbo. *Omenaani* is the means by which traditional Igbo societies enforce conformity. Culturally speaking *omenaani* is the means by which the social ethos is measured, the values of the society are continued from one generation to the other, and the process of socialization through the education of the young ones are facilitated.

## 5. Rites of Passage in Igbo Traditional Religion

Rites of passage are groups of ritual which celebrate transition from on phase of life of an individual or a community to another. Fairchild (cited b Kanu, 2015) sees rite of passage as "the ceremonies which cluster around th great crisis of life, periods of transition from one status to another, notabl, birth, puberty, marriage and death" (p. 165). The performance of a particula rite of passage would mean that the person involved had moved from on stage of life to another, and since the Igbo universe is a religious one, all rite of passage have religious undertones Madu (2011) believes that rites o passage ensures a change of condition from one religious or secular group t another, and that each stage is an outburst of new life due to the interventio of the divine. The divine order is recognized, acknowledged and actualized i the rites and these rites are reenactment of the archetypal patterns of th divinities.

Rites of passage have great educational value. The occasion marks th beginning of acquiring knowledge, which is otherwise not accessible to thos who have not been initiated. It is a period of awakening to so many things, period of dawn for the young. According to Mbiti (1969):

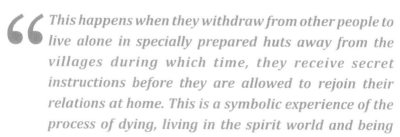

> *This happens when they withdraw from other people to live alone in specially prepared huts away from the villages during which time, they receive secret instructions before they are allowed to rejoin their relations at home. This is a symbolic experience of the process of dying, living in the spirit world and being*

*reborn. The rebirth, that is the act of rejoining their families, emphasizes and dramatizes that the young people are now new personalities, they have lost their childhood, and in some cases they even receive completely new names. (p. 159).* **"**

These rites take a glaring place in the life of the Igbo, as it is an issue that forms the Igbo lifestyle. This is at the base of so many problems that Igbo youths are experiencing today. The absence of such forum for learning has left a vacuum. The rite among the Igbo include: pregnancy, birth, puberty, marriage and burial.

## 1. Pregnancy Rites

The Igbo understand pregnancy as a period of transition from conception to childbirth. Pregnancy rites facilitate the birth of the child and protect the mother and child from evil powers and malignant persons through offering a sacrifice. Metuh (cited by Kanu, 2015) maintains that:

**"** *It is a rite of separation of the child from the world of the ancestors and incorporation into the world of human beings; it begins as soon as the woman misses her period. Among the Igbo the oracles are consulted as soon as a woman conceives and sacrifices offered to Ala. (p. 168).* **"**

Ezenweke (2012) adds that oracles are consulted because it is generally believed that children have come from the divine with a message for the community, consultations with the diviners help the community to know the message the child has brought and if possible to take precaution when necessary.

## 2. Birth Rites

There are two stages of birth rites: purification rite and naming ceremony. The purification rite begins after the woman has given birth; she a n d  t h e child are secluded for purification. It is only after the purification that she can begin to move around in the community. It is usually a ceremony of days, the number of days depends on the custom to establish the community ownership of the child, the umbilical cord connecting the mother and the child is cut as sign of the incorporation of the child into the community. After the purification rite, the naming ceremony begins which humanizes and socializes the child, making him a member of the human family. During this rite, the ancestors are consulted to know which of them has reincarnated. If the ancestor who has reincarnated is established, the name of the ancestor is given to the child. If no reincarnation is established, the paternal grandfather gives the child a name. The name given to the child is usually monumental or prophetic.

3. Puberty Rite

Puberty rite in both boys and girls is an announcement that they have reached adulthood. It introduces the child from the world of dependence to that of independence with the rights, privileges and duties of adulthood. It is a sign that they are ready for marriage and have reached a biological maturity necessary for reproduction. The rites for boys and girls differ according to their particular roles in the society as husbands and wives. While the women are taught folktales, dances and songs, the men are taught roles that they would play as head of the home. This is a period of learning for both men and women. At the end of the rites, the women are beautified and brought to the village square where they could display their beauty and dances to the admiration of men. Men who are in search of wives usually find this period very interesting. The boys are also initiated into secret societies and masquerade cults. They undergo great hardship so that they may learn through suffering, especially to prepare them for the challenges that would come with being a father. After this period, the boys come to the open and eat with the elders as sign that they have arrived. Their seclusion and public appearance are symbolic: it symbolizes the death of the child and the birth of the adult, the death of dependency and the birth of independence.

## 4. Marriage Rites

Among the Igbo, marriage is between families and not between individuals. Real discussion about marriage begins when the two families consent. When the man and the woman accept and the families refuse, the marriage would not hold. To show the hold of the family on the individual in the issue of marriage, there are times when the parents or family decide who the child would marry, sometimes even before the child is mature enough to choose a partner. The declaration of marriage intentions is usually spoken of in parables. When accepted, the bride price is paid along with the appropriate sacrifices and ceremonies.

## 5. Rites for the Dead

The rite for the dead can be divided into two: burial rites and funeral rites. The nature of a burial is determined by who has died: if it is a child or a young person who has died, the burial is not displayed. There is usually little or no ceremony accompanying such burials. This is based on the fact that it is regarded as a bad death.

During the rites, the dead is usually washed. The purpose of this rite is to strengthen the deceased as he or she embarks on a journey to the spirit world. In some cases, if it is a man, the *okpara* (first son) performs the rite, and if the person has no son, a male from the extended family does that. If it is a woman, the *ada* (first daughter) performs the rite.

After washing, a fowl is strangled and the head cut off. The blood is rubbed on the body of the deceased; the blood is sacrificed to the deities to accompany the dead to the spirit world. When the ritual-washing is over, the body is taken to the grave for burial. If it is suspected that the deceased was killed by someone, sometimes cutlass could be put in the coffin so that he or she can revenge. This is based on the belief that the dead still lives.

Part of the rites for the dead is the funeral rites. This usually comes not necessarily immediately after the burial. It is not a second burial as some falsely refer to it; it is rather a continuation of the rite for the dead. It is a rite of incorporation of the dead into the world of the ancestors. This rite also helps the dead to secure his rightful place in the world of the living-dead. This is also marked with celebrations. It is a kind of thanksgiving. These rites for the dead are responsibilities that the living owes the dead. ∎

## 6. Conclusion

Religious festivals and rituals such as new yam festivals, harvest seasons, hunting seasons and planting season festivals are activities that demonstrate and express belief and faith respectively in *Chukwu* and the spirit world. During these ceremonies, what God or the divinities have done for the people are commemorated; rituals are executed and powers obtained from the spirit world. Religious festivals sustain and generate the myth underlying the believe system of the people, while it also binds the people together socially. ∎

# References

Achebe, C. (1986). *The world of the ogbanje*. Enugu: Fourth Dimension.

Awolalu, J.O. & Dopamu, P.A. (1979). *West African traditional religion*. Ibadan: Onibonoje.

Basden, G.T. (1983). *Among the Ibos of Nigeria*. Lagos: University Pubishing Company.

Chidili, B. (2012). Religion, healthcare and Africa herbalism. In E.O. Ezenweke & I.A. Kanu (Eds.). *Issues in African Traditional Religion and philosophy* (pp. 207-225). Jos: Fan Annieh.

Idowu, E.B. (1973). *African traditional religion: A definition*. London: S.C.M.

Ejiofor, L.U. (1982). *Igbo kingdoms, power and control*. Onitsha: Africana.

Ejizu, C.I. (1986). *Ofo: Igbo ritual symbol*. Enugu: Fourth Dimension.

Ezenweke, E.O. (2012). Rites and rituals in African ontology. In E.O. Ezenweke & I.A. Kanu (Eds.). *Issues in African Traditional Religion and philosophy* (pp. 121-146). Awka: Fab Annieh.

Idowu, E.B. (1973). *African Traditional Religion: A definition*. London: S.C.M.

Ilogu, E. (1985). *Igbo life and thought*. Onitsha: The Varsity.

Ilogu, E. (1974). *Christianity and Igbo culture: A study of the interaction between Christianity and Igbo culture*. Enugu: NOK.

Kanu, I.A. (2015). *A hermeneutic approach to African Traditional Religion, theology and philosophy*. Jos: Fab Annieh.

Madu, J.E. (2011). *Rites of passage in traditional and modern Igbo society*. Unpublished lecture note on African Traditional Religion. Nnamdi Azikiwe University, Awka.

Mbiti, J. (1969). *African religions and society*. Nairobi: Eastern Educational.

Metuh, I. (1987). *Comparative studies of African Traditional Religions*. Onitsh: IMICO.

Ogbukagu, I.N.T. (2008). *Traditional Igbo beliefs and practices*. Enugu: SNAP.

Onuwa, U. (2005). *Studies in Igbo traditional religion*. Obosi: Pacific.

Ugwu, C.O.T. & Ugwueye, L.E. (2004). *African traditional religion: A prolegomenon*. Lagos: Merit.

# CHAPTER 10

GEORGE E. ONWUDIWE

## Some Igbo Traditional Cultural Practices
## And Institutions

## Summary

*In normal life, every human being conforms to certain norms common to the society to which he or she belongs. These norms are systems, techniques and tools that make up their way of life; and they can be broadly classified into material (concrete) and nonmaterial (nonconcrete) aspects of their culture. In Igbo culture, the material aspects of the culture include the Igbo type of houses, clothes, food and cooking utensils, farm implements, war and hunting weapons, chieftaincy attires like the red cap, etc. The nonmaterial aspects include the language (Igbo), Igbo customs and tradition (including greetings and their types), beliefs (including worship and ways of worship), values, occupation, politics and any other behaviours that members of the various Igbo communities learn from their elders. This chapter has as its focus some of these cultural and traditional practices and institutions. These include customs like greetings, kola nut, nzu and their ceremonies; festivals like the new yam festival and Ofala festivals, religious institutions and beliefs; as well as social institutions such as marriage and marriage rites; and political institutions like umuokpu, inyom di, otu ogbo and its initiation ceremonies. Although these traditional cultural practices and institutions contribute to distinguishing the Igbo people from other ethnic groups in Nigeria, they are nevertheless subject to the influences of the modern times, some of which are not particularly positive.*

## 1. Introduction

CERTAIN PRACTICES, SOCIAL, CULTURAL AND RELIGIOUS PRACTICES and institutions that are customary to the Igbo people cut across all Igbo land and are recognised and understood by every Igbo person. Although they are subject to slight variations from community to community, each represents the same aspect of the culture.

## 2. Some Cultural Practices

2.1 Greetings and Respect

*2.1.1 Greetings*

Greeting is so highly regarded in Igbo culture that anybody who is not in the habit of greeting others is regarded as not having good home training. Greeting precedes every interaction, between individuals, within a group, or during ceremonies and festivities.

In traditional Igbo setting, the child or the junior person owes it as a duty to greet the elder or senior first. Also, the woman greets her husband first, as the children must greet their parents and seniors first. For instance, no junior greets his senior tucking his hands in his pockets. In the same way, Chiefs and titled men are greeted first, often hailing their chieftaincy titles. But among the elders, no one is under strict obligation to greet the other first except in the case of proven seniority.

The Igbo have different greetings for different people, different times/periods, conditions and different occasions. They consider morning greeting as very important and significant, because it ushers one into a new day or dawn. Therefore, failure to greet or respond to someone's greeting in the morning is uncustomary and viewed with disfavour. One who neither greets nor responds to morning greeting is assumed to have an ill will towards the other person. In some areas, the recipient of this uncultured behaviour may have to go back to bed and wake up a second time to ward off the purported ill luck. Below are some of the greetings that are for specific periods/times of the day:

## (i) Morning greeting

This varies from community to community. The most common forms (with their literal meanings) are given below. Also note the verb sources indicated in the brackets.

(1)    *Ị bọọla chi?* 'Have you cut open the day?'
       [source verb: *ịbọ* 'to cut/slice open']

       *Ị saala chi* 'Have you washed the day?'
       [source verb: *ịsa* 'to wash']

       *Ị pụtago ụra* 'Have you come out from sleep?'
       [source verb: *pụta* 'come out']

       *Maa mma* 'Be beautiful!'
       [source verb: *ịma mma* 'to be beautiful']

       *Ị pụtakwara ụra?* 'Have you also come out from sleep?'
       [source verb: *pụta* 'come out']

All these serve as the cross-dialectal equivalents of the English 'Good morning'. It is important and noteworthy that the Igbo have no special greeting for the afternoon like the English, French and some other tribes in Africa like the Hausas and Yorubas (Ekwealor, 1998; Onwudiwe, 2020). Instead, Igbo greetings in the day depend on the condition or the activity the recipient of the greeting is engaged with at the time. Therefore, such greetings as *'Ndeewo', 'Daalụ', 'Deeje', 'Maa mma',* etc., can be given as the English 'Hallo' and are usually greeted after the time for the morning greeting is over, till evening. For evening and night, the reserved greeting can take any of the following forms:

(2)    *Ka chi bọọ* 'let the day break'

[source verb: *ịbọ* 'to cut/slice open]

*Ka chi foo* 'let the day become clear'
*Ka abalị chee anyị* 'let the night watch over us'
(Onwudiwe, 2017).

From the foregoing, it should be noted that the Igbo have special greetings only for morning and night. However, a new trend in many Igbo communities is the literal translation of the English greetings as (1) *Ụtụtụ ọma* (for Good morning); (2) *Ehihie ọma* (for Good afternoon) and (3) *Uhuruchi ọma* (for Good evening). These are definitely deviations from the traditional forms and are adapted from the English language. Surprisingly, it is now often heard in Igbo language radio broadcasts. While some native speakers who oppose such a development describe it as an absurdity that does no originate in a consensus of the Igbo speech community (Onwudiwe 2017:265), one cannot say in advance whether the form has come to stay as one of the forms of greeting in Modern Igbo. Below are other forms o greeting and the occasions they are used:

*(ii) Journey Greetings*
This form of greeting can be given either at the point of departure, or at the point of return from a journey. With regard to the first, the departure point could be in front of the house as the traveller either walks away or enters any type of vehicle, or even at the motor park as the vehicle departs. It is expressed at the point the separation sets in between the traveller and the speaker. The last examples below however, are used when the traveller returns home.

- *Ị gawala* (have you started going? = Have you set out on a journey)
- *Jee nke ọma* (go well = Safe journey)
- *Laa/Naa gboo* (Come back in time/early)
- *Nnọọ* (Welcome), etc

A slight distinction is sometimes made between the above forms of greeting and another form that is used when the person is embarking on a distant journey. In such an instance, some of the following forms can be used:

- *Ka o mesịa!* 'Let it be done = Farewell!'
- *Nọdu nke ọma!* 'Stay well!'
- *Ka ọ dịzie!* 'Let it then be = Farewell!'

*(iii) Greetings at Formal Occasions and Festivities*

These are greetings at social events, like Village/Town meetings of any form. The examples below are not exhaustive:

- *Igbo mma mma nụ!* 'Igbo be beautiful!'
- *Oha/Ọra obodo ekelee m unu!* 'Community, I greet you all!'
- *Igbo birikwa nu!, etc.* 'Igbo, you shall live!'

*(iv) Greetings to a Benefactor*

Here, the benefactor can be any person; the main point is that the recipient has been given something by the giver/benefactor:

- *Daalụ* 'Thank you!'
- *I meela* 'You have done well (noble)'
- *Anwụchula* 'Don't die a sudden death!'
- *Chukwu gọzie gị, etc.* 'May God bless you!'

*(v) Greetings to People at Work*

This is usually for people working, whether one accidentally meets the people at work or one is visiting the work site.

- *Jisie ike!* 'hold on to the strength = Well done!'
- *Daalụ ọrụ!* 'Thanks for the work = Well done!'
- *Deeme!* 'Be doing = Well done!'
- *Dịike!* 'Be strong!'
- *Ị dị ike* 'You are strong!'

*(vi) Greetings for the Sick*

This refers to all forms of greeting to indicate sympathy/empathy and commiseration.

- *Kasiwe* 'Be strong (at heart)/Endure'
- *Jisie ike!* 'Cling to the strength = Be strong!'
- *Ndo* 'Sorry!'

- *Dịwa mma* 'Start becoming better!'
- *Gbasie ike, etc.* 'Grow in strength!'

*(vii) Greeting to the Bereaved*

A form like *Ndo!* Can be used for both the sick and the bereaved, as can be seen below and compared with the example above. However, all the forms below are exclusively for the bereaved:

- *Ndo*
- *Kasie*
- *Diwe*
- *Chukwu kasie gị*
- *Ebezila, etc.*

In addition to the above forms, greetings can also be demonstrated in Igbo culture through *handshake* or *hugging*. But it is equally important to state that it is usually the elderly that initiate greeting through handshake or hugging. Secondly, though hugging is mainly carried out by women, it is more for close relatives. Men, particularly the titled and the elderly, receive homage from the young ones who bend to receive a pat on the back as they greet them.

Finally, another form of greeting which does not apply in all parts of Igbo land is the *hail greeting*. This is a form of greeting made to titled men, Chiefs, warriors and other great men like great farmers, hunters, wine tappers, native doctors, wrestlers, etc. According to Ekwealor (1998), this form of greeting is common among the people of Onitsha, Awka and Ọmambala areas in the present Anambra State; Udi, Nkanu in Enugu; as well as Ihite-Mbaise and environs in Imo State. To these people, it is disrespectful and no greeting at all, to greet such highly placed people in the conventional way. In some of these places, the wife of these chiefs will first hail them in the morning as a routine. A few of the names used for *hail greeting* includes *Ogbuefi, Omeifeukwu, Ogbuagu, Ezeji, Akataisiebue, etc.*

## 2.1.2 Respect

Greetings generally signify respect, regard, loyalty and knowledge of the norms of a people. Different forms of Igbo greetings are accompanied by some forms of gesture and tone, which signify respect. Greeting is one of the main signs of respect in Igbo tradition, and anybody that does not greet is seen as one who lacks respect. Respect is therefore a significant attribute of the Igbo people. Below are some of the acts and behaviours that indicate respect or disrespect.

Firstly, in addition to the young or a junior person greeting the elder or senior, there are other ways of demonstrating respect. For example, in Nnewi and Anaedo clan, including some neighbouring Idemmili communities like Nnobi, all in the present Anambra State, the young ones accord respect to the very aged through special greetings. For a very old man, they usually greet Nnaa ọm!, while the aged woman would be greeted Nne omoo! The response from any of these elderly ones, with the accompanying gesticulation and voice modulation such as ọ̀ọ̀ nnwa m!, indicates acceptance of the respect and the concomitant blessing that follows. It is also a sign of respect for a younger person to get up from his seat for the elder, while it is an abomination to shout down an elder or a titled man in a public gathering.

There are also some acts or forms of behaviour that are seen as disrespectful. For example, no Igbo woman drinks palm wine standing erect before her husband or other titled men. It is similarly an act of disrespect to palm wine tappers for a none-wine tapper to drink holding his gourd with his left hand. In some parts of Igbo land, such an act attracts a penalty. Another act that indicates disrespect is when a young man performs the ceremony for the breaking of kola nut in the presence of his father or elders, or for a woman to break the kola nut in the presence of a male, even if it were an infant.

However, respect is not a one-way affair as it is bifocal. Just as the young person respects the elderly person, the elderly does not despise the young or treat him with ignominy. Rather, the old accord the young their due respect by providing for and protecting them, whether they are their own children or not. Hence, the Igbo saying that nwa bụ nwa ọha 'the child is the community's child', meaning that nobody should overlook or mistreat a child simply because he is not his child. This attitude helps to inculcate in the child the legacy for respect.

## 2.2 Ọjị na Ịwa Ọjị (Kola Nut and the Breaking of Kola Nut)

Kola nut is the seed of a kola tree. But, in the Igbo culture, it is more than a mere seed in the sense that the Igbo people accord a high regard to it. This is not because of anything special about it, nor because of its delicacy or even nutritional value. In fact, the taste is simply bitter. Nevertheless, these attributes do not count in its cultural role amongst the Igbo people when communing with their creator or ancestors.

There are two species of the Kola nut. One is mainly purple in colour, while the other is cream coloured. This purple coloured species is generally called **ọjị Igbo** (Igbo kola nut), and the cream coloured species is called gworo or **ọjị Awụsa** (Hausa kola nut). The two names, **ọjị Igbo** (Igbo kola nut) and **ọjị Awụsa** (Hausa kola nut) are of no major significance.

The tradition of using the purple coloured species arose from the fact that the Igbo as a tradition use it because it grows in Eastern Nigeria. It has therefore become a tradition over the generations to venerate or chew the purple species, or use it in ceremonies such as marriage ceremonies, peace accord, chieftaincy ceremonies and sacrifices, and in oath taking.

The traditionalist Igbo man uses the kola nut to pray every morning, to thank God for protecting his family and to request him to guide, protect and provide for him and his family throughout the day. Kola nut therefore has a strong cultural-cum-spiritual significance amongst the Igbo. This however does not mean that they do not use the cream coloured Kola nut, **ọjị Awụsa** or **gworo**; instead, the Igbo chew it and can also offer it to a visitor, but without any form of the traditional ceremony accorded the purple coloured kola nut.

### 2.2.1 Kola Nut and the Significance of Number

Kola nut is not just served; it is first presented for the guest to see, after which follows the Kola nut blessing, the breaking and shearing.

Generally, before any traditional ceremony, kola nuts are presented in certain numbers. This differs from community to community. In Nnewi, for instance, kola nuts are presented in even numbers. In big ceremonies the number is usually not less than four. This is because the community is made up of four quarters. Other communities could have the same four but attach the significance of the number to the four market days.

The next very significant aspect of the kola nut is the number of its lobes when it is broken. Normally, a kola nut of whichever species is made up of lobes. Whereas the gworo is almost always made up of two lobes, ọjị Igbo can be made up of three lobes, four lobes, five lobes or even more. Each number has its significance in Igbo culture. Prominent among the number of kola nut lobes and their significance are **three, four, five, six** and **seven**. Kola nut with any of these number of lobes are regarded as portending good omen.

A kola nut of **three lobes** is called **ọjị Ikenga**. Here **Ikenga** signifies a tripod used to sit a pot when cooking. Hence the saying, akwụkwa naatọ, ite esiri. A kola nut of three lobes is also referred to as **ọjị dike**. A kola nut that has four lobes is again taken to be a good one as the four lobes signify the four market days - Eke, Orie, Afọ and Nkwọ - which constitute the Igbo weeks (**izu**). It therefore signifies completeness. Hence, when such kola nut is broken the person that performs the ceremony will normally announce that the kola nut signifies ahịa naanọ, izu naanọ 'four market days, four weeks'.

Furthermore, a kola nut that has five or six lobes is regarded as portraying wealth, blessing, etc. Such kola nut is at times said to foretell many children for the benefactors. For a kola nut that has seven lobes and more, this is usually not eaten immediately, because it calls for ceremony. Hence, it is called ọjị mmemme. In such situation, the presenter of the kola nut will kill either a fowl or even a goat for celebration for the good omen it portends.

### 2.2.2  Ịwa Ọjị (Breaking of Kola Nut)

The verb ịwa simply means 'to slize/cut open'. One would therefore expect ịwa ọjị to be nothing else but the cutting up of the kola nut; but it is not so simple, because the ceremony that takes place before the actual breaking of kola nut in Igbo land is a very serious one and sometimes contentious where the right procedure is not followed. That is why in more recent times, soft drinks, biscuits and garden eggs are presented at some occasions when it is felt that the processes involved in the breaking of the kola nut might constitute a source of disagreement. Nevertheless, most Igbo communities adhere to these processes, some of which are discussed below.

In most parts of Igbo land the oldest or a titled man performs the ceremony as well as does the breaking of the kola nut, while in some, the oldest or the titled man performs the ceremony and the youngest breaks as well as shares the kola. Also, a stranger does not break kola nut before his host. In the same vein, an in-law or nephew does not break kola nut before his fathers-in-law or his grand fathers. However, the host often has the exclusive right to perform the first (or morning) breaking of kola nut in his house. It is important to add that in the home, the man calls on his wife to bring kola nuts for their visitor(s); and in public functions, like marriage ceremonies, it is the women also who bring the kola nuts that are used for the occasion.

During the kola nut breaking ceremony, the performer calls on God and all the ancestors of the community, including the deities of the land for blessing, long life, wealth, children, protection and provision of all their needs. After the ceremony and breaking of the kola nut, the performer takes a lobe first called aka ọjị (kola nut hand). Then, the youngest amongst them checks whether the remaining lobes will go round the people. Otherwise he cuts them before carrying the kola nut plate (ọkwa ọjị) round for others to pick, often in order of seniority.

## 2.3 Nzu na Ịtụ nzu

Nzu is 'white kaolin', a whitish soil formation. Some species are not so white, but it generally has the texture of clay. Nzu is regarded as a sacred object and is used to demonstrate purity of heart to the visitor.

In the presentation of nzu to a visitor, the Igbo person can present it in place of kola nut, or along with kola nut. The activities connected with it are ịtụ nzu/ịka nzu and ịma nzu. With regard to the first, ịtụ nzu/ịka nzu, when nzu is presented to a visitor, the host first takes it, draws lines on the floor in prayer, and then rolls it to the visitor who does same and rolls it back to him or to another visitor in that order. The lines drawn signify one's wish or request. Some people draw four straight lines signifying the four Igbo market days of Eke, Orie, Afọ, Nkwọ. Some also draw images that signify one thing or the other to them. The variation in the names ịtụ nzu or ịka nzu, is the result of the two perspectives from which the activity is viewed. The first perspective is from the verb ịtụ 'to throw', whereby ịtụ nzu codes the process of 'throwing/rolling' the nzu over to the next person. The second perspective is from the verb ịka 'to draw a line (on a hard surface)', whereby ịka nzu codes the process of drawing a line on a hard surface, which is the floor of the house. Ịtụ nzu ceremony does not cover every part of the Igbo land. The traditional rulers, leaders and Chiefs - Ndị Obi, ndị Eze, ndị Igwe, ndị Ichie, ndị Nze, etc, predominantly observe it. Other people that observe the ịtụ nzu ceremony are the elders and the native doctors.

The other form of the ceremonial use of nzu is ịma nzu, which involves rubbing it on some part of the body. For example, the visitor can simply rub the nzu on his toe, instead of using it to draw a line. Nzu is also rubbed on the body of anybody who is about to take the Ọzọ title to proclaim his cleanliness, while the native doctors rub nzu on their eyelids to enable them see the spirits. Some pregnant women also chew it. It is also rubbed on a child's body as a form of protection against heat rashes.

Finally, it is necessary to note that modernisation and Christianity have negatively affected these aspects of the Igbo culture, particularly among the youths. Nevertheless, there are still remnants of the activity in different forms, like the use of "modern white powder" by Christians. The 'modern white powder' might replace the nzu, but its symbolism remains.

## 3.0 Some Social Institutions

Igbo Social Institutions are those aspects of the Igbo culture that discuss various mutual relationships that exist among people. Here, we shall present and discuss, such major Igbo social institution as *marriage* (*alụmalụ*), *ọmụgwọ* and *nwadiala.*

### 3.1 Alụmalụ na mmemme alụmalụ (Marriage and marriage ceremonies)

Marriage is a union between a man and a woman, and it has a prime position in the affairs of the Igbo people. Hence, traditionally, they respect those who are in that union more than those who are of age to marry but fail to do so, whether male or female. This second group are even sometimes deprived of certain privileges in the community. The purpose of Igbo traditional marriage custom and practise is primarily to beget children and increase the manpower in a man's household for the purpose of his occupation that was mainly farming. As a result, Igbo traditional culture permitted and promoted polygamy. However, the actual marriage itself involves some steps that could vary from community to community.

First, before any marriage union can take place, the man first searches for a lady of his desire. When he finds one, he asks her for her hand in marriage. Even if it is her wish to marry the man, Igbo tradition demands that the lady should consult her parents, usually her mother first before openly assenting to the proposal. And when she does, the man full of joy gives the good news to his own parents, usually to the father first. Then, after the preliminary investigation about the nature of the family of their proposed in-law, they will go with their kinsmen to the parents of the lady with drinks for a formal marriage proposal which many Igbo communities call *iku aka nwanyi* 'to knock on the door for a woman'. This step opens up other crucial steps in the process that could include any or all of the following:

(i) to determine the social status of the two families.

(ii) establish whether the two families have blood relationship, and whether one of them is known for any crime.

(iii) whether any one of them is known for sudden death, whether any one is under any curse.

This activity is called in some communities *iju ese,* and in some others *igba nju/iju ajuju, etc*

The outcome of the investigation, determines whether the other stages can follow; and this is preceded by *ime ego nwanyi* 'the payment of the dowry or bride price'. The man's family carries palm wine and other drinks with his father and selected members of their kindred to the proposed in-law's house who too will be waiting with his own kinsmen. This stage is very remarkable in the sense that it is here that the lady will formally assent to the marriage before the two families. If it turns otherwise, the marriage procedure stops.

At the decision of the bride price to be paid, few selected men from the two families, excluding the fiancé withdraw behind closed doors, coordinated by *Onye uko* or *Nwa ndu uzo* 'the intermediary'. The actual bargaining, called *ido akirika*, is made using either goat droppings (*akpuru ewu*) or broom sticks (*mkpirisi aziza*). When an agreement is reached, the representative of the fiancé hands the dowry over to the father of the lady or his representative.

Some remarkable things about the bride price is the fact that the amount paid for the dowry is not announced (as in some communities). Generally, the fathers do not collect all the money negotiated for the dowry, while some may simply take a little amount from the dowry and give back the rest to the in-law. Part of the thinking behind this approach is the belief that marriage is only an expansion of relations, hence the saying that *ogo bu ikwu ito*. Also, many believe that high bride price or collecting all the bride price is a complete sell-off of the girl and will also reduce her to a mere commodity that can be used by the buyer as he likes. Another reasoning is that the in-law should realise that they have not completed the payment for the bride price. As a result, they have no total rights over their new wife; for the little token of the bride price can always easily be returned and the daughter recalled. Again, it should be noted that these beliefs and actions do not apply in all parts of the Igbo land.

The grand finale in the customary marriage is the traditional marriage, variously called *Igba nkwu nwanyi, Igba mmanya nwanyi, Ikwà nkwu nwanyi, Ibu mmanya nwanyi, etc.* This is the biggest ceremony in the marriage procedure of the Igbo people. No wonder it is accorded the highest regard by the kinsmen. Hence, any of their in-laws that fails to carry out the traditional marriage of his wife is taken to be owing his in-laws and is not applauded by his kinsmen.

At the traditional marriage ceremony, the two families or communities are fully represented. The ceremony is where the groom formally declares her bride to people. That is why after welcoming the visitors, the head of the groom's kinsmen or her father as in some communities will pour palm wine into a cup, give to their daughter and then ask her to sip and give to her suitor for everyone to know him. When she locates her suitor, she kneels down before him, sips the palm wine, and offers him the wine. When the man receives it and drinks there will be cheers and jubilation by everyone present. The man will aid his wife to stand up and two of them will return the cup. In some communities, the man will return the cup with some money. The man and his wife will kneel before them for their prayers and blessing. From there, they will assume their seat in the front, and the general merriment commences.

The next very important ceremony is the bride's father's blessing of his in-law and his daughter called *Igo ofo* in most communities. This ceremony is performed at the centre of the arena. The girl's father and some of his kinsmen will sit in a circular formation, while his in-law and his wife will kneel at the centre. After blessing the couple and their marriage, and wishing his daughter the best of a married life, prominent among which is good and prosperous children (*ozuzu Eke, Ozuzu Orie, Ozuzu Afọ na Ozuzu Nkwọ*), he presents to her and her husband household gifts to aid them in starting their new home. The mother of the bride and her co-wives, friends and other relations also present their gifts. Among these gifts are basic household items like cooking pots, mortars and pestles (big and small), smoking basket, domestic animals for rearing, such as she goat, hen, etc. The father of the girl will later hand her daughter over to his son-in-law with a request to take good care of her. He also declares the roads to their home *uzọ mmiri* 'the road to the stream', meaning that the two families should be visiting each other frequently. This ceremony marks the end of the traditional marriage. After that, the young man takes her wife home to start a new life and rear a new family. The girl's sisters and friends escort her to her new home when they are going.

Another traditional ceremony that follows the traditional marriage, and the church wedding as is presently the case is the formal hosting of the girl's husband at his in-law's home. This is called *ikpọlu ndi ọgọ ulọ* 'bringing home of the in-laws' or *Ọgọ malụ be* 'the in-laws getting to know the home (of their new in-law)'. There are other designations for this by different communities. Many communities and in-laws, especially the titled men take this ceremony very serious to the extent that if it is not done, they refuse to visit their daughters' married home. I will not fail to mention that the marriage ceremony and its various stages as well as the seriousness attached to them do vary from one Igbo community to another. Some have more stages than others; while some include more stringent conditions than others.

## 3.2 Ọmụgwọ and Ile Ọmụgwọ

The major reason for marriage in the general Igbo belief is to get children and increase the number of their households. Therefore, once a man's wife gets pregnant, both are very happy and the man starts from then to prepare to welcome his new baby and celebrate his wife. As the pregnancy progresses, he begins to prepare by saving money or purchasing some necessary items.

When the baby finally arrives, and the mother alive and strong, there is joy and jubilation in the man's house. The next is to visit his in-law with the good news and to invite his mother-in-law. In the visit, he will go with items as the custom of the people stipulates. On receiving the good news, his mother-in-law rejoices and circulates the good news to her neighbours and co-wives. Next is her preparation to go to her in-law to help and take care of her daughter and grandchild, the new baby (*Ije ọmụgwọ*). If the man's mother-in-law is incapacitated or dead, the woman's sister can go. In her absence, the husband's mother or any other of the woman's relations can go.

The woman's mother or any other person that goes is expected to take few necessary things needed which may include dried fish, *ụda, ụzịza,* etc. At her daughter's house, she will assist her in her duties, but especially in cooking, bathing the baby and attending to her daughter's health needs. In some communities, a fresh plantain trunk is placed at the entrance door to where the woman and her baby are. Any visitor entering the room is expected to step on it before entering. This is believed to protect the tender baby and the mother from any possible infection.

During this period, the young mother has ample time to rest and feed her baby. She also eats what she likes and what is best for her at the time. She attends to her visitors most of who would bring some gift items to her, ranging from foodstuffs, dried fish, money, clothes, etc. The visitors are given *nzu* or powder as is mostly the case at present. Most importantly, the woman's husband always ensures that his wife eats mainly body-nourishing food for the well-being of the mother and the new baby. Some even slaughter goats for their wives. Hence, the woman gets fully refreshed. The official period for *ọmụgwọ* is twenty eight days, (*izu asaa* i.e. seven traditional weeks).

When the man's mother-in-law gets ready to return to her home, her son-in-law presents some gifts to thank her for the care she gave to his wife and new baby. The gifts depend on the financial strength of her in-law, but most often include cloths, money and tubers of yam. Other items may include jewelleries, shoes, drinks, etc. After the official period of *ọmụgwọ*, the woman makes a public appearance commonly called *ikupụta nwa* 'bringing out/showing the child (to the community)' or *ịzụ ahịa nwa* 'going to market with the child'.

## 3.3 Nwadiala

*Nwadiala* 'maternal nephew/niece' in Igbo culture is a grandchild in the family and town of his or her mother or the father's mother. It could be in his or her own town or in another town. In this family and town, while his or her mother's father and relations regard and call him or her *Nwadiala,* he or she regard and call them *Ndị Nna ochie* 'grand fathers'.

*Ndị Nwadiala* (i.e. the plural form) enjoy immunity as they are regarded as sacred. Hence, they are free to take anything they like at their maternal grandfathers' homes. They also participate in many cultural activities in their maternal grandfathers' towns such as *àlụlọ mmụọ/mmeya mmụọ* 're-enactment of the covenant with the spirits of the ancestors', etc. At such feasts, they enjoy with their grandfathers. One important gain of such get-together is that it creates forum for familiarisation among grandchildren, and will prevent such taboos as incest.

*Ndị nwadiala* also perform important social functions such as settlement of disputes in their grandparents' families. They settle inter community disagreements. Most importantly, they wield into, and quench inter town wars on the strength of the held belief that *agha adighị eri nwadiala* - 'no grandchild is consumed in any war in his maternal home', because those in his maternal home cannot kill him because he is also a child of their child and as such one of them. In some communities, the female *ụmụdiala* can also become the *ụmụdiala ọkpụ*. In that case, they assume the position of *nwaọkpụ* at their maternal home. This honour makes them feel very proud. Some even brag to their fellow female *ụmụdiala* who are not *ụmụdiala ọkpu*. ∎

## 4.0 Some Administrative institutions

The Igbo political institutions are those aspects of the culture that aid governance in Igbo land. Of interest here are the Age grade system (*Òtu Ọgbọ*), *Òtu Ụmụọkpụ* and *Òtu Inyomdi*. These groups contribute in various ways in the governance of their various communities. Let us now discuss them one by one.

### 4.1 Otu Ọgbọ (Age Grade)
This is a group of people born within the same period. They may be exactly of the same age or within a specified age range as agreed by each group. Also, in some communities both male and female belong to same age grade. Furthermore, some age grades comprise of those born within two or three years' interval or even more; and they have rules that govern their age grades.

As already said, various age grades in each community contribute in the political matters of the community. For instance, in some communities, the age grade of the elders help to formulate laws for their communities, they also adjudicate over matters of inter-community relationship and clashes and wars, as well as ensure that there is peace in their communities including land matters and land disputes.

On the part of the youth age grades, they handle matters that require physical strength, vibrancy, etc. For instance, this group often handles road construction in their various communities, reconstruct existing ones, construct and reconstruct bridges, etc. Others functions are representing their communities in inter-tribal or inter community wars, collecting fine from defaulting members of the community, at times using masquerades. Through these efforts, they help to fight crimes in various communities.

Finally, the age grades generally enhance unity and social interaction in various Igbo communities. Their cultural relevance is that they not only provide recreation, but they especially promote several aspects of their culture through active participation in the festivals, like *mmọnwụ* festival, new yam festival, *ọfala* festivals, marriage ceremonies, etc.

### 4.2 Otu Ụmụọkpụ (Ụmụada)

This is a group of women born into one family, one kindred, village or town. They may be married or unmarried; and may be married within the community or outside the community. In most parts of Igbo land, they are organised at kindred levels. In other words, those born within one kindred, whether married or unmarried belong to this organisation. They help to foster peace and unity among their parents, their fathers' wives, their brothers' wives, their kindred and even between their parents (kindred) and their husbands. They equally work for their own good and benefits. Their position is mostly felt at funerals of their relations. For example, it is their responsibility to perform the tradition of bathing the body of their dead relation and traditional cleansing of the house after funeral.

In some communities, they form smaller units of Ụmụọkpụ, either on the platform of those married from one town, village or kindred into another town, village or kindred. Those from one town and married in that same town call themselves *À mụrụ̀ n'ụlọ bi n'ụlọ* 'the home-born that live at home'.

Finally, in most Igbo communities, *Otu ụmụọkpụ* is an organ to reckon with as they pose to be so formidable that most members respect them and try to avoid any clash with them. However, many still accuse them of being unnecessarily overbearing, especially in matters that will benefit them.

### 4.3 Otu Inyomdi

Like *Òtu Ụmụọkpụ*, *Òtu Inyomdi* is a group of women married within one kindred, one village, one town or one family. But, unlike *Ụmụọkpụ* many of them come from families, towns, villages and kindred outside their kindred of marriage. Therefore, their interest is more on those issues that will benefit them in their marriage.

*Òtu Inyomdi* is mainly organised at kindred levels. *Òtu Inyomdi* is formed at town level in many Igbo communities as the women's wing of the town government structure.  They concentrate in attending to matters that benefit them, their husbands and their children. For instance, they can wield in to bring peace between their co-wives and their husbands and amongst themselves. They also assist their husbands in some projects in the kindred and in some communities, they form cooperatives to assist themselves and their families.

## 5.0   Some Religious Practices

Igbo religious practices here are the practices that involve objects that aid the Igbo man in communeicating with and worship the Supreme Being, *Chukwu*. In this discuss, we shall look at two major aspects of the Igbo institution that aid good relationship between God and man. These are *Òfò* and *Ìkengà*.

### 5.1   Òfọ na Ijì Ọfọ

*Ọfọ* is both a metaphor and an object. First, it is the branch of an *Òfọ* tree. In this case, it is an object and a symbol. On the other hand, it is a metaphor or an idea which the Igbo hold of the behaviour or attitude held or expected to be held by an individual or people to show piety or uprightness to God and to man.

As a metaphor, it is believed to bind the spirit of all the ancestors. In this case, it stands to judge and reward everyone according to his deeds. In other words, anybody who thinks or does good receives good reward, while the reverse will be the case for anyone that thinks or does evil. It is also believed that Ọ̀fọ links together and unites the spirit of all the ancestors in a family, kindred, village or town; and that it wields great spiritual powers. As a result, they beckon on it always for justice and fairness in all they do or require anybody to do. Also, they believe that anyone who does not get involved in any evil thought or act against his brother is always protected by the spirit of their ancestors from any evil plan from another man. Such disposition is generally regarded as *iji ọ̀fọ*.

As a symbol, *Ọfọ* is kept at the house of the eldest in the family, kindred, village or town. It is brought anytime they want to meet or take any serious decision. It is highly valued and respected by the Igbo. Hence, whenever any Igbo man performs the breaking of kola nut, or a native doctor wants to commune with the ancestors, he first re-enacts his uprightness before making his requests.

## 5.2 Inwe Ikengà

*Ikengà* is another object of worship in Igbo land. It is a carved wooden object with two horns. An *Ikengà* holds a machete up with the right hand. All these portray it as brave and a warrior. An *Ikengà* represents one's personal god. Therefore, the owner believes that his *Ikengà* protects him and brings him fortune.

*Ikengà* is owned only by the men, and each man has his own *Ikenga*. Hence, he determines the size of his own *Ikengà* which may be big or small, as well as beautifies it as he likes. It is usually painted with *nzu, uhie, etc.* When the owner of an *Ikengà* dies, his *Ikengà* dies with him. Therefore, once any man dies, his *Ikengà* is destroyed as it is not transferable.

## 6.0 Some Leadership Institutions

Chieftaincy is a revered institution in the Igbo culture. It is the aspect of the culture that marks one out among others in any community. Any man who takes or is given a chieftaincy title counts himself as having arrived. He automatically moves from the class of those that contribute ideas in the community to the class of those that make decisions.

There are different chieftaincy titles for men and women; and they have hierarchy, from the junior to the senior. Again, some are awarded, that is some people are selected for certain chieftaincy titles, while some graduate from the junior titles to the higher titles. In any case, the benefactor must be qualified for it through screening by the Council of Chiefs (*Ndị Nze na Ọzọ*) and the King makers of the community.

Some of these titles are *Ezè* or Traditional Ruler, *Ọzọ* and *Lọọlọ titles*. While the *Ọzọ* and *Ezè* titles are mainly for males, the *Lọọlọ* title is for the women. Now, let us discuss these chieftaincy titles one by one.

### 6.1 Eze

The position of *Eze* 'traditional ruler' is the highest of all leadership positions as in many other communities that are not Igbo. As stories have it, the Igbo community were not known for having traditional rulers like their neighbours – the Binis, the Igalas, the Idomas, etc. As some reports have it such neighbouring communities influenced them a lot. Hence, communities like Onitsha, Ugwuta, Nsukka, Nri etc were among the early communities in Igbo land that had traditional leaders due to the influence of their neighbours and contacts.

However, presently, every community in Igbo land has a traditional ruler that goes by the name that they choose. Such names as *Obi, Eze, Igwe, Ọluọha*, etc are chosen by each community based on some historical reasons. So, the name with which each community's traditional ruler will be known and addressed is decided by the entire community, and not by the benefactor of the position. This is because, he is owned by the whole community. It is not like the *Ọzọ* title that the aspirant has the right to determine his title name.

All the same, the traditional ruler position is so important to any community that it is not an open contest for aspirants. Therefore, each community contributes in selecting and approving any candidate to be coroneted the traditional ruler of their town. In most communities, such a candidate must have attained the highest title of the land, which is usually the *Ọzọ* title. In some, he should be the oldest man. Generally, a candidate for the traditional ruler position must be a person of impeccable character, he must be approved by his immediate community, and must be well established.

When finally a candidate for the post of traditional ruler of a community is selected, he is coroneted at the community square by all the titled men of the town (*Ndi Nze na Ọzọ*), including other traditional rulers from neighbouring communities invited. The major events at the coronation are dressing the candidate in his regalia. Then followed by putting his crown or cap on his head which usually is done by the oldest man of the community. Others are giving him his staff of office, his hand fan, an elephant tusk etc. and sitting him on his traditional stool. All these are done at the public glare and, at the end of the coronation other fanfare follow. These include dancing to the prestigious *Igba Eze* 'the royal drum' round the square. This is latter followed by gifts from friends and well-wishers.

Finally, different communities have different ways of determining who their traditional ruler will be. Whereas some pick theirs from one particular family as in Nnewi and Agbor, other communities rotate theirs from one village to another. These days, the selected candidate is subjected to the approval of the state government before he could be crowned the next traditional ruler. It is again not surprising to hear that a traditional ruler has been deposed by the State Government, which was never the case before.

## 6.2 Ọzọ

*Ọzọ* title is regarded very highly in the whole of Igbo land. It is a title that admits the benefactor into the group of decision makers and king makers of his community. In most Igbo communities, the leaders, including the traditional rulers, are selected from among the Ọzọ title holders. More importantly, it is a revered title as it is not an all-comers title. Hence, to qualify for Ọzọ title taking, the aspirant must be a full son and a free born of his community. He must not be a man of questionable character. He must also be wealthy enough as the demand of the title taking is enormous.

The process for initiation into the Ọzọ titled men takes a long period of time. In some communities, like Nnewi it lasts for upwards of ten years, while in some other towns, it lasts for a fewer number of years. In any case, it has to last for a long period as an aspirant must first pass stages where he is expected to take some junior titles which are preparatory to the Ọzọ title that is regarded as the epic of them all. In fact, some aspirants fail to get to the top due to one reason or the other, one of which may be death. Other important things to note is that no man takes ọzọ title before his father or elder brother(s). But where he desires to take the title before them, he should ensure that they are initiated first.

According to Ofomata (2012), there are two types of Ọzọ title; the junior and the senior Ọzọ titles. The junior Ọzọ title is also called family Ọzọ, while according to him the senior Ọzọ title is that which initiation and jurisdiction covers the entire town or community. His report further has it that what distinguishes the two grades of Ọzọ titles is that a community Ọzọ wears Ọzọ thread round his ankle and has an eagle feather pinned to his red cap, but the junior or family Ọzọ does not wear any of these insignia.

During the Ọzọ title taking proper, the aspirant undergoes several initiation stages. These include taking him round major deities in his town where he has to offer sacrifices to them. Also, he undergoes certain purification rites where he will perform ịsa ire (washing of tongue) which empowers him to speak the truth always after the final initiation. Furthermore, he is taken to his town's market to perform what is called *Ịpụ ahịa ozo* 'going to the market like an *Ozo*' or *Ịzụ ahịa ozo* 'buying things like an *Ozo*'. This is to present him to people as a full *ozo* title holder.

At this time, he is dressed in his full *Ozo regalia* which include his chieftaincy dress, red cap with eagle feather pinned onto it and *Ozo title thread* worn round his ankle. Others are elephant tusk, rattle spear (*Oji*), his *ozo* bag which some call *akpa nwaehi* 'small cow bag' and his *ozo* hand fan. He also wears a bell on his waist which announces his appearance. As a highly respected title, there are a host of things that an *Ozo* title holder is banned from doing. These include:

· he must always speak the truth
· he should always stand by his words
· he must not steal
· he should not engage in certain jobs such that involve climbing of trees
· in some communities, an *Ozo* title holder does not touch a corpse
· he does not eat everywhere
· he does not eat any food bought from the restaurant, while some do not even eat any food that is not cooked by their wife or daughter
· he does not have sex with another man's wife
· he does not swear falsely
· he does not take another person's property by force, etc.

When an *Ozo* title holder dies, the community sees it as a great tragedy. This is not only because of his death, but more because of the demand for the funeral. In fact, the funeral of an *Ozo* is a replication of all the things done and spent during his initiation. This is why it is an imperative that anyone who wants to be initiated into the *Ozo* title should be very wealthy and even provide for his burial while alive.

In conclusion, *Ọzọ* chieftaincy is purely a traditional Igbo culture and is highly respected. No wonder many individuals do not aspire for it due to their Christian faith. The deep traditional content of the *Ọzọ* chieftaincy may also be the reason many individuals and communities seldom organise *Ọzọ* chieftaincy initiation today as many do not accept that there is Christian *Ọzọ*.

## 6.3 Lọ̀ọ̀lọ̀ or Ịyọ̀m

*Lọọlọ* or *Ịyọm* is to women what Ọzọ title is to the menfolk in the Igbo title ranking. In other words, it is the highest female title in the Igbo communities where it obtains, such as Okigwe and Owerri where they call it *Lọọlọ,* and in Onitsha, Awka and Oyi areas, where they call it *Ịyọm.*

In all these communities, the aspirant must be of proven integrity and must be well established in the society. In the olden days, they were expected to come of age. But today that has been de-emphasized as what matters to them more is having the capability to meet the demands of the title. Therefore, once the aspirant passes the screening of the leaders, she moves on to the initiation into the *Lọọlọ* or *Ịyọm* title.

On the initiation day, the aspirant dresses in a very gorgeous attire. Then the leaders will pull through the *Ọdụ* (ivory) to her wrists and ankles. Thereafter, she sits on her title chair while guests, friends and well-wishers pay homage to her with various gifts items. Other members of the group will then relax and feed on the sumptuous entertainment provided by the new initiate. She is also expected to give a huge sum of money to the organisation for the members to share among themselves.

Members of the *Lọọlọ* and *Ịyọm* title organisation serve as adjudicators in disputes among the womenfolk of their communities. They also assist the men in some aspects of governance of the community. Apart from the prestige and status elevation it gives to the initiates, they are exempted from the works done by the women in the community, such as sweeping the market and the village square or cleaning the community stream.

## 7.0 Cultural Festivals

The Igbo communities have some notable festivals that bind them together. These festivals go by different names in different communities. Similarly, they are celebrated at different times in different communities. Some of such festivals which we shall discuss here are the *Ọfala/Ịgụ Arọ* and *New Yam Festivals*.

### 7.1 Ofala/Ịgụ Arọ

*Ọfala* is a relatively new ceremony among the Igbo communities. It is an annual festival celebrated by the traditional rulers. In some Igbo communities, like Enugwu-ukwu and Nri, it is called *Ịgụ Afọ/Ịgụ Arọ*, as they also use that occasion to recount the failures and successes of the community in the passing year. The occasion is also used to plan for the incoming year.

Furthermore, the occasion is an anniversary to celebrate the coronation and enthronement of the reigning traditional ruler. Since this other reason is by far the major aim for the festival, the *Obi, Eze,* or *Igwe* takes the front stage in planning and executing the *Ọfala* ceremony. Hence, he starts early to plan for it through his *Ọfala Advisory Committee*. A date is fixed, finances sought for, and invitation sent to selected guests, including masquerades and dancing troupes that will perform at the ceremony.

On the said day, canon shots are fired at the palace to announce the day's event. The number of shots varies from community to community. In some, it is twelve, in others, it is twenty one. By this time, the ceremonial *ufie* (wooden gong) will be sounding, with the player performing, hailing and praising the *Obi, Igwe or Eze* and the guests as they arrive.

When it is time for the Royalty's first outing to the Ofala arena, he is ushered out by his guards and Cabinet Chiefs. He dresses in his ceremonial regalia. He will dance to the beating of the traditional *Igba Eze* music round the arena before taking his seat. At this time, his Cabinet Chiefs will formally greet him. Then presentation and breaking of kola nuts will take place. Other guests, including other invited Traditional Rulers, government officers and other dignitaries join the ceremony. Around midday, the Igwe or Obi and his Cabinet Chiefs come out again to dance to the traditional *Igba Eze* round the arena to the cheering of his guests. This is his major outing. In most cases, he dresses in a different regalia, and his traditional dance lasts longer in this outing. After the Igwe's performance comes welcome address, usually presented by the Chairman of the Ọfala Planning Committee. Responses may follow, especially from the Governor of the State who often is the chief Guest of Honour. After that the Igwe or Obi will honour some of his subjects and friends with Chieftaincy titles. In some communities, like Nnewi, Ọfala Ceremony is a two-day occasion. In such a case, general masquerade and dance performances are reserved for the second day. In Nnewi too, it takes place about the same time every year. The Igwe, in this case uses the same occasion to celebrate his birthday.

Finally, the Ọfala ceremony is more or less a feast for people to eat, drink and be merry. Gifts are presented to the Igwe. It also serves as an opportunity for what is called *mass return*, which refers to a period when the members of a town or local government spread all over the country and even in diaspora decide to return home for at least one to two weeks. Many use that opportunity to meet old time friends from within and outside, as well as create opportunity for many to meet the Igwe face-to-face.

## 7.2   New Yam Festival

This is one festival that is celebrated in all Igbo land. It is meant to honour yam which is regarded as the chief crop on one hand, and to thank God for a successful farming season. New yam festival is given different names by different communities. However, the aim of the celebration still remains the same.

In some communities, it is called *Iwa ji* 'the cutting of yam', while others call it *Iri ji* 'eating of yam' or *Ahiajioku* in honour of the god of yam. Yet, there are communities that call it *Mmemme Ọnwa Asaa* 'festival of the seventh month' or *Mmemme Ọnwa Asatọ* 'festival of the eight month' because it is celebrated on the seventh or the eighth month of the year. Again, some communities like Nnewi and neighbouring towns like Nnobi and Awka-Etiti that celebrate something similar call theirs *Afia Ọlụ*. They hold theirs between the seventh and ninth months of the year.

Some outstanding peculiarities in these festivals are the duration of the festivals that is four days in all the communities. Another peculiarity is that they are celebrated before harvesting the new yam. In fact, people feel free to harvest and eat their yam only after the new yam festival.

Some Igbo communities have *Ihejiọkụ priest* whose duty it is to announce the date for the new yam festival in those communities. *Ihejiọkụ* is the god of yam. So, on the selected date, all farmers are expected to harvest their yams and take one tuber each, fowl and kola nuts to the *Ihejiọkụ priest*. Some tubers of yam will be cooked and some of the fowls killed and the blood spilled on the *Ihejiọkụ deity* by the chief priest as sacrifice. The fowls will be cooked with the yams.

When the yam is done, the Chief priest will take some and put in an earthen pot for the deity before others present join to eat the porridge. After this ritual, people go back to their homes. From that moment, they can embark on celebration of new yam festival. In some communities, it is the head of the Ọzọ title holders that will announce the date for the new yam festival. On the day of the festival which takes place at the village square, yam could be roasted or boiled as porridge. But the yam to be used for the actual ceremony is usually roasted. After cutting the roasted yam by the Igwe with the people present hailing and thanking God for a successful farming, canon shots are fired. Then, the pieces of yam will be served with red oil and sliced oil bean seeds (*ụkpaka*). This is followed by masquerade displays, dances and visitations.

This marks the climax of the ceremony. People of the community are from that day free to celebrate their own new yam with their family members, in-laws and friends. In-laws and grandchildren visit their in-laws and grandfathers. Ụmụada and their children visit their parents, many with food and other gifts. In appreciation, the parents and their neighbours and friends will present gifts to their children and grandchildren. On the fourth day which is the last day of the festival, all the big masquerades in the town display at the central playground, as well as dance troupes. Some towns organise wrestling contest, football competition, greatest yam farmer of the year contest, etc. on that final day.

In conclusion, the main aim of the festival is to thank God for a successful farming year. It is also meant to encourage farmers, as well as challenge others to join in farming which is the main occupation of the Igbo people. ▣

### References

Ekwealor, C.C. (1998). *Omenala na Ewumewu ndị Igbo*. Onitsha: Palma Publishing & Links.

Ofomata, C. E. (2012). *Omenala na Ọdịnala ndị Igbo*. Enugu: Format Publishers.

Ọgbalụ, F. C. (1079). *Omenala Igbo.* Onitsha: University Publishing Company.

Onwudiwe, G. E. (2017). "Meaninglessness in Language: The case of the Igbo Language", in *Ogirisi: a new journal of African studies, Vol. 13. Pp. 256 – 276.*

Onwudiwe, G. E. (2020). "The Igbo Lexicon: A veritable Igbo thought and philosophy for training and sustainable development", in *Journal of African and Sustainable Development, Vol. 3, No. 5. Pp. 100 – 115.*

Onwudiwe, G. E. (2020) "Vagueness for Specificity in the use of Igbo Language", in *Odezuruigbo: Journal of Igbo, African and Asian Studies. (Forthcoming).* ▣

# Chapter 11

Chike Okoye

## Igbo Masquerades And Festivities

1. Introduction

2. Some variations in the *Mmọnwụ* Phenomenon

3. What is Known about *Mmọnwụ*

4. *Mmọnwụ* Categories and Festivities

   4.1 The Night Mask

   4.2 The Day Mask

5. *Mmọnwụ* Chants and Mimetics

6. Summary and Conclusion

## Summary

The Igbo have many traditions and accompanying festivals that they are known for. One of the most common that cuts across numerous Igbo communities is the **New Yam Festival**, which involves the agricultural god or deity of the yam crop, **Ahiajoku, Ifejioku, or Fejioku.** Another agricultural feast is the **Ede Aro**, which is celebrated on a lesser scale and by fewer communities in honour of the staple food **Ede** 'cocoyam'. Different from these agricultural festivals is the annual **Ofala** festival, at which the king or Igwe of a community celebrates his royalty. This is marked by pomp, regality, and pageantry, and it is often lively and seldom solemn. Many and more of these festivities are widespread in the majority of Igbo communities domiciled in Anambra, Enugu, Imo, Abia, Ebonyi, and the Igbo speaking parts of Delta and Rivers states of Nigeria, but they vary in degree of components, spectacle, rites, duration, seriousness and/or levity, depending on the tradition of the community and the scope of community participation. During such festivals, the representatives of the ancestors from the spirit world visit their former abode of the living as masks, masquerades, **mmonwu, mmanwu, mmuo,** etc., and join in the festivities, all of which contribute to the enrichment of the Igbo cultural heritage.

## 1. Introduction

THE CULTURAL HERITAGE OF THE IGBO IS GENERALLY RICH. The masquerade, masking or mask institution is one of the most revered and sacred of them. When masquerade or masking is mentioned, it has little similarity with the mask carnivals that are for fun and revelry. The Igbo phenomenon is an ancestral and dynamic portal of spirit world representation and intervention, practiced over many years and still relatively potent. It is referred to as *mmọnwụ, mmanwụ, mmụọ*, and is seen as a physical and tangible representation of a masked entity assuming diverse shapes but most often taking after the human physiognomy and believed to be ancestral spirits that visit the world of the living occasionally. It is accorded regard, respect, reverence and awe. The Igbo ontology and culture lend it significance and credibility because it is believed that the dead, living, and unborn are always in close proximity, owing themselves mutual respect. They appear to the living with marked peculiarities common to the spirit world: ancestral wisdom, cryptic messages, entertainment, social justice and security, etc. They are a common sight during individual and communal festivals – dance festivals, burials, ritual feasts, community communions, harvests, commemorations, funerals, etc.

According to Ugonna (1984) in addition to the generally sacrosanct view that the *mmọnwụ* is an ancestor come-back-to-life, different Igbo communities have different ways of viewing the *mmọnwụ*, all of which could be summarized as follows:

a.　A mask with supernatural powers, regarded as a visible spirit in the community and accorded all spiritual awe and respect;

b.　A spirit coming from the underground in a masked form;

c.　A spirit masked, deified, sacrosanct and not to be

touched or approached by humans, inhibiting under the ground and

d.     An age-old form of mask supposed to come to man's world from the spirit world. (2)

However, these views are more aptly captured in the title of Onyeneke's work *The Dead Among the Living: Masquerades in Igbo Society*, which buttresses the fact that the *mmọnwụ* are the dead that have come back as masquerades. That is why in his introduction to Onyeneke's book, Arazu concludes that the masquerade in Igbo tradition is the direct result of the Igbo man's belief in life after death (vi).

In a nutshell therefore, the basic notion is that the *mmọnwụ* for the Igbo refer to ancestral spirits operating in the world of the living as (ancestral) masks. One might think their visitations as akin to the ghoulish monotony of zombie-like manifestations, or mere carnival entertainment skits – far from that; they instead are actively engaged in the community. They are involved in community policing, maintenance of law and order, social engagements such as initiations and entertainment (through dance, play, satire, etc.); and also ensure gender differentiation as masking is mostly an all-male affair (Onyeneke, pp. 75-89). The entertainment aspect is usually marvelous to watch, especially in the masquerade's to-and-fro movements, forward dashes and abrupt stops, in addition to its negating or affirmative head nods, and dignified spins, all of which rhythmically align with the masquerade's chants, narratives and songs.

## 2.   Some Variations in the Mmọnwụ Phenomenon

The Igbo speaking region has been noted for a variation in its dialects. Similarly, the *mmọnwụ* in Igboland is not an exception to such a variation, because different Igbo communities have different names and conceptions of the mask phenomenon.

the masks of the riverine south-western Igbo where they are known as the *Owu* and *Okorosha* and are associated with the water deity, *Echere*. Onyeneke explains that

 *...the goddess 'Echere' is venerated at night. An Owu masquerade...is raised at the shrine and is inducted by the pilgrims from the shrine.... These masquerades dance to music and they do not talk. They play for about four market weeks and retire, thereby making room for a swarm of youthful masquerades of various types called (the) Okorosha. (34)*

Around the south-east of the Igbo, among the neighboring Efik and Ibibio ethnicities, we find a tradition domiciled within the Ngwa and Umuahịa-Bende parts of the Igbo which has been influenced by the masking traditions known as *Ekpe*, *Ọkọnkọ*, and *Ekpo*. These are slightly different from the masked deities, for they are associated more with the influence and execution of political power. Their manner of operation involves strict secrecy, security, violence, and highly secret codes in operation and communication. The Igbo of the central area of the Anambra Awka-Nri-Ekwulobia axis and environs practice the tradition popularly known as mmonwu which has a mystical progenitor in the mythical *Nwazenọgwụ* character who is said to be the founder and father of all *mmọnwụ*. This is the masked tradition known as the ancestral mask – the ancestors coming back periodically to the human world.

## 3. What Is Known about Mmọnwụ

The masquerade institution dates back to a long time in Igbo history when it was a very powerful aspect of the society, especially in issues of entertainment, security, rules, keeping of order, and adjudication. However, it has lost most of those mentioned roles and qualities leaving behind only the entertainment aspect due to the debilitating effects of Christianization, civilization and modernization. Generally, the history of *mmọnwụ* can be described having passed through the stages of an initial, unperturbed existence, through the period of missionary-cum-colonial denigration, to the recent renaissance and reappraisal.

The early Christian missionaries and white imperial forces who made contact with, and lived amongst, the peoples of West Africa and the Igbo in particular during the subsequent colonial era quite naturally took it upon themselves to understand the life and culture of the "savage natives" and consequently churned out volumes of anthropological research; with many on the *mmọnwụ*. It is important to note that these mainly British colonizers were adequately armed with the authority of the church and the force of administration and could almost always muscle their way through most traditional obstacles; and the *mmọnwụ* tradition was not spared their unravelling and demystification of the hitherto dreaded and revered institution. This eroding of the awe and aura of the *mmọnwụ* cult was most times done ungraciously in the full glare of the community – the uninitiated males, women, and children – whose previous belief in the mystical, supernatural, and potent powers of the mask most certainly came down to an end. It was obvious that the colonizers were not impressed by the natives' belief system and *mmọnwụ* culture; in fact they could not hide the sneer and disdain in some of the reports they made. The following comment is attributed to G T Basden, a pastor of the CMS in his book, *Among the Ibos of Nigeria:*

*The Iboman undoubtedly thinks that the ceremony of making maw has somehow transformed the man and endowed him with extraordinary qualities. Moreover by virtue of the unassailable status of a spirit, a maw was "onye-nwe-obodo" and equivalent title for our 'Lord of Creation'. (237)*

Of course other colonial researchers and anthropologists continued more or less this style of documentation for the mask tradition. Onyeneke presents G I Jones' important, objective, and insightful discoveries in his report "Masked Plays of South-Eastern Nigeria", and it is paraphrased thus:

> *G I Jones reported as a District Officer. He underlined the three common elements in the masquerades of south eastern Nigeria, which were always mixed together: (a) the religious and magical elements where supernatural and religious awe are attributed to masquerades; (b) the disciplinary element where secrecy is maintained and initiation formalities are demanded; (c) pageantry and display in so far as masquerades provide an enjoyable show and spectacle.... For him, the institution was undergoing a serious transition in Igboland: "today, masked plays with much secrecy or religious ritual have died out in the more sophisticated communities and those of a spectacular nature remain" (1945, p. 199).*

There are reasons for the progressive dearth of the reclusive and religious ritual aspects of the tradition. The major reason for the dying out could be attributed to the threat to authority which the colonial masters felt it posed to their court and police arms of suppression. The colonial missionaries and administrators would not tolerate any native challenge in any form, not to talk of the mask institution against their trade, control, governance, and missionary missions in the Igbo country. They would not tolerate the use of force against any peoples under their care or watch as colonial overlords. According to Jeffreys (1949) in "The Bull Roarer Among the Igbo" published in *African Studies*,

 *Complaints of murder, of violence and of destruction of property brought before the District Officers during the mmo season resulted in posse of police arresting and de-masking the mmo members, thus shattering locally the awe in which the society was held. Under such political hostile environment, the power of the mmo died: its ability to hold Ibo society together …has gone, never to return. (23)*

Obviously, this sad note for the future of the mask's powers in the society simply got aggravatingly worse and has steadily continued to date. But as the political and religious/ritual powers continue to diminish, other aspects (including those bordering on entertainment) have more or less remained and some colonial anthropologists and researchers also captured these other aspects. For example, the colonial anthropologist Meek (1930) captured the legal system roles of the *Odo* and *Omabe* of the Nsukka area, while Boston (1960) looks into "the genres, magical powers and the night mask category" of the Umueri, Nri, and Awka axis. Onuora Nzekwu (cited in Okoye, 2019, p. 101) toed the line of the colonial writers by unveiling the long-held secret of the mask's distorted voice contraption

As if signaling the end of colonial scholarship in the mmonwu phenomenon, Nzekwu's work also opened a floodgate of works from well-educated indigenous researchers who avoided the colonial tone and sought to present the tradition as a veritable and interesting institution full of art but in full cognizance of the "nuances, values and taboos surrounding masks and their operations" (Okoye, 2010, p. 101). This disposition and the academic preparedness could very possibly be the reason for the many thorough and focused researches that are now available on the subject. For Onyeneke (1987), studies of these kinds gently shifted from unraveling the secrets and internal mechanism of the mask operations and concentrated "on phenomenological analyses of the shape, form, dance, song and dramatic qualities manifested in the performance session of the masquerade" (8). Hence, the study of the mask tradition began to shift away from the colonial denigration to an appreciation of the uniqueness of its drama, its supernatural aspect, and its aesthetics and elements of spectacle, art, song, dance, and mimicry.

In this new phase, some Igbo scholars started seeing the masked performance as indigenous drama, quite distinct from European concepts of drama. Echeruo, for example, believes that it can only be drama enough when it moves away from its ritual content, while Ugonna sees the Ozubulu area type of the *mmọnwụ* ensemble as full opera with lead actors. Simon Ottenberg presents the *Okumkpo* mask of Afikpo as a full play with morality and comic reliefs as highpoints, similar to James Amankulor's explanation/analysis of the *Ekpe* of the Ngwa people and the *Odo* of the Nsukka area as truly complete African theatre.

Another view is the re-orientation on the ritual and supernatural aspects of the mask practice by Enekwe (1987). He explains that the animal to be represented by a particular spirit is usually identified by the *dibia* and sacrificed, and its blood spilled on the mask to which magical objects and talismans are attached. The power in the mask is manifested through the performer, who makes tangible the imagined presence of the dead or supernatural. Through this, the masked performance is seen as a union of the religious and magical with human skill and ingenuity (pp. 78-79). In other words, there has to be that element of awe which the supernatural element provides; otherwise, the mask, without inducing fear of possible harm in the African juju way, will be disregarded as nothing.

The aesthetic view of the masks is represented by Aniakor (1985), who has endeavoured to analyze and explain what the head-pieces or headdresses of masks and their carvings signify. He sees the mask images as actually functional art and laden with messages and not just arbitrary art. He used the *Ijele* mask to showcase the wonderful symbolism of art in the Igbo king of masks – the *Ijele*. He explains that the mask head-dresses act as microcosmic representations of what the full masks are about. Hence, in the masks, "the Igbo bring into close social and functional relations, the world of the living, the dead, the forest, rivers and other elemental forces, all revolving around man as the supreme agent in the cosmic mission" (*Nigeria Magazine* 91). For example, according to Okoye (2019), the *Agaba* mask's head-dress is easily decoded in the presence of horns, leopards, lions in a mix of carvings but with man placed atop to still signify control of the violent elements around and underneath. Again, the *Ijele's* leading spirit quality is showcased in the head-dress as all noted Igbo masks are murals on it, therefore heightening the mystic aura of the *Ijele*.

Finally, there is also a sociological approach to the *mmọnwụ* by Onyeneke (1987). He explains that the masking tradition and structure is a microcosm for a better understanding of the Igbo country macrocosm, because it guarantees a clearer and more easily comprehensible insight into the Igbo. Hence, it is an indicator of social values and community consensus and is structured in such a way as to "ensure a successful preservation and continuation of the existing and living community... (and) the external manifestation of these in a symbolic action is the masquerade" (Onyeneke, 1987, p. 17).

## 4.   The Categories of Mmọnwụ and Their Festivities

The two broad categories of masquerades among the Igbo are: (1) the ones that strictly appear only in the dead of the night, the night masks; and (2) the ones that operate by daytime and the others.

### 4.1  The Night Masks

The night category is generally called *Mmonwu Abani* (masks of the night/night mask) and is not as accessible as the daytime counterparts as per participation and free audience. It is strictly more reclusive and secretive and more often than not requires extra initiation to be able to participate in its arts. All *mmọnwụ* traditions in Igbo land are categorized and broken down into subgenres with very many of them bearing identifiable names.

In general and especially among the Anambra Igbo, the night mask tradition is broken down into three different styles or types which prevail in certain loosely marked community clusters. The Igbo of the mostly Anambra South senatorial zone practice what is known as the *Ogbaagu* (leopard clan), while the Central zone have more of the *Ajikwu/Achịkwu* tradition and finally the Anambra North Igbo are more at home with the *Ayaka*. Each has distinct qualities that make them what they are but they all have these in common – they operate by night, their viewing and entertainment are for a very select few, they have a propensity for violence, instill terror in most people, and engage in almost inexplicable and ingenious feats in the dead of the night. They are given to very engaging satire and satirical music, and make chilling, weird sounds through clever means. However, they mostly vary in their degrees of interest and expertise. The *Ajikwu*, for example, plays skeletal but still engaging music, but are more given to vigilante services than any other thing. The *Ayaka* are known for very clever satirical pieces delivered melodiously; while the *Ogbaagu's* musical ensemble is the best, with a complete music system and mostly in unison. All these however overlap and making a hard and fast rule of their performance would be difficult to achieve.

In any of the types of *Mmonwu Abani*, there are characters and other entities such as the *Ọgbazuluobodo, Ọganigwe, Agụmmụọ, Odegiligili, Omenikolo, Ajịkwụ Ikpo, Isimpki, Ajịkwụ Ọhịa, Ajịkwụ Ụnọ*, and others of the same ilk that could be found anywhere amongst them. Onyeneke (1987) describes the *Ọgbaagụ* as a

> ❝ ... *group of night masquerades (that) are strictly for dance entertainment and are not part of the village guard system. It is ... they (that) often play at the compound affected at funerals of members and their dependants. An ogbagu performance in the Aguata area is considered an entertainment dance play of the leopard family, (Onyeneke (1987, pp. 22-24).* ❞

In his comment on the night mask's audial spectacle, Enekwe's (1987) maintains that the *Ayaka* appears only at night, with "Voice" at the centre and no masks worn. He explains this voice ingenuity of audial spectacle as follows:

> ❝ *By means of sound created by highly trained voices, voice disguisers, ankle rattles, a*

> *netted calabash, studded with cowries and nuts (worn by the leader of the group), and bull-roarers (odegili-gili), the maskers create a ghostly atmosphere which makes the blood of the initiated and uninitiated alike tingle with fear... the Ayaka speak a peculiar language, which is supposed to be that of the spirits, (Enekwe, 1987, p. 81)* **99**

## 4.1  The Day Masks

There are proper explanation needed here, which would help further the comprehension of the *mmọnwụ* concept. I am from the Agulu community of the Anambra central are, a community known for veritable mask practices and naturally my charity of knowledge reasonably takes root and begins from my homebred knowledge of the mask phenomenon. We refer to a single ancestral spirit entity performing to be a mask as *mmọnwụ/mmanwụ*, and if accompanied by humans, they are referred to as *ndị mmọnwụ*. But when the masks are more than one and not performing in an ensemble or concert, then they are *umu mmọnwụ* ie, masks; and when they perform as an organic and linked group, they become a masquerade group (*otu egwu mmọnwụ*; literally: dance group of masks). This helps in both the Igbo delineations and the English usages of "mask" and "masquerade" for these purposes, (Okoye, 2018, p. 41).

In the categorization of Igbo masks below, Enekwe's (1987, p. 42) veritable diagram has been paraphrased and reproduced with Okoye's (2019) infusions showing different Igbo masks, their activities and significations:

| | MASKS INVOLVED | ACTIVITIES | MEANING/SIGNIFICANCE |
|---|---|---|---|
| 1 | *Agbọghọ mmọnwụ* (maiden/ female spirit); *Ọgbangbada* (antelope dancer); *Ojiọnụ* | Highly expressive dancing, movement and mime | Beauty, elegance, suppleness, chastity |
| 2 | *Ijele* | Dancing, movement | Beauty, mobility, wealth, royalty, regality |
| 3 | *Agaba-Idu* (lion); *Omenike* (force); *Okwomma* (machete wielder); *Mgbedike* (time of the brave); *Ọtawalụikpo* | Aggressive movement, uncontrollable force | Force, violence, and the uncontrollable factor in human life |
| 4 | *Big belle* or *mmọnwụ torch* | Mime, gesture, chanting, the comic | Comic spirit, joy |
| 5 | *Ọganachi; Akụ-ezu-ilo; Eze-ahịịlị m* | Mime, Dance | Ugliness, moral deformity and agency |
| 6 | *Ọkụmkpọ; Odo Okolaz; Ojimkpa* | Satire, Lampoon | Moral agency, rectitude |
| 7 | *"Wonder"; Nwaọta m; Ekpe* | Dance | The wonderful; magical power |
| 8 | *Amadị Odo; Ọkụnagba Achalla* | Chanting | Ancestral wisdom |
| 9 | *Ụdọ; Az ụzụ; Samba; Akpala Mmọnwụ* | Racing; pursuit | Athleticism, lithe youth, energetic living |
| 10 | *Agụ-na-ada-aja; Ikwiikwi; Okwuanyiọnụ; Akịka-ata-okwu* | Chanting, singing | Ancestral wisdom; moral rectitude |

These classification is not rigid, because there are also overlapping, and nothing is cast in stone for the assumed activities and scope of performance or responsibilities of these masks. Below are a few pictures of some masks.

|*Ikwiikwii 'owl'*

|*Okwuanyionu*

*Omeluonye omechafu*

*Mmonwu Poliisi*

*Adamma*

|*Ekwe Mbe*    |*Ololo*

## 5.   The *mmọnwụ* Chant and Mimetics

Another spectacle the *mmọnwụ* is known for is singing and chanting poetry. As a result of the fact that the *mmọnwụ* is seen to harbor and dispense wisdom through the oral tradition of speech, its utterances and narratives are listened to with respect and reverence.

When looked at from the perspective of its chanting activity, the mask produces an aura of the unknown, hence an "elder, ancestor, sage...whose wisdom once voiced should be digested and adhered to"; also "mask utterances are very important for the positive development of the Igbo psyche and polity" (Okoye, 2016, p. 60). It is important to note that while certain parts of the Igbo prefer and practice the mask traditions that are more physically expressive than vocal, other parts savour the more vocal types because of the beauty and memory of their songs and chants that sublimely distil ancestral wisdom. The songs are known as *egwu mmọnwụ* while the chants are known as *mbem mmọnwụ*. The songs and chants are delivered mostly through a reed-like contraption that disguises the voice and gives it a guttural, otherworldly quality, and filled with features of traditional, oral, Igbo poetry. These renditions are generally poignant, and "the poignancy is felt when one is an initiate of the mask cult because it manifests in varying meta-language levels, mostly codified and encrypted for the benefit of a select few (mostly initiates)" (Okoye, 2016, p. 62). The tonality of the Igbo language contributes to the effects of the *egwu* and *mbem*, giving them a conspicuous rhythm that tends to have a gradual downward slope in pitch towards the end of a line. Sample lines will be featured below, first from the *Odogwuanyammee* (Red-eyed brave) of Arondizuogu town of Imo State. This mask is known for derring-do, dark magic and charms. It likes to present itself as invincible, and its chants and songs are accompanied by melodious music marked by the heavy rhythm of the bass tom-tom. In the chant below, the *Odogwuanyammee* recounts a mystical journey of metaphysical proportions:

| Igbo | English |
|---|---|
| Mgbe m na-eje wee pụta n'Ezinanọ | When I came up to the four-road junction |
| Obu ekuo m wee nee anya na-ene Danda | Discovery dawned, I looked it was Danda |
| Danda wee gwaba m okwu | Danda started talking to me |
| Wee sị na ya e gbugo ichi n'ihu gbuo n'azụ | Saying he has scarified his face and his back |
| Wee dịka dike na-adị ma ọ kwado agha | And that he is now like a battle-ready warrior |
| Na ọ bụ ile ọma ka ejule ji a ga n'ogwu | A sweet tongue sees the snail through thorns |
| Na a na-eji ego a kpa nzu | Money is spent in applying kaolin chalk |
| Were nzu e wunyere ndi nwụrụ anwụ | And kaolin chalk is used in burying the dead |
| Na ọ bụ ndom ngha ka e ji e jide agụ dị ndụ | The perfect mist is used in capturing the leopard |

| Igbo | English |
|------|---------|
| Mana ihe na-eku ume na-anwụ anwụ | But every breathing thing is prone to death |
| -ka m kpacahara anya | -that I be careful |
| Mgbe ahụ ka m ji nee anya n'ihu nee n'azụ | That was when I looked in front and looked behind |
| O nweghi onye m fụlụ | I did not see anyone |
| M wee je were igbe e ji ejeọgụ gbanye n'aka ikenga | I then took my war bracelet and put on my |
| m: | ikenga hand: |
| Sị onye gbaa n'aka ikenga m | A foe on my ikenga hand |
| Ọ bụrụ ya ọnwụ | Meets his death |
| Onye gbaa n'aka ibite | But if one meets my left hand |
| Uwa adịrị ya mma! | His world will be better! |

Another mask, the *Akika-ata-okwu* from Agulu in Anambra State whose name means "speech defies termites", underscoring the permanency of the spoken word which moves from generation to generation even after the demise of men; defying ordinary termites that can only consume material things, is known for cryptic, witty comments and satirical pieces delivered with no musical accompaniment. Below is a short excerpt of its chants:

| Igbo | English |
|------|---------|
| Ọ dịka mụ gụlụ obodo | I have the urge to clutch the people |
| Mụ gụlụ nwa | And clutch the child |
| Ọ dịka mụ gụlụ nwarobunagu | I have the urge to clutch the childin-the-wild |
| Anya ọbụla fụlụ ugo | The eye that sights the eagle |
| Ya jakene ugo daa | Let it hail the eagle always |
| Na anya adị afụ ugo kwa daa | For the eyes seldom see the eagle |
| Nkili nkili ka a na-ekili ododo | You can only admire velvet |
| Sị ejikwene ododo eni ozu | It should not be used as a burial shroud. |

The Igbo mask is also a veritable dramatic character and most moves it makes in a performance contain elements of the dramatic. These dramatic actions sometimes accompany the poetic chants while at other times it is more of a pantomime with the act being accompanied by only music (and a little bit of singing from the human troupe). Even its gestures on certain circumstances constitute drama.

*Agaba* or *Okwomma* mask which is known for force, violence and aggression, also embodies poetry in motion, which is seen in this skit where it encounters a human intruder. It takes dramatic strides to and fro, all the time thrusting its machete in a warning and menacing motion. Suddenly it stops with both legs together quivering and bobbing its shoulders up and down as it speaks in guttural voice:

| Igbo (Narration) | English (Translation) | Action seen |
|---|---|---|
| Ọ bụ nche ka I na e che m? | Are you waylaying me? | Takes the forward steps |
| Ka ọ bụ anwa ka Ị na-anwa m? | Or are you trying me? | Takes the backward steps |
| Ka o bu ka I   mara ebe m na | | |
| edobe isi m? | Or you want to know where I keep my head? | Moves forward again with the accompanying shoulder movement |

The spectacle above is cast as minimalist drama played out spontaneously in the said context of meeting a hapless human careless enough to stand in the tracks of such an aggressive ancestral spirit.

The *Ogbangbada* mask is another that is highly expressive in its mimetic act, because it

... entertains the audience by dancing expressively to the message of the flutist in the accompanying music of the troupe. Through supple dance movements, this mask enacts various domestic kitchen chores especially the hilarious act of mashing breadfruit called 'I macha ukwa' or 'igwe ukwa'.

Sitting on the bare floor, it spreads its legs in the normal female position of mashing breadfruit but in addition to the rhythmical back and forth movements of its hands supposedly mashing the breadfruit in the space created by the spread legs, it also involves the buttocks which bob up and down grindingly to the rhythm of the grinding, much to the amusement of the surrounding audience, (Okoye, 2018, p. 45).

## 6. Conclusion and Things to Note

This write-up has attempted to briefly explain the mask tradition among the Igbo, taking into consideration, its nature, characteristics, history of documentation and studies, geographical and community specifics, categories and types. It also went into the classifications that approximate their types, roles, actions, and significations of the actions, though the concentration is mostly on the Anambra Igbo – this again being a testament to the vast and difficult terrain of *mmọnwụ* studies.

The chapter also attempted an introductory survey of the highly secretive and dangerously reclusive night mask, roughly dividing it into the three main sub-traditions of the *Ogbaagụ, Ayaka,* and *Ajikwu.* Again, there are illustrations of mask chants and descriptions of dramatic skits which are merely what they are – skeletal examples; because there are many exhaustive texts, records, and practices of *mmọnwụ* drama, songs, and chants all over Igbo land. Therefore, a single chapter such as this cannot do justice to the vast and ancient institution of the Igbo *mmọnwụ* tradition.

It is easy to see that the terms *mmọnwụ,* mask, and masquerade have been used interchangeably to generally refer to the same entity and phenomenon of the tangible ancestral spirit that visits and communes with man from time to time by honoring festivals and other occasions. There are also occasions that are slated for masks specifically, and not only festivals that masks are invited to or just appear to colour as spectacle. The state-organized *Mmanwụ Festivals* are such occasions. Certain communities also celebrate masks for their sole sake for days and even weeks on end.

An interesting thing however, is that this topic is fluid and vast. Many aspects are not cast in stone – instead variations can be confirmed in different Igbo communities. Take for instance an important mask like the *Ajọ Ọfịa* of Nnewi, *Atụmma* of Abagana, and some other ancestral masquerades that take the shape of animals common to the community locales where they are actuated; eg, the *Mmọnwụ Enyi* (Elephant Mask),

*Mmọnwụ Akụm/Atụ* (Hippo/Buffalo Mask), *Mmọnwụ Ugo* (Eagle Mask), and so on which all defy clean and clear categorization. Such "serious" masks are often known by the calibre of the guides or followers, the strange juju paraphernalia attached to its costume, daunting magical feats attributed to it, legends about its occult and ritual escapades, its name or character and other tell-tale signs. Such masks are generally referred to as *Nnukwu Mmọnwụ* (big masquerade).

This chapter did not discuss the government and security/law and order function of the *mmọnwụ* tradition, because this function has been almost totally taken over by the modern administrative white collar government. Nevertheless, that does not remove the fact that many rural communities at least still apply the *ọmụ mmọnwụ* (the do-not-touch-or-pilfer tender palm frond warning sign) put on fruit-bearing trees that often get ravaged by rascally kids and youths. In such violations, the *mmọnwụ* goes to the home of the defaulting rascal and enacts a fine in which absence, a goat or sheep or any other property of value will be seized from the defaulter's home as punitive measure for the *ụdala*, mango, or orange, or any tree bearing the *ọmụ mmọnwụ*. This measure till date is still very effective.

Satire is also still applied especially by night masks to date. These are usually aimed at wayward and irresponsible members of the community with an aim to shame them into correction and as deterrent for other potential perpetrators. It is important for us and posterity that this veritable institution be revived and reinvigorated and people's minds disabused about what the mask stands for among the Igbo. It is a deep well of cultural norms, mores, and heritage; handed over through generations but now at the verge of extinction due to colonial mentality, modernization, over-religiosity, lack of interest, and inferiority complex. More festivals should be organized and dance, drama, and chant competitions put up solely for masquerades for the purposes of revival, reappraisal, reintegration, preservation, posterity and enhancement of cultural identity.

# References

Aniakor, C. (1985). Igbo Art as an Environment: The Example of Mask Head-dresses. *Nigeria Magazine* 53(4), pp. 90-97.

Basden, G T. (1983). *Among the Ibos of Nigeria*. Ibadan: University Publishing Company,.

Boston, J.S. (1960). Some Northern Ibo Masquerades. *The Journal of the Royal Anthropological Institute of Great Britain and Ireland*, 90(1), pp. 54-65.

Enekwe, O. (1987). *Igbo Masks: The Oneness of Ritual and Theatre*. Lagos: Nigeria Magazine.

Jeffreys, M D W. (1949). The Bull Roarer among the Igbo. *African Studies*, 8, pp. 23-54.

Okoye, C. (2019). "The Igbo Mask and the Elements of Sound and Darkness in the Night Mask Phenomenon", in S. Ododo &

Chike Okoye. *Liminal Margins: Performance Masks, Masquerades and Facekuerades*. Awka: SONTA, p. 93-114.

Okoye, C. (2018) "The Igbo Mask as Solo Performer". Eds. G. Mbajiorgu & Amanze Akpuda. *50 Years of Solo Performing Art in Nigerian Theatre: 1966-2016*. Ibadan: Kraft, pp. 31-48.

Okoye, C. (2014). *The Mmonwu Theatre: Igbo Poetry of the Spirits*. Saarbrucken: LAP Lambert.

Okoye, C. (2016). "Poignant Poetics: The Aesthetics of Mask Chants". *Igbo Scholars International Journal*, 3(1), 56-71.

Onyeneke, A. (1987). *The Dead Among the Living: Masquerades in Igbo Society*. Nimo: Asele Institute.

Ugonna, N. (1984). *Mmonwu: A Dramatic Tradition of the Igbo*. Lagos: Lagos University Press.

## Some Igbo Masquerades From Nsukka

| *Akatakpa Group*

| *Akatakpa Group*

| *Akatakpa Group*

| *Akatakpa Group*

Akatakpa Group

Akatakpa Group

Akatakpa Group of Masqurades

Egbe Ocha (Masquerade of Omabe Cult)

Ekpe Masquerade

Ochiajagba

Odogwu Masquerade

Agbeji (a masquerade of the Omabe cult)

Odogwu Masquerade

Odum Masquerade

# Igbo Music And Igbo Musical Instruments

1. Introduction

2. Igbo Musical Instruments and Their Types
   *Ọja, ụbọaka, ịgba, ogene, une, udu, ọdụ ekwe,*
   *ufie, ikoro, ikeremkpo, ịchaka, okpokoro*

3. Some instrument - Specific Pieces

4. Some Igbo Folk Songs: *Ikpem (egwu ikpem), akwụeke, mgbala*

5. Some Igbo Musical Ensemble

6. Conclusion

## Summary

Igbo music, which is the music of the indigenous Igbo people as developed in the Igbo culture area, includes instrumental, dance, and folk music. Igbo music however, is not cast in iron, for it continues to expand, to absorb and indigenize the rhythms of the modern world, the same way that the Igbo cultural universe continues to expand as it grapples with the ever-changing currents of the modern world. That is how Igbo music rhythmically contributes to the resilience of Igbo culture. Traditionally, the Igbo child is exposed to Igbo music from the point of conception. When the child is born, it is welcomed with music, and music accompanies it as it goes through several stages of formation and joins various social and cult groups in the course of its development. Igbo societies generally vibrate to the rhythms of Igbo music, because music is an essential part of the life of the Igbo people, and most of the celebrations in Igbo land – festivals and feasts alike – always have Igbo musical accompaniments. As a brief introduction to this aspect of Igbo life and culture, this paper is focused on Igbo traditional music and especially Igbo musical instruments, their types and the kinds of music they are used for.

## 1. Introduction

**M**USIC PLAYS A MAJOR ROLE THROUGHOUT THE LIFE OF AN IGBO PERSON. Okafor (2017, p. 16) explains that "music features in many different settings within Igbo traditional society: palm wine drinking, hunting, games, and sports, harvesting and others aspects of agricultural work, birth, marriage, death, funerals and so on." Music therefore does not just pass for fun and mere pleasure, but most importantly, it is also an edifying means, pleasing as it instructs. Igbo music serves as accompaniment to various social activities and as such it is rare if not impossible to have any event without music in Igbo land. It is pertinent to observe that the Igbo do not just hold music important, they equally participate in it, actively or passively, as part of a communal experience. That is why in the traditional setting music is didactic, therapeutic and wholly edifying.

Music in every Igbo community also reflects the aesthetic appeal in the form of styles that have "aesthetic values" (Ebighgbo, 2006, p. 61). This expression of aesthetics can be seen in the choice of notes, text, instruments, and mode employed in musical performances. In addition, music in Igbo land resonates basically to teach, reecho, and celebrate the societal beliefs and values, as well as enhance human interaction amongst the people of a given Igbo community. Thus the aesthetics of Igbo music within its cultural context is only a means to an end. Onyeji (2011) reaffirms this assertion in his view of the African man's conception of music:

 *In every African music type therefore, there is the entertainment aspect of the music and the main social issue it addresses. The former assists in the delivery of the later. Entertainment is then the subtle means of reaching its major objective in aesthetically appealing form. There must*

*always be a social intention that gives meaning and value to the music beyond mere entertainment for it to be rationalized as a creative art of social importance (p. 29).* **"**

Another aspect of Igbo life and music is the fact that there are Chains of festivals across a year and these festivals do require music as part of the activities of the festival as well as indication of the context of the festival. Hence, Igbo traditional music does not just occur because one wants to hear music or dance to it. Aside incidental music which may occur to ease the tedium of work while one is at work, most Igbo music types are performed within the context of the Igbo musical calendar. Okafor (2005) describes the cultural implications of the Igbo musical calendar thus:

 *'A drum is not beaten without cause', a nụhọ eti igba nụ makala, na e tirọ igba na nkịtị". The cause as well as the avenues of expression of music in Igbo land can easily be traced to the ceremonies, festivals, rituals and social activities, which not only are replete in Igbo life but also are integral with their attendant music and humanly organized sounds. Therefore, the Igbo musical calendar does not exist because the Igbo society wants to hear such music or watch such a dance at an appointed time. It exists because of certain ceremonies, rituals, festivals and other activities which appear in appointed order, which have music or dances and usually both as a sine qua non. Igbo musical calendar is therefore not an academic expression but an Igbo cultural essence and reality (p. 126).* **"**

## 2. Some Igbo Musical Instruments and Their Types

According to Echezona (1964), "Ibo (sic) musical instruments are made from a variety of materials ranging from clay as in *udu*, gourd as in another type of *ubọ-aka*, wood as in drums, elephant tusks as in *ọdụ*, and metals as in the prongs of *ubọ-aka.*" This does not imply the production of musical instruments with only these materials. In fact, it has been noted that producers of musical instruments generally turn the materials in their environments to musical instruments, thus making the instruments to be imbued with some form of the local (Onwuekwe 2011). That is also why "the instrumental resources at the disposal of performers naturally tend to be limited to those in which their respective communities specialize" (Nketia 1974, p. 67). There are indeed many Igbo musical instruments, but this chapter shall focus on the most common and well known, which include *ọja, ubọaka, igba, une, ogene, udu, ọdụ, ekwe, ufie, ikoro/ikolo, ikeremkpo, ịchaka/ọyọ and okpokoro.* All these musical instruments have been grouped into four categories by Curt Sachs and Erich Hornbostle's system of classification of African musical instruments. These are the *ideophones*, the *membranophones*, the *aerophones*, and the *chordiophones*. In summary, the *idiophones* are the musical instruments that produce sound by the vibration of the body of the instrument; an example is *ubọaka* 'thumb pano', made from gourd and metals prongs. The *membranophone* produces sound by the vibration of the membrane fastened across a hallowed wood, for example *igba* 'drum'. The aerophones produce sounds by the vibration of their air column, for example, *ọja* 'flute'; and the chordiophones produce sound by the vibration of plucked strings, for example, *une* 'stringed bow'. However, the different musical instruments shall be presented below without tying them down to this categorization.

*Ogene* is a 'metal gong'. The Awka people of Anambra State are known for blacksmithing, and they have the robust culture of *ogene* music. There are the additional sub-types of *oke ogene* 'male ogene (lead ogene)' and *nne ogene* 'female ogene (supporting ogene)'. *Ogene* is generally used in various Igbo communities by town criers to summon the attention of the community, regardless of the existence of blacksmithing in such communities. The instrument as such is not restricted to communities that have blacksmiths.

Figure 1. (a) Single Metal Gong

Figure 1. (b) Double Metal Gong
ogene mkpi naabo 'twin ogene'
ogene nne na nwa 'mother and daughter ogene'

Ọja 'flute' is one of the prominent instruments of the Igbo. It is made of wood with four holes, two by the sides. It also has a hole at the bottom and another at the top where the mouth is placed. Oja and opi which are speech surrogates are like "the akpele of the Aniocha people which makes use of prosodic features of speech to enhance its style of expression" (Mokwunei 2005, p. 46). Oja music is imbued with magical mysteries and beauty, and can be associated with the mbem mmọnwụ 'masquerade chants' which in the words of Okoye (2014), contains "the encrypted form of the Igbo essence, portrayed in rhythmical lines of verse."

Ụbọaka 'thumb piano' is made up of a calabash which serves as the resonator, a wooden sound board, metal prongs and two bridges that hold the metal prongs.

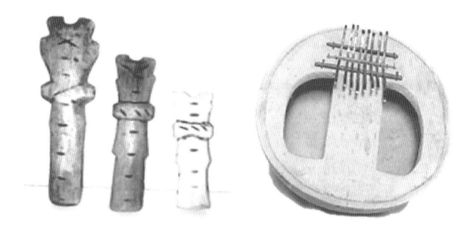

*Figure 2. (a) (Oja aerophone)*     *Figure 2. (b) Uboaka (Thumb Piano)*

Ekwe is a wooden slit-drum that also serves the medium of communication as speech surrogate. It appears in various sizes. The bigger sizes are called Ikoro/Ikolo. Some Ikoro are so big that a house is built around them and they cannot be moved around. According to Achebe in Okafor (2017, p. 16), ikolo "is a mythical symbol of office and power, regarded as ritual or sacred and enveloped by myths, legends and cults by the Northern Igbo communities." Ufie is an emsemble of a pair of ekwe. In his detailed explanation of the nature of the Ufie instrument and

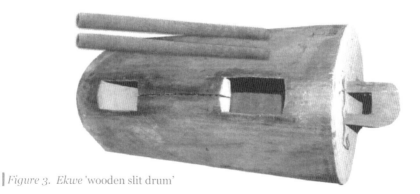

*Figure 3. Ekwe 'wooden slit drum'*

its function, Onwuka (2012, p. 48), describes it as "a pair of wooden drums, which is usually carved out of cylindrical logs of resonant wood". He also explains that it is primarily used to play "rockable persuasive rhythms". In musical performances, it plays the role of a master instrument, dictates movements, communicates signals, and announces "the arrival or presence of notable citizens at a social gathering by calling out their praise-names and extolling them for their achievements and exploits" (p. 48).

Ngedegwu 'xylophone' is an ideophone which consists of wooden slabs and a resonator.

| Figure 4. Ndedegwu 'xylophone'

| Figure 5. Igba 'wooden drum'

Udu 'pot drum' is an ideophone instrument made of clay or aluminum. It is often used to store water. It is a popular instrument used in Ogene, Egedege and Mkpǫkịtị ensembles.

Figure 6. *Udu* 'pot drum'

Figure 7. *Ichaka* 'rattle'

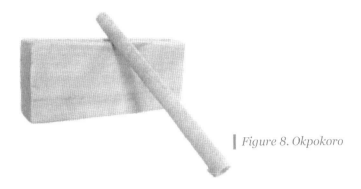

Figure 8. Okpokoro

Whereas some Igbo musical instruments can stand alone as solo instruments played by a master instrumentalist, they collectively play vital roles in dance ensembles as accompaniment to dance and also purely orchestra music (that can also be danced to). According to Onwuka (2012)

> *The roles include the principal (lead or dominant) and communicative, played by the master instruments, supportive (accompanying or subordinate), motivational, ornamental (decorative), indicative and symbolic. (p47)*

This role of the lead instrument is also reflected in the names given to the instruments. For example, *ogene* has the *oke ogene* (letral: male ogene) and *nne ogene* (female ogene), the same with other musical instruments.

Echezona (1964) acknowledges that Igbo musical instruments are not museum pieces. "They are part of the daily lives of the people in Nigeria, Africa." Hence, an ensemble of Igbo musical instruments is better understood from the background of a balanced understanding of the society that owns the music. According to Akpabot in Onwuka (2012, p. 46), "all African orchestras are constituted on the basis of their societal utility, function, gradation of tones, rhythmic colour and symbolism." Within the Igbo culture musical instruments play various roles which may be musical or extra-musical. Igbo musical instruments like the *ogene* are mainly used by town criers for communication, in the sense that once it is played, it summons the attention of the members of a given Igbo community.

Igbo Instruments serve as guide for the community. This role seems to be fading away since most persons find it difficult to decode the message of the *oja, odu, and ekwe* for instance. Instruments like *oja, odu, ekwe* are esoteric in nature and the enjoyment of the music could be for all, but to decode most of the messages, one needs to belong to the masquerade cult or other sacred institutions like the *ozo* cult.

## 3. Some Instrument-Specific Pieces

There are some musical performances that are meant for specific instruments, and not just an ensemble of various musical instruments. In this section we present a few instruments and the pieces that they can be played with.

The first is the *oja*, which like several Igbo musical instruments, can function as speech surrogate. The *ogbu oja* (flutist) can use it to engage in social commentaries. The example below can be used to indicate that there is danger, although the sentence is in the past: *Ebelebe gburu* 'calamity has happened'.

Ebelebe gburu

Scripted by: Gerald Eze

The tune is a melody by a solo *oja* performer to decry evil. It is played just as it is spoken. People may respond to this as they do to *oja* tunes by saying such words as (*eeyi!, ọ ka-emerọ!, ana m anụ!, ebelebe gbukwere!*). A musical response is usually not obtained here. The tune can be played in free rhythm or in any rhythm chosen by the flautist who is a "performer-composer".

The second is the *ụbọaka*, the thumb piano. The tune below is performed with the one octave *Ubo-aka*[5].

Egwu Ubo

Played with the Ubo-aka by: Emmanuel Nwukwor
Scripted by: Gerald Eze

Allegro ♩ = 200

Although the *ụbọaka* is plucked, it is percussive in nature and it adapts to the rhythm of the special drum *ịgba eze* 'the royal drum'. It is especially because of this unconscious association with royalty that Mr. Emmanuel Nwankwo usually sings the following song while playing this tune: *Ịgba na-ekwu, Igba na-ekwuru ndị nwerụ ego* 'the drum is speaking, the drum is speaking for the rich'. Is it not surprising that the singer refers to the *ụbọaka* 'hand piano' as 'drum' here, even though it is plucked with the thumb.

The next instrument is the *ngedegwu/ekeremkpọ/ikeremkpọ* 'xylophone'. The instrument is made of about 5 to 6 woods placed on banana trunks, with the performers facing each other. In some cases, it is

---

[4]Refer to the website: http://acif-igbo.org/
[5]Refer to the website: http://acif-igbo.org/
[6]Refer to the website: http://acif-igbo.org/

played alongside the Igbo *une* 'musical bow', which is an instrument that has almost gone into extinction in Igboland. In Umuchu town of Anambra State, *ekeremkpọ* is used in social activities like *egwu onwa* 'moonlight dance/play'. It is sometimes used in *ilu akụ oyibo* 'throwing of coconuts', which is a festive occasion where young men play games with the coconut and anyone who is able to break more coconuts than others by throwing each one into a dug hole, goes home with lots of coconuts and cheers as reward. A well-known player of *ekeremkpọ* in Umuchu is Mr. Chidi Onuigbo, who is well versed in the cultural role of the instrument, the playing techniques, and the music of the instrument. One of the popular musical tunes played with the instrument is presented below[6]:

## 4. Some Igbo Folk Songs

Folk songs are usually traditional songs of a community or region. Okafor (2017: 17) explains in detail that a folk song is "a composition that has grown with a race or a nation or even a community and whose authorship is enshrined in the midst of antiquity, that is, whose origin is unknown but which can claim community authorship because generations of the race, the community or the nation have grown with it and added to it." However, such songs were not created by "nobody"; instead, they were created by some gifted persons but because of the communal style of living in the African societies, the composers do not claim authorship. Each person in the village is free to interpret the music his or her own way without deviating from the basic nature of the tune. As a result, "...a folk song is never static; it grows in the performance and in re-performance" (Okafor 2017, p. 17).

Igbo folk music comes in various forms and styles, from lullaby to satirical folk songs used to condemn a wrong, but with contextual and community-bound variations. Below are examples some Igbo folk songs.

*Ikpem*

It is a satirical form of folk music realized in Umuchu, a border town between Anambra State and Imo State, but within the present Aguata Local Government Area of Anambra State. The word *Ikpem* has as its root in the verb *ikpe* 'to complain/to judge', which is nominalized as *ikpe* 'judgement', but realized as the critical-cum-satirical folk music *ikpem*, otherwise called *Egwu Ikpem* 'ikpem music'. To perform such satiric songs involves the use of the verb *iṭụ* 'to throw', which gives rise to the form *iṭụ ikpem* with the literal meaning 'to throw ikpem', but the English equivalent of 'to satirize'. Hence, *ikpem* songs involve satire and derision, outright teaching of morals, as well as a means of social control to enhance morality. A good example is *Mgbala* presented below:

| Igbo Text | English Translation |
|---|---|
| Nwa agbọghọ ga ịgba mgbala ya bụrụ ụzọ gbawa di ya. | If a young girl wants to be chivalrous, she should start with her husband. |
| Ọ'ụ kwanọ di wụ mgbala, | It is indeed the husband that is chivalry, |
| di anoghị mgbala adashaịshịa. | if there is no husband, chivalry will be shredded. |
| Oooo, oo ịya, oo ịya, oo ịya. | Oooo, oo iya, oo iya, oo iya. |

Ikpem songs can be performed during recreation, and within this context it would be used as fun and not particularly to deride anyone. It can be performed by a professional group of singers. There are also cases where a group of singers who are usually women and adherents of traditional Igbo religion may go to an offender's house, place of work or any appropriate place to satirize and chastise him or her. Ikpem songs are sometimes created on the spur of the moment by gifted singers within the community to respond to specific urgent issues. Hence, various ceremonies and festivals can be enriched or charged by a spontaneous performance of ikpem music. Another Igbo folk song Akweke Orima, is presented below.

| Igbo Text | English Translation |
|---|---|
| *Akweke orima akweke orima* | Python-egg *orima*, python-egg *orima* |
| *Dorimariri dorima* | *Dorimarimari dorima* |
| *Akweke orima akweke orima* | Python-egg *orima*, python-egg *orima* |
| *Dorimarimari dorima* | *Dorimarimari dorima* |
| *Akweke mụ deberụ n'ọnwa na ahụhị mụ* | Python-egg that I kept there has disappeared |
| *Dorimarimari dorima* | *Dorimarimari dorima* |
| *Akweke mụ deberụ n'ọnwa  na ahụhị mụ* | Python-egg that I kept there has disappeared |
| *Dorimarimari dorima* | *Dorimarimari dorima* |

## 5. Some Igbo Musical Ensemble

There are various Igbo musical ensembles. The instruments in these ensembles are built according to the materials available to the community that own the music. The ensembles can also be created because of the influence of neighboring communities or communities that are encountered through trade and other form of relationships. The ensembles are usually to entertain and edify the members of the community. There are many of such ensembles, but only two will presented here.

*Figure 9. Instruments of the **ogene ensemble***

## Egwu Ogene (Ogene Music)

Egwu ogene is a popular instrumental music. It is usually a male ensemble and consists of the *oke ogene* (lead ogene), *nne ogene* (supporting *ogene*), *ichaka* or *oyo, oja* or *opi, udu,* and *okpokoro*.

The *nne ogene* and the *oke ogene* often operate in call and response pattern. The *ichaka* enriches the texture of the ensemble. The *oja* embellishes the ensemble with tuneful melodies as well as social commentaries. The *oja* can be used to greet a great person in the societ. The sound of *oja* often flows contrapuntally with the singing of the *ogene* boys but most times when the singing stops, the *oja* peels out tuneful melodies and subsides again for the singing to continue. Some groups prefer to use the *oja* while some like *Ogene Mkpakija* of Enugwu Ukwu use *opi*. The *udu* 'pot drum' punctuates the pulse, usually at the strong beats, and also syncopates.

### Igba Mmanwu:

This is another ensemble that is peculiar to the Amiyi area, and does not literally mean "the outing of the masquerades", as it would be in many other Igbo communities. *Igba mmanwu* literally means 'the drum of the *mmanwu*', which involves 'engaging in *mmanwu* performance' at a big arena featuring various types of *mmanwu*. The focus however is on the *mmanwu igba* 'the dancing masquerade'. It is popular in various Igbo communities and still retains its communal purpose and appeal. It is usually a day's event and starts in the late afternoons/ in the evenings.

The *Igba mmanwu* performance is used to mark festive periods, both traditional Igbo festive periods and Christian festivities such as Christmas. It is not done particularly to celebrate Christ, but because many people who live in cities return to the villages during Christmas. Hence, some traditional festivals, which normally take place within other

*Figure 10. A flutist and a masquerade heading for the dance arena for Igba mmanwu*

periods of the year, or would have required some Igbo cosmological considerations to fix their occurrence, are now made to happen because majority of the indigenes are in the villages to celebrate Christmas. Generally, *Igba mmanwu* is a communal theater which however excludes women. It is usually performed at designated village squares and arena.

In Umuchu, the four major instruments usually played for the performance are: *ọja, igba, ọyọ*, and *ogene*. There are of course variations in different towns, like Akpo and Amesi that add *ekwe*, and *udu*. The rhythms of the drum is exactly what the flute plays and this is also what the *mmanwu* dances. So the lead drummer and the flautist will be focused on the *mmanwu* to properly play the tune it has chosen. The dancing *mmanwu* directs the orchestra; it demands for faster rhythm or change in tune by gesturing for such changes. While one *mmanwu* is performing at the centre of the square, every other *mmanwu* usually steps aside or simply keeps quiet. In Umuchu, the only *mmanwu* allowed to stand while the dance is ongoing is the *Ogbuọtụrụgo*, which is the *mmanwu* that is in charge of the arena. It is the only *mmanwu* in the arena that holds cane and it is allowed to flog anybody or another *mmanwụ* who disrupts the flow of the event.

Finally, just as there are variations in the nature of the instruments used for *ịgba mmanwụ*, there are also lots of variations with regard to the nature of the performance and how it is executed in different communities. For example, there could be the presentation of Kola nut, which helps to re-establish or renew the social structure, relationships and communality of the people and the spirit world manifested in the *mmanwụ*. The variety in *Ịgba Mmanwụ* performance is such that each community's *Ịgba Mmanwụ* would always have something peculiar. That is why *Ịgba Mmanwụ* is best experienced than narrated, and the more the varieties experienced, the better[7].

## 6. Conclusion

In conclusion, music is an important part of Igbo life and culture. That is why Igbo music is still very much around, creating and gaining influence. Many studies have been done in various areas of Igbo music to teach the resources as well as to explore the potentials in the music. This chapter is simply an overview of Igbo music based on the experiences of the author, since Igbo music is better experienced than read. It is therefore apt for every student or enthusiast of Igbo music to listen to and utilize the music, even while studying it. Without the experience, the full essence in the music may never be appreciated. "Perhaps the best way to preserve and certainly the best way to present African traditional music is to play it" (Ekwueme 2004: 53). Indeed, several musicians have drawn from the rich resources of Igbo music to create pop and art music. This is a pointer to the fact that Igbo music is there to nourish anybody who seeks it.

---

[7]Refer to the website for some *Ịgba Mmanwụ* performances : http://acif-igbo.org/

# References

Agu, D. C. C. (2011). *Forms and analysis of African music.* (2$^{nd}$ ed.) Enugu: New Generation Books.

Agu, D. C. C. (2017). *Utilizing the power of music in contemporary Nigerian.* Onitsha: Noben Press Ltd.

Ebighgbo, C. (2006). The trumpets-okike, odu-mkpalo, eneke as ethnography in Igbo social commitment. *Nigerian Musicology Journal (NMJ).* 2, 59 – 69.

Echezona, W. (1964). https://journals.sagepub.com/doi/abs/10.2307/3390123

Ekwueme, L. E. N. (2004). *Essays on the theory of African music.* Lagos: Lenaus Publishing Ltd.

Ibekwe, E. U. (2018). *Children's folk songs in Igbo society.* Awka: Fab Education Books.

Muokwunyei, J. N. (2005). Linguistic foundations of African music: The Aniocha Igbo example. *Interlink: A journal of research in music.* 2, 42-51.

Nketia, J. H. K. (1982). *The music of Africa.* Great Britian: R. J. Acford Ltd, Chichester, Sussex.

Nnoli, O. L. (1999). *The culture – history of Umuchu.* Enugu: Nolix Educational Publications Nig.

Okafor, R. C. (2005). *Music in Nigerian society.* (3$^{rd}$ ed.) Enugu: New Generation Books.

Okafor, R. C. (2017). *A study of Igbo folk songs.* Enugu: Academic Publishing Company.

Okoye, C. (2014) *Mbem mmonwu theatre: Igbo poetry of the spirits.* Saarbrucken: Lap Lambert Academic Publishing.

Onwuekwe, A. I. (2011). The socio cultural implications of Nigerian vegetation and production of indigenous musical instruments. *Awka Journal of Research in Music and Arts (AJRMA).* 8, 54 – 65.

Onwuka, U. A. (2012). *A basic text for dance education in Nigeria.* Onitsha: Jenson Publishing Company.

Onyeji, C & Onyeji, E. (2011). A perspective on the philosophy of African Music practice and creativity. *Awka Journal of Research in Music and the Arts (AJRMA).* 8, 19 – 31.

Umeogu, B. U. (2019). *Kolanut in Igbo metaphysics: a phenomernalysical research into its symbolismic universe.* Onitsha: Noben Press Ltd.

Umezinwa, E. C. (2008). *Identity, freedom and logic in Igbo music genres: The resonance of The Metaphysical Essence Undefended (Towards a Philosophy of African Music).* Unpublished dissertation presented to the Department of Music, Nnamdi Azikiwe University, Awka. **L**

NICHOLAS C. AKAS

# Dance In Igbo Culture

## Summary

*Dance is a prominent and integral part of Igbo cultural activities, both in the mundane and in the sacred. This chapter is focused on the nature of dance as an aspect of Igbo culture. It goes into the function and the role of dance, in addition to giving an overview of the different types of dance. Through this, one can begin to recognize the traditional role of dance in Igbo culture. It must also be noted that, so long as many of these traditional practices or ceremonies persist, the dance accompaniment also persist, both of which shall continue to contribute to the resilience of Igbo culture, in spite of the intermittent incursions of the modern hip-hop music. In fact, the deliberate inclusion of some of the Igbo dance steps and movements by some modern Igbo pop musicians definitely adds a cultural flavor to the modern dance but without diminishing or obliterating the cultural mainspring.*

## 1.  Introduction

GENERALLY, THE FACT THAT EVEN A LITTLE BABY CAN SHAKE ITS little body to a rhythm it hears makes one think of the word *dance* as too obvious a phenomenon, almost too 'childish', to need a definition. Nevertheless, there have been several efforts over the years to give an appropriate definition to it. Some scholars see it as mere movement of the body, others as a form of relaxation and exercise, while another group sees it as a mere communal activity. Initially, dance was seen as being just for exercise, entertainment, and body relaxation, but in the course of time research into dance started indicating that there is more to it when choreographed, ranging from cultural identification to expression of ideas, exploration of the self, to cultural identification.

Koff Susan (2012) defines dance as "the sequential explore and learn because it allows for the expression of ideas and images without words." This definition presents the Choreographer as a super communicator with his/her body as the instrument of communication. It is through the styles of manipulating and communicating with the body that the message, theme, and mission are felt by the audience. Every dancer is thus an embodiment of artistic reflections on human wants, desires, and intended achievements. In contrast to this view, William (1996, p. 7) explains dance in the light of its role in the almost prehistoric traditional societies: "The dance of primordial societies gave them source of cultural identification both in their professing myth and life style. At this point, communities' trade, norms and cultural values can be identified through their dance".

Within the Nigerian context, notable Nigerian scholars in dance, have also tried to define dance, but on the basis of social, political, environmental, and religious factors.  Ojo (1994, p. 30) defines it as "rhythmic movement of the body in time and space to make a complete statement based on political happenings and beyond". He argues that every dancer must be able to mirror the situation of things in the country and not just be appreciated as a street entertainer. Simlarly, Udoka (2012, p. 23) defines dance as "The Choreographic reflection of immediate environmental problems through the dancer's body". He maintains that choreographers should not impose other cultural and environmental problems on us; rather, they should always look inwards and make do with own problems. By so doing, we become true ambassadors of ourselves and not that which was imposed on us. To Ugolo (2007, p. 56) dance is the "socio-watchdog that mirrors, both the ruling and the ruled". This shows when those who we elected refuse dialogue, and then art (through dance) becomes another harmless tool to pass the intended message across. There is also a spiritual dimension to dance. This has been aptly captured by Ossie (1994) who explains that

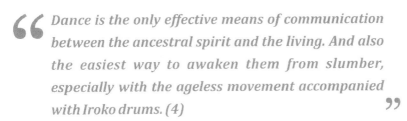

> Dance is the only effective means of communication between the ancestral spirit and the living. And also the easiest way to awaken them from slumber, especially with the ageless movement accompanied with Iroko drums. (4)

Dance in traditional Igbo cosmology is not static; rather it changes based on thematic potency which always centers around the communal mythological belief system. Dance in this context highlights the experiences of the community at any point in time. The experiences could be fully portrayed in the accompanying songs, costumes and movements.

Another relevant point is the communicative potency of traditional Igbo dance. This depends solely on every artistic ointment or design on the body of the dancer that, when interpreted, portrays the choreographer's innermost intentions. Akas (2015, p. 42) observes that "Motifs on the dancer's body teaches social patterns and values, and help the people work, grow, praise or even satire members of the community. The choreographer can express his/her inner thoughts in any form or style, all of which could become manifest through the dancer's body in the form of motifs that often have their origin in the choreographer's experiences, observations, gossip or even ordinary inter-personal interactions with people or his environs. At this point, what he assembles could serve as a lampoon, a mirror or a corrective watchdog.

Finally, although all of the above views of dance apply to various aspects of dance in Igbo land, there is still something unique about every Igbo dance: the cultural undertones, which serve as sources of identification for the different Igbo communities. It is through these that the different types of dance in Igbo land also get their names, because they can often be traced to a particular tribe, village or lineage, and understood as the socio-cultural methodology around its existence. In the next section we shall go into the functions of dance. ⌐

## 2. Types of Igbo Dance

In Igbo land there are different types of dance, and each has a communicative message it passes across. Although their types and functions are explicit from their names, their actual performance involves more than can be expressed in words. Some of the dance types are: ritual dance, social dance, initiation dance, age grade dance, and purification dance. Each is briefly described below.

### 2.1 Ritual Dance

Generally, ritual dance performance is an indispensable communicative tool in Igbo cosmology, where it is believed that ritual activities are made acceptable to the gods through dance and music. In the course of performing some of these rituals, the ritual dance is executed, involving definite kinds of physical movements connected with the particular ritual. According to Omigbule (2017), the dance at a ritual festival

> " *"Serves as a connecting link between the living and the dead. It is through the iconic festival (ritual festivals) that the living seeks for blessing, guidance, and protection from their ancestral fathers in their day to day activities (before, during and after the festival) (Omigbule 2017: 48)* "

The level of spirituality in any ritual performance depends so much on its due process, which is usually in these three-dimensional transformations: Village Dance, Festive Dance and Ritual purification. The *Village Dance* is simply any new dance merely for celebrations such as child-birth, marriage and chieftaincy titles, and coming of age. In village dance, the communicative interpretation of dance is de-emphasized; rather, what matters most are entertainment and aesthetics, body flexibility and mastering of movement pattern in harmony with the particular social event. Every dance at this stage must be able to use environmental factors as its creative metaphor. The *Festive Dance*, though the same as village dance in performance, is different in artistic ideology. The core artistic ideology for such performance is centered around such activities like *iru mgbede* 'coming of age of womanhood', and *ịma mmanwụ* 'initiation into the masquerade cult'. One unique thing about this type of performance is that it is the members are selected and trained seriously for the performance. The major training at this stage is to make them understand the guiding principles of the performance, especially the dos and don'ts. This training earns them the respect of the community as custodians of the truth. Also, the performance during *iri ji* 'New Yam Festivals' and *ịkwa ozu* 'final burial rites' belong to this group of *Festive Dance*.

However, it should be mentioned here that Christianity, Westernization and Globalization have contributed immensely to diminishing the significance and actual performance of ritual dance in Igbo land. Nevertheless, some communities that still value it still stick to it. Some of the rituals involving ritual dance include the following: *Egwu Onwuike* (untimely death), *Egwu Ịkpu Aru* (cleaning of the land), *Egwu Ikpe Azụ* (Dance of Last funeral rites) and Incarnation Dance in Igbo Cosmology. All these ritual dances have a serious communicative value both in their dance movements, when they are performed and why they are performed.

*Egwu Ọnwụuike* (Untimely Death) is a highly dreaded ritual dance in Igbo culture, because is a sign of bad omen. In Igbo land *ọnwụ ike* (untimely) is not acceptable in any form at all. It is believed that the deceased has not completed his assignment before the untimely death and requires serious ritual purification; otherwise, such deaths might keep recurring more into the next generation. There are different types of death that can be classified as *ọnwụ ike* (untimely death) in Igbo land such as: accident, death through any form of poison (including food poison), death in the hands of kidnappers, sleeping and not waking up, death resulting from a fight, and assassination. These types of death are tagged evil death in Igbo custom and must be cleansed with a specialized dance movement, songs and costumes.

The dance movements are not choreographed at times because the deceased age grades are not happy that someone so dear to them died without any form of ailment. So, during the purification dance the age grade can be seen dancing energetic steps with the coffin, which shows the person that passed away was once alive and full of energy. They will run around the village with these energetic movements portraying their anger. But it is important to note that, the dance movement differs at times especially with the case of assassination, or death in the hands of someone or kidnappers. The dance movement involves a circular movement round the coffin with hot drink, knife and utterances of some incarnation. The instruments used during this circular movements are very symbolic. The dry gin hot drink is used to charge the spirit of the deceased to arise and seek for revenge; the knife is placed inside the coffin which the deceased is to use and fight back, while the incantations seek the help of other spirit to assist the deceased in the fight for justice. The circular dance movement is sign of spiritual bond with the death that if he seeks their assistance those alive, he should say it and they will also fight for him.

*Egwu Ikpu Aru* (cleansing Dance) is another symbolic a ritual dance that is performed when some actions and activities are seen s abomination and totally against the norms and values guiding the community. Examples of abominations that would require this type of dance include the following: incest, murder, beating a titled man, theft, and so on. These offences are highly punishable by customary law, while some require purification dances. The style of dance movement here is customized and meanat mainly for those who committed the offence and the lead dancer (chief priest) who is carrying out the act. The offender is expected to be naked and wrapped with palm front and rubbed with *Nzu* 'lime stone'. The lead dancer (chief priest) costumes himself in red cloth which portrays danger. The nakedness on the part of the offender is to indicate remorse and contrition as we all as the desire for forgiveness cum acceptance into the community again. The chief priest dances slowly side by side while flogging the palm front around their body. The chief priest's symbolic movement of side by side signifies three things in purification dance of

*Fig. 1. Iduu Ritual Dance*

Ikpu Aru: to cleanse away such action(s) from the victims, to be sure the remains of such action do not touch the clean members of the community and to ask his *chi* not to allow the aftermath of this particular offence to befall him and his family after the cleansing.

Egwu Ikpe Azụ (Last Funeral rites) is performed after the funeral of a titled man. The dance is believed to be a means of saying farewell to the dead tilted man and also for easy acceptance into the ancestral world. It is believed that any Eze (king) or notable titled chief that did not receive such last funeral dance will keep wandering in the spirit world until such performance is carried out. It is also believed that some of the dead that did not get the Egwu Ikpe Azụ at times continue to cause havoc in the community until the dance is being performed for them. The dance is purely a celebration involving the children, family members, and well-wishers dancing and celebrating the dead. It is often the case that one of the children is costumed like the diseased so as to imitate the walk and dance movements of the diseased as if he were still alive. In such instances, this would mark the climax of the event.

Incantation Dance is mostly used by the chief priest or any other strong person in the community. It is a dance movement used to invoke spirits to join the functions or intercede in serious occasion. This type of dance normally surfaces during power tussle, seeking for truth, and calling out for magical performance. The dance movement is highly reflects the nature of the entity being invoked. For example, those who believe in owu mmiri 'marine spirit' always dance as if they are swimming, while those who believe in mmụọ ikuku 'wind spirit', always use magic to invoke wind and dance in it. Those who believe in fire spirit, always dance like fire destroying things and while those who believe in birds, always dance as though flying in the air.

## 2.2 Social Dance

This type of dance is purely for entertainment, as can be witnessed in various communities during festive periods or occasions. Indigenes perform this type of dance either to express their joy for a life well spent, celebration or for a reunion. In this type of dance, the movement is highly personalized because the dancers are excepted to be expressive in their movements based on how they feel at moment: it is not choreographed. What matters most here is the individualized form of expression in trying to depict their subjective emotions towards the cause of the dance. In this type of dance, there is this believe that the individual dancers are engaged in the struggle to out shine one another in the performance.

*Fig. 2. A Social Dance Group*

There are different types of social dances and why, where/when they are performed in the community. Some of them are: marriage dance, festive dance, worship dance and child birth dance.

*Egwu Igba Nkwu* refers more specifically to the dance performance during *Igba Nkwu* which is the traditional marriage event; but is also includes *Marriage Dance* in general. *Egwu Igba Nkwu* is performed during traditional and white weddings; though the traditional wedding is the more remarkable in terms of dance performance. The man or woman performing the traditional marriage rites is believed to belong to a particular age grade, and members of the age grade are expected to perform on that day. The dance movement is usually well choreographed, based on the vision, mission, and ideology of the age grade. The costumes of the age grade also plays an important role in the whole performance. During the dance movement, the celebrant, who is also a member of the age grade, is expected to perform his/her own dance style. The dance movement is patterned in such a way that everybody is always identified with a particular movement or the generalized choreographed dance movement of the age grade. Some of the dance movements vary; some are fast, slow or stylish, depending on the individual performing at the particular time.

*Egwu Mmemme* 'Festive Dance' is a well-rehearsed performance that is executed during special occasions in rural communities. Such occasions are: during fund raising ceremonies, community dance competitions, Christmas festivities, send forth parties, and welcome parities. The dance movements here are strictly based on what was learnt during the rehearsal process and how it should harmonize with the particular occasion and the audience.

*Worship Dance* is realized in both the traditional and the modern settings. While the modern setting is that of the church, the traditional setting involves the shrines of the particular deities as the case may be. This type of dance requires personal free willed dance movement based on the individual mood and status. Each of the places of worship determines the type of movement to be performed. For example, those in church can dance any movement especially contemporary westernized movement just to express their joy and belief in the Almighty God based on what believes that the Most High has done for him, and in his desire for more. This is slightly different from the traditional worship dance, which involves stylized movements that are not in line with modern dance movements, and with a lot of praise chants thanking their *chi* for guiding and protecting them and seeking for favor. The only difference between the Christian dance in church and the traditional dance at the shrine is that the westernized contemporary movements are not welcome in the traditional sacred groove all in the name of dance.

*Child Birth Dance* is highly celebrated by mother and father, if the child is a boy. It is believed that the arrival of a boy signifies two things: (1) the woman has secured her place in her husband's house and (2) while the man now has his heir. Apart from this attachment to the male child, the arrival of any child is generally celebrated with a dance. In this type of dance movement, everybody is expected to be dance freely, singing and jubilating. White powder is usually shared around on such occasions. It is also remarkable that any person on the road with a lot of white powder around the neck and face must surely be coming from a visit to a home that has a new born child. The sharing of the powder is an indication of the welcome of the new baby with a pure heart.

## 2.3 Initiation Dance

This is one among the sacred dances in Igbo land. It is a unique dance purely meant for a select few, usually people that want to belong to any of the respected groups in their community. Some of the groups include for example, *Ndị Nze na Ọzọ* 'the group/class of the nobles and titled men', *Ndị Eze* 'the Chiefs', *Otu Mmọnwụ* 'the Masquerade cult', and so on. In this type of dance, in addition to their dance movements, costumes are of great significance.

*Fig. 3. Owummiri Initiation Dance*

During the process of initiation, the initiates are in their ordinary clothes or bare bodies while trying to understand the rules and regulations guiding the group. It is in this process that they are taught the dance movements and costumes. Immediately they are initiated, they can dance the peculiar dance of their group and wear the costumes of the group. In some groups the aesthetics or entertainment value of the dance is de-emphasized, because this type of dance is of some spiritual significance and only full initiates can understand the body movements. In addition, the initiates are being presented to the gods in their raw forms for immediate transformation. The initiation dance performance can be in various forms. What matters so much is to understand each initiation process and what it signifies. With that one can appreciate the cosmic totality embedded in initiation dances. Some of the examples of initiation dances are: initiation into masquerading, initiation into titled men/women and initiation into the sacred or occult.

*Egwu Ima Mmanwu* 'Initiation dance into the Masquerade Cult'. The initiates of the masquerade cult are usually a select few who are ready to maintain the secret rules and regulations of the cult. The initiation into the masquerade cult is usually done at night for two reasons: to prepare the initiates in the right frame of mind towards the journey they are about to undertake and present them to gods for cleansing and acceptance. The dance movement seems abstract in nature and always scary because it is believed that at the point of initiation, the initiates seize to be human and become half human and half spirit. So, they are not expected to have a choreographed or patterned movement. This contrasts with some masquerades that have patterned choreographed movement because they perform some entertaining functions. Such masquerades with some entertainment value are: *Adamma* (daughter of beauty), *Police Masquerade, Ugo* (big eagle masquerade), *Izaga* (the tall masquerade), *Nwaanyị Dị Ime* (Pregnant woman masquerade), and other occasional masquerades. The dreaded masquerades that feature because of the terror and dread they spread around them are: *Owumiri* (king of water), *Ajọ Ọfa* (Evil forest), *Anya Nme* (Bloody Eyes), *Akwa Ike* (Cry of danger), and *Abalị* (Night). The initiates in these dreaded masquerades are not expected to have any patterned movement at all because they are no longer human.

*Initiation into Class of Titled Men/Women.* Those who belong to this group must done well in the service of the community. During the initiation the initiates are guided step by steps into the rules and regulation guiding the particular title, especially the dance steps, the costumes, the meeting point, and the byelaws. The dance movements here are strict, and the initiates are not allowed to dance another except the approved one. The dance movement itself can be in various forms: circular (which shows unity), straight line (which shows boldness), and curve (which shows defense). The initiates are allowed to be innovative in their dances but not to westernize it.

*Initiation into the Occult* is where selected few with one like minds decided to form a secret group either for positive or negative reasons. Everything about is structured to be totally different from other publicized groups both in their dressing, singing, shaking of hands and dance movements. The dance movement and songs are structured to suit them in a way that none initiates can understand. They normally perform at times especially when their member dies or is celebrating anything. At their point of performance, none-initiates are not allowed to partake or record their performance, if done it might lead to death or serious spiritual attacks.

## 2.4  Age Grade Dance

This is another unique dance meant for a selected few who belong to a particular age grade. For one to belong to this age grade, he/she must be within a particular age bracket, most often, 40 years and above. It is

*Fig. 4. Iduu Women Age Grade Dance*

another form of social dance; the only difference is that it's not meant for everyone. The dance movements are also well choreographed to suit the vision, mission and ideology of the group. Just as it is in the Initiation dance, costumes are of essence. The essence of costume is to give them a sense of belonging as a group.

## 2.5 Purification Dance

This is a sacred dance in Igbo land and is part of the ritual dance. The lead dancer is usually the chief priest who performs the cleansing or purification. Some of the purification acts could be done to achieve any of the following:

(1) *to break of curse*

(2) *to appease the spirits, especially those causing havoc*

(3) *to take an oath*

(4) *to atone for an evil practice like burying someone alive or killing of the child gotten from incest.*

These types of situations are seen as bad omen that requires urgent attention. The dance movement is not meant for everybody, but strictly for those who committed the atrocities. The performance venues are always designated and the lead dancer is the chief priest. The chief priest is the custodian of the law and is expected to be ready to intercede at any given point. The offenders here are expected to perform the purification dance in the designated arena (such as river and forests) so as not to infect others while been cleansed.

The dance movement is always slow and shows signs of remorse, pleading for the ancestral fathers to forgive them. During the purification dance, the offenders are meant to bring with them various gift items that are supposed to appease the gods to forgive them. The dance of the Chief Priest cannot be compared to any of the already identified dance forms. It usually comes up once in a while, and whenever it does, the person, family or community involved must have committed an abomination. It is believed that if the purification process is not done, the aftermath would be disastrous. During the performance of this purification dance, the chief priest wears a red costume and later changes into white costumes. The two colours have symbolic meanings. The red indicates danger before the cleansing, while the white is to indicate that the purification is successful.

## 3.  Conclusion

Dance in Igbo culture is not restricted to entertainment or the pure display of well-choreographed body movements, but also involves the sacred. Each Igbo community uses its dance to showcase who they are and what they believe in. As a result, this has led to a very fruitful and highly enriching cultural practice, *ibute egwu*, which involves travelling to other Igbo communities to learn their newly

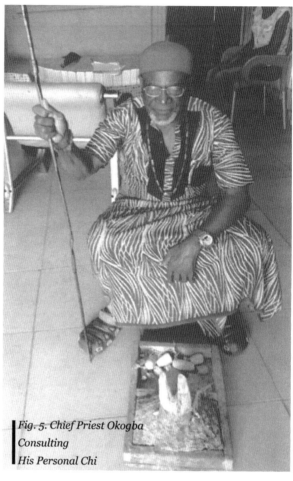

*Fig. 5. Chief Priest Okogba Consulting His Personal Chi*

developed musical instruments and rhythm, as well as the new dance steps accompanying such developments. Hence, every Igbo dance not only has a message, but it also has a history and serves as a source of unification. In choreographing Igbo dance aesthetics are de-emphasized rather socio-communicative values becomes the order of the day, especially in the communities wherever they exist. It is especially this fact that makes dance a very important part of Igbo culture.  ∎

## References

Akas, N. C. (2015). A sociological tool in a child's moral development: dancing master and Uzo as example. *Global Journal of Human Social Science,* 15(2), 38 – 48.

Enekwe, O. (2009). *Theories of dance in Nigeria.* Nsukka: Afa Press Publication. Marcel, D. (2009). *Understanding media semiotic.* London: Hodder Arnold Publication

Omigbule, M. B. (2017). Rethinking African indigenous ritual festivals, interrogating the concept of African ritual drama, *Journal of African Studies Quarterly,* vol 17(3). pp 72-88.

Ojo Bakare (1994). *Rudiments of choreography* Zaria: Zaria Publication. Umarhabila, D.D.(1996). Ritual as dance and dance as ritual: the drama of Kok Nji and other festivals in the religious experience of the Ngas, Mupun and

Mwaghavul in Nigeria, *Journal of ScriptaInstituti Donneriani Aboensis,* Vol 16(1). pp 28-27

Ugolo, C. (2006). Dance documentation and preservation in Nigeria. In *Yerima,* A., Rasaki, B., & Udoka, A. (Eds.), *Critical perspective on dance in Nigeria* (pp. 56-63). Ibadan:Kraft Books Ltd.

Udoka Arnold (2016): *Dances of Africa: from lived experience to entertainment.* Ibadan: Kraft books.

Koff Susan (2012): Professionalism in dance education, *Journal Research in Dance Education,* Vol13 (no1)

Purcell, P. (1994). *Man and dance.* London: University of London press.

Willam Gerritsen (2017). *The sun dance of the Shoshone Bannock.* London: University London press.

# Part Four

# IGBO MENTALITY

# Onye Aghana Nwanne Ya Mentality Among The Igbo

1. Introduction
2. Mentality and the Igbo Cosmogram
3. The *Onye aghana nwanne ya* maxim
4. The Practical Applications of *Onye aghana nwanne ya*
5. *Onye aghana nwanne ya* within the Nigerian Context
6. Conclusion

## Summary

The Igbo's existential orientation, which characteristically builds a pervasive strong social support systems, is captured in the exhortative maxim **Onye Aghana Nwanne Ya** 'no one should abandon/leave behind a relation'. This is not just an aphorism but also a mentality, since 'mentality' stands for a characteristic way of thinking of a person or a group that describes the attitudes that define their personality and social interactions. **Onye aghana nwanne ya**, is like a pervasive call to the Igbo not to abandon one another, but to take care of one another in every circumstance. It motivates helpful and protective behaviour, as well as pro-social engagements among the Igbo. Hence, it has been perceived as the bedrock of the Igbo collective strength, business successes, and near uncanny ability to surmount seemingly intractable environmental obstacles to survival. This existential orientation is anchored on the triangular cosmogram of the endocosmos, the mesocosmos, and the exocosmos, which are the three different levels at which harmony or harmonious relationships significantly affect social behaviour. Although religious denominationalism seems to be cracking the walls of the **onye aghana nwanne ya** mentality, it is still very relevant as a 'cognitive force' for effective group mobilization towards societal development.

## 1. Introduction

**A**T THE HEART OF THE IGBO WAY OF LIFE IS THE BELIEF IN the unseen Almighty God: *Chi ukwu* 'the great Chi' (written as *Chukwu*), the omnipotent, omniscient and omnipresent Being that created all things and has the power of infinite discretion, though benevolent. This *Chi-Ukwu* must be obeyed to be able to enjoy His protection and benevolence. Accordingly, the chief characteristics of Igbo could be located around the injunctions of this God among which are: honesty, hard work, respectful exploitation of natural resources, family, and care for others (altruism). This belief and associated values translate to rendering support to humans and taking care of one another's needs, hence the description of the Igbo as partly communist in orientation. It is within this orientation that *Onye aghana nwanne ya* is anchored.

For the rest of this chapter, we shall adopt the methodical approach of first introducing and discussing the concepts of mentality and the *onye aghane nwanne ya* in the Igbo person's cosmos. This shall be followed by an exploration of a possible theoretical origin of *onye aghana nwanne ya*, to be rounded off with some practical aspects of this mentality.  ▪

## 2. Mentality and the Igbo Cosmogram

The concepts, mentality and the person's cosmos, interrelate to the extent that an attitudinal disposition could be related to a certain personal existential orientation, which for the Igbo seems to be captured in the maxim, *Onye Aghana Nwanne Ya.*

### 2.1 Mentality

Mentality means a characteristic way of thinking of a person or group. The word could be used in relation to particular issues or behaviour as well as in a broad sense that describes attitudes which define a person's personality or social interactions. An attitude is not an observable entity, it is an underlying construct that must be inferred, and it possesses three central characteristics of always having an object, being usually evaluative, and relatively enduring. Krech, Crutchfield, and Ballachey's (1962) definition of attitude as an enduring system of positive or negative evaluations, emotional feelings and pro and con (action tendencies) with respect to a social object, are in tandem with Myers (2006 p. 36) explanation of attitude as a favourable or unfavourable evaluative reaction towards something or someone, exhibited in ones beliefs, feelings or intended behavior. Hence, *onye aghana nwanne ya* amongst the Igbo is also a mentality, because it also represents a set of related attitudes that underlie a range of social actions and reactions.

## 2.2 Igbo Cosmogram

According to Ebigbo (2017, p. 22), the world of the individual is his *cosmos*, which has three aspects: the *endocosmos*, the *mesocosmos*, and the *exocosmos*.

The *endocosmos* is the biophysical and the first level. It represents the biological self and how one reacts to internal stimuli, one's personality, self-concept, and intuition regarding one's own and other's mental states. It envelops how beliefs and mental states/mind govern behaviour. The second level, the *mesocosmos*, is the bio-psycho-social component of the individual's world, which is contained in the interactions with the physical and social environment. It involves all relationships within the ecosystem; it is at this level that the consciousness of the significance of others becomes imperative. The Igbo understand the need for, and practically builds rewarding relationships across the levels of their operations. This is fostered by various initiation/introduction rituals/ceremonies into family, peer (age grade), or community meeting groups and titles. These groups represent significant agents in members' lives, because each member expects trust relationships and welfare benefits as in a brotherhood (*nwanne* 'sibling' (literal: 'mother's child')/

*umunne* 'siblings' (literal: 'mother's children'.)

The *exocosmos* is the third aspect of the Igbo person's cosmos. Here we have the spiritual components of the individual's world: the ancestors (ancestral spirits), deities, sacred elements, and of course, the Supreme Being (*Chi-Ukwu*/God). The important thing to note is that each phenomenon at the exocosmos is a powerful determinant of conscious behaviour at both inter personal and inter group levels, since this embodies the mores, myths, legends and the mystic. It is within the context of this embodiment that brotherhood is further strengthened since people who share the same ancestral beings are bonded accordingly, much like those who honour the same deity are strongly bonded by the values attached to the deity. In practical terms, they become *umunne*: the Deity being the 'exocosmic mother/parent figure'.

It is based on the above conviction that Ebigbo (1995) formulated the *Harmony Restoration Therapy* and observed that disharmony in any of these aspects of the individual's cosmos would lead to maladaptive behaviour. According to him, abarticulation of strings of bonds occasioned by negative actions that may include non-compliance with expected pattern of interaction (unethical responses) may lead to problematic emotional states and behaviour. This paraphrased means that hurting the *nwanne* bond by violating norms at any level has unpleasant consequences that are commensurate to the size of the violation. In effect, the bond must be regarded... relations should care for one another. Hence: *Onye aghana nwanne ya*!

## 3.   The *Onye Aghana Nwanne Ya* Maxim

### 3.1  The Meaning of the Maxim

Literal translation of *Onye agha na nwanne ya* is 'let no one leave behind/abandon his/her sibling', which means that everyone should 'carry the sibling along'. It is a maxim among Igbo, a commonly accepted rule for sensible community life that fosters the brotherhood/fraternal feelings among the people. *Onye aghana nwanne ya* is one maxim that is pervasive and applicable at various levels: intimate family, extended family, peer groups, village, community, and national level. This is so because *nwanne* 'sibling (literal: mother's child)' has the applicable meaning relevant to the mother in context: biological, ancestral or even mother deity. Among Igbo, *nwanne* was ranked as an inestimable value; such that many parents had to name their children *Nwanneka* 'sibling is the greatest', perhaps as a constant reminder of the irreplaceable place of siblings in each other's lives, since no value could be of comparable 'price'. Indeed, a common saying that '*ozu sibe isi, enyi ka nwanne anaa*' (literal: when a corpse starts smelling, even the person who is a closer friend than the sibling absconds) i.e. decaying dead bodies do not have friends, only friends do abscond at extremely difficult times, but family never does).

The point being stressed here is that there are shared relationships at various levels, hence it is common for an Igbo person to call another *Nwannem* (standard orthography: *nwanne m* 'my sibling' (literal: "my mother's Child") in all sincerity. We must note that *Nwanne m* 'my mother's child' and *Nwanne anyị* 'our sibling' (literal: "our mother's child") are not exactly the same. The first person singular pronoun, *m,* in the first form is used more often to indicate that the relationship is at the endocosmic (immediate family) level, while the first person plural pronoun, *anyị*, connotes the 'larger families'. Also, *Nne m* means 'my mother', while *Nwa nne m* 'my mother's child. Hence this 'mother' could be the mother deity or the ancestral mother.

The Igbo are unequivocally convinced that they all originated from the first homosapiens to inhabit this part of the earth. This position was subscribed to by a foremost traditional institution in Nigeria: The Ooni of Ife, Oba Adeleye Ogunwusi, who during the 2019 Aje festival stated categorically that the Igbo are among the oldest peoples of the world, the first to discover prosperity and wealth from Divinity, and how to nurture and celebrate same[8]. He also attested that the Igbo have close affinity and possible consanguineous relationship with some present day Yorubas, lived along side Yorubas in prehistoric times, but moved eastwards due to their enterprising prowess. On the obvious similarity between the cultures of the Igbo and Jews of Israel, this revered source holds that the Igbo are the progenitors of Israel, arguing that the Igbo race is 'way older' than the Jew. A contrary view has been expressed by another Yoruba Oba, Oba Fredrick Akinruntan, the Olugbo of Ugbo, who sees the explanation as an attempt to rewrite the history of the Yorubas[9]. In spite of such disagreements, Oba Ogunwusi's statement seems to be fully in line with the growing tendency towards a rapprochement between the different ethnic nationalities of southern Nigeria based on perceived century old cultural relationships. With regard to the postulated connection between the Igbo and the Jews of Israel, the resilience and ingenuity of both groups, and the attachment style and group strength are the expression of the *Onye aghana nwanne ya* attitude.

## 3.2 The Theoretical Underpinnings of the Maxim

As implied in the paragraph above, human behaviour and thought processes have been evolving since creation (Igbo believe that *Chineke*, the *Chi Ukwu*, is the creator of all natural things, including humans). However, in agreement with evolutionary theorists and scientists, even human cell morphological advancement is deemed to have been largely due to the impact of environmental factors that engineer adjustments requisite for survival. Indeed, Darwin's theories of evolution captured in the aphorisms of natural selection and survival of the fittest aptly show that for a species (in this case a race or nation) to survive in an ecosystem (geographical or social environment), the species must develop both biological features and response patterns that confer advantage on it over competing members of the ecosystem.

Being an aboriginal race, it is indubitable that the Igbo were faced with very daunting environmental challenges, and had to eke out solutions in successive generations. Thus each successive generation became an improved nation/race: more intelligent, more resilient, more adventurous, and with improved quantity and quality of brain cells and experience. In a sentence, each generation became better developed both in biological and psycho-social apparatuses that enhance survival and proper adjustment in their ecosystem. We imply that at the centre of the astonishing ability for positive adjustments to multiple environments by the Igbo is the *Onye aghana nwanne ya* maxim which confers friendly disposition that engendered approach behaviour among other peoples they came in contact with. ◼

---

[8] https://www.thenigerianvoice.com/news/275814/the-ooni-of-ife-confirms-the-jews-are-from-igboland.html
[9] https://guardian.ng/news/yorubas-have-no-ancestral-link-with-igbo-olugbo-tells-ooni/

## 4. The Practical Applications of *Onye Aghana Nwanne Ya*

A major characteristic of the Igbo as mentioned above is the near uncanny ability to 'conquer' environmental obstacles to survival, and even turn some possibly negative factors to their own advantage hence they operate profitably in environments that many other races would not dare. An obvious source of this strength resides in the maxim under discussion. The Igbo across developmental stages already know that self-preservation is akin to security: these two words could be said to be the 'nearest' in meaning to every true 'son of the soil'. Consequently, since it is given that security in all its connotations and perspectives is the whole goal of humans, we shall hinge further discussions on it.

### 4.1    Onye aghana nwanne ya as a Maxim for security of lives and prosperity

Okoye (2020) contemplated that *onye aghana nwanne ya* (or its derivative) is a near everyday slogan among Igbo that dates back to prehistoric times in Awka South area of Anambra State. He opines that it's frequently spoken variety around Awka and Nibo towns is *Ọnụlụnụ kaalụ ibe ya* (he who hears should tell the next person/share with another person the information you have received). Accordingly, every citizen is duty bound to disseminate information regarding community security, rules, actions, presence of strangers, and any threat or even emerging events. It follows that it is a civic responsibility among Igbo to carry everyone along:  no one should be left in the dark regarding emerging events and issues in the community, including outbreak of diseases. In this regard, one calls to mind that such 'slogans' were used by the Radio Biafra during the Nigerian Civil War to remind the citizens regularly to be vigilant and stick together.

It should also be stated here that this security maxim applies at all social levels: the nuclear and extended family, the village and town, and the Igbo nation. The motivation is 'preservation of the species'. It is a primitive and subsisting belief among Igbo that a formidable threat to one person's life is a threat to 'his brother': Family members, community members or another National. It is in this connection that the common saying *oru fulu ka e ji mbazu eni ibe ya malukwa na o ga-adi ya otu ahu otu ubochi* (a slave that sees another slave being buried should realize that it shall soon be his/her turn) is a concomitant expression to *onye aghana nwanne ya*. It is meant to activate the passion to defend one another against threats to life and property. People are thus 'engineered' to protect one another at both individual and group levels. By this maxim also, it is expected that no citizen should be a part of any conspiracy to harm another, and no citizen should keep silent or conceal information regarding threat to another's life or property to which he/she is privy, else, both the perpetrator and the conspirator or indolent are treated as criminals and are punished accordingly. Hence, the saying: *Ogbalu nkiti kwelu ekwe* ('He who is silent is in agreement' => silence is consent/agreement/reinforcement).

Finally, *igwe bu ike* ('the mass (of people) is the strength' => unity in strength/together we conquer/united we stand and divided we fall) is another concomitant saying to *onye aghana nwanne ya* just as *ibu anyi danda* 'with enough hands, every weight could be lifted'. However, it is taken for granted by the Igbo that the hands must be willing and potent, and must work in synergy to be effective in achieving the desired goals and aspirations of a secure and peaceful society.

## 4.2 Onye Aghana Nwanne Ya as a Paradigm for Peaceful Cohabitation

Food, food security, cohabitation and health are four intertwined factors that are also motivated by the spirit of *onye aghana nwanne ya* as a driving force amongst the Igbo.

Igbo do realize that physical security of lives and property is not possible except within an atmosphere of peace. They also hold firmly that *aguu bu ọya* 'hunger is disease', and that *agụụ na-akpasa uche* 'hunger breeds confusion/cogitative insufficiency', and of course that a hungry man is an angry man. Hunger is therefore treated as a dire 'enemy' by Igbo hence the serious investment in the discovery of uncountable number of dishes from available agricultural products, which explains partly the array of rich dishes in Igboland. This achievement must be a resultant of the onye aghana nwanne ya mentality, which is here paraphrased to *onye rie, ya nye nwanne ya* 'as you eat, you share with your siblings/person', since he who eats alone dies miserably.

Highly educative is the following traditional practice which is also a fall out of the *onye aghana nwanne ya* maxim: traditionally eating together. In the past, the Igbo freely ate from one another's bowls and no child of those days ever lacked food except there was no food at all in the entire neighbourhood... a very unlikely event except during wars. Furthermore, in many Igbo communities certain crops may be plucked and eaten by hungry passersby and it was a not crime, just like some farm products may be taken by neighbours without permission yet they were not reprimanded. However only the rightful owners of these crops or products could harvest more than a meal quantity or sell any quantity. People were only punished in accordance with extant rules and regarded as misfits if they failed to contribute anything at all to the community but kept plundering other person's farms.

It is pertinent to note that in traditional Igboland, servants naturally ate from the same pots (and the same meals) with their masters. Even a paid labourer was entitled to at least a meal during work hours. It is also considered as ill-mannered of an Igbo person to be on table while someone plays the spectator without requesting the company of such a person. The expectation is the compulsory greeting: *Bia, ka anyi rie nri* 'Come, let us eat'. Interestingly, this is also one of the very first sentences that neonates usually learn in Igbo. This Author readily recalls an occasion he was punished by his mother for refusing to share his *akara* 'bean cake' with two of his younger siblings "because they had taken their own while he was still busy with chores so should not take double portions". He was taught that under no circumstance should one refuse to share one's food with one's *nwanne* 'siblings'. It was *njo* 'sin'! Indeed, the *onye aghana nwanne ya* served as a cultural paradigm for the eradication of hunger (and perhaps meaningful anger control).

From the foregoing, it is evident that with the maxim internalized by everyone, food security was almost assured. Again, the practice of co-operative farming, which was commonplace in those days, was also another extension of the *onye aghana nwanne ya* maxim. Men and women organized themselves in groups (friends or families) that enabled cultivation of large farmlands. Although in some arrangements merchant traders had to hire labour, the  major practice was for the 'group farmers' to cultivate one another's farm land in rotation: *Ummunne* worked for each other so no payments were made except for provision of food and drinks by the host. Thus, the average person in the village never complained about inability to cultivate his crops due to cash squeeze: every citizen thus had some kind of investment in his name.

Another form of co-operation was in cases where people who had much of seedlings but inadequate land mass had to exchange seedlings to lease portions of land. Igbo were therefore organized into a win – win situation except for persons with psychological or physical decrepitude, which number must have been very insignificant. It is important to note here that even to this day; land constitutes a great asset to the Igbo. Igbo in most non-urban communities still preserve common heritage of large land areas: this most important economic resource must not be taken over by a few, rather, by communal management, equal access is therefore guaranteed for all. This must be a part of the reasons why no Igbo man or woman was programmed for poverty. The level of poverty being experienced by some Igbo at which meals are jumped, and people are virtually homeless and hopeless, has not been known among Igbo if not in the Nigerian context. The Igbo' natural craving for landed property as a major achievement even up to this moment and in whichever settlement form they find themselves, must be rooted in the *onye aghana nwanne ya* maxim: they settle down where they achieve a certain level of economic independence, but within the in-group inter dependence.

Akin to hunger as a security factor is health care. Among the Igbo, the most revered 'prayer episode' is done in the context of *kolanut* ceremonies, and some of the words that no elder ever missed when he raised the *kolanut* are some of these expressions: *Ndu!* 'Life!', *Onye wetelu ọjị wetelu ndụ.* 'He who brings kolanut brings life.', *Ndu na arụike* 'life and good health'... and so on. The prayer for good health points to the fundamental place of healthy living in the continued existence of the race and it's direct bearing on economic and physical security. Indeed, health care in those days occupied a central place in the exocosmic forces in the well-being of the people. The strongest support to the traditional Igbo health care system, which is anchored in the spirit of *onye aghana nwanne ya*, is that Igbo traditional, medical and surgical treatments were not commercialized. Instead, herbalists and orthopedic practitioners seemed programmed or anointed to serve the people selflessly. Skills were transferred within families as if they were genetically engineered and, in overwhelming number of cases, they do not give bills for their services; rather, the patients' families were required to express gratitude in concrete terms that are commensurate with the condition treated, and in tandem with their economic status. This approach is a form of social security that is anchored on the *onye aghana nwanne ya* maxim, because it achieves a social balance through a form of redistribution of resources whereby the rich, through their greater remuneration, contribute to the health and wellbeing of the poor. This is an in-built health insurance system that was not readily corruptible. People had near equal access to health, so poverty was not a determinant factor for the access. Nonetheless, in cases of disharmony at the exocosmic level wherein sacrifices may be required to appease the spirits, elements for such sacrifices were required of the patient or family concerned.

Finally, in spite of the above positive impact of the *onye aghana nwanne ya* maxim on the traditional and modern Igbo societies, there is also a negative aspect. This could involve dragging along the ụmụnne 'siblings' on the way downwards, the same way that the positive aspect of the maxim involves not forgetting to take along the ụmụnne on the way forward. As a result, families can be stigmatized in any ungodly event, misconduct, crime, or inefficiency in role performance, because of the conduct of one member of the family. A check on this negative aspect of the maxim is the tradition of mentoring and empowerment, which is the subject of the next section.

## 4.3 Onye Aghana Nwanne Ya as the Nucleus of Mentoring and Empowerment

Mentoring is a fundamental form of human development where one person invests time, energy and personal know-how in assisting the growth and ability of another person. Thus, mentoring is a process that always involves communication and is relationship based: between the "mentor" and the "mentee.". The mentor passes on valuable skills, knowledge and insights to the mentees, to help them develop their career. Mentoring can help the mentees feel more confident and self-supporting, and develop a clearer sense of what they want in their careers and their personal lives. In terms of the impact on the group, it expands the group's skills base, helps to build strong teams, and can form part of a well-articulated plan for succession. Through their deeds and work, mentors help people to move toward the actualization of their potentials. They develop greater self-awareness and see the world and themselves, as others do (Ehigie, 2014). Mentoring has a unique place in the traditional life of the Igbo, for it is highly pervasive in all aspects of

Igbo tradition and culture, and it is firmly connected with empowerment, which aligns more with 'allowance and dispensation'. The mentor not only takes the mentee through the skills acquisition process, but he also initiates her/him into the pertinent attitudinal requirements for actualization of goals, and to dispensation because the Igbo mentee receives allocation of sufficient implements to move on as an independent entrepreneur. It is often said that the kind of mentoring relationship indigenous to Igbo is unique and positive. In fact, mentees already set free do remain under close watch of the mentors until they become fully established and have mentees under themselves. This paradigm will be illustrated below using the most popular field of excellence among Igbo, which is commerce.

The first is Dr. Chike Nwankwo's tale of the post war experience by *Nanka* people who migrated to Lagos soon after the war in 1970. Theirs is a practical example of the *onye aghana nwanne ya* maxim. The narrative in Nanka village is that Chike Nwankwo was among the first Igbo who found their way back to Lagos through a tortuous journey. He was able to get a low class accommodation within a few months and settled down for business. His fluency in Yoruba language facilitated his fast adjustment, hence he was able to secure a big shop in which he sold every available legal item. He took in several young men from his community in the months that followed: many Nanka families sent their children to him only on the recognition of his being 'from Nanka' … not anything more! Another similar story that is still being narrated in Nanka village up to the present is that of a public servant popularly called Ezeliora, who provided shelter and guidance to everyone said to have come from Nanka. I do not intend to enumerate the steps such people from across Igbo land took to mentor others in their hundreds, however, it suffices to add here that most of the people they mentored had no immediate family relationships with them, and that they (the mentors) gave them equal opportunities within the same business arena. In no time, each person so treated had to replicate his training, at least to members of his extended family, hence in the years that followed, Nanka people became popular and dominated the building materials and electronic trade.

This narrative is similar for most communities in Igboland: *Oraukwu* and *Alor* communities for instance, came to be known for fabrics business (Abada/Wax), *Awka* for metal works and *Agulu* for confectionary and general goods. It is commonplace information that the first most successful transporter in West Africa was the late Sir Odumegwu Ojukwu of Nnewi. Sir Odumegwu did not only engage young men of same origin as employees, he mentored them into the business and helped them mature into independent businessmen transporters; hence, many later day transport moguls, including *Ekenedilichukwu* and *Izuchukwu* transport companies, were products of this mentoring.

This mentorship paradigm persists in modern day Igbo business tradition: the culture of bringing up young ones in their mentor's line of business. Everyone who receives training and empowerment replicates the same for others. The mentee in most cases is absorbed into the mentor's family so that it is not only the business strategies that are learnt but 'home keeping' and other manner of responses that impress positive adjustment to the ecosystem as an independent, successful Igbo person. In this way, at the point of completion of the mentorship period, when the mentee is usually given reasonable capital for take-off, the likelihood of success is already pre-programmed.

Finally, this mentorship paradigm is peculiar to Igbo and is a factor in the Igbo cosmos. It marks the Igbo as a people who have a high sense of self-efficacy and an overall higher-order understanding of the complexity of the cycles of wealth; they can look beyond the seeming gains of selfishness and monopoly. Only a people who are innovation driven and can see co-operation within competition can practice this level of mentorship.

## 5.   *Onye Aghana Nwanne Ya* Within The Nigerian Context

Prior to the amalgamation of Northern and Southern Nigeria, Igbo were residing in all parts of the North and South, as well as in other parts of Africa where they worked with, and for, their hosts in commerce especially, but also in shaping society for good. In many parts of Nigeria, even post amalgamation, they contributed immensely to the development of the places. They integrated themselves in their host communities and mentored those who were willing to accept their pattern of business life. Driven by the maxim and attitude under discussion, Igbo usually increased progressively in any place, area, or trade they got into, hence their positive activities become consequential sooner than later. This also played out in the Nigerian political arena in which Igbo initially formed a formidable pro-democracy group.

Igbo were the most widely spread breed within the geographical space of Nigeria, thanks to *onye aghana nwanne ya*! It was also the maxim that motivated the Igbo during the Nigerian hostilities to attempt to become independent. For example, it was not the plan of the Igbo to go to war or to become independent: these were forced on them by the genocide against them which up to the present time remains unjustifiable. That is fact of history. Although the political influence of the Igbo has been significantly watered down by the combined craft of the former Colonial Master and the Northern Nigerian oligarchy, this Author is of the view that the little that is still left of the political and economic relevance of the Igbo is the product of the *onye aghana nwanne ya* maxim.

Finally, the remnants of the *onye aghana nwanne ya* orientation is currently serious threat from various quarters, way beyond what it had experienced in the past. The first is the threat of pretentious, self-serving and most dangerously colonized indigenous religious leaders and their

Machiavellian unscrupulousness. The psychological effect of this group on the followers is their holier than thou affectation through which some now prefer to identify themselves as Catholics, Pentecostals, or Anglicans, for political gains; instead of emphasizing God's endowment that strengthens and preserves them as a people. That is why Okoye (2007) sees Anambra State, with its religious pretensions, as a state that is sitting on a keg of gunpowder. The second and more devastating threat is political prostitution and corruption, both of which have been seriously undermining the selfless orientation of the age-long tradition of community self-help of the *onye aghana nwanne ya* spirit. It is in recognition of these negative effects that effort is being made once again to reinvigorate the *Association of South East Town Unions* (ASETU), which is a union of many town unions that immensely contributed to the development of their various communities before, during and immediately after the Civil War. Even this recent effort is in itself a manifestation of the *onye aghana nwanne ya* spirit, inviting one's siblings to go back to the original orientation that contributed to the growth and development of Igbo land.

## 6. Conclusion

*Onye agha na Nwanne Ya* is a mentality, a behavioural set and an aphorism among Igbo which dates back to the earliest days of the Nationality. As a mentality, it describes the peculiarity of the Igbo's mind set regarding how to feel, think about, and act or react towards one another. It embodies feelings that are consistent with liking and admiration; thoughts that are consistent with understanding, constructive reasoning and unbiased appraisal of one another's words and deeds, and actions or reactions that are consistent with synergic application of resources and positive approach behaviour. The attendant behaviour is usually with the intention to render assistance to the needy at the point in time, to alleviate suffering, to prevent hardship, and indeed to improve wellbeing of one another in various domains of security (food, health, physical and social security). Being a primordial aphorism, this maxim finds significant attachment to every mother figure at all existential levels of the Igbo cosmogram. It is therefore a very potent force that ignites and sustains group action in every situation, especially when group mobilization is desired. In spite of the fact that acculturation and political prostitution and corruption are threatening the potency of this aphorism, one is persuaded to see *onye aghana nwanne ya* as an enduring song from the heart of the Igbo Nation. ■

### References

Ebigbo, P. O. (1995). Harmony restoration therapy: An African contribution to Psychotherapy. Being an invited paper to the annual scientific meeting of The royal college of psychiatrists, Riviera Centre, England.

Ehigie, B.O. (2014). Mentoring and Academic development. In Obi-Nwosu, H. & Ajaelu, C. (eds) Mentoring and academic development. Awka: SCOA Heritage.

Krech, D., Crutchfield, R., and Ballachey, E.

(1962). "Individual in society". New York; McGraw.Hill.

Myers, D., G.,(2006)." Social psychology". New Delhi; Tata McGraw-Hill.

Newcomb, T.M., Turner, R., and Converse, P. (1965)." Social psychology". New york; Holt.

Nwankwo, C. (2020). Family day talk rendered at the Chapel of Redemption, Nnamdi Azikiwe University, Awka, (June 14). Unpublished paper.

Okoye, I, 'k. (2007). The 2007 desiderata. Awka: Mecury Press ■

# CHAPTER 15

OKEY IKECHUKWU

# E Kere Ọrụ Eke

## Summary

*This chapter is focused on the Igbo saying **E kere oru eke**, whose English equivalent is "there is division of labour". The saying is traditionally an anchor point for the assignment of responsibilities within the Igbo World, an almost unconscious guiding principle. It is a concept that finds expression in the functioning of the family, in interpersonal relationships, arts and craft, societal role-play, and in leadership and followership. It is like the lubricant that smoothens the functioning of the Igbo society and gives it its republican-egalitarian character. Although modern day crass materialism is strongly gnawing at the root of this concept in the psyche of modern Igbo society as it battles for survival in the present day Nigeria, it nevertheless intermittently emerges when issues of rightful assignment of responsibilities and duties are to be resolved. This single fact not only confirms the continued existence of this concept, but also the fact that it belongs to those core values that should be upheld in the resuscitation of Igbo traditional values.*

## 1. Introduction

**T**HE IGBO EXPRESSION *Ẹ KERE ỌRỤ EKE* IS A SIMPLE declarative sentence whose beneficial effect is like that of an engine oil that lubricates and smoothens the functioning of the machinery of the Igbo society. This section first explains the makeup of the expression as a language structure, before introducing some of the issues connected with it that shall be presented in the subsequent sections of the paper.

First of all, the expression *Ẹ kere ọrụ eke* can be broken down as follows:

| Ẹ | kere | ọrụ | eke |
|---|------|-----|-----|
| 'someone(indefinite)' | 'divided' | 'work/labour' | 'divide' |

The literal translation is 'Someone divided work divide', but the appropriate English equivalent is 'There is division of labour'. The essence of the expression goes back to the Igbo verbal structure *ike ọrụ*, made up of the verb *ike* 'to divide' and the noun *ọrụ* 'work/labour'. The activity of *ike ọrụ* involves the assignment and allotment of tasks based on the principle that not everyone may carry out every available task. The concept of *ike ọrụ* as a guiding principle comes from the underlying idea in the Igbo world that tasks and responsibilities are usually assigned to people based on their skills, both natural and acquired, gender, background, general inclinations, temperament, and ability to manage situations or challenges. This includes their understanding of standards of propriety in the society. That is why in Igbo culture[1], for example, a woman does not climb a palm tree at all, not to talk of cutting a palm head or tapping palm wine from the tree.

In contrast to the order and sense of propriety in *ike ọrụ* is the concept of *ịzọ ọrụ* 'to grab at tasks/jobs' or *ịlụ ọgụ ọrụ* 'to fight/struggle over tasks/roles'. The latter refers to role usurpation and the desperate determination to take on tasks and responsibilities for which one may not be well suited. The attitude of *ịzọ ọrụ* or *ịlụ ọgụ ọrụ* engenders a disregard for Rules of Engagement in any particular endeavour, or a disposition to act with impunity and impose one's will, and impropriety and undue self-inflation the standard for determining right and wrong. However, such impropriety is checked by the declarative saying: *Udene na Egbe anaghi azọ nri*[2] 'the kite and the vulture do not fight over food'. Because the vulture is a scavenger, it does not have the instincts and nature of the kite, which is a predator. It often has tattered feathers and an overall ambience that is without dignity. So, the saying urges self-respecting individuals not to demean themselves by grabbing at or fighting over roles and thereby competing below their level.

The subsequent sections of this chapter use this concept of *E kere ọrụ eke* to throw light on various issues and activities in Igbo society, thereby highlighting the traditionally positive impact of the saying, but also laying bare the opposing negative modern undercurrents that are now converging as a flood. These two trends can be confirmed in the breaking of kola nut, in the new-found and wrong understanding of the concept of *Igbo enwe eze*, in the manifestation of charlatans and heroes in present day Igbo society, and in the role of the Igbo person in present day Nigerian politics.                                                              ∎

## 2.   E kere ọrụ eke in the Kola nut Ceremony

The kola nut ceremony, or the breaking of the kola nut before every occasion, is a well-known practice in Igbo land. In addition to the fact that not every kind of kola nut is used for the kola nut breaking ceremony, it is also not everyone that is deemed qualified to break the kola nut for others to eat. Why? Because E kere ọrụ eke! There is a traditional division of labour, both in the plant species itself and in the ceremony of breaking it.

With regard to the plant species, it is the purple coloured species, usually called ọji Igbo (Igbo kola nut), that is used for all Igbo traditional ceremonies, and not the cream coloured species which is called gworo or ọjị Awụsa (Hausa kola nut). The two designations are merely of geographical significance in terms of their origin, and nothing more. The purple coloured species is used because it is the predominant traditional species in Eastern Nigeria. As a result, it had always been the traditional kola nut the people have been used to for many generations. Any other species was therefore unusual, and even deemed inappropriate, for the traditional kola nut ceremony. Meanwhile, both species can otherwise be eaten for the purely biological effect they have in common, for example to keep one awake.

The kola nut ceremony itself is divided into two parts, namely, the kola nut prayer or toast and the breaking of the kola nut itself. Both activities might or might not be carried out by one and the same person. In most parts of Igbo land, for example, the oldest or a titled man says the toast and also breaks the kola nut. Some believe that titled men and elders are likely to be taken more seriously by the gods to whom the people pray, while others impute other reasons for their preferred person to play the traditional sacramental role of breaking the kola nut. In some areas, the oldest or the titled man performs the ceremony, while the youngest breaks and shares the kola nut, in line with their communities' Rules of Primogeniture. Generally, it is inappropriate for a visitor to break the kola nut before his host. The same applies to an in-law, or nephew, breaking the kola nut before his fathers-in-law or his grand fathers. In every case, and instance, there are Rules of Engagement[3], because E kere ọrụ eke. That this is a solemn ceremony, during which all are in the mood of supplication, signifies that this 'nut' is a symbol of communion. It helps to weld the community together, as it is used to constantly remind everyone of the oneness of life. It is not a snack.

The kola nut is never shared or eaten without first calling on the gods and forces of nature for blessing. The gods and good ancestors are invited to partake and join in protecting and guiding the living. This makes the presentation of kola nut, first and foremost, the presentation of an opportunity for prayers. The process itself is called usoro ịwa ọjị[4] (the way the kola nut is broken, shared and eaten) in Igbo land. And since prayers bring blessings and strengthen life, whoever brings the kola nut has brought an opportunity for life to be strengthened. This is the basis for the opening statement by the person blessing the kola nut: Onye wetere ọjị wetere ndụ 'He who brings kola nut, brings life'. Had it been that the notion of 'life' is literally understood in terms of getting up and walking about as we do every day, then the Igbo would simply feed kola nut to a dead man, in order to revive him. Thus, the life that is 'brought' with the kola nut is not life in the literal sense. That is why the person calls on 'He Who Lives above, the Giver of life,' for protection and guidance.

Because the principle E ekere ọrụ eke permeates the Igbo understanding of nature in every way, the kola nut ceremonies always emphasize interdependence in every community and among all living things. That is why it is said, during the breaking of the kola nut Mmiri atana, ma azụ achọkwana mmiri ọ ga-egwu 'May the river not dry up and may the fish not lack water to swim in.' This is a call for reciprocal goodwill. It rests on the fact that the river looks more beautiful because of the fish, while the life of the fish depends on the steady flow of the river. Since nature, human life and the full complement of living things will be diminished if the river were to dry up, an appeal for mutual goodwill is a prayer for continuity in nature. Beyond that, there is also, during the kola nut ceremony, an opening good-will prayer like: Ndị okenye, Ndụ unu! Ndi okorobịa na agboghobịa, Ndụ unu! Unu ga-adị! 'The elders shall live and the young shall live as well.'

## 3. E kere ọrụ eke in Igbo Enwe Eze

The prayers preceding the breaking of the kola nut are usually the first event in every serious gathering of Ndị Igbo. It shows that Ndị Igbo have always been an organized people, with a sense of community and social responsibility. What the Igbo traditional political system lacked in absolute monarchy is replaced by a republicanism that rests on the basic principle of E kere `ọrụ eke. It is a worldview that uses the Council of Elders, titled men, age-grade associations, women groups, etc., to create a framework for seamless division of labour that permeates the entire society. That is how the society arrives at community decisions that are endorsed by all.[5]

The question that may perhaps arise here is: Whence comes the much-advertised claim that Ndị Igbo are fundamentally individualistic in a socially and politically disruptive sort of way? This notion has largely been attributed to the fact that the absence of an entrenched feudal system, with monarchs and all, easily suggests disorder to those with a feudal background. This counter narrative is captured in the now-notorious saying Igbo enwe eze 'the Igbo do not recognize kingship'. This saying has helped to reinforce the image of a disorganized, unruly and probably ungovernable people; whose individualistic inclinations completely overshadow any attempts they make to build cohesion and consensus on any matter.[6]

But this perception, or supposition, is grievously mistaken. Looked at more deeply, especially against the background of the theme of this chapter, the assertion Igbo enwe eze simply refers to the fact that no single feudal authority governs the Igbo society without consultations, consensus and group endorsement. It is because E kere ọrụ eke that no single person can, arbitrarily and in the name of a presumed superiority conferred by title, overrule the community, or visit tyranny on the people unchallenged. He cannot do that because the principle of E kere ọrụ eke, flows through the titled men, elders, age grades, etc., and permeates the entire society. That is why there is also the Igbo saying Arụsị kpawa ajọ ike, e gosi ya osisi e jiri pịta ya 'when the wooden god starts becoming too powerful (as to begin to give signs of having a life of its own), then it must be shown the wood from which it was carved' – to sober it up. This is said with particular reference to individuals who begin to overrate the community. They are then shown where they came from, because E kere ọrụ eke!

Thus Igbo enwe eze does not mean disrespect for constituted authority, the way some people try to misrepresent it today. It is a way of saying that the collective right and might of the people, their authority as owners of the land, as embodied in the Laws of the Land and also in various platforms that represent them, should be invoked to remind anyone with tyrannical aspirations that Dike bu dike oha 'a hero is always a people's hero', and not a hero unto himself. That is also why an Igbo proverb says Mmọnwụ pịasaa ndị egwu ya, ọ kwụsị ịgba egwu 'A masquerade that flogs and scatters its drummers and followers must cease to dance (because it is then abandoned).' Thus, it should be clear that the Igbo concept of power and authority rest more on respect for the consensual decisions that define the various groupings making up any Igbo community, than on the whims of any individual. It is also for the same reason that the true Igbo concept of success is anchored on respect for Omenala 'the laws of the land'. The word Omenala can be broken down as follows: O 'it' me 'does/happen' n' 'on' ala 'earth/ground' = 'that which happens/takes place on the ground/earth'. This refers to something that has become a regular and reoccurring pattern, and as such a subsisting and recognized guiding principle or Law, in the life of the people as their tradition. The success of the individual usually harmonizes with such core principles.

The Nze title, for instance, used to be given only to the most upright of men, who neither bore false witness nor endorsed evil of any type. The saying A fụ onye Nze e bie okwu 'disputations end, once an Nze title holder intervenes on any matter' is rooted in this understanding. It is the people, guided by the laws of the land, who always determine the differences between right and wrong. Therefore, the nexus between usoro omenala, 'the traditional pattern', and ike oru stand out in bold relief. That is also why the Igbo say 'A sọkarịa eze anya, e kpuchie nkata n'ihu wee gwa ya nke bụ eziokwu' 'There is a limit to the extent of the respect you give to a crowned leader, beyond which you must use some veiled means (of covering your face with a basket) to tell him some home truths'.

Every leader symbolizes transcendental authority, beyond the mere person on whom rulership is temporarily conferred. It would, therefore, be wrong for anyone, no matter how highly placed in the society, to walk up to the community leader and insult him. It is just not done, no matter what the ruler may have done. You must first be briefed by the community and formally sent to admonish the leader, in the event that such a thing has become necessary. Once you are sent in this way, you no longer represent yourself. Thus, you are stepping forward as the messenger of the community, sent by the community. Just as a man is presumed to have transcended to the immaterial world, and thus becomes part of the spirit world, once he is dressed up as a masquerade,[11] the person who covers his face with a basket to rebuke a leader is deemed to be other than human. This presumably mysterious being from the beyond is speaking for the gods and for men, but is using the voice of a man. It is because he has thus transcended the world of mortals, by this symbolic covering of the face, that whatever he then says does not diminish the dignity of the office of the leader. The act of covering the face with a basket is not out of fear of the leader, because the life of the speaker is never on the line in such circumstances. Instead, the act even affirms the office of the leader further, because it demonstrates that no one may insult this office in his capacity as a mere mortal. It is a special job, that must be executed in a special way by a specially chosen person, and through a special means, because E kere ọrụ eke.

## 4.  E Kere Ọrụ Eke Amongst Igbo Heroes and Charlatans

It is against the background of the foregoing that Ndị Igbo make a distinction between heroes and charlatans. For even the distinction between the two is based on the division of labour, because *E kere ọrụ eke*.

A hero is a person of courage, who dares incredible things in the name of, and on behalf of, the people and their cherished values. He is not a violator of the laws of the land, nor oppressor of the people. His strength is brought into service, to strengthen the feelings of oneness and the idea of *Onye aghana nwanne ya* 'Let no one abandon his kith and kin'.[7] A true hero may even sometimes be unpopular, especially from the perspective of the uninformed and those who love ephemeral successes and advantages. He will not follow the majority when the latter is wrong. He may even be physically weak, in which case his strength, or heroism, is not purely physical. It may sometimes express itself in the possession and imparting of knowledge, in his convictions about the rightness of a less trod path, or simply in his resolve to continuously resist *ndi akalogeli/ofo ogeli* 'the never-do-wells and layouts' and *ndị ọ bata o su* 'rabble rousers', by always speaking out and standing out. This is moral heroism, as a counter narrative to those whose presence, or arrival, anywhere in the community, heralds confusion and aggravated misconduct.

We can say, by way of definition, that a hero for Ndị Igbo is anyone who displays courage and the readiness to make sacrifice for the common good, when faced with clear danger and adversity. The operative words here are: (1) courage, (2) sacrifice, (3) common good, (4) danger, and (5) adversity. Not everyone elects, or is called, to play the hero. It is only for the lionhearted. Therefore, *E kere oru eke!*

In contrast to these positive attributes are the negative attributes of bad manners, debauchery or barbaric display of strength that characterizes the charlatan. The latter attributes do not build up, strengthen, or  add value to, the community. For example, the person who boldly rigs elections, kidnaps a governor, or confiscates the money allocated to a state, and then later displays the material benefits of his abominable acts is not a hero for the Igbo. Yes, such a person may have demonstrated courage and readiness to die while executing all the evil deeds he perpetrated. But they all have a selfish motivation and were in direct violation of everything that held the society together.

The major trademark of the traditional Igbo charlatan is that nothing he does can ever lead to sustainable development, or a healthy communal, religious or family life. He is dangerous to social morality and the economic life of the people; because he is an *Ọ kpata o titaa* 'one who quickly consumes whatever comes his way' in his approach to on life. *Ọ kpata o titaa* is literally someone who goes scouting for kernels, and cracks and eats each one he finds, without any thoughts about saving for the future. Also, as a justification for his always following his whims, whomever he can parasitically grab from, the Igbo charlatan parrots proverbs like *Ewu na-eso onye bu igu* 'a goat always follows whoever is carrying the palm fronds'. He uses it to justify his being like an uninvited goat following the person carrying the palm fronds and tearing off the leaves from it any moment it has the opportunity. He proudly proclaims that this statement is true and confirmed by experience, but he will not be quick to proclaim that the saying applies exclusively to goats and any other living thing that behaves like a goat, including himself. Such a saying, which was originally meant to warn people against thoughtless materialism and immorality as a philosophy of life, is now appropriated as a philosophy of life by those who do not know that *E kere ọrụ eke*. That is why, today, the proverb is freely used to justify irresponsibility, unfaithfulness and every form of tomfoolery. To live by the saying that only the person who offers immediate material satisfaction deserves loyalty is to abort all norms.

In Igbo land, where the cardinal communal philosophy is *Mmadu abụghị ewu* 'A human being is not a goat', any saying that urges people to assume the mentality, lifestyle and profile of a goat is antithetical to the core notion of *E kere ọrụ eke*. Only a goat acts and behaves like a goat. Therefore, anyone who exhibits the irrational reflexes of a goat as a trademark is less than human. The fact that this saying and others like it are becoming popular in Igbo land in recent times shows that the region is actually being taken over by the dregs of the society. Those who will do everything possible to overturn our core traditional values are now taking over! They tend to forget that while it is true that a goat eats wherever it finds the things on its natural menu, including yam, it is rarely served yam; but if it gains access to a barn of yams, it simply eats its fill without seeking for permission; after all, yam belongs to its natural menu. However, if the goat is found dead in a barn of yams, it is taken for granted that it most likely did not die from hunger, or overfeeding, but from the wrath of the barn owner. Hence the proverb *Ewu nwuru n'ọba ji abụghị agụrụ gburu ya* 'A goat that died in a barn of yams surely did not die from hunger'. Our traditional values are being desecrated with impunity, because the desecrators are also Ndị Igbo. The values they are desecrating belong to them, like the yam is an item in the natural menu of a goat. Can it be that a rebound of Igbo core values will be their undoing someday, like the goat dying from the wrath of the owner of the barn of yams? Is it possible that the activities of modern day Igbo politicians may yet yield a harvest of calamities for the never-do-wells in Igbo land? ◾

## 5. The Igbo Ignorance of *E kere ọrụ eke* in Nigerian Politics

Part of the danger facing the Igbo worldview today is that a new breed of Ndị Igbo, driven by presumption and impunity, are over-running the land.[8] At the national level the fabric of the Igbo world is facing merciless assault from Igbo political office holders, nouveau-riche economic actors, fraudsters with substantial financial muscle and desperate power seekers and their collaborators. That is why an Igbo political office holder easily forgets that *e kere ọrụ eke* and presumes himself to be qualified to participate in a meeting to which only titled men are invited. And, at the village level, uncouth young men with more money than brains can now walk into meetings of elders uninvited, sit and down and join the discussion. Gradually, everyone is endeavouring to conveniently forget that *ụsụ abụghị nnụnnụ* 'the bat is not a bird', and that shouting at a bamboo pole *Ide ji ụlọ!* 'Pillar of the House!' cannot turn the bamboo pole into the pillar that holds a magnificent edifice. The Igbo rhetorical question/proverb *Onye ajụ na-ebu ọ na-aza "Ide Ji Uno"?* "Do you give the title of 'Pillar of the house' to a drowsy person?" is also rooted in this understanding. Surely, a drunken man who does not have full control of his faculties, as he also does not have full control of even his physical movement, should not be the person to handle certain responsibilities that call for sobriety, full personal dignity and the mandatory sense of propriety. The embarrassing scenario of power hungering and power mongering ineptitude that is replicating itself in different forms everywhere, with the uncouth Igbo village youth practicing at the village level what his Igbo political counterpart is manifesting in Abuja, portends ill for the Igbo world. And it is because the two sometimes converge, as a form of handshake of leadership idiocy between the village and the city, that '*Ewu na-eso onye bu igu*' has become the new mantra in some places.

When the depraved children of a family achieve and maintain political prominence and visibility in the village square, their conduct and image will rub off on the entire family. This will progressively stigmatize the family members before the rest of the community, as people with questionable moral and political credentials. If we extrapolate this to the wider Nigerian society, it becomes somewhat easy to see why Ndị Igbo are sometimes considered too temperamental and politically naïve and predictable in the Nigerian political firmament. This is because their prominent sons and daughters, especially those enjoying the most media visibility in the Nigerian political space, seem to be mostly people who focus on personal gains whenever they have access to political power. And because Ndị Igbo are represented and led, particularly in Abuja, by an emergent elite with wrong ideas about leadership and social responsibility, the Igbo are disconnected from national political issues. Very few of them seek, or bother, to draw popular Igbo support for an 'Igbo Position' on any issue. The reason for this unfortunate state of affairs is quite simple: they do not know that *E kere oru eke.*

It is in the light of this ignorance that, seeing themselves as very important "Igbo leaders" (though thoroughly ignorant), they seek and obtain endorsement from outside Igbo land and measure their importance by the ease with which they can terrorize and silence anyone who has a dissenting voice from within Igbo land. This class of new leaders are not connected to their roots, except through their likes in Igbo land. Worse still, they do not constitute any form of new, forward-looking force that is rooted in 21$^{st}$ century values at the personal or group level. They are also not genuine products of the old, core values that define Ndị Igbo. They can be described as a curious high breed of characters with questionable antecedents, committed to ensuring that the worst in Igbo land stand forth as epitomizing the best. They deliberately have to act this way, because they know that nobody sent them, and that no Igbo family or kindred sends out its mad offspring to represent it in the village square as *Ọnụ na-ekwuru ọha* 'The voice of the people'. Igbo core values make a clear distinction between the sublime and the ridiculous, based on the basic principle of *E kere ọrụ eke.* The mad and ridiculous cannot replace propriety and dignity.

Ndị Igbo have lost a lot of respect in national politics because they are now mostly seen as a people who thrive in the most reprehensible brands of non-inclusive home politics; and who are brash, ruthlessly materialistic, avaricious and hard to govern. Any mention of the South East in Nigerian politics today immediately brings up thoughts of political degeneracy, the enthronement of money and the belief that everyone is available for a fee. And this is all because those who know that *E kere ọrụ eke* are being marginalized. The Igbo man now walks the Nigerian political landscape with an unsteady gait, unstable at home and misrepresented at the national level. He faces a crisis of relevance and identity. Even when platforms that are supposed to represent the cream of Igbo elite speak, there is a frightening cacophony of voices. Nothing authentically Igbo, or credible, seems to emerge. Today Ndị Igbo are contending with what can best be described as the Years of Locust that have not ended, even now.

At the village level, a barely literate young man that is loaded with a lot of money and a corresponding quantity of bad manners, can stagger into a duly constituted village meeting and, in the course of discussions, shut up any speaker (no matter how refined or informed) by simply saying: "I am using this ten thousand naira to tell him to close his mouth." Why is it that this display of debauchery, as seen in his tendering of money in order to prevent someone from making his contributions during a discussion, automatically translates into the 'victim' being ordered to sit down and speak no more. Why is this unsound practice that runs counter to the principle of *E kere oru eke* now endorsed by some supposedly rational adults in many places? A little attention to the wisdom of *E kere oru eke* would have made this impossible. It would have made it clear that the job of making contributions in meetings is not a function of cash capacity, but of knowledge, wisdom insight, exposure and understanding of the *mores* of the land. This singular fact is borne out by the underlying philosophy of the Igbo worldview, as evinced also in 'the kola nut ceremony.'　　　　■

## 6. Back to the Core Values of *E kere ọrụ eke*

To restore the basic traditional philosophical outlook of Ndigbo, which emphasizes propriety in role-play, a return to *E kere oru eke* is now mandatory. It is with this that a move from the culture of leadership charlatanry to genuine role assignment must begin. This calls for a strategic response to the political profile, economic rating and attitudinal excesses now associated with the Igbo leadership elite of today.

What is needed is a simple, but fundamental, focus: To restore the values of effective/responsible leadership and citizenship, which held Igbo communities and people together before the colonial era; and which persisted on an even wider scale after independence, as manifested in the *Igbo Union*. But such group solidarity can only be achieved by quietly creating and nurturing new political values that will change the expectations of the people from Government and Government Officials. One basic truth we all struggle to deny today is that the people are often the greatest danger faced by public office holders who wish to do the right things while in office. That is because, many people now have the wrong expectations regarding what a leader should or should not, do for them. One way out of this is to now use all avenues and platforms as opinion moulding machines to project new values and influence positive action that would bring social change. It is in this way that we can create the needed critical mass of Ndị Igbo who will one day say: "Thus far and no further". This will require the following:

(1) Identifying the power centres in the region and galvanizing them for collective action

(2) Quietly initiating consultations with leaders who control these centres of influence

(3) Building linkages and networks with all centres of influence

(4) Evolving aggressive, innovative and issues-based messages targeted at the centres of influence and the entire spectrum of stakeholders

(5) Identifying and focusing on the critical 20% that gives the 80% result

(6) Embarking on person-to-person contact and communication, to build buy-in

(7) Setting agenda in the media through print media, radio and television discussions, issues-based advertisements and 'teasers', etc.

What we now need in Igbo land is a reaffirmation of the principle of *E kere oru eke*, which should manifest in the following areas:

*Attitude to work*

Every workman must (1) know his trade, (2) keep to his trade, and (3) ply his trade to the best of his ability. This means recognizing the fact that not everyone is suitable for every task. Do not because you are a prominent politician tell a medical doctor how to do his work. Do not because you own a car tell a well-trained mechanic how to do his job. It also means that mass endorsement of what is wrong will not, and cannot make, it right. *E kere oru eke!*

### Social Occasions

Religious gatherings, village meetings, etc., have rules and procedures. They also have roles assigned to specific individuals by their natural abilities, experience and exposure. Respect these attributes, simple. Do not change the rules for the breaking of the kola nut, because there is a "big man" or a "big politician" who wants to break the kola nut. Do not give the *Igwe* title to a n'er-do-well, simply because he has enough cash to throw around.

### Interpersonal Relationships

How a person relates to his in-laws, what roles are expected of a wife, a husband, a son, a daughter, an in-law, etc., rest on the principle of *E kere oru eke.* In all situations of conflict, misunderstanding and social tension, you will always find a violation of this principle as a major causative factor.

### Family meetings

Family meetings and filial engagements are not exempt from the mandatory need to respect the principle of *E kere oru eke.* This includes the relations between siblings, according to age. Rules of inheritance, headship of the extended family, etc. Material wealth does not automatically qualify anyone to be head of a family. Once this fact is ignored and a new breed of triumphant value-violators are allowed to take charge, the moral fabric of that family is ruined; because this single violation will create new generations of violators. Once the principle of *E kere oru eke* is thrown to the dogs, everything else that constituted the foundation of values in the Igbo world is also thrown out with it.

# References

[1]Ihe Igbo sọrọ nwaanyị ime - BBC News Ìgbò - BBC.com (www.bbc.com › igbo › afirika-45397445)

[2]Ogbalu, F. C. (1965). Ilu Igbo: The Book of Igbo Proverbs. Onitsha: Varsity Press. [http://www.columbia.edu/itc/mealac/prit chett/00fwp/igbo/proverbs/index.html]

[3]https://www.britannica.com/topic/rules-of-engagement-military-directives

[4]Osuagwu, B.I.N. (2004). *Ndi Igbo na Omenala Ha.* Ibadan: Macmillan Nigeria Publishers Limited.

[4]"The Symbolism of Kola nut in Igbo Cosmology: A Re-Examination". *International Journal of Research in Humanities and Social Studies* 2 (8), 51-56

[4]Chidume, C. G. (2014). The symbolism of Kolanut in Igbo Cosmology: A Re-examination. *European Scientific Journal*, 2, 547-552.

[4]Obineche, J. O. (2017) Kola Nut: Revisiting the Igbo Socio-Cultural Values and Identity. *International Journal of Arts and Humanities(IJAH)*, . 6(2), 94-107.

[5]Ibenekwu, I.E. (2010). Igbo Traditional Political System and the Crisis of Governance in Nigeria. *Ikoro Journal of the Institute of African Studies*, 9(1&2).

[6]Okoli, K.I. (2020). Understanding Republicanism in Igbo Pre-Colonial System of Governance: The Viewpoint of Igbo Enwe Eze. *ODEZURUIGBO JOURNAL*, 4(1), pp. 251-265.

[7]Okoro, C.D. (2019). Unveiling the Paradox of Igbo Indigenous Ethic of *Onye Aghala Nwanne Ya* in the Context of Infertility in Marriage. (PhD Dissertation Lutheran School of Theology at Chicago)

[8]Okoye, V.O. & Okoye, C.R. (2014). Corruption and Self-Interest in Igbo Leadership. International Journal of Business and Management Review, 2(2), pp. 33-42. ■

Part Five

# Igbo Economy
# and Politics

# A Linguistic Note on *Ígbā Bọ̀yí*

*Summary*

**Igba boyi** *is a well-known modern Igbo expression. It is seen as the anchor point or foundation for the success of the Igbo entrepreneurial system. This brief chapter is on the linguistics of the expression. It first examines its structural make up as a verbal expression of the language, before going into the origin of the expression, as well as the nature of its semantic relation to another well-known Igbo expression that has a comparable meaning:* **igba odibo**. *The overall insight is that while* **igba odibo** *had always existed as the designation for the traditional Igbo tutelage system ,***Igba boyi** *is the modern expression for the adaptation of the system to the modern times, but without the loss of the altruistic core of the traditional tutelage system.*

## 1. Introduction

**T**HE IGBO EQUIVALENTS OF THE FOLLOWING ENGLISH WORDS have something in common. They indicate how the Igbo language uses two words to express what the English language expresses with one word:

(1)   *to run* 'ígbā ọsọ́'        *to dance* 'ígbā égwú',
      *to wrestle* 'ígbā mgbá'     *to sue* 'ígbā ákụ́kwọ́'

In the above examples, the Igbo language combines the verb *igba* with different nouns to express the equivalent of one verb in English. There are also instances where the Igbo language combines a verb with a prepositional phrase: *ígbā n'èzí* '(i) to be a layabout [for male]; (ii) sleep around [for female]'. These combinations, which can be summarised as V+N and V+PP respectively, are the well-established patterns for forming verbal structures in the language. They are also used for encoding the handling of new objects that enter Igbo land. For example, *to play football*, *to buy a ticket*, and *to travel by air* are activities that did not exist within traditional Igbo society. Consequently, there were no Igbo designations for them before the colonial experience. However, with the entrance of these activities into Igbo land, the V+N pattern was used to form the verbal structures for expressing them in the language. Hence: *ígbā bọ́ọlụ̀* 'to play football', *ígbā tíkēètì* 'to buy ticket', *ígbā ụ́gbọ́élū* 'to travel by air'. An example of this V+N pattern but with a different verb root is *ítụ̄ vóòtù* 'to vote'.

The V+N pattern is also the linguistic basis for the formation of the Igbo expression *Ígbā bòyí*. This involves the combination of the verb *Ígbā* with the modified English noun *boy*, igbonised as *bòyí*. The structure, *Ígbā bòyí*, now exists in the Igbo language for the expression of a particular type of modern day Igbo entrepreneurial training whose details are presented in the next chapter. The focus in this short chapter is the linguistics of the expression *Ígbā bòyí*. This shall take the form of further elaborations of the identified pattern, to be followed by the examination of the origin and semantics of the expression in addition to its comparison with the traditional Igbo expression for tutelage/mentorship/training: Ị́gbā ọ̀dìbò.

## 2. The Linguistics of Ị́gbā bọ̀yị́

### 2.1 The Igbo V+N Pattern

Generally, many Igbo verbs are formed through the combination of a verb root with a noun or a prepositional phrase, which can be summarised as V+NP or V+PP respectively. However, because this short chapter is focused on the verb root *gbá*, whose infinitive form is *ị́gbā*, the combinations of this verb root with different nouns shall be used for all the illustrations here. For this reason, the V+PP pattern which is the less dominant pattern, shall not be further discussed. Below are some examples of the combinations.

| Verb Root + Noun | | Igbo Verb | English verb |
|---|---|---|---|
| 1. ị́gbā | + ọ́sọ́ 'race' | => ị́gbā ọ́sọ́ | to run |
| 2. ị́gbā | + égwú 'dance' | => ị́gbā égwú | to dance |
| 3. ị́gbā | + àkwụ̀nà 'prostitute' | => ị́gbā àkwụ̀nà | to prostitute |

*(2) (a) Verb + Noun (V+NP)*

| Verb + Preposition + Noun | Igbo Verb | English verb |
|---|---|---|
| ị́gbā + nà + èzí => | ị́gbā n'èzí | to be a layabout/to sleep around |

*(b) Verb + Prepositional Phrase (V+PP)*

Definitely, one is bound to ask about the meaning of the verb *ị́gbā* in the above examples. The effort here is not to delve into the discussion of the semantics of this verbal element. Suffice it to say that the verb contributes such notions as MOTION, EXPLOSION, etc., in addition to being the base for the formation of other verbal categories like tense and aspect. (More on the nature of the meanings expressed through the verbal component of the Igbo V+NP pattern, see Uchechukwu, 2011, *Igbo Verb and Cognitive Linguistics*).

## 3. The Origin and Semantics of *Ígbá bòyí*

The word *bòyí* is a phonologically adapted form of the English word *boy*, which was originally used by the colonial masters for their African servants, no matter how young or old the servants were. The new phonologically modified form, *bòyí*, became conventionally accepted across Igbo land and became part of the new designations that were used to encode conceptual differences between old and new objects and activities that entered Igbo land.

The best illustration of this process of forming new designations to differentiate between the old and the new objects and activities that have entered Igbo land is the Igbo word *ụ́gbọ́* 'canoe'. Originally, there existed only *ụ́gbọ́* 'canoe' in the language. However, with the arrival of the colonial masters and their bigger boats and ship, there arose the need to differentiate between the new arrivals and the traditional *ụ́gbọ́*. The new was simply called *ńnúkwú ụ́gbọ́* 'big canoe', while the old now became *óbéré ụ́gbọ̄* 'small boat'. Common to both the old and the new is the manner in which the human being embarked on them: step in, sit down, and be conveyed to wherever you want.

In addition to *ńnúkwú ụ́gbọ́* 'big canoe', the colonial authorities also brought in another means of transport that the human being must step into and sit down to be conveyed to where he wants: vehicles. The vehicles, as new objects, had to be differentiated from the existing *ńnúkwú ụ́gbọ́* 'big canoe' and *óbéré ụ́gbọ̄* 'small boat'. To achieve this, its surface of movement, *àlà* 'ground/earth surface', was combined with *ụ́gbọ́* to form *ụ́gbọ́ àlà*, which means 'the *ụ́gbọ́* that moves on the ground'. As there was no tarred road then, the *ụ́gbọ́ àlà* moved only on *àlà*; but with the introduction of tarred roads, *ụ́gbọ́ àlà* became *ụ́gbọ́ kòròtá*, which means 'the *ụ́gbọ́* that moves on the tarred road' (coal tar = *kòròtá*). This choice of 'surface/area of movement' to specify the new objects, was now extended backwards to the already existing *ńnúkwú ụ́gbọ́* 'big canoe' and *óbéré ụ́gbọ̄* 'small boat', by using their surface of movement, *ḿmírī* 'water', to further specify them as *ụ́gbọ́ ḿmírī* 'the *ụ́gbọ́* that moves on the water'. When their sizes are taken into consideration, they were further specified as *óbélé ụ́gbọ́ m̀mírí* 'small water boat' and *ńnúkwú ụ́gbọ́ m̀mírí* 'big/large water boat'.

Much later, another kind of *ụ́gbọ́* came in view: the aeroplane. It offered the human being the same procedure for conveyance, which all the other *ụ́gbọ́* before it had: walk in, sit down and be conveyed to wherever you want. However, while the *ụ́gbọ́ m̀mírī* moved on water and the *ụ́gbọ́ àlà* moved on the earth surface, the new *ụ́gbọ́* had the sky as its area of motion. Therefore, to differentiate it from the previous *ụ́gbọ́*, its area of motion, *élúígwē* 'the sky', was combined with *ụ́gbọ́* to form *ụ́gbọ́ élū* 'the *ụ́gbọ́* that moves in the sky'. The Igbo word *Ígbā bòyí* is involved in this pattern of word formation for the purpose of further differentiation an already existing object or activity.

The original Igbo expression for undergoing a traditional tutelage/mentorship or training involves the use of the noun *òdìbò* 'servant' to form *Ígbā òdìbò* which means 'to serve a master/mentor'. This does not mean working as an ordinary servant or as someone's slave! It means to serve a mentor and, through that, learn from the mentor. With regard to slavery, the word for slave is *óhù* and it is not combined with the verb *Ígbā*. Instead, it is combined with a more complex verb *ígbápụ̀tà* 'to redeem' to form *ígbápụ̀tà n'óhù*, which means 'to redeem from slavery'. A slave, *óhù*, is therefore not an *òdìbò* 'servant', and cannot therefore be described as being engaged in *Ígbā òdìbò* which involves some form of tutelage or mentorship while serving the master. It is in the midst of this traditional system of mentorship and training that the colonial master introduced a new system of house servants made up of 'men and boys', with all being addressed as 'Boy!', i.e. 'house boys'.

Finally, to differentiate this new and foreign form of 'servitude with minimal tutelage' from the traditional tutelage of *Ígbā òdìbò*, the expression used by the colonial master for his servant, *bòyí*, was incorporated in the V+NP pattern to form *Ígbā bòyí*. Therefore, the verbal structure, *Ígbā bòyí*, was formed to conceptually differentiate it from the already existing traditional tutelage system of *Ígbā òdìbò*. This is similar to the gradual differentiation between *úgbọ́* => *úgbọ́ ṁmírī* => *úgbọ́ àlà* => *úgbọ́ élū*. It is therefore not surprising that this differentiation is further seen in the fact that the new word, *bòyí*, can be used as an insult by calling someone *Bòyí! bòyí!* or *nwá bòyí*, both of which mean 'a stupid, slavish servant!'. However, this usage as an insult does not seem to apply to the traditional expression, *òdìbò*, which does not easily lend itself to being used for insult. This fact points to the traditional understanding of *òdìbò* as 'a servant trainee' and not as an 'ordinary house servant'. It is a servant trainee with the goal of being sent off by the master after the completion of his training.  It is also interesting to note that this idea of 'servant trainee' associated with the word *òdìbò* has become so fully integrated in the meaning and usage of *Ìgbá bòyí* that *Ìgbá bòyí* now covers both the domains of training and apprenticeship that initially existed in *Ìgbá òdìbò*. For example, *Ìgbá òdìbò* included undergoing training by both male and female 'servant trainees'. Similarly, *Ìgbá bòyí* is not restricted to boys. Instead, it has now become a generalised term like *òdìbò* for any form of 'servant trainee' relationship, regardless of whether girls or boys are involved. Hence, girls and boys undergo *Ìgbá bòyí*, as a period of apprenticeship for whatever profession or craft they lean towards. But no girl undergoes *Ìgbá gìèlí*, because the expression has been blocked by *Ìgbá bòyí*, which generally stands for undergoing apprenticeship, whether by a boy or a girl.　　　　　　　　　　　　　　■

## 4. Conclusion

*Ịgbā bọ̀yị́* is an expression that goes back to the period of servitude under the colonial administrators. Contrary to expectation, the expression did not exit from the Igbo language at the exit of the colonial masters from Igbo land. Instead, it became infused with all the ideas of mentorship, grooming, setting up and aiding the growth of the mentee; all of which are the ideas that existed in the traditional mentorship system expressed through *Ịgbā òdìbò*. Hence, *Ịgbā bọ̀yị́* can be seen as a very good illustration of the well-known Igbo attitude of always adapting and moving on with the new but retaining the noble essence of the old that is expressed through the word *Ịgbā òdìbò*.

# Chapter 17

Ikechukwu Anthony Kanu

## Ịgba Bọyị: An Igbo Indigenous Structure For Community Development And Social Welfare

1. Introduction

2. The Fundamental Principles of *igba bọyị*

3. The Nature of *igba bọyị*

4. Examples of *igba bọyị*

5. Conclusion

## Summary

Among the Igbo of South-Eastern Nigeria, there were traditional structures with which they prospered the community and improved on the social welfare of the people, and some of these structures that became more obvious after the Nigerian Civil war, have endured to this day. One of them is the **ịgba bọyị** incubator system for wealth creation. This chapter is focused on the contribution of the **ịgba bọyị** system of commerce to the development and improvement of the welfare of the Igbo society. It also explains how the Igbo social structure of reality, the Igbo think-home ideology and the Igbo spirit of resilience shape the this apprenticeship system, which has been the driving force in the creation of wealth among the Igbo over the years. The beauty of it is its simplicity. It is a system that does not take equity or require raising huge capital. It is simply driven by a human-platform and is based on the Igwebuike philosophy that understands the other as a part of me, thus making me responsible for the other. Finally, this chapter recommends that the government should heavily invest in this incubator system for the creation of wealth and for the tackling of the problem of unemployment.

## 1. Introduction

IN ADDITION TO THE STUDY OF GENERAL ECONOMIC POLICIES and strategies for economic prosperity, there has also been an increased interest in indigenous models or frameworks for community development and social welfare. It is this increased interest in indigenous economic models or frameworks that motivated this paper on *igba bọyị*, which is an indigenous framework that has the Igbo socio-cultural background as its base. ∎

## 2. The Fundamental Principles of 'Igba Boy' Apprenticeship System

There are three fundamental principles that shape the Igbo apprenticeship system. These principles include the Igbo social construction of reality, the Igbo philosophy of resilience and the Igbo think-Home ideology.

### 2.1 Igbo Social Construction of Reality

A social construction of reality, according to Kuhn (1970), "is the entire constellation of belief, values, techniques and so on shared by the members of a given community" (p. 175); or "a belief system that prevails in a given scientific community at a given time in history" (Grenz 1966, pp. 54-55). The idea of Igbo social construction constitutes the Igbo worldview. It may be described as "a unified picture of the cosmos explained by a system of concepts which order the natural and social rhythms and the place of the individual and communities in them" (Kalu 1978, p. 39). It is therefore, not surprising that Oguejiofor (2010), in his understanding of worldview, includes ideas about both material and spiritual realities and their relative importance, the origin and destiny of humanity, the end of life and what is conducive to this end.

Among the Igbo of Nigeria, the life of a human person is circumscribed within the *ụwa* (the world), which is composed of the physical and the spiritual, the abode of humans and spirits. In the contention of Oguejiofor (2010), these dimensions of the world are not separated or divided by chasm, but rather "there is interconnectedness between the two enabling contact, between the deities and spirits, and human beings. This unitary conception of reality pervades the Igbo world in a remarkable way" (p. 21). The Igbo person, therefore, does not see himself or herself as an individual without noticing immediately the need for the other. No wonder he often warns the other: *onye aghana nwanne ya* (No one should leave his brother/sister behind). This thought is also caught in some proverbs of the language that express this sense of mutual dependence and support:

1. *Ọha nwe nwa; otu onye anaghị azụ nwa.* (The community owns the child; one person does not raise a child: It takes a village to do so)

2. *Oke osisi anaghị emewe ọhịa.* (A giant tree does not make a forest.)

3. *Ngwere hapụ ukwu osisi, aka akpara ya.* (If a lizard stays off from the foot of a tree, it would be caught)

4. *Otu mkpịsị aka anaghị atụtụ ihe.* (A single finger cannot pick up things from the ground)

## 2.2  Igbo Philosophy of Resilience

The Igbo world is not a bird of roses. It is a world of struggles that begins from birth, noticeable in the cry of a little child as soon as it is born. Circumscribed to the *uwa* (world), the human person is faced with difficulties and frustrations. Diseases like small pox, aids, leprosy, malaria, etc., are present vying for a central place in the human person. This makes survival in a tolerable way a major concern for the Igbo, and to Oguejiofor (2010), this to a large extent determines the Igbo attitude to life. Nwala (1998) views the desire for *ndụ* 'life' and its preservation in Igbo ontology as the *summum bonum* (the supreme good), and every other thing is expected to serve its realization. Hence, the prominent appearance of *ndu* in Igbo proverbs, parables and personal names projects the nature of the value that the Igbo place on life and the need to make every effort for its preservation (Kanu 2012).

If the Igbo person must qualify to live in the world of the ancestors, he needs to achieve personal success, which is economic, social, moral and biological (long life). Failure in any of these implies exclusion from the community of life, both earthly and otherworldly. This explains why the Igbo adapt themselves to any condition no matter how difficult to achieve their aim. Thus, the Igbo person sees life as a struggle in which he must put all he has in order to live a successful life. If he is observed as hard working, competitive and admires personal achievement, it is because these attributes have great weight on his ultimate destiny. After all, "No live code of behaviour is possible unless the meaning of life is sensed (Tempels 1952, p. 10).

Given that this achievement must be personal, not based on those of your father or brothers, the Igbo develops a social and political ethos that is distinguished by egalitarianism and competitiveness. The spirit of the Igbo person was captured by Basden (1966) when he described Igbo immigrants to the west of the 1920s as follows: "Whatever the condition, the Igbo immigrants adapt themselves to meet them, and it is not long before they make their presence felt in the localities where they settle" (p. ix).

It is this spirit that makes the Igbo to understand suffering, not purely in a negative sense, but also positively as any kind of work or difficult experience resulting from situations or painstaking efforts to achieve difficult objectives. Hard work is at the centre of the Igbo spirit. This is illustrated in the following Igbo proverbs *Onye rụọ, o rie!* 'He who works must also enjoy', and *Aka aja aja na-ebute ọnụ mmanụ mmanụ* 'It is the hand that is frequently soiled in hard work that gives rise to the mouth always looking well oiled'. It is something the individual willingly undertakes for himself with a view to benefitting from it. Other proverbs that capture the same axiom are as follows: *mmiri mmadụ kwọsara onwe ya adịghị atụ ya oyi* 'the water a person deliberately pours upon himself does not bring him or her cold' (because he knew what was to follow before going into it). *onye ọbụla chọrọ ihe mara mma ga-adị nkwadobe ikuchara ya okpofu n'ihi na ọ dịghị ije ọma na-ada n'elu* 'one who desires great things must be ready to work hard for them'. *Ọ bụ naanị ụkwụ gbara apịtị na-eri ihe gụrụ ya* 'It is only the leg that has been soiled with mud that enjoys whatever it likes'. Hard work is not seen as a curse or unjustified suffering, but as something that attracts blessings from the gods, because greatness is achieved through hard work.

## 2.3 The Igbo *Think-Home* Philosophy

The Igbo, even before the Nigerian Civil War, have never forgotten home. This sense of attachment to home not only applies to the physical presence of visiting home but also to the idea of one's wealth also reaching home. That is why the Igbo exhortation: *Akụ ruo ụnọ!* 'Let wealth reach home' i.e. 'Wealth must reach home!' The implication of this is that, if a person is known all over the world but not known in his hometown, then he is not known at all. If a person does not make an effort to return home or at least have a link with the home base, he or she is referred to as an *efuru efu* 'the lost one'. However, with the Nigerian Civil War, after which the property and wealth of the Igbo were seized by the Nigerian government, the Igbo were stranded and couldn't access anything and had to begin all over again, the philosophy of *Cheruo ụnọ became more popular among the Igbo.* The exhortation *Cheruo ụnọ* literally means 'think reach home', but with the appropriate translation of *'think towards home',* or better still, *Think Home!*

*The Igbo person does not claim the citizenship of any state except his hometown. No matter where he travels to and no matter the number of houses he builds elsewhere, he ensures that he has a home in his village, even when there is no one to live there in his absence. Home is home for them and so they are at home for the celebration of festivals like Christmas,*

*New Year, Easter, New Yam Festival. More interesting is that many who are not able to travel during these seasons have one Igbo association or the other to which they belong in the various cities where they live. Home is so important that, although the Igbo can be born in Lagos, Abuja, Sokoto, Katsina, Benue, Benin, etc., when he or she dies, the corpse must be taken home. The corpse needs to get home to rest well. So the Think Home philosophy is not restricted to physical visit of home or ensuring that one's wealth reaches one's home; it also applies to one's dead body returning home to be buried when one dies.* ▰

### 3. The Nature of *Igba Boyi* as an Indigenous Apprentice System

The Igbo apprentice system popularly known as *Igba Boyi* 'to serve/work as a servant while learning a craft/trade', is a major factor in any discussion about the Igbo wealth creation or commerce. But it also has other lesser-known designations or near equivalents that could create confusion for the uninitiated. They therefore need to be distinguished, one from the other, in order to bring to the fore the overarching importance of *Igba Boyi*, before going into how people have looked at the significance of *Igba Boyi* in wealth creation.

The two related designations are *Imu Olu* 'to learn a craft/handiwork' and *Imu Ahia* 'to learn trading (in goods of any form)'. The full form of *Imu Olu* is actually *Imu Oluaka* with the full designation 'to learn handcraft'. This is slightly distinct from the second designation, *Imu Ahia* 'to learn trading (in any form of goods)'. These designations can actually be used interchangeably, but without the distinctions becoming blurred. The reason for this is that *igba boyi* is the overarching concept, but can be realized in specific environments of either learning a craft or learning how to trade. The core point is that someone can be engaged in *imu olu* 'to learn a craft/handiwork' or *imu ahia* 'to learn trading (in any kind of goods)' without being engaged in *igba boyi* 'to serve/work as a servant while learning a craft/trade'. The reason is that neither *Imu Ahia* nor *Imu Olu* has the intimacy or closeness of *igba boyi*. It is this intimacy or closeness that forms the basis for mentoring in wealth creation in the larger Igbo society.

## 3.1 How Does *igba bọyị* Function

There are many good descriptions of how *igba bọyị* functions, but most of them are focused on its present day Igbo business communities, leaving out the fact that it is part of the traditional Igbo educational system. This section presents two recent descriptions of *igba bọyị*, before going into it as a traditional system of wealth creation.

Maleke (2018) describes *igba bọyị* as an "apprenticeship system that purports responsibly established businessmen [the nurturer] in a town, street or locale to pick up teenagers-young adults [the apprentice] from their homes and give them an informally formal, but raw and practical, cutthroat business education" (n.p). This teenager might be a relative, a sibling or a non-relative from the same region. Maleke further explains that "The idea centres around taking them off the streets and the perilous tendencies of an idle mind to give them a purpose, worthy of emulation, so they can also continue the trend when they are established" (n.p). Another explanation of how *igba bọyị* functions is Crescent's (2019) summary:

> " *The Igbo Apprenticeship System is an unpaid business apprenticeship/incubator model that lets people learn business from a master for a certain number of years (5-8) [...] and at the end of their apprenticeship tenure, get cash infusion and support to start their own business. There is no salary paid during the time of the apprenticeship tenure but meals, clothing and t-fare are provided for by the master. When the years of learning are over, the boy is as good as his master.* "

However, there is more to say about the origin and the driving force behind *igba bọyị*, because it is a system of commerce that was with the

Igbo before the Nigerian Civil War, and with it they created wealth across the Nigerian nation. Moreover, even after the Civil War, when the Igbo world faced the terrible legacy of the war that marked by great poverty, halting of livelihood, scarcity of funds and human capital and hopelessness, it was the *igba boyi* apprentice system that pulled majority of Igbo families out of poverty within two years after the Civil War. The system turned their troubles into a model of financial prosperity worthy of study and adoption. Furthermore, through the *igba boyi* system, many Igbo families took their financial destinies into their hands and forged ahead, in spite of the 20 pounds policy of the then Nigerian Government, which gave only £20 to every Igbo person to survive on regardless of what they had in the bank before the war. In spite of this unfavorable condition, the Igbo created wealth through her apprentice network that has continued to be a matter of intrigue speculation and wonderment for many.

The *igba boyi* apprenticeship system of commerce is unique to the Igbo, and is anchored on her social structure and spirit of resilience. This is not to say that other cultural groups in Nigeria do not have their apprentice systems, but it is only to say that there is something unique about the 'Igba Boy' system of apprenticeship. For instance, among the Yoruba of Western Nigeria, at the end of the apprenticeship of a candidate, which usually lasts between two to three years, he or she pays the master a 'freedom fee', and purchases drinks and throws a party to celebrate the end of his or her apprenticeship. This is an important part of the apprenticeship which has to be done before the candidate can begin to trade officially. After this party, the candidate is presented with a certificate to show that he or she has graduated. During these two or three years, the apprentice does not necessarily live with the master, and so the master does not necessarily have the responsibility for the feeding, clothing and housing of the apprentice.

This is very different from the Igbo *igba boyi* apprentice system. Here, the apprentice is like the son or daughter of the master. The apprentice, therefore, leaves his parents and comes to live under the care and supervision of an established business Igbo person who becomes his master and he the servant. He takes care of his master for the agreed number of years, and does every chore that the master assigns him. He serves his master not only in the shop or in relation to the business but at home as well, like washing of cars, cleaning the home, washing and ironing his master's cloth, etc. He has no right to travel home without the consent of the master, even if the parents live in the same city with the master. He must work hard to win the trust and favour of his master, as it is the master who would make an appraisal of his service in the growing of the business venture and in non-business related areas. At the end of the apprenticeship, the master gives the apprentice a take-off fund for the hiring or purchase of a shop, goods, equipment, where necessary and in some cases, accommodation for a given period of time. This take-off fund does not in any way mean that he ceases to collaborate with the master, the master still assists him or her with goods procurement to reduce overhead importation cost, knowing fully well that the apprentice has a weak purchasing power.

Through the different responsibilities that the master places on the apprentice, the master prepares him for the future. In what seems like a tough time, the master exposes the apprentice to a future reality that is tough, and which can only be overcome through hard work. It is not in all cases that the master stays with the apprentice in the same shop or business premises, having gathered some experience, the master can decide to open a shop elsewhere, different from the location where he might be. In this case, the apprentice manages the business branch for the master, representing him even at business negotiations with foreign trade partners. This seeming independence of the apprentice in management does not only help the master expand his business and thus make more profit, it equips the apprentice with an ownership mindset that gives room for trust, building of his confidence and exposure, which is necessary for the apprentice if he must succeed in the future.

Once an apprentice graduates and is settled, he has a responsibility of doing for others back at home what his master has done for him. He, therefore, goes to the village and picks another apprentice who would serve him. Meanwhile, before his graduation, his master must have gone home and picked another apprentice who would learn the trade before his final graduation. It is thus a model that keeps engaging the young. The Igbo traditionally frown at the young roaming the streets in idleness and refer to as *efulefu* 'a lost one'. The *igba boyi* apprentice system ensures that if a child is unable to go to school, instead of staying back at home, he learns a trade - usually the type of trade that his family people have been involved in. The two basic principles, according to Crescent (2019) that drives the Igbo apprentice system are:

1.  Get every Igbo child busy with something and discourage laziness

2.  Give helping hands to someone running a business and in turn transfer the knowledge to ward.

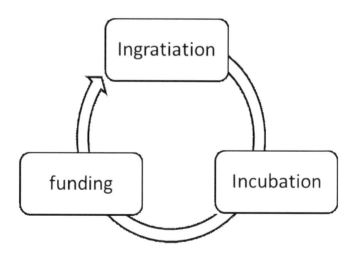

*Figure 1: Cycle of **igba boyi***

In summary, it all begins with Ingratiation, which involves the processes of the master going to the village, picking a relation and introducing him to the system, their duties, roles and overall workings of the system. It is also a period of orientation. This is followed by the period of incubation, which offers the apprentice the business spaces of learning to mature in the business, in co-creation, trainings and cultivation of business models. The incubation platform is full of risks, but especially practical in nature. It is during this period that the apprentice is trained, nurtured, and mentored; during which time also honesty, accountability and work ethic are the core principles. The final stage is funding. This is when the master settles the apprentice to begin his own business. This is dependent on the financial capability of the master and the commitment of the apprentice to the success of the business during the incubation period.

It should be emphasized that at the picking up point and the settlement/funding point, there are no written documents or court papers to sign. It is all done on trust. According to Neuwirth (2018):

> *The interesting thing is that nothing is in writing, it's all done on trust and credibility. The boy's family would usually come together and meet with the master at the commencement of the arrangement. And at the end of the apprentice period, the master will also bring the boy home and settle him in the presence of his family. Government cannot replicate that. They can only complicate it. (Ted, November 2018)*

### 3.2 Checks and Balances in the Success of *igba boyi*

In spite of the absence of clearly written laws to guide the relationship between the master and the apprentice, this system has succeeded over the years. This success is based on a college of factors. The first reason why it succeeds is that the apprentice treads with caution, knowing fully well that if he fails or ruins his masters business, his own future would be ruined. He treads carefully in managing the affairs of his master and tries to prosper the master's business because he knows that his destiny is tied to the economic destiny of his master. This fear, according to Okoro (2018) engenders honesty during the years of apprenticeship, as every established acts of theft, diversion of fund and flamboyant use and wastage of business finances terminates the arrangement. Second, while the apprentice does his best to avoid the termination of the apprentice arrangement, the master is also careful to avoid a bad labeling from his community where he has picked the son of a brother or relation. To dismiss the apprentice on grounds that are not substantiated or failing to keep to the terms of apprenticeship after the agreed number of years of service can incur the wrath of the community back at home.

Thus, the *igba boyi* apprenticeship system is not just an arrangement between the master and the apprentice, it is a community or family affair. Masters who are notorious for not settling their apprentice hardly get apprentice to work with them because the story of every master's treatment of his apprentice is generally known. And these stories, good or bad, last for generations among the members of the community or family. No wonder some masters have more applications for apprenticeship than others. According to Okoro (2018), insincere masters run the risk of having their businesses or fortune ruined by the apprentice's personal deity, known as the *Chi*. This is why every master does his best to give a take-off package to the apprentice after the fulfillment of the agreed years of service. At this point of settlement the blessing of the master is indispensable. The blessing of the master is more important than the financial package, because it is believed that the financial package without his blessing ends in ruin. At this point, therefore, the Igbo apprentice system takes up a spiritual dimension.

## 4.  Some Products of *ịgba bọyị*

As the Igbo continue to create wealth in different parts of Nigeria, the apprentice system is at its base. Neuwirth (2018) visited the Alaba International Market in Lagos dominated by the Igbo and observed that:

> *This mutual aid economy still exists, and we can find examples of it in the strangest places. So, this is Alaba International Market. It's the largest electronics market in West Africa. It's 10,000 merchants, they do about four billion dollars of turnover every year. And they say they are ardent apostles of Adam Smith: competition is great, we're all in it individually, government doesn't help us. But the interesting reality is that when I asked further, that's not what grew the market at all. There's a behind-the-scenes principle that enables this market to grow. And they do claim — you know, this is an interesting juxtaposition of the King James Bible and "How To Sell Yourself." That's what they say is their message. But in reality this market is governed by a sharing principle. (Ted, November 2018)*

It is a system that depends on the other. Everyone becomes who he is because of who the other is to him and what the other has done for him. Thus, Neuwirth (2018) says further:

> *Every merchant, when you ask them, "How did you get started in global trade?" they say, "Well, when my master settled me." And when I finally got it into my head to ask, "What is this 'settling?'" it turns out that when you've done your apprenticeship with someone you work for, they are required — required — to set you up in business. That means paying your rent for two or three years and giving you a cash infusion so*

> *you can go out in the world and start trading. That's locally generated venture capital. Right? And I can say with almost certainty that the Igbo apprenticeship system that governs Alaba International Market is the largest business incubator platform in the world. (Ted, November 2018)* "

The Igbo apprenticeship system has produced more millionaires and billionaires than the entire Nigerian University economic system has produced. Neuwirth (2018) observes that the Igbo multi billionaires were the products of this business incubator platform:

 > *Innoson, Cocharis, Ibeto, Chikason, Ekenedilichukwu, are all from our great city of Nnewi. None of these men ventured anywhere near the gates of a secondary school, some didn't even finish primary school, but control multi-billion dollar empires. It starts with an apprentice system where a master takes a young boy of about 10 years, the boy serves his master for about 7 years. At the end of the 7 years, the master settles the boy with some capital. Most times depending on their relationship, the boy remains in the master's house even though he is now free, eats there and sleeps there for the next 2 years or so, to save money. In addition to the capital, the master also extends credit facilities to the boy and gives him goods on credit to sell. (Ted, November 2018).* "

These millionaires: Innoson, Cocharis, Ibeto, Chikason, Ekenedilichukwu are not just millionaires for themselves, they make millionaires every year through the apprentice incubator platform. The system is such that there is always a millionaire waiting to be born. It is a beautiful circle, with each circle preparing for the birth of a millionaire- who is either being ingratiated or incubated or funded.

## 5. Conclusion

This chapter has tried to present the significance of *igba boyi* as part of the indigenous structure for wealth creation in the Igbo community development and social welfare. The beauty of it is its simplicity. It is a system that does not take equity or require raising huge capital. It is driven by human-platform. It is a human network that the Nigerian government can deepen through the provision of capital. If the government can deepen these human-platforms, she can comfortably fix the unemployment problem that is affecting the young and the economy of the country, and ultimately improve the nation's social welfare and community development.

## References

Aleke, M. (2018). The Igbo apprenticeship system that builds wealth and started the incubation system, https://www.pulse.ng/gist/imu-ahia-the-igbo-apprenticeship-system-that-builds-wealth-and-started-the-incubation/q50ps44

Aligwekwe, P. E. (1991). The continuity of African traditional values in the African society: The Igbo of Nigeria. Enugu: Snaap.

Basden, J. T. (1966). Niger Ibos. London: Frank Cass.

Grenz, S. (1966). A primer on post-modernism. William B. Eerdmans: Grand Rapid.

Gudtalent Chrisent (2019). What Is Imu Ahia/Igba Boy – What The Igbo Apprenticeship Is, History, Thought and Terms. https://www.entorm.com/opinion/imu-ahia-the-igbo-apprenticeship.

Isichei, E. (1976). A history of the Igbo people. London: Macmillan.

Kalu, O. (1978). Precarious vision: The African perception of his world. O. Kalu (Ed.). African cultural development (pp. 28-41). Enugu: Fourth Dimension.

Kanu, I. A. (2014). Suicide in Igbo-African Ontology. Developing Countries Studies. Vol. 4. No. 5. USA. pp. 27-38.

Kanu, I. A. (2014). Suffering in Igbo-African Ontology. Research on Humanities and Social Sciences. Vol. 4. No. 5. pp. 8-13.

Kanu I. A. (2017). Igwebuikeconomics: Towards an inclusive economy for economic development. Igwebuike: An African Journal of Arts and Humanities. Vol. 3. No. 6. 113-140.

Kanu, I. A. (2012). The concept of life and person in African anthropology. In E. Ezenweke and I. A. Kanu (Eds.). Issues in African traditional religion and philosophy (pp. 61-71). Jos: Augustinian.

Kanu, I. A. (2012). Towards an Igbo Christology. In E. Ezenweke and I. A. Kanu (Eds.). Issues in African traditional religion and philosophy (pp. 75-98). Jos: Fab Anieh.

Kanu, I. A. (2019). Collaboration within the Ecology of Mission: An African Cultural Perspective. The Catholic Voyage. Vol. 15. pp. 125-149.

Kuhn, T. (1970). The structure of scientific revolution. Chicago: University of Chicago Press.

Njoku, E. E. (1990). The Igbos of Nigeria: Ancient rites, changes and survival. New York: Edwin Mellen.

Nwala, T. U. (1998). Igbo Philosophy. Lagos: Literained Publications.

Oguejiofor, O. (2010). Globalization and the Resilience of traditional paradigms: The case of the Igbo of Nigeria. In A. B. C Chiegboka, T. C. Utoh-Ezeajugh and G. I. Udechukwu (Eds.). The humanities and globalization in the third millennium (pp. 15-25). Anambra: Rex Charles and Patrick.

Okoro, C. (2018). What makes the Igbo Apprenticeship model tick and critical considerations before taking it mainstream. In https://techpoint.africa/2018/11/07/igbo-apprenticeship-system-for-startups

Onwuejeogwu, M. A. (1987). Evolutionary trends in the history of the development of the Igbo civilization in the culture theatre of Igbo land in Southern Nigeria. A paper Presented during the Ohiajioku Lecture, Owerri.

Neuwirth, R. (2018). Igbo apprenticeship system is world's largest business incubator platform – Robert Neuwirth reveals. https://www.informationng.com/2018/11/igbo-apprenticeship-system-is-worlds-largest-business-incubator-platform-robert-neuwirth-reveals.html

Tempel, P. (1952). Bantu philosophy. Paris: Presence Africaine.

Uchendu, V. C. (1965). The Igbos of South East Nigeria. London: Rinehart and Winston.

# Part Six

# THE NDỊ IGBO
# AND THEIR NEIGHBOURS

# CHAPTER 18

BROWN GRACE N. M. & T.B. MICHAEL

## The Igbo-Niger Delta Relations: From The Past To The Present

1. Introduction

2. Pre-Colonial Igbo-Niger Delta Relations

    2.1 Economic Relations

    2.2 Cultural Relations

    2.3 Political Relations

3. The Essence of Igbo-Niger Delta Relations

4. Conclusion

## Summary

*Some historians, sociologists and anthropologists consider the Igbo and the Niger Delta ethnic groups as people that have had good and cordial relationships and complemented each other over the ages. This chapter examines the nature of this relationship, from the pre-colonial times to the present, with a view to highlighting how the groups have lived in the past as well as the factors that facilitated mutual co-operation between them. Historical oral analysis, written and ethnographical evidences were used for this study. It can be ascertained that the Niger Delta ethnic groups and the Igbo have since pre-colonial times always related mutually and complemented each other in many endeavours. However, this is contrary to the present day antagonistic and unfavourable political sentiments that colour the political space of the two groups, and which could be traced to the complications arising from the inherited colonial political structure, in addition to the creation of the Niger Delta States, and the 1966 – 1970 Nigeria Biafra Civil War. Although politicians of both the Igbo and the Niger Delta ethnic groups intermittently exploit these complications to stoke political crisis and disagreements, the age-old mutual social inter-ethnic relationships between the two groups have not diminished on that account. Instead, the relationships continue to live a life of their own, as though immunized against political manipulations.*

## 1. Introduction

THE HISTORIOGRAPHY OF INTERGROUP RELATIONS is aimed at unearthing and highlighting the things that promote intergroup cooperation and coexistence, especially in multicultural states that are in search of nationhood. Such an effort is unavoidable with regard to the Igbo-Niger Delta intergroup relations, which are presently faced with intermittent politicization of issues that seem to negate or deny century-old relationships that were bound to naturally arise from the geographical contiguity of the different ethnic groups of the region.

The Igbo are predominantly found in the south-eastern region of Nigeria which is divided into two parts, an eastern part (which is larger) and a western part. Igbo land as such comprises sub-linguistic and cultural groups such as Anioma, Aro, Abiriba, Ngwa, EddaEgbebu, Ezaa, Ibeku, Ohuhu, etc. (Isichei, 1976). However, these sub-groups are generally subsumed under a common Igbo identity with the central Igbo language as the dominant lingua franca. The Igbo also constitute a significant proportion of the population of some states in the South-south region of Nigeria such as Akwa Ibom, Cross River, Delta and Rivers State. The Niger Delta on the other hand, is inhabited by some ethnic groups such as the Itsekiri, Urhobo, Isoko, Ijaw (Izọn), Ogba, Ikwerre, Ahoada, Etche, Engenni, Abua/Odual, Ibani (Bony and Opobo), Ukwuani, Kalabari, Okrika, Ogoni, Eleme, Epie-Atissa, Obolo, Ibibio, Efik, yakurr, Edo, and others. The coastal Niger Delta area is bordered in the north by the rain forest belt where the Igbo are predominantly found. Thus, nature has placed the Igbo and the Niger Delta peoples in a confine where mutual interactions at the socio-cultural, political and economic fronts are inevitable.

## 2. Igbo-Niger Delta relations in the Past

Historical accounts of the relations between the Igbo and the Niger Delta people suggest that the Igbo-Niger Delta relation was characterized by a relatively high degree of mutual cooperation, interdependence, peace and equality (Davey, 2015). Ejituwu (2007) noted that Igbo-Niger Delta relations were characterized by symbiosis of economic relations and cross-cultural borrowings, in addition to the borrowing of political structures.

## 2.1 Economic Relations

Before the trans-Atlantic slave trade, Igbo-Niger Delta relation was more localized and more intense in areas where the two groups shared common borders or are connected by fresh water bodies.

The Niger Delta peoples, by virtue of their proximity to the Atlantic coasts, were among the first people in Nigeria to come in contact with the European merchants. The role of the Niger Delta people in the Euro-African trade which followed the European discovery of the Gulf of Guinea was more pronounced during the Trans-Atlantic Slave trade. The Niger Delta merchants served as middle men in the trade and related with other Igbo middle men who supplied slaves from the rain forest hinterland to Niger Delta merchants for sale to the European slave merchants. During the slave trade, powerful and autonomous War Canoe Houses which were micro political units in the Niger Delta emerged and competed in the slave trade. The Igbo middlemen were the major trade partners of the coastal merchants. The Aro oracle, popularly known as Ibini Ukpabi, was a major instrument for the procurement of slaves (Njoku, 2016). The fame of the oracle was known throughout the Niger Delta and beyond. The Aro slave traders, through the instrumentality of the oracle, established settlements in some parts of the Niger Delta hinterland region such as Isiokpo and Igwuruta in Ikwerre Local Government Area of Rivers State. Oral interviews conducted in these communities revealed that the two groups have co-existed peacefully till date. The slave trade period can be described as a watershed in the Igbo-Niger Delta relations; slave dealers from both sides cooperated effectively in the trade thereby ensuring the sustenance of the trade even beyond the period of its abolition (Njoku, 2016).

Another trade that thrived within the period was the palm oil trade. Following the abolition of the Trans-Atlantic Slave Trade in 1807, and the reintroduction of trade in non-human commodities, Niger Delta merchants repositioned themselves for the new trade and still maintained the same channel of supplies as the slave trade. Palm oil was obtained from Igbo hinterland by the Niger Delta Middle men who dealt directly with the European merchants and exchanged African produce for European finished goods. Some Eastern Niger Delta traders also established trading posts in some Igbo communities. For example, Opobo and Bonny traders established trading posts in Akwete, Ohambele, Azumini, Umuogor, Okoloma and others in the present day Ndoki in Abia State.

The great fortune made from the palm oil trade led to the rise of powerful political units in the Niger Delta in the 18th century. Noble houses in the Niger Delta such as the Ama Pepple House of Bonny and later the Jaja of Opobo and other prosperous trading houses emerged as a result of the great fortunes made from the oil trade. The Niger Delta merchant supported palm oil producers in parts of Igboland by giving them facilities such as big pots and containers for processing and storing oil (Davey, 2015). Davey (2015) also reported that Douglas Jaja, the son of Jaja of Opobo, while tracing his father's connection with the people of Amaigbo, was able to find traces of big vessels for oil processing which his father had given to oil producers in Amaigbo, in present day Imo State. Hence, this proves that oil merchants in the Niger Delta cooperated with their Igbo oil producers. Nevertheless, there was also the movement of some Igbo into the Niger Delta region, propelled by the search for greener pastures, especially during the colonial period. The Igbo who came into the Niger Delta during this period took up many employments: some were employed in the colonial civil service; some engaged in businesses, some were labourers, some teachers, some stewards, some artisans, while some were drafted into the army or police. The Igbo explored every available economic opportunity in the Niger Delta and were not discriminated against.

The post-colonial period which spanned from 1960 to present, witnessed the influx of indigenous Igbo people to the Niger Delta region for commercial activities. This could be attributed to the oil boom in the region. Both groups have had cordial, friendly, and harmonious relationship. The creation of the defunct Eastern Region in 1960 provided ample opportunities for more intensive interaction between both groups. Some Niger Delta indigenes worked and lived in Enugu, the capital of the Eastern Region, and also engaged in different forms of economic activities. Likewise the Igbo also lived, worked and established businesses in other commercial centres in the Niger Delta region such as Port Harcourt, Calabar, Uyo, Yenegoa, Benin, Warri and others. They built and owed shops and residential houses.

Despite the cordial and harmonious relationship that existed among the Igbo and the Niger Delta people after the Nigeria-Biafra Civil War, Igbo – Niger Delta relationship was strained due to suspicious moves made by both groups on the issue of abandoned property policy of the federal and state governments in the post-civil war years. Although these were pockets of skirmishes between both groups, such minor disagreements did not result in open aggression or serious conflicts. Hence, since the 1970s to date the economic interactions between the Igbo and the Niger Delta people have remained cordial and stable. Trading activities have been on the increase and there have been complimentary processes. For example, Niger Delta traders travel to Aba, Onitsha and other popular Igbo markets to buy and sell their wares. On the other hand, the Igbo traders and merchants also travel to different markets in the Niger Delta region such as Calabar, Yenegoa, Warri oil mill market, creek road market, and mile one/railway market in Port Harcourt and others to sell their goods.

More State capitals emerged due to creation of new states after the Civil War. This paved the way for the establishment of commercial centres in cities like Asaba, Calabar, Port Harcourt, Yenegoa and others, attracting Igbo traders and merchants. For instance, Ikokwu Spare Parts Market Port Harcourt, Port Harcourt Building Material Market, Mile Three Market, Yenegoa Motor Spare Parts Market, among others, are dominated by the Igbo. The border communities have shared long years of peaceful coexistence, good economic relation, inter-group marriages, political affiliation and socio-cultural ties. Hence, Igbo – Niger Delta economic relations over the years have been more peaceful than confrontational.

## 2.2   Cultural Relations

Great cultural transformation occurred in the Niger Delta during the second article of trade period that succeeded the era of Trans-Atlantic Slave Trade. This could be traced to a mixture of social and religious factors.

From the social angle, many Igbo domestic slaves in the Niger Delta that became free at the end of the slave trade era gained prominence and began to influence the lives of the Niger Delta people. For instance the city of Opobo which was founded by an ex-Bonny slave of Igbo Origin, Jaja, was a place where Igbo infiltration led to significant cultural changes. The *Ibani* language that is spoken in the area is a variant of the Ijaw (Izon) language that resulted from Igbo influence. Also Igbo names became common in places with significant Igbo presence such as *Opobo, Bonny, Okrika, Eleme* and others. The Igbo on their part adopted certain cultural practices of the Niger Delta peoples, including new vocabularies and dressing habits such as the Ijo*hombre hat* that became popular among Onitsha-Igbo chiefs. The high proportion of Igbo men in this region resulted in inter-marriages between the Igbo and their neighbours. Oral traditions claim that women of *Andoni, Degema, Efik,* and *Ibibio* descent entered into short- and long-term relationships with thousands of successful Igbo male entrepreneurs of servile background, and *Efik, Ibibio* and *Kalabari* men favoured Igbo women due to their fair complexion and beauty. *Andoni* men in particular were fund of marrying Igbo women from Umuahia area (Njoku, 2016, pp. 125-127). These intense social relations between the Igbo and their Niger Delta neighbours led to significant cultural transformations and complex hybridization.

From the religious angle, the Igbo people that accepted Christianity and Western civilization accompanied some missionaries that came to the Niger Delta, served as clerks, stewards, catechists, teachers and servants for the missionaries. In some Anglican and Roman Catholic churches that had Igbo catechist or teachers attached to them, Igbo was used as the language of the church. In places like *Ikwerre, Etche, Ahoada, Ogoni, Obolo* where the missionaries were assisted by Igbo teachers, many persons learnt and spoke the Igbo language. The Igbo were held in admiration by the people of the Niger Delta as a result of their privileged positions in the missions and colonial milieu.

However, it is note worthy that the Niger Delta people were not as itinerant as the Igbo; their cultural effect on Igbo heartland is therefore not as intense as that of the Igbo on the Niger Delta people. Population explosion and unsustainable agricultural farmland in many parts of Igboland were among the factors that gradually propelled the Igbo to exit from the Southeast into the Niger Delta region. Such conditions did not exist within the Niger Delta environment; hence, most of the Niger Delta people continued to stay in their locality. Nevertheless, both groups have coexisted peacefully for long and have attained high level of mutual understanding. Following the many years of mutual existence, the Niger Delta people have come to regard the Igbo as part of them, though not in the political sphere.

## 2.3 Political Relations

The different peoples of Nigeria have lived as independent states like in other parts of Africa before the advent of colonial rule. The introduction of colonialism altered the structure of pre-colonial administrative units in Nigeria. In 1906, the colony and protectorates of Southern Nigeria were created by the colonial government and three provinces were carved out namely: Western Province with headquarters at Lagos, Central Province with headquarters at Warri and Eastern Province with headquarters at Calabar. Three commissioners were appointed accordingly to administer these provinces. Notably, the Igbo and some parts of Niger Delta were grouped into different political units with their Igbo neighbours in the Eastern Province. For example, the Eastern Province constituted of Afikpo, Arochuku, Bende, Calabar, Obubra and others. (Effah-Attoe, 2013). After the amalgamation of Southern Nigeria and Northern Nigeria into one Nigeria in 1914, the Igbo and the Niger Delta neighbours continued to share political affiliations.

By the time Nigeria attained independence from Britain in 1960, the Igbo under the Eastern Regional Government, had established such a strong influence in the Niger Delta that the minority groups in the Niger Delta began to feel uncomfortable and to see them as overbearing (Davey, 2015). The earliest formal complaint of Igbo domination of the Eastern Region occurred in 1953. The complaint was precipitated by the expulsion of Eyo Ita, one of the foremost nationalists, from the NCNC by the Nnamdi Azikiwe led executive of the party. The minority groups in the Eastern region which included most Niger Delta people agitated for the creation of Cross River-Ogoja-Rivers State (C-O-R). In response to the complaints and agitations of the ethnic minority groups, the colonial government created the Wilkins' Commission to look into the claims of ethnic domination by the Igbo to establish the facts and make recommendations to the colonial government. The commission rejected the agitation for the Creation of a separate state, thus laying the foundation for future agitations.

After independence and during the Nigerian Civil War (1966-1970) between the defunct Eastern Region and Nigeria, the Niger Delta fought alongside the Igbo against the Nigerian army. The civil war inflicted much grief and agony on the minds of the affected states especially the South East and South-South, which contributed to distancing the Igbo from their Niger Delta neighbours. Abandoned properties were one of the devastating effects of the war as the Nigerian Government promulgated the abandoned property edict. This emboldened the governments of each state to enact laws relinquishing the rights, title or claim to any property abandoned during the war. The federal government enacted the "Abandoned Properties Act, 1979, Cap. 1, Laws of the Federation of Nigeria". The East –Central States (old Anambra and old Imo States) also enacted "Vacant Premises Edict", while the South Eastern State (old Cross River and old Rivers State) enacted "Abandoned Properties Edict" in imitation of the federal government edict (Abandoned Property Matter File No. LS/TD/VOL. 11:1030, National Archive). Rivers State's "Abandoned Property Edict" and the Land Instruments Registration Law were enacted by the military Governor of Rivers in 1969 towards the end of the Civil War.

At the end of the War, many Igbo gradually returned to the Niger Delta areas and continued in their various endeavours. However, the administration of the abandoned properties in the former Eastern States and Rivers State created a lot of acrimony, dissatisfaction and animosity among the Eastern States resulting in numerous petitions and counter petitions between the affected states. This further aggravated the tension between the Igbo and their Niger Delta neighbours. Nevertheless, the Igbo presence in the Niger Delta region continued to expand. Places such as Port Harcourt, Onne, Bonny, Warri, Ughelli, Yenagoa continued to swell with Igbo presence. Some Igbo became employed by the oil companies and in other establishments in the Niger Delta, others engaged in personal businesses while others were casual labourers. Some authors are of the view that the Igbo are more at home in the Niger Delta region than in other parts of the country outside their home state. The mutual relationship between the Igbo and the Niger Delta people is the facilitating factor for this, but it has also given rise to a lot of cross-cultural borrowings in the forms of dressing, language, food, and other things.

## 3. The Essence of the Igbo-Niger Delta Relations

According to some historians, art historians and anthropologists, the pre-colonial relations between the Igbo and their Niger Delta neighbours witnessed exchange of ideas, artifacts, religion and socio-political institutions between the two groups (Ijoma, 1984; Shelton, 1971; Afigbo, 1987, 1981; Oguagha & Okpoko, 1984; Kolapo, 2004; Ohadike, 1994; Onwuejeogwu, 1981). The core of Igbo-Niger Delta relations lies in these cross-cultural borrowings. Some of the borrowed customs and practices have gradually become so deeply entrenched in the various communities that they are no longer recognised by the majority of the present generation of the various ethnic groups as borrowed. In other words, the cross-cultural borrowings can be seen as having contributed to some cultural norms and practices that can now be described as a *common cultural heritage of the Igbo-Niger Delta region.*

In areas where the Igbo shared common boundaries with some people of the Niger Delta such as the *Ikwerre, Abua, Ahoada, Eleme, Ukwuani, Engenni, Ogba*, and others, great cultural borrowings occurred. Also, ideas of political and social organization were borrowed. The Anioma Igbo, the Onitsha Igbo and other Igbo groups that closely associated with the Niger Delta borrowed and domesticated the political institutions of the Niger Delta. For instance, the various Anioma Igbo groups and Onitsha Igbo established well-defined monarchical structure that was typical of the Niger Delta city states (Ikime, 1985). The rest of the Igbo groups in the rain forest heartland which maintained a republican system and functioned without kings or paramount rulers during colonialism adopted the Niger Delta monarchical model of political and social organization which was hitherto unknown in their culture.

All these borrowings by the Igbo contrasts with the borrowing of religious and cultic artefacts from the Igbo by some Niger Delta groups. For example, the Niger Delta borrowed some Igbo rituals connected with agriculture and the services of some powerful oracular institutions (Obichere, 1982). The Ibinu Ukpabi oracle has been described as the most powerful oracle in pre-colonial West Africa whose influence extended into Ibibio, Ijaw, Edo, Idoma and Igala. The oracle was a well-known and revered phenomenon in pre-colonial Niger Delta (Ikime, 1985). Also, the Igbo *Ikenga*, a carved image that symbolizes the spiritual force behind male achievement, was introduced into the Niger Delta areas of Ijaw, Isoko, Urhobo and Itsekiri by the Igbo (Chuku, 2018; Odita, 1973; Boston, 1977). The similitude of cultural artefacts among the Igbo and western Niger Delta groups has also been used to argue that the Igbo and western Niger Delta people exchanged ideas in the crafts (Isichei, 1976). Some sculptures and carvings discovered in the Obi of Eze Nri bear remarkable similarity with some artefacts found in the ancient Benin kingdom.

From the language angle, the similarity between the Igbo language and the languages of some Niger Delta groups is not seen as mere coincidence but as a pointer to sustained cultural relations in the past. For instance, the word "ise", which is normally echoed by the Igbo in response to the traditional prayer before breaking of kola nut and other rituals, is similarly used by the people of the ancient Benin kingdom which include some Niger Delta people. Although lack of written record makes it difficult for one to establish whether such words were borrowed from the Igbo or the Igbo borrowed them from the Niger Delta, the words still remain indicators of cultural relations that existed between the Igbo and their neighbours in the Niger Delta area. An aspect of the language that can be confirmed in the present is the expansion of local vocabularies of some Niger Delta people as a result of the infiltration of freed Igbo slaves into the Niger Delta. It has been confirmed for example, that Igbo names were given by parents of non-Igbo ancestry often as a result of the admiration that such parents had for the Igbo people who had excelled to become very prosperous in the Niger Delta environment (Dike, 1956, Isichei, 1976). However, the name-borrowing is not all that one-sided, because the Igbo also borrowed some Niger Delta names. For example, the Igbo of Ndoki in present day Abia State borrowed from the *Ijaw* (Izọn) of the Niger Delta. Hence, *Ijaw* names like *Erefa, Ibiene, Furo, Ibiwari* etc, are found in *Akwete* in Ndoki. Soup that is called *fulo* in the *Ijaw* language is also called *fulo* in *Akwete*. *Ndoki* communities speak *Igbani Igbo*, which is a dialect of the Opobo and Bonny people in Rivers State. The *Nwaotam* masquerade display of the *Igbani* people (Opobo and Bonny) originated from the *Ndoki* people. (*Nengia Harold in Eber Opubo, 150 years anniversary edition, 2020*).

The exchange of culinary ideas is one area that has persisted up to the present, although one would expect a certain levelling after many decades of mutual coexistence. Both sides have adopted various food varieties of each other into their traditional menu. In Igbo land meals that were originally associated with the Niger Delta are served. Also in the Niger Delta area, meals that are associated with the Igbo are extensively served, such as *Abacha* (popularly known as African Salad) thus, proving that culinary cultures from both sides have intermarried and will continue to complement each other.

Finally, one could conclude from all of the above that the Igbo and the Niger Delta have developed some form of social bonding. In cities such as Port Harcourt, Yenagoa, Warri, and others, the Igbo relate with the indigenous people in almost all fronts: they belong to the same social clubs, attend the same events, eat the same kind of food, and dress alike. This is an indication of a great level of social and cultural integration between the Igbo and the Niger Delta groups.

## 4. Conclusion

There were relatively harmonious relations between the Igbo and the Niger Delta groups in the past. Culturally, the two groups enriched their respective cultures through cross-cultural borrowings. Political ideas and forms of social organization were also borrowed. Both groups occupied and participated in the economic space of each other without any significant form of discrimination. Before the colonial period, the two groups had strong economic relationships and complemented each other through effective trade relations. However, the feeling of separateness between the two groups was initiated and entrenched by the colonial government, which not only divided the people into ethnic groups, but used the ethnic grouping as a base for political units, thus, inventing ethnic sentiments in places where such was non-existent. The political structure made the minority ethnic Niger Delta to feel insecure by their attachment to the Igbo dominated Eastern region. Hence, they began to clamour for a separate political unit. This division along ethnic lines, which was later adopted and further solidified through the creation of states in Nigeria and the division of the core Niger Delta people into the states of Delta, Bayelsa and Rivers, further strengthened ethnic consciousness in the Niger Delta. These divisions heightened the tension in the relation between the Niger Delta and the non-Niger Delta peoples. The Niger Delta people as a result, began to see the Igbo as foreigners who had no stake in their political affairs. But ... back home in Igbo land, the Igbo also began to treat the non-indigenous people, including the Niger Delta, the same way. It is noteworthy however, that this feeling of political separateness has not been extended to the economic space to this day, as the economic environment has always remained open for equal participation on both axes. Also, socially and culturally, the Igbo and the Niger Delta have continued to interrelate and intermarry, in spite of all the different forms of ethno-political differences and separation championed by politicians on both sides.

| s/n | NAME | SEX | AGE | OCCUPATION | STATUS | LOCATION | DATE |
|-----|------|-----|-----|------------|--------|----------|------|
| 1 | Isaiah Onwuka | male | 65 | Teacher | Chief | Ohambele | 05-12-2020 |
| 2 | Mrs. Evelyn Eruba | Female | 70 | Trader | Women leader | Akwate Ndoki | 05-12-2020 |
| 3 | Joy Nnadede | Female | 45 | Teacher | - | Akwate Ndoki | 14-11-2020 |
| 4 | Dr. Chibuzor Nelson | Male | 52 | Lecturer | Chief | Port Harcourt | 13-01-2021 |
| 5 | ThankGodJaja | Male | 56 | Business man | Elder | Port Harcourt | 13-01-2020 |
| 6 | Helen Peters | Female | 62 | Trader | - | Port Harcourt | 16-01-2021 |
| 7 | Mrs. ChidiChinda | Female | 50 | Civil servant | - | Port Harcourt | 17-12-2020 |

*List of Oral Informants*

## Archival Sources

Abandoned Property Matter, File No. LS/TD/VOL. 11:1030, National Archive, Enugu. Abandoned Property File No.Go/Sc/146 Vol. 111:113m National Archive, Port Harcourt.

## Written Sources

Boston, J. S. (1977).  Ikenga Figures among the North-West Igbo and the Igala.London: Ethnographica.

Brown, G. M. (2013). Abandoned Properties in Nigeria: The Effect of Civil War in the Nigerian State in Icheke Journal of the Faculty of Humanities, Ignatius Ajuru University of Education, Port Harcourt.Pp. 13 – 24, Vol. 11(1).

Chuku, G. (2018). Igbo historiography: Part I, II, & III. African Studies, UMBC.

Davey, J. M. (2015). Replanting the seeds of home: Slavery, King Jaja, and Igbo connections in the Niger Delta, 1821-1891. A Thesis submitted to Michigan State University in partial fulfilment of the requirements for the degree of Doctor of Philosophy in History.

Dike, K.O. (1956). Trade and Politics in the Niger Delta, 1830-1885; An Introduction to the Economic and Political History of Nigeria. Oxford: Clarendon Press.

Effah-Attoe, (2013), From Ethnicity to Federalism: A Study of the Biase of the South/South Geo-Political Region of Nigerian Pre-independence times" in Okpeh O. Okpeh, Jr. Christopher B. N. Ogbogbo (eds.), Federalism in Historical Perspective. Aboki Publishers, Makurdi.

Ejituwu, N. (2007). Thesis, Antithesis, Synthesis: Niger Delta Historiography in Time Perspective. In ChimaKorieh& Femi Kalopi (eds.), The aftermath of slavery: Transitions and transformations in South eastern Nigeria. Trenton: Africa World Press. Pp. 207–27.

Ijoma, O. J. (1984). "Evolution of Kingship among the West Niger Igbo Chiefdoms with Particular Reference to Benin Influence."Ikenga, 6, 34-46.

Ikime, O. (1985). In Search of Nigerians: Changing Patterns of Inter-group Relations in  an Evolving Nation State. Lagos, Nigeria: Impact Publishers.

Isichei.E. (1976).A History of the Igbo

People.London: Macmillan Press.
Kolapo, F. J. (2004). The Igbo and their Neighbours during the Era of the Atlantic Slave-Trade. Slavery and Abolition, Vol. 25, pp. 114-33.

Njoku, R. C. (2016). "Becoming African: Igbo Slaves and Social Reordering in Nineteenth-Century Niger Delta."In Igbo in the Atlantic World, eds. ToyinFalola and Raphael Njoku, 123-134. Bloomington: Indiana University Press.

Nengia Harold (2020) "Culture" in EberOpubo, 150 years anniversary edition. Obichere, B.I. (1982). Studies in southern Nigerian history: A festschrift for Joseph Christopher Okwudili Anene 1918-68.Routledge.

Odita, O. E. (1973). "Universal Cults and Intra-Diffusion: Igbo Ikenga in Cultural Retrospection." African Studies Review, 16, 73-82.

Oguagha, P. &Okpoko, A. (1984).History and Ethnoarchaeology in Eastern Nigeria: A Study of Igbo-Igala Relations with Special Reference to the Anambra Valley.Oxford: B.A.R.

Ohadike, D. C. (1994).Anioma: A Social History of the Western Igbo People. Athens, OH: Ohio University Press.
Onwuejeogwu, M. A. (1981). An Igbo Civilization: Nri Kingdom and Hegemony. London: Ethnographica.

Shelton, A. (1971). The Igbo-Igala Borderland: Religion and Social Control in Indigenous African Colonialism.Albany: State University of New York Press.

# CHAPTER 19

EKANADE OLUMIDE

# The History Of Yoruba-Igbo Intergroup Relations

## Summary

Right from the pre-colonial period to the present, various forms of intergroup relations have always existed between the Yoruba and the Igbo. The Vicissitudes of the colonial period, the struggles of the independent era, the conflicts of the civil war, up to the present politically motivated atmosphere of almost mutual distrust, have not been able to entirely wipe off this long standing relation. Instead, the tides of time have intermittently reached peaks of pure ignorance of such Yoruba-Igbo intergroup relations, apparently throwing up huge and suffocating fumes of prejudices on the shores of our social lives, to be followed most often by heart-warming recollections of the positive aspects of the relations, which form the fine sea shells and peals deposited by the ebbing tide on the shores of our social time. The radiance of these shining peals have a debilitating effect on the manipulative propensities of our political class, who should rein in their selfish desires and pursue the general good of the citizenry regardless of ethnic persuasions.

## 1.  Introduction

INTERGROUP RELATIONS REFER TO THE WAYS IN WHICH PEOPLE in groups (ethnic or religious) perceive, think about, feel about, and act towards people in other groups (Hogg, 2003). It also refers to interactions between individuals in different social groups, and to interactions taking place between the groups themselves collectively. Intergroup relations between states could be harmonious, congenial, friendly and mutually beneficial. In other instances it could be conflictual, hostile and cantankerous. The avenues and platforms for the conduct of intergroup relations among states and communities ranged from trade to diplomacy to socio cultural and political arrangements.

For Nigeria and most third world countries, the primordial culture has been creating problems for inter-ethnic coexistence unlike the prevalent civic culture well established in the Western Europe and North America which has enhanced mutual coexistence in such climes. It is important to state here that without meaningful intergroup relations among the various ethnics that constitute the Nigerian state, there can be no meaningful socio- political and economic development. Thus it is imperative to know what factors from pre-colonial times have shaped and enhanced intergroup relations between the Yoruba and the Igbo, points of divergence and reconstruction of such relationships for better results. My specific purpose here is to interrogate the inter-ethnic relations and interactions between the Yoruba of South-West Nigeria and the Igbo in South East Nigeria from pre-colonial times to the present. Present conclusions of glotto-chronology suggest that languages now spoken by Igbo and Ijo of Southeast Nigeria originated some 5,000-6,000 years ago along with sister languages like Igala, Idoma, Edo, and Yoruba, all in Kwa linguistic sub group from an ancestral stock with homeland in Niger Benue confluence from which point diffusion subsequently started(Afigbo, 1978, p.54).

## 2. The Pre-colonial Period

The pre-colonial period refers to the era before British colonisation of the Nigerian state. Long before 1500, much of modern Nigeria was divided into societies identified with contemporary ethnic groups. These early societies included the Igbo kingdom of Nri, the Benin kingdom, the Yoruba City states, including the kingdom of Ife, Igala Kingdom, the Hausa City states and Nupe kingdom. Historically, the earliest known contact between the Yoruba and Igbo ethnic groups was in the pre-colonial period. There are various hypotheses describing the initial contacts between the Yorubas and the Igbo. One tradition asserts that the Igbo were ancient inhabitants of Ife. The Igbo connection to Ife according to this tradition of origin is evident in the traditions preserved in oral narratives of Ile Ife itself and in the extant lineages of the Igbo still present in their habitations inside the Ooni of Ife's palace (Vanguard, 2019). The most probable is that tradition of origin which affirms Benin as the medial culture between the Igbo and the Yoruba. Indeed, the Benin suggest that Izoduwa was Oduduwa, and they know precisely when he left Ani-Idu (Benin City). So, who indeed are these people? There is the Nok hypothesis which suggests a coagulation that broke off at the Niger-Benue valley, with the Jukun, the Igbo, the Yoruba and the Igala, and possibly the Idu, moving apart into their current settlements. The Idu, who call themselves Benin today, are part of the larger Igbo, and are possibly the bridge with the Yoruba (Ibid). It is important to note that trade and politics were important determinants of intergroup relations between the Yoruba and the Igbo in the history of their various interactions.

Interestingly, introduction of slave trade and the transformations that took place in Benin in the 16th and 17th centuries caused large scale population movements into western Igbo land. In addition, some Edo speaking people fleeing from political and religious persecution came into Igbo land as refugees and were soon joined by a number of Benin warriors and hired Yoruba mercenaries of Oba of Benin (Ohadike, 1991, p.23). With the extensive rise of slavery in the 16th and 17th centuries, strangers, provided they were not slaves who had been captured, kidnapped, or purchased were welcome throughout western Igbo land where they were incorporated into the society as free men and women. In this regard, the Yoruba mercenaries in Igbo land brought with them their language, their food culture and general way of living which they introduced to the Igbo people and even engaged in cross cultural marriages with their Igbo landlords. The arrival of large numbers of strangers through the centuries caused the people of Western Igbo to develop certain characteristics not often found in other parts of southern Nigeria. For instance they were able to combine elements of the Igbo kingship system with Edo (Benin), Igala and Yoruba monarchical structures to build small-scale, autonomous chiefdoms and republics. Unlike the Igbo of the East of the Niger, but like the Edo and Yoruba, they preferred to settle in urban centers where they combined the Edo kingship system (under a paramount chief called Obi) with Igbo title system (sometimes called the Ozo or Eze system) to produce political structures that were neither Igbo nor Edo (Ibid, p.24). In essence, the dynamics of the dispersal and movement of the Yoruba, Bini and Igbo from one place to the another, necessarily brought them into close contact with each other, providing the basis for a cultural rubbing off which was fundamental to the subsequent evolution and development of the Igbo kingship system.

Furthermore in pre-colonial Igbo land, blacksmithing was adjudged the most useful and valuable craft. It was an economic activity in Awka which flourished as a protective device and a regulatory instrument through the guild system and, as such, was confined to Awka people. Itineration on a rotational basis by members of each guild was another basic feature of the blacksmith guilds in Awka. Really, itinerancy had profound root in Igbo blacksmithing traditions. However, Awka smiths travel organization differed from that of other Igbo groups in one significant way. The land beyond Awka was divided into trade zones and a trade zone was assigned to each blacksmith guild and her members for occupational tour. The respective blacksmithing territories were arbitrarily fixed and respected by all the sub-villages in Agulu. For instance Agulu villages maintained various zones one of which was *Umuogbu* whose itinerant blacksmiths migrated to areas such as Benin, Urhobo, Itshekiri and some Yoruba areas (Anaemene, 2018, p.140) such as Igbomina and Ikale land. The itinerant blacksmiths from Awka who moved into Ikale land developed a rigid system of trade unionism which jealously guarded their secrets and persistently resisted any attempt to usurp their privileges. The Awka blacksmiths practiced their vocation under this guild system manufacturing hoes and cutlasses for farming, kitchen utensils like metal basins and knives, dane guns for hunting and were also involved in trade, agriculture and traditional healing practices in Ikale land . Interestingly, Ikale men and women married off their daughters to the strong medicine men (among the Awka blacksmiths) who healed them and their daughters of certain infirmities. With the intermarriage between the itinerant Awka blacksmiths and Ikale women in Yorubaland, settlements (however short-lived) and mutual cultural borrowings, impacted on one another. This has helped to solidify cross cultural allegiance among the Yoruba and Igbo thereby promoting intergroup relations. The Awka blacksmiths also took advantage of the abundance of palm produce in Ikale; they bought palmoil from Ikale land, moved and sold them in Lagos for profit, then moved their profit back to Awka as they prepared for subsequent trips back to Ikale land (Anaemene, 2021).

## 3. The Colonial Era

Colonial period refers to the age of British subjugation and eventual colonization of subject peoples in the territories seized by the external colonial order. Colonial rule had important implications for intergroup relations in Nigeria, not only among the Igbo and their neighbours but also in the wider Nigerian federation. Colonialism caused forced cohabitation. It meant among other things that people now had to take into account, ideals, ideas, interests, and institutions arising not only from their indigenous experiences and sanctioned by their traditions and usages, but also of others introduced and imposed by new colonial rulers (Afigbo, 1987, p.79).

There was apparent indifference on the part of the colonial rulers during colonial era to ethnic and cultural differences as this affected the delimitation of administrative boundaries. Thus the boundaries of the districts, divisions and provinces into which regions were divided in this period did not seriously or at any rate generally aim at respecting any need to preserve the honor of linguistic or ethnic groups. For instance the Central province included Edo, Itshekiri, Urhobo, some Idoma, the rest Igbo, Ishan and some Yoruba groups. By implication, the Central province became a melting pot for all these cultures as the different peoples lived and interacted with one another. These close interactions helped to dispel notions of stereotypes which before now caused conflicts among the different ethnic groups. Really, the British accorded little or no priority to cultural homogeneity and ethnic kinship as criteria for establishment of boundaries of the administrative units which they created – be they provincial, districts or native court boundaries(Okpeh, 2007/2008, pp.130-131). Indeed if anything, colonialism created wider horizons and opportunities for closer interaction amongst 'strange bed fellows', though with intermittent contradictory results.

With the rise of nascent urban centres around administrative headquarters,- divisional or provincial headquarters, colonial conquest of Igbo land saw the influx of a small army of non Igbo subordinate staff (bureaucratic staff), clerks, interpreters, messengers, teachers, policemen and soldiers, at first mostly Ijo and Efik, some Sierra Leoneans into Igbo land. With the building of East Railway after 1913, some Yoruba too came in (Afigbo, 1987, p.83). The arrival of the Yoruba in the urban centres added flavor to the cultural mix as most of them occupied the middle and lower echelons of the bureaucracy in Igbo land and subsequently intermarried with the autochthonous Igbo. This promoted intergroup contact and integration in this period.

After 1930, pressure on land, the effects of colonial education and the need to acquire the British currency (which was the only medium of exchange) to pay colonial taxes saw massive Igbo migration in significant numbers as far as North- Kano, and West- Lagos. They went into Yoruba and Edo geographical spaces as farm hands in cocoa and rubber plantations. In other words, the full implications of British colonial rule for intergroup relations in the economic sphere began being recognized more and more after about 1930 as effective use came to be made of the network of road and railway transport which had been constructed during the preceding three decades. The new roads and the railway made long distance travel easier, safer and more attractive than previously. Not only were distant centres of economic enterprise visited, but the traditional centres along the borders were even more intensively exploited than hitherto. In this period the neighbours of the Igbo ceased to be just those with whom they shared common territorial borders. They now conveniently included any Nigerian ethnic group whose homeland offered opportunities for business or whose venturesome sons found scope for business in Igbo land (Ibid, p.85). These infrastructures became the medium for exchange of goods, services and ideas between the Igbo and the various ethnic groups they came in contact with, the Yoruba inclusive. A valid assumption from the dynamics of intergroup relations in the colonial period is that contact and relationship between ethnic groups in Nigeria were controlled by the external colonial order in line with her entrenched economic and commercial interest (Okpeh, 2007/2008, p.131). In addition, the era also marked the evolution of the phenomenon of labour migration in Nigeria. Interestingly, the discriminatory practices, divide and rule structures and policies created by the external political order necessitated the gradual emergence of nationalist forces in Nigeria.

## 4. The Platforms for Intergroup Relations

### 4.1 The Political Platform

Nationalism can be understood in the context of the attempt to build a nation. In nation building, men and women of different ethnic nationalities contribute to the building of a cohesive nation. Adu Boahen defines Nationalism as the collective consciousness on the part of individuals or groups of people to achieve social, cultural, political and economic freedom. Nationalism can either be ethnic or civic as it deals with primordial and western forms of agitations based on rationality, law and democracy. In all, nationalism has three basic components. These are historic territory, a legal political economy, and a common civic culture and ideology.(Okonkwo, 2020, p.173).

In the attempt to forge a common civic culture, the amalgamation proclamation of 1914 which created the Nigerian state provided a geopolitical focus for the activities of the elites of different ethnic groupings in Nigeria. The Clifford constitution of 1922 provided the legal framework for their involvement in party politics (forming political parties) (Iweriebor, 2003, p.88-89) which was a melting pot for diverse cultures in their attempt to forge a common ideology.

The dawn of party politics in 1923 and the nationalist struggle for independence after 1945, inaugurated yet another dimension in inter-group relations in colonial Nigeria. The socio psychological climate generated by nationalist agitations of the late 1940s and 1950s brought different ethnic groups together in the form of political parties and pressure groups as we will now discuss. The first political party that responded to the new reality was the Nigerian National Democratic Party (NNDP) inaugurated by Herbert Macaulay, a Yoruba man on July 24, 1923 and the party dominated the politics of Lagos at the period. By 1934, the Lagos Youth Movement (LYM) was formed and it transformed into Nigerian Youth Movement (NYM) which signified a transition from Lagos politics to national politics with branches across the Nigerian federation. The founding fathers of NYM were J.C. Vaughan, Samuel Akinsanya, H.O.

Davies and Ernest Ikoli. In 1937, Dr Nnamdi Azikiwe, an Igbo joined the NYM(Osadolor, 2003, p.139) as Chief Obafemi Awolowo, a Yoruba also became the Secretary of the Ibadan branch of the party. This goes to show the historic and historical nature of the political alliance between the Yoruba and Igbo which dated back to 1937 well before any form of political alliances between the Igbo and Hausa or Yoruba with the Hausa. By 1938 the party won the elections to the Lagos town Council and the three seats in the Legislative Council. For the first time since 1923, the combined efforts of these Yoruba and Igbo political elites ensured the dislodgement of the NNDP at the polls. The success was no doubt a vindication of the new party's national orientation. The NYM represented the new nationalism, and its countrywide focus stood in marked contrast to the local and limited politics of the NNDP. By implication the NYM fashioned good social and political understanding and relations between the Yoruba and Igbo in Lagos and by extension across the Nigerian federation strengthening intergroup relations between the two ethnic groups. The NYM enjoyed good fortunes until 1941 when the NYM President, Ernest Ikoli and his deputy, Samuel Akinsanya, both indicated their desire to contest a vacant elective seat in the legislative council recently vacated by Dr K.A. Abayomi. The ensuing tussle for nomination created a division in the party with Azikiwe an Igbo supporting Akinsanya a Yoruba man while Chief Obafemi Awolowo another Yoruba man supported Ernest Ikoli an Ijaw who won the nomination. Consequently, in protest, Azikiwe and many Igbo members left the NYM. Fundamentally, this was the first major instance of parochialism in national politics and it set a precedent for the future (Adeleke, 2006, pp2-3).

Despite this turn of events, Azikiwe worked well with Herbert Macaulay and took over the leadership of the National Council of Nigerian and the Cameroons after the death of Herbert Maculay. With Lagos as his political base and given his detribalized disposition, Azikiwe won an election into the Western House of Assembly in 1952. Considering the ethnic nationality question in Nigerian politics today, one would wonder how an

Igbo could win an election into the Western House of Assembly in the heartland of the Yoruba ethnic group. The time was different and the Nigerian political landscape was equally different and tolerant to the extent that Chief Adeniran Ogunsanya, a Yoruba, was and remained one of Nnamdi Azikiwe's closest confidantes and that relationship became a major bridge over the ethnic gulf that had polarized the western and eastern parts of Nigeria from the first republic (Nwauwa, 2015, pp.16-18). In the same vein, TOS Benson, another Yoruba, served Nnamdi Azikiwe well in the politics of Nigeria's first republic (Igbokwe, 1999, p.233). It need be mentioned here that a lot of Yoruba youths and Yoruba intelligentsia such as Dr Olorunnimbe the late Hezekiah A. Oluwasanmi (who later became the second Vice Chancellor of University of Ife) were drawn to Nnamdi Azikiwe and his party because of the ideological pinning and posture of his party, the NCNC and his Newspaper, the West African Pilot (Ige, 1995, p.15).

Interestingly, in the build up to Nigeria's independence, various political parties emerged to jostle for power in the centre. The three major parties that emerged were the National Council of Nigeria and the Cameroons, (NCNC) (which later metamorphosed into National Council of Nigerian Citizens, following the exit of Cameroons from Nigeria), formed in 1945, the Action Group, established in 1951 and the Northern Peoples' Congress which also emerged in 1951. These were all regional and ethnic based parties as each had their support base and followership strongly established in their regions of domicile. These three parties formed during the pre independence era remained the most formidable parties throughout the first republic. Two of them NPC under Ahmadu Bello and Tafawa Balewa and NCNC under Nnamdi Azikiwe formed the coalition government after the 1959 general elections with AG as the official opposition party under the late Chief Obafemi Awolowo (Akinboye & Anifowoshe, 1999, pp.246-247).

In the political activities leading to independence and first republic, the NCNC ably led by Nnamdi Azikiwe gained wide acceptance among the

Yoruba of Southwestern Nigeria. To this end, the NCNC established strong foothold in places like Oyo under the Alafin Adeyemi ll holding a third of Oyo city and Iseyin. Beyond Oyo and Iseyin, the NCNC had strong presence in Ilesha town where between 1954 and 1964 the NCNC, an Igbo party consistently won elections in Ilesha Central, with B. Olowofoyeku being usually the first to have his results announced in the Western region (Ige, 1995, p.15). Part of the fall out of this was that many Igbo natives, especially traders settled in Ilesha and married Ilesha women and products of these conjugal relationships cannot trace their Igbo ancestry (Alo, 2021).

The NCNC also made a strong showing in Ikere over a chieftaincy dispute and in Akoko, where D.K Olumofin entered the Western House of Assembly in 1952. Two other areas where the NCNC waxed strong between 1955 and 1959 were Ife district and Ibadan. Here, Fani-kayode under the auspices of NCNC won elections to the Western House of Assembly up till 1965 and in Ibadan Azikiwe found an ally in Adegoke Adelabu who through the influence and platform of NCNC dominated the politics of Ibadan between 1955 and 1958 (Ige, 1995, pp. 156-163). From the foregoing it is very apparent that the Yorubas in Western Nigeria could probably have decided to join NPC but were quite receptive to the Igbo ideas and ideals of governance and politics which was ably represented and gained expression in NCNC at that time.

Before the periodic federal elections 1964, the NPC/NCNC coalition broke down leading to realignment of political forces and emergence of new alliances. Here the NCNC an Igbo party went into a coalition with the AG, a Yoruba based party under United Progressive Grand Alliance (UPGA) in their attempt to wrest political power from the dominant NPC which had also by now gone into another alliance with the NNDP under NNA. Though unable to appropriate federal power from the NPC, the UPGA disputed the 1964 elections and the UPGA alliance between Yoruba and Igbo continued with the formation of another alternative government under Adegebenro at the Western region which continued till 1966 (Nwauwa, 2015, pp.22-23).

With the outbreak of the Nigerian Civil war in 1967, the Igbo, like other ethnic groups, lost lives and property across the federation. However on their return to Lagos after 1970, the then governor of Lagos state, Brigadier Mobolaji Johnson ensured that most of the properties left behind by the Igbo traders in Lagos (where the Igbo had huge investments) were returned to them after the war (Igbokwe, 1999, p.233). This perhaps was in the spirit of reconciliation and rehabilitation prevalent at the time. This is a far cry from what happened to Igbo properties in other climes where they were declared 'abandoned properties' and taken over by government in places like Rivers state. The important thing to note however is that Mobolaji Johnson's actions further enhanced mutual coexistence between the Yoruba and Igbo in Lagos and by extension across other Yoruba areas.

## 4.2 The Markets and Commerce Platforms

Historically, markets have been central to the development and promotion of cordial relations among peoples of diverse ethnic backgrounds who come to the market space to carry out one form of trade transaction or extra market activities. In other words, the market is a vibrant space necessary for the nurturing of inter-ethnic relations and fostering peaceful coexistence and strengthening communal ties among diverse ethnic groups that occupy the trade space(Ekanade, 2019, pp.79-80). In the course of such interactions, untoward notions about the other, misconceptions about attitudes and dispositions of other ethnic groups are dispelled, while new forms and bonds of friendship are cemented across ethnic lines.

Be that as it may, Lagos, the commercial nerve centre of Nigeria, holds lots of commercial attraction for the Igbo, a peripatetic people who naturally are given to trading and are also known for their commercial prowess.

Given the exigencies of the Nigerian civil war which devastated Igbo lands (destroying vast arable lands meant for agriculture), the young and agile Igbo men seeing no future in farming famished lands migrated to Lagos to source for new livelihoods, engage in trading and extra market activities. This massive Igbo influx into Lagos and by extension, Mushin started in 1970 after the civil war.

Beyond the civil war, the need to migrate for the Igbo had to do with the need to survive. The struggle to survive increased in a quickly monetizing capitalist economy and with subsequent economic down turn, their ranks swelled in Lagos. In addition, this emerging informal economy was also about the only survival response to the depression in the Nigerian economy as it required little or no education and minimal capital outlay which the Igbo youths could comfortably fit into (Olutayo, 1999, p.150). For Meagher, the lack of state assistance in the reconstruction process of Eastern Nigeria after the civil war combined with disadvantageous state policies governing the economic re-absorption of Biafra, fractured the Igbo involvement in the formal economy and deepened their focus on the informal sector of the Nigerian economy(Meagher, 2009, p.37). It is within this circumstance that Ladipo market comes into the picture. The question then arises as to why this work is focusing on Mushin for Yoruba/ Igbo intergroup relations? The answer is that essentially, Mushin, a suburban area of Lagos, is host to the Ladipo Automotive spare parts market, (a trading space which has a preponderance of Igbo traders cohabiting with Yoruba landlords, artisans and traders) which is the largest automotive spare parts market in West Africa that attracts customers from Chad, Cameroon and Burkina Faso (Ekere, 2007,p.15, Ukpebor, 2015, Grossman, 2017,p.2, Ogboo, 2011). As Sandra Barnes aptly captures it, as at 1972, much unlike Lagos metropolis, Mushin neighborhood was more ethnically balanced than the rest of the city amounting to about 15% fewer Yoruba and 15% more Igbo speaking residents (Barnes, 1975, p.77). It is important to note that unlike other ethnic groups, the Igbo, the second largest in Mushin after the Yoruba, had culturally ingrained themselves into the social, religious and recreational milieu of Mushin. According to Sandra Barnes again, "for the ordinary people (hosts and immigrants), residence was a social melting pot'. The metropolitan area housed one of the most heterogeneous concentrations of people in the nation. Houses and neighborhoods reflected this heterogeneity with one exception: the Hausa who often lived in fairly homogenous enclaves (Barnes, 1986, p.14). One inference that can be drawn from this description as rightly observed by Biko Agozino and Ike Ayannike, is that the Igbo usually immersed themselves into the culture and practice of their host communities, learning the hosts' language in no time as they will need it in their market transaction, adopting the manner of their hosts' dress sense (Aso Oke), enjoying their staple foods, making it obvious that the Igbo culture is one adaptive to change (Agozino, Ayanike & Ahia, 2007, p. 240). These inter ethnic interactions have led to the development of hybrid identities and identity renegotiation in a more positive sense (Watson & Studdert, 2006, p.3) which was subsequently carried over into the market space in Ladipo Automotive market, Lagos. Activities in Ladipo Automotive market reveal an aptitude for economic survival, shared profit motive and wholesome business development as the basis for building ties across ethnic and religious divides without rancor through their self governing unions and institutions.

Ladipo automotive market is a microcosm that can be used to dramatize economic interactions, intermarriages, politics, administration and conflict resolution and other inter-ethnic dealings between the Yoruba and Igbo. There are institutions and structures created in Ladipo market that manage intergroup relations in the market space. They range from the Ladipo Central Executive Committee (LACEC) to Public Complaints Commission (PCC) which engages Alternative Dispute Resolution (ADR) methods to resolve disputes. LACEC is an overarching traders' association which aggregates and articulates traders' demands in negotiations with government, engages in lobbying government for fair tax regime and deals with insecurity in the market. It manages relations within the market and its executive comprises an Igbo President, Yoruba secretary with other sensitive posts shared between the two ethnic groups. LACEC in late 1993 federated the original five unions that have now transmuted into over forty automobile spare parts associations comprising Igbo and Yoruba traders. Essentially, within these associations social relations are established and this facilitates informal interactions amongst traders of different ethnic persuasions. The layers of authority relations starting from the small units to different associations, the federated nature of LACEC and holding of periodic democratic elections (where all shades of ethnic, religious and secular opinions are represented) have all helped to diminish incidences of conflict in the market and ensured that elected union/ association leaders develop relationships that reinforce peace and unity among the Yoruba and Igbo traders.(Ekanade, 2019, pp85-86).

Furthermore, since disputes are integral parts of human interaction, managers of Ladipo market established a community court also known as Public Complaints Commission (PCC) in order to manage conflicts and ensure traders have a greater sense of social inclusion in the market. In adjudicating over disputes between Yoruba and Igbo traders, the LACEC President constitutes the community court headed by an elderly trader who by virtue of wisdom and experience sits in as Chief Judge (CJ) assisted by other sectional heads within the market, including elders from ethnic associations if parties to the conflict belong to different ethnic groups. About five of the adjudicators sit together with the (CJ) to hear the case, confer together and pass judgment. The primary goal of the court ruling, asides ensuring fairness, is also not to foist retributive or punitive measures on the guilty but rather, the focus is restorative justice where healing is the key concern. The further aim is to promote and strengthen a viable community characterized by empathy, trust, and commitment to rebuilding communal relations (Ibid, pp91-92). This attitude has inspired confidence in the system and strengthened inter ethnic relations in Ladipo market. Hardly do inter ethnic crises break out between the Yoruba and the Igbo which gain media attention. Interestingly, the two ethnic groups find a common ground in the profit motive of their business engagements which is mutually beneficial. Any crises between them would disrupt the flow of material gains that should accrue to the two parties. To that extent, they would explore all available options to checkmate inter-ethnic crisis. However, in South west there are a plethora of reported cases of inter-ethnic clashes between Hausa and Yoruba traders over market spaces where they have had to cohabit and this has led to loss of lives, properties and disruption of business activities in the contested spaces.

Given their successes at trade relations, the two ethnics have also made enormous progress in politics emanating from the market space. Also, given that politicians regard traders in markets as vote banks, the informal market space has become a space of intense political lobbying and competition for professional and aspiring politicians. For instance, the gubernatorial elections of 2007 and 2011 amply demonstrate the strength of LACEC and Igbo traders in mobilizing Igbo votes for Babatunde Fashola, who through this support conveniently won elections then as Governor of Lagos state. In addition, the accommodative nature of Lagos politics permitted the emergence of Igbo candidates in the 2015 national elections where they won three federal House of Representative seats in Lagos (Ekanade, 2017). This development is unprecedented given the culture of exclusivity in Lagos politics. However the cordial relations between the Igbo and the Yoruba allowed for this performance.

Given its unique role in trading vehicular parts, Ladipo Market has led to a dynamic trade culture, and a systematized apprenticeship that has improved lives and social relations among traders. It has produced a symbiotic relationship in which Yoruba have remained largely as landlords and artisans with Igbo as leaseholders and traders. Continuous informal market operations have deepened market governance and the artisanal skills of traders and blurred ethnic boundaries among the different ethnicities that constitute the market space, thereby fostering peace among the different ethnicities in Nigeria.

On a final note in the area of culture, the Olu of Mushin from time to time gives chieftaincy titles to prominent Igbo sons who have contributed to the development of Mushin as a society. He also uses his prerogative to appoint a prominent Igbo son domiciled in Mushin as the Eze Ndigbo of Mushin in an elaborate installation ceremony. This is followed by a festival like procession where prominent Igbo sons and daughters, their Yoruba friends and members of the Mushin traditional council all join in the performance. Subsequently there are cultural displays by Igbo and Yoruba cultural troupes to entertain guests during the ceremony. Beyond this, there are periodic carnival performances in Mushin and other Yoruba towns by Yoruba and Igbo sons and daughters at different times of the year. Ceremonies like these have strengthened the bonds of understanding and cordial relations between the Yoruba and Igbo in Mushin and by extension other states in Yoruba land. The impact is that it has helped to diminish incidences of conflict between the Yoruba and Igbo wherever they have had to live together.

## 5. CONCLUSION

Drawing a curtain on this write up, the work has interrogated the broad outline of intergroup relations between the Yoruba and Igbo. Inferences that can be drawn from the article are that the Yoruba and Igbo belong to the Kwa Congo group of languages and initial contact between the two groups was through the Benin peoples who carried the Yoruba to Igbo land as mercenaries. Subsequently, the Yoruba forms of governance (monarchical and gerontocratic system) rubbed off on the Igbo and influenced their political orientation. Also in the precolonial period, Awka blacksmiths migrated to areas like Ikale and Igbomina in Yoruba land to practice their vocation and in the process engaged in intermarriages with the Yoruba women producing cross-cultural offsprings. The incursion of colonialism fast-tracked the pace of intergroup relations amongst far flunged Nigerian peoples such as the Yoruba and Igbo through the instrumentality of colonial transport infrastructure and imperial capitalist policies. Beyond this, colonial policies on governance also impelled nationalist fervor among political elites of different ethnic orientations who forged a united front in the quest for independence. Here the socio-psychological climate generated by nationalist agitations brought different ethnic groups together in the form of political parties, pressure groups and cultural associations to ease out the colonialists. In the immediate post independence years, seemingly ethnic party like the NCNC made bold foray into the heartland of Yoruba territories and gained good acceptance among the locals. Finally, trade and commerce, with the preponderance of markets like Ladipo market (where goods and services are exchanged in addition to extra market activities) has become a veritable platform for the intermingling of the Yoruba and Igbo peoples which has resulted in mutually beneficial relationship for the two ethnics with enormous social harmony. Just as Okpeh Okpeh commented, the contemporary conglomerate nature of the Nigerian society and the scope and forms of relationships existing between the Yoruba and Igbo and the complementarity which characterizes this relationship has given meaning and significance to the dictum 'unity in diversity'(Okpeh, 2007/2008, p.134). The challenge for functional and productive intergroup relations in our quest for communal harmony in Nigeria lies in the ability of the political class to rein in their selfish manipulative propensities across ethnic divides in order to pursue the general good of the citizenry regardless of ethnic persuasions.

## REFERENCES

Adeleke, A. (2006). 'The evolution of Party politics in Nigeria 1914-2000' *University of Lagos Monograph series* No. 2, 2006. Lagos; University of Lagos Press.

Afigbo, A.E, (1987). '*The Igbo and their Neighbours: Intergroup Relations in South Eastern Nigeria to 1953'*, Ibadan; University Press.

Agozino, B., & Ayanike, I. (2007). Imu Ahia: 'Traditional Igbo Business school and global commerce culture'. *Dialectical Anthropolgy*, Vol 31, No 1/3, Springer.pp.233-252.

Akinboye, S. & Anifowose, R. (1999). Nigerian Government and Politics' in Remi Anifowose and Francis Enemuo,(eds.), *Elements of Politics,* Lagos: Malthouse. *P244*

Anemene, B. U. (2018). 'Precolonial Guild System in Igboland: The Example of Awka Blacksmith Guilds' *RUN Journal of Cultural Studies.* Vol (2) pp 135-150.

Barnes, S.T., (1975), Voluntary associations in a metropolis: The case of Lagos, Nigeria, *African Studies Review*, Vol. 18, No. 2, pp. 75-87.

Barnes, S.T., (1986). *Patrons and Power: Creating a political community in metropolitan Lagos*, Manchester: Manchester University Press.

Discussion with Anaemene Benjamin, University Lecturer, Adult, 20/05/2021. Discussion with Dr Alo Lawrence, University Lecturer and indigene of Ilesha, Adult 23/05/2021.

Ekanade O. (2017) From an Invocation Space to a Commercial Emporium: The Evolutionary Dynamics of the Ladipo Auto Spare Parts Flea Market in Lagos, Nigeria: the 1950s to 2016. *Afrika Zamani, CODESRIA* Publication (Senegal) No. 25, pp 125-145.

Ekanade O. (2019). The Dynamics of Spare parts trade and market Associations' Mediatory Role in Resolving Conflicts: Evidence from Lagos. *Kaduna Journal of Humanities*, Vol. 3 No 1, Kaduna State University, pp 79-99.

Ekere, N. (2007). 'Automotive Electronics - Opportunities and challenges for Nigeria's Auto Sector, Paper delivered at National conference and workshop on automobile electronics', on 16th August 2007, http://www.nac.org.ng/NAC_Conferences/Workshop_on_AMT/NdyEkere%20%20AutoElectronics_Paper_for_NAC_Conf_16August2007.pdf

Grossman Shelby (2017). 'The politics of order in informal markets: Evidence from Lagos', Stanford University, Centre on Democracy, development and rule of law

Hogg, M. (2003). *Handbook of social psychology*. John Delamater, ed. Kluwer: Academic Plenum publishers, New York, 479-501

https://en.wikipedia.org/wiki/Intergroup_relations
Igbokwe, J. (1999). *Heroes of Democracy*, Lagos, Dynotech.
Ige, B. (1995). People, Politics and Politicians of Nigeria (1940-1979), Ibadan: Heinemann Books.

Iweriebor, Ehiedu, E.G. (2003). 'Nationalism and the struggle for freedom, 1880-1960' in, Adebayo Oyebade (ed.), *The Foundations of Nigeria; Essays in Honour of Toyin Falola*. Trenton, NJ Africa World Press, Pp 79-106

Meagher, K. (2009). The informalisation of belonging: Igbo formal enterprise and national cohesion from below, *Africa Development*, Vol.XXXIV, No 1, 2009, pp 31-46

Nwauwa, A. O. (2015). 'Nnamdi Azikiwe: High Priest of National Unity' in Apollos O. Nwauwa and Julius O. Adekunle (eds.), *Nigerian Political Leaders; Visions, Actions and Legacies*. Glassboro, New Jersey; Goldline and Jacobs, 2015, pp 11-30

Ogboo, A.N. (2011). 'The geography of automobile spare parts and trade ASPMDA and LADIPO automobile spare parts market, Lagos Nigeria', *MA thesis* submitted to the Department of Geography, Miami University, Oxford, Ohio.

Ohadike, D. C. (1991). 'The Ekumeku movement: Western Igbo resistance to the British conquest of Nigeria 1883-1914'. Ohio University Press, Athens.

Okonkwo, U. (2020). 'Herbert Macaulay as the father of Nigeria's nationalism: A Historical misnomer and misogyny regarding the role of Igbo women in the decolonization process'. *Journal of International women's studies,* 21 (1) 172-184.

Okpeh, O. O. Jnr (2007/2008). Patterns and Dynamics of Intergroup Relations in Nigeria, 1800-1900 AD, *Journal of Historical Society of Nigeria*. Vol.17. Pp 123-137.

Olutayo, O. A. (1999). 'The Igbo entrepreneur in the political economy of Nigeria'. *African Studies Monographs*, 20 (3): September 1999, p147-174.

*Vanguard*, Lagos, 08/ 2019  'Ooni of Ife and the Igbo- Yoruba Relationship'. https://www.vanguardngr.com/2019/08/o oni-of-ife-and-the-igbo-yoruba-relationship/.Accessed on 02/05/2021

Osadolor, O. B. (2003). ' Understanding the Nationalist Issues in the Colonial Central Legislature' in Adebayo Oyebade (ed.), *The Foundations of Nigeria; Essays in Honour of Toyin Falola*. Trenton, NJ Africa World Press p127-152

*The Guardian Newspaper,* (Lagos), 7th , February, 2015 http://guardian.ng/sunday-magazine/cityfile/ladipo-a-market-begging-for-attention/.

Ukpebor, H. I. (2012).  Exporting Of Used Automobile Parts From Finland To Nigeria, Bachelor's thesis December 2012 Degree Programme in International Business Tampereen Ammatikorkeakoulu, Tampere University of Applied Sciences http://www.theseus.fi/bitstream/handle/1 0024/52520/Ukpebor_Humphrey.pdf

Watson, S., & David, S. (2006). *Markets as sites for social interaction*. Bristol: Policy Press.

# CHAPTER 20

## Reveries Of The Eastern Melodies: Expectant '50s, Emergent 60s And... *A Dream Deferred?*

1. Introduction

2. The Keynotes of the 50s

3. The Rhapsodies of the Independence

4. The Staccatos of Decolonization

5. The Dying Cadence of the Unsung Melodies

6. The Finale of the Eastern Melodies

*Summary*

The past was not a dream, but a reality gone by. real dance to the tune of a real music, played by real human beings. It was the onset of a harmonious performance, a joy to the eyes of the observers, old and young, moving the young to boisterous movements and stirring the old to the recollections of their youth. It was an unspoken promise about to be fulfilled in its simple performance. And suddenly, the music came to an abrupt end, and the performance stopped, with human beings scampering about for safety. But ... it could have lasted longer! It could have become better, more harmonious, and more melodious; but it never did, and we are still asking why? Our unresolved past is still with us in the cacophony of the present, whose loudness has now dimmed the soft and harmonious sounds of the past melodies. The inner values of the past, nurtured through peace, hard work and a natural sense of balance, is now besieged by the present, whose brutality is indicating that the way forward if to nurture the indwelling inner values of peace, harmony and natural sense of balance.

## 1. Introduction

**I**T IS PROBABLY NOSTALGIA IF YOU LIVED THROUGH IT, **and seems like fantasia if you read or heard enough about it to conjure up an image in your mind as to what it must have been like. Either way, it brings alive reminiscing notions in the minds of those who can *(or old enough to)* recall the place(s) and the times; stirs the imaginative senses of those who have built an impression of what that reality must have been and evokes a curious combination of both for folks my age, who straddle both versions of that storied existence.**

What we all have in common though, is that we ponder, *just what might have been...?* Could it have been sustained and if it had been, what heights would have been attained? Or was it always going to be just a flash of brilliance in a history mostly of turbulence and eventual failures - or worded less harshly, under-achievements? The deflating reality is, we would never know.

However, reflecting on those times - far gone enough to be past the inevitably subjective excitement that comes with 'being in the midst', yet recent enough to interrogate accurately with facts and figures – even if not entirely objectively – we should be able, at the very least, to gain some insight; draw on some caveat; attain some wisdom, that might prove helpful at the minimum and pivotal at best – in this very critical time in our collective history as Nigerians first, but also as Easterners past.

Let us take a walk back in time to a place that has been described as, beautiful, rich and vibrant; but also, serene, peaceful and laden with hope. A place where a people that were industrious, learned, urbane and proud; lived, worked, collaborated, reveled and thrived with the common objective: to achieve the best their Region could, in an emergent Nation excitably pulsating with promise – not unaware of the myriad of challenges before them, but not deterred by them either. Let us take a reflective stroll back to The Eastern Region of Nigeria.

## 2. The Keynotes of the 50s

### 2.1 Where is the Eastern Region of Nigeria?

Along the shores of the Atlantic Ocean's Gulf of Guinea and through the yet unadulterated creeks (Ikot Abasi, Opobo, Port Harcourt, Ogoniland, etc.) of the riverine south, into the bustling commercial hubs (Aba, Owerri, Onitsha) and then ricocheted by the boundary of the Great River (the Niger); eastward across the distinctive red soils peering through the gaps up and down the non-conforming topographies in the North (Udi, Enugu, Nsukka); traversing the savannah plains (Abakaliki, Ogoja); up the picturesque landscapes of hills and onto the temperate plateaus (Obudu plateau, Oban hills) and then back down south through the dense tropical rainforests (Boki, Akamkpa) and minerally rich soils (Akwa Ibom) straddling Nigeria's shifting border with the Cameroons (Bakassi) and then through more rivers (Bonny, Calabar, Forcados, Imo, Nun, Orashi), emptying into the Atlantic like deformed fingers crisscrossing as they reach for the ocean, in classic delta form.

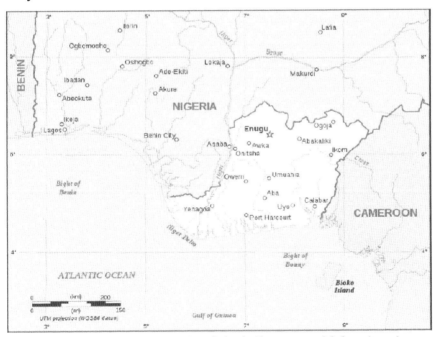

|Figure 1. Map Showing the Eastern Region of Nigeria (Source: www.globalsecurity.org)

All that fall within these bounds – indeed, the lands, waters, skies and all therein that make up most of what is labelled, "the 'South-South' and the entire 'South-East' geopolitical zones" today - constituted the Eastern Region of Nigeria *effectively* between 1939 (constitutionally 1954) and 1967.

## 2.2 Who Were the Easterners?

The people were indigenous to the Region and as diverse as the geography of the Region, with literally dozens of distinct clans and ethnic/language groups (Agbo, Andoni, Etche, Nembe, Ogbia, Oron, Yakurr, etc.) dotting the region, at times interspersing and adding a seeming buffer in their amalgam of adaptiveness between the dominant Igbo and the other significant tribes – the Izon (Ijaw), Efik, Ibibio, Annang, Ejagham, Ikwerre, Ogoni, Qua - and even the non-central Igbo like the Waawa, the Aro and Ndoki.

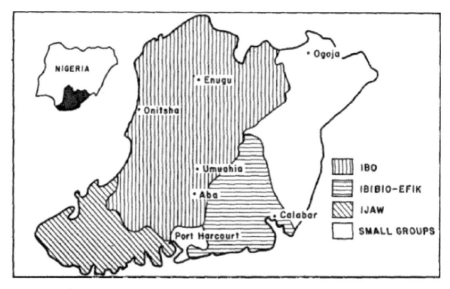

|Figure 2. Ethnic Groups in Nigeria's Eastern Region (www.nigerianmuse.com)

In speaking of the people of the East, I will interject that although there were calls to varying degrees; at various times and by different groups, for greater representation, more autonomy and even separation on the basis of fear of domination, oppression and for the right to self-determination, there never seemed enough of a disadvantage to enough persons or groups for such clamouring to take significant hold or to create an imbroglio detrimental to the status quo or to the progress of the Region.

Perhaps the most telling gauge of the state of the relationships that history allows us the liberty to glean on the matter of the formation of a separate region is that the Sir Henry Willink Commission, which was appointed in 1957 by the colonial government, to inquire into the fears of minorities and largely in response to demands for the formation of 'minority regions' from the three regions, did not deem it necessary to recommend so in its (the Willink Commission's) 1958 Report. It could be argued that the powers that were – i.e., the colonial government in its seemingly strictly worded mandate to the Commission; and the dominant indigenous political leaders of the period in their stance against it, especially when tied to the possible delay of the realization of independence – did not leave the Commission the option to recommend the creation of new region(s). The Commission's conclusion that the solution(s) to the concerns of the minorities did not lie in the creation of states could not however have been said to have lacked merit. Indeed, considering the diversity that existed in most parts of the region, even outside of the major ethnic groups, there would have been need for several more states to have been created if it was ruled that the only way a minority group could exist equitably was to be the dominant ethnic group in its region.

There also was not the persistent push by the minorities in the Region and the consensus with the dominant Igbos as there was between the minorities of the Western Region and the Yorubas leading up to, and resulting in, the creation of the Mid-Western Region from the Western Region - post independence, in 1963. This would seem a buttressing to the suggestion opined earlier that such a separation was not, at least at the time, a priority to most. Moreover, looking at the growth and development agenda embarked on by the government of the day, it is clear that fragmentation was not anticipated, nor was its likelihood given much consideration. Plantations, roads, social welfare and other governmental structural models were imminently planned across the region on the basis of factors such as exigency and comparative advantage rather than in a segregatory manner or with the expectation that such developments may eventually turn out to have been wasteful or in some way, not be contributory to the entirety of the Region.

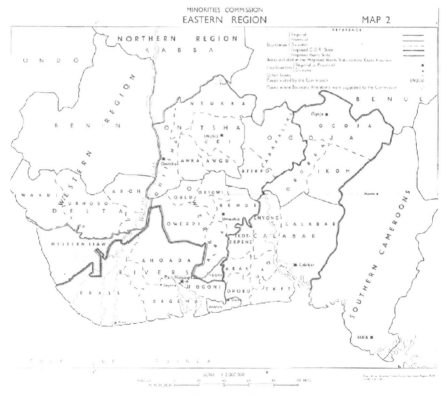

*Figure 3. Regions proposed for creation by the Willink Commission (1957 – 58)*
(http://www.waado.org/nigerdelta/maps/willink_commission/willink_commission_east.html)

While the tide may have turned subsequently – perhaps fueled by an increase in disparaging equity and divergent opinions on any number of social, economic or other issues that could have arisen, festered and even boiled over amongst the variant communities, peoples and groups - it could be asserted that, up until the beginning of the civil crises the Country experienced in the mid-1960s, such an escalation had not been reached, or even neared; and that indeed most of the East was fine with being a part of the East. In postulating what may or may not have happened down the road, it could also be opined, considering the manner in which the Eastern Region had progressed, that it was poised to avoid, but if necessary, manage the ills associated with the threats of discrimination, maltreatment and marginalization by the dominant Igbos over the minorities of the region. This, not necessarily because of the kindness or benevolence of the majority, but more than anything else for the purpose of exigency and the natural tendency of self-preservation. The plantations that lie in today's Cross River and Rivers States, the

*Figure 4. Eastern Development Commission Projects in 1955*
(https://www.nairaland.com/attachments/6921110_fbimg1522731604400_jpeg9ee392740b6ef40e776208075b9eb12b)

access to the Atlantic and the accompanying benefits that the port cities of Bonny, Brass, Abonema, Calabar, etc. offered, etc. – and subsequently the potential that the discovery of oil and gas on and off the shores of the Region portended, were all critical facets to the success of a plan to attain the heights in growth, development and to provide for the welfare of its people that the leadership believed was achievable across the entire region. Actions that would propel the peoples of these other tribes to feel so apprehensive as to consider withdrawal from the union a viable option, thus threatened the attainment of the Region's founding fathers' (many of whom themselves were from these minority tribes) vision, and they would have done all that they could to eclipse such a threat.

## 2.3  The Eyo Ita Matter

It would be evasive at best, but perhaps disingenuous for a 'child of the East' whose place of origin is in today's Cross River State, in the South-South geopolitical zone, to write of the people (*and politics*) of the Eastern Region and not as much as make *even* a cursory mention of, or allude to, the political confrontation that resulted in Professor Eyo Ita - the Head of Government Business of the Eastern Region – leaving the ruling party of the period - NCNC (National Council of Nigeria and the Cameroons and subsequently, National Council of Nigerian Citizens when Southern Cameroon seized to be a part of Nigeria) to form the National Independence Party (NIP).

Two general views persist as to exactly what led to this debacle:

The more salacious and perhaps therefore more recounted is that having being defeated in his bid to become the Premier (actually, Head of Government Business as the term 'Premier' was not reflected in the Constitutions by which the country was governed until 1954) of the West through political machinations supposedly based primarily on tribal sentiment – a factor that until then was said to have been largely irrelevant at that level of Nigerian politics – that Dr. Nnamdi Azikiwe, being of Igbo origin, returned to the East and dealt Professor Eyo Ita, from the minority Efik tribe, a similar hand as he had purportedly been dealt in the West.

A keener unfurling of the trends of the period however suggests the origins of the misunderstanding were in the locking of horns on the implementation of a strategy for dealing with the MacPherson Constitution promulgated in 1951, and therefore, had more to do with disagreements around definitive political matters than that it was an ethnically inclined putsch.

Agitators for complete self-rule and total independence – a cause for which the NCNC was founded and had resolutely stood – were bent on not allowing the MacPherson Constitution, which was drawn up by the Colonialists, to stand - the thinking within the leadership ranks of the Party being that the so-called 'semi-responsible governance' it perpetrated would hinder the march towards Nigeria's full independence (Sklar, 1963). Some members of the NCNC - including Eyo Ita, but also several Ministers of Igbo origin - refused to toe the party line to frustrate the Constitution's workability in a broad strategy that included the resignation of Ministers.

Being that the remainder of the Parliament still constituted a majority, they, compliant to the Party's dictates, were still able to advance the strategy of making the Constitution unworkable by stopping the passage of every bill brought to the floor of the House. The MacPherson Constitution eventually collapsed under the determined application of the tactic that had by the time also been adopted by the then ruling party in the Western Region – the Action Group.

With the dissolution of the Parliament in 1953, Prof. Eyo Ita and the rest of the 'sit-tight ministers' - as they were then dubbed, since refusing to resign their ministerial positions - left the NCNC and formed the NIP. While many of them won their respective seats in the elections that followed later that year, the NIP was defeated as the NCNC remained overwhelmingly in the majority in the Eastern House of Assembly. Consequently, Eyo Ita lost the position of Head of Government Business to Zik, who - as National President of his Party, the NCNC - had contested for and won the seat in his home Province of Onitsha defeating Barr. Louis Mbanefo of the United National Party. Professor Eyo Ita became the leader of the opposition.

The argument could be made that even if this crisis had not rocked the NCNC and the Eastern Assembly, the preceding occurrences in the West which caused Zik's NCNC Party to lose out on its efforts at gaining control of the Western House of Assembly - where the Party's leadership intended to deploy the same tactics of frustrating the MacPherson Constitution - would still have resulted in him returning to contest for, and in all likelihood, winning the Onitsha seat in the 1953 elections. He probably would still then have become the Head of Government Business of the Eastern Parliament – but then, perhaps with Eyo Ita's support, as his deputy in the Party.

In the thick of the discord, Professor Eyo Ita included the propagation for the formation of a COR (Calabar-Ogoja-Rivers) Region to the agenda of the newly formed Party.

Professor Ita eventually returned to the NCNC in 1956 - in his own words, *"...according to the dictates of my conscience and in obedience to the chiefs and members of my constituency..."* Eyo Ita further stated that events that led to his leaving the Party did not warrant the action. It must be noted that the creation of a separate COR Region was *not* a primary reason for the discord. It was a position that he later adopted and would subsequently rescind.

## 3. The Rhapsodies of Independence

### 3.1 Politics, Governance and the Economy

The Lyttelton Constitution in 1954 instituted a federal governance system in Nigeria with the regions – Northern, Eastern and Western - to function with significant autonomy of a Central government. The country's attainment of Independence in 1960 ushered in the long sought-after concept of 'self-rule' and on the 27th of May 1967, in the bid to avert what would become the inevitable calamitous outcomes of the '1966 crises', the military administration, headed by General (then Lieutenant Colonel) Yakubu Gowon, created three states from the Region – East Central, South-Eastern and Rivers – in the nation's new twelve-state political structure.

### 3.2 Pre-Independence

It should be noted that indigenous Nigerians had for decades prior to Independence engaged in models of representative (although not always elective), deliberative governance. In 1922, the Hugh Clifford Constitution - the country's first formal constitution - provided for a partially elected Legislative Council. The concept was however limited to the South and functioned only in an advisory capacity. There were no Nigerians ('Africans' – as we were then referred to) in the more relevant Executive Council and the (Colonial) Governor held veto powers.

With the adoption of the Richards Constitution in 1946, greater participation by Nigerians was achieved in the three Regions that had been created by Sir Bernard Bourdillon in 1939; and by the promulgation of the MacPherson Constitution in 1951 Nigerians were somewhat running the affairs of government even if still under the scrutiny of a colonial Governor who retained veto authority.

## 3.3 Post-Independence

Like most countries emerging from British colonialism, we adopted a hybrid Parliamentary system in line with a constitution deliberated on and agreed to in multiple conferences held in Lagos and London, at which representatives from the political parties active in the country at the time participated. The Independence Constitution sought to address perceived defects from previous iterations. It was ambitious – reflective of the desire and optimism of its protagonists who intended for it to be a catalyst for the building of a bold new independent Nation.

*The Parliamentary System*

The Centre and the Regions would continue to have an Executive Council chosen from Parliament with a Prime Minister at the Centre and a Premier in the Regions, acting as Head of Government Business. The offices of Governor General and later, President (at the Center) and Governor (in the Regions), though above the Prime Minister and Premier, respectively, were largely ceremonial.

The House of Representatives (at the Centre) and the House of Assembly (in the Regions), alongside the Senate (Centre) and the House of Chiefs (Regional), formed the primary deliberative bodies.

Traditional governance systems, prevalent in most ethnic cultures of the East before the incursion of Western entrants and the subsequent advent of colonialism, were indeed variants of representative (even if not via a democratic elective system) deliberative bodies. The King of Opobo ruled with a council of advisers - who it was expected spoke for their kin - as did the Obi of Onitsha; and the Ekpe Society literally governed the communities along the Cross River from Creek Town to Arochukwu and as far up north as Obanliku (on the Benue border) - as well as in other parts of the West and Central African Atlantic coastline - in which it was prevalent – to name a few examples.

Like the colonial system prior, the transitional and post-colonial authorities recognizing their value, sought to accommodate such institutions in the Constitutions justifying the formation of the House of Chiefs in which traditional rulers deliberated alongside the House of Assembly in the 1951 Constitution. While its role changed – in fact, diminished - over time, the House of Chiefs remained a deliberative body in Eastern Nigeria until its dissolution in 1967. Interestingly, the diminishing capacity of the institution while individuals from their ranks sought to augment their own influence as they identified increasingly with the stronger political parties, may be an area to delve more into when we call into question some of the choices we have made as a people over time.

*The Local Government*

Local governance concepts transited from what was termed 'Indirect Rule' in the colonial system – where traditional rulers held sway in local matters during the country's period of colonization - to more structured models during decolonization and thereafter.

The Eastern Nigeria Local Government Ordinance of 1950 introduced a robust 3-tier local government system – County, District and Local Council (Egbe 2014).

Over time, the local governance structure would evolve, becoming more entrenched even as the role of the House of Chiefs seemed to wane. A more aware, participatory and expectant populace recognized failures, opined and sought to address, rather than disregard them or seek ways to circumvent the challenges they engendered – either of which would have been detrimental to realizing the objectives for which there was a local governance system in the first place.

The system was continually adapted or modified. By the time of attainment of independence, an efficient and better managed single-tier District system which functioned with established operational procedures and was accountable to a Parliamentary Minister was in place and remained the Eastern Region's model for local governance until the dissolution of the Region in 1967.

## The Judiciary

Pre-independence, Nigeria operated a unital Judiciary system. As the decolonization process unfolded and with the formation of regions, it became imperative – or perhaps, expedient - that the Judiciary become regionalized. The Judiciary was also a hybrid modeled largely along the lines of the British legal system but with cognisance of, and accommodation for local (native) legal considerations.

## 4.   The Staccatos of Decolonization

Considering Britain's interest in and dependency on Nigeria's vast resources (predominantly agricultural at the time); and the potential that these portended, the attainment of Independence was never going to be as simple as a request and a handover. But also, learning from past experiences – especially hers in Asia and that of the French in North Africa - Britain recognized that Colonialism could not be perpetual either. Dialogue thus became the vehicle through which the road from Colonialism to Independence (self-rule) was traversed. Progress along that road was measured largely by way of gains made in attainment of influence, representation and participation in the political process, and subsequently, governance - during the 'decolonization' period.

Whether or not it was so intended, the seemingly dithering manner by which progress towards Independence and self-governance was achieved – whereby Nigerians' roles in decision-making and governance progressively increased during the period prior, rather than an abrupt 'takeover' - turned out to have been of great benefit to the emerging Nation and its Regions.

Most of the key strategists and activists in Nigeria's struggle for Independence from British colonial rule – many of whom were well-trained, articulate, accomplished professionals – had become drawn into politics driven by two key objectives: (1.) The desire to gain Independence and (2.) The need to ensure 'their people' are properly represented.

With the attainment of Independence and inherent self-rule, this cadre of Nigerians - many of them lawyers, doctors, academicians, and the like - would become the champions for and drivers of the actualization of the vision *they* had begun to mold from the onset of their struggle for independence and with measured steps, through various roles in advocacy, politics, policy-making and actual governance. They, thus quite naturally, *and I daresay*, readily, transitioned into the political class of the country's immediate post-colonial era – from 1960 until 1966/67.

The developmental and economic successes recorded as having taken place from independence in 1960 in the Regions of the country were therefore, outcomes or the manifestations of strategic plans largely developed prior to Independence acted upon by the originators of the blueprint ensuring implementation in their amplified roles as doting custodians of the vision.

In Eastern Nigeria, this vision was to build a Region that expanded well beyond the growing of agricultural cash crops such as oil palm, cocoa, rubber, etc. for export - which was the colonialist government's unabashed prime interest. Virtually all ancillary development prior - from the railway to whatever rural development had been attained during the colonial period – was intended to foster the achievement of this objective.

At Independence, the leadership recognizing the potential to achieve their more robust, egalitarian vision and accepting that the destiny of their people was literally in their hands sought to drive a developmental agenda steeped in the universally accepted doctrine that all citizens should have the opportunity to do well or at least, aspire to – an ideal that has from the beginning of civilization been a basis by which progress and development in society is measured; and has thus been fostered, and its attainment sought, in societies that seek to excel. Critical in seeking to achieve this paradigm is the establishment and indeed, the concretization of the fundamental principle of inclusiveness. In this instance, this meant that no area, people or resources were to be omitted in the Region's scheme for development and that no individuals, institutions or other entities are to be exempted from conforming to its established dictates for the achievement of such growth. This is neither a far-fetched notion nor is it one that should be difficult to apply as it is bound in the ideals of reciprocity, fairness and discipline – all elements at the core of a strategy for development on the basis of the more recently coined term, 'comparative advantage'.

The post-colonial Eastern government saw the development of a viable and sustainable economy as pivotal to achieving the ideal of building a region in which its vision would thrive. The plan was thus to develop an ecosystem around its potentials in vast & mostly arable lands, mineral resources, population and intellect. The key to achieving the objective of enhancing not only the Region's earnings (GDP), but just as importantly, the impact thereof on its peoples' socio-economic well-being, was thus going to be through deliberate strategies to increase productivity, largely by facilitating industrial growth and developing the latent capacity in its populace.

4.1    The four legs of the Economy: Agriculture, Commerce, Industry and Education.

Agriculture would remain an integral building block in the paradigm; however, with the emphasis now being to feed a proposed processing industrial base where value would be added in advance of products being exported or distributed locally, as well as to catalyse a more advanced regional industrial complex – all of this in contrast to growing primarily for export - as was the preoccupation of the colonial government. The reasons for this shift were obvious.

Agriculture, viewed in this perspective assured it remained pivotal and made its sustenance even more critical. Ancillary key concepts derived directly from this thinking - the first being: 'Farm Settlements'; where all that was required to keep the proper manpower requisite not only to farm, but enhance product quality and yield were situated – schools for the workers' children, health centres, electricity, access roads, laboratories for primary product sample collection and testing, as part of a larger research initiative, etc. This approach would have served the equally important purpose – especially at the time - of 'rural development' as most of the plantations were in remote areas where government may have been challenged to provide these amenities had the added benefit of serving to sustain the revenue-generating plantations not existed.

The second direct benefit was the creation of crop research institutes which resulted not just in the desired effects of improved crop yield and product quality, but also, the emergence and growth of a research profession and culture. Mechanisms for mutually beneficial collaborative networking were being developed through the fostering of interactions between field laboratories, governmental agencies and institutions.

Following regionalization, in line with the implementation of the 1954 (Lyttleton) constitution, the government of the Eastern Region took the onus in 1955 to establish the School of Agriculture, Umudike on grounds which hitherto had been an outpost Provincial Experimental Farm of the Agricultural Department of the colonial government. The entire resource now a regional asset, the facilities would in 1956 be structurally integrated to form the Eastern Nigeria Agricultural Research and Training Station (ARTS), Umudike (https://nrcri.gov.ng/who-we-are/).

At the pinnacle of the network was the already acclaimed Department of Agriculture at the University of Nigeria, Nsukka which was at the time attracting research grants from and entering into and fostering beneficial collaborative agreements with international agencies and multilaterals.

Industry as a focus would increase earnings while creating employment opportunities for skilled and semi-skilled labor – an important trigger towards growing the necessary well-sized middle class by whom the new economy was intended to be anchored. Industry was not limited to the processing of agricultural produce and bye products. In anticipation of attainment of its objectives in physical development and recognizing the presence of mineral resources such as limestone, increase in demand for building materials was anticipated and strategically planned for. Cement factories were sited in Nkalagu, Port Harcourt and Calabar. The Nkalagu factory may have been the first built in Africa and was functional as early as 1957. The Port Harcourt factory also was functional before the Civil War but the Calabar factory, although completed prior to the outbreak of the war, was commissioned in 1970 by Col. U. J. Esuene, the military governor of the South-Eastern State – one of the three states that had been created, largely from the defunct Eastern Region. Other factories of note set up in the region were the steel and the roofing sheets manufacturing factory in Emene as well as tropical Africa's first aluminum mill and a glass factory in Port Harcourt.

Port Harcourt - which had the access to the Atlantic Ocean; Aba - which was located along the Enugu – PH railway line and exhibited the natural industrial traits and Enugu - where a coal industry had since thrived *and* was proximal to Nkalagu and where, by virtue of being the administrative capital, a significant market would exist, became the Region's key industrial cities.

The area that made up the Eastern Region had flourished in trade for centuries before colonization as geographically it fell within the natural route for the trade of various goods at different times in history. Commerce was thus naturally adapted. After the abolition of slave trade in the 19th century, places like Calabar and Bonny would become the ports through which non-human resources – cash crops mostly – would leave the shores of the Region perhaps in some of the same vessels and on the same routes that some of our ancestors would have been conveyed in the middle passage. The location of Onitsha along the Niger made it a historical trading post that served all of West Africa. Its relevance in this regard only grew as the economic success in the Region increased.

The increased autonomy derived from the 1954 Constitution saw the management of the Marketing Boards transferred from the Federal government to the Regions. Although there remain questions as to whether the functions of the Marketing Boards could have been better handled - since their role as middlemen came with certain inherent disadvantages - the benefits that accrued from having them closer to the farmers and the watchful eyes of a government whose revenue derivation was directly impacted by their activities, far outweighed any reservations there may have been to their existence. Perhaps, better ways would have been devised to achieve the objectives for which they existed that could have resulted in their curtailment of the negative practices, or perhaps, their utilization as a whole.

Education formed the fourth leg of the table built for the attainment of the vision of the leaders of post-colonial Eastern Nigeria. Quality education at all tiers was critical to the success of their agenda and a multipronged approach was embarked on to achieve this. The Eastern Region just like the West, had adopted a free elementary education policy. Missions had achieved great success – especially in primary and secondary levels as had communities. Government support was extended to ensure their success but also to encourage their increased participation and improvement. Technical education was prioritized with as many as 24 trade schools planned across the Region by 1964 (Imoke, 1964) Agricultural and teacher training schools were added to expand the reach at the secondary level while the University of Nigeria in Nsukka – the crown jewel in the Region's plan for academic excellence had opened with pump and pageantry in 1960.

In an unequivocal statement on the Region's intent to restate its priorities, the Eastern Nigeria Development Plan, 1962 – 1968 - the first developed in the post–colonial period - a whopping £80,235,000 (or 74% of the proposed expenditure) was allotted for these sectors in the following breakdown: Primary Production - 34%; Trade and Industry - 12%; Education - 28%.

| Sector | Capital | % of Total | Recurrent | Total | % |
|---|---|---|---|---|---|
| Primary Production | 30, 361 | 40 | 6, 460 | 36, 821 | 34 |
| Trade & Industry | 12, 930 | 17 | 586 | 13, 516 | 12 |
| Electricity | 600 | 1 | – | 600 | 1 |
| Transport | 8, 850 | 12 | 1, 350 | 10, 200 | 9 |
| Water (Urban & Rural) | 5, 100 | 7 | 1, 100 | 6, 200 | 6 |
| Education | 8, 805 | 12 | 21, 091 | 29, 896 | 28 |
| Health | 1, 819 | 2 | 1, 381 | 3, 200 | 3 |
| Town & Country Planning | 3, 306 | 4 | 275 | 3, 581 | 3 |
| Social Welfare | 534 | 1 | 724 | 1, 258 | 1 |
| Information | 450 | 1 | 190 | 640 | 1 |
| Justice | 250 | * | 190 | 440 | <5 |
| General Government | 2, 067 | 3 | 382 | 2, 449 | 2 |
| Financial Obligations | 120 | * | – | 120 | <5 |
| Total | £73, 192 | 100 | £33, 731 | £108, 923 | 100 |

Table 1. Eastern Nigeria Development Plan, 1962 – 1968 (Iwuagwu, 2006)

The decolonization period – the era covering the years leading up the end of colonial rule, and the period immediately after – mostly coincidentally occurred in the midst of Western Europe's massive rebuilding period following the end of the Second World War funded largely by the United States of America under the Marshall Plan.

This period also marked the beginning of the Cold War between the United States and the Soviet Union. Significant about that time, and an intrinsic outcome of the war, was the establishment of the United Nations, the World Bank, the International Monetary Fund and like multilateral institutions.

Although the countries emerging from European colonization did not directly benefit from the historic Marshall Plan, the convergence of these incidences - pivotal to the shaping of the global economic, social and political landscape for the foreseeable future - would greatly impact the vision and strategy for development in the nascent African and Asian Nations. Nigeria was no exception.

Understanding and aligning relevancies as reflected in the economic developmental planning models and principles considered to be the norms of the times assured viability internally as well as acceptance abroad. Emerging Asian and African nations thus had the opportunity to ride the crest of that wave of reconstruction if they were properly situated – structurally.

Crude oil reserves had recently been discovered in parts of the Eastern Region but its extraction was yet at preliminary stages. I make bold to say that with the sort of economic sagacity that prevailed at the time and the disciplined and structured manner in which government functioned, the inclusion of the extensive petroleum and gas deposits we now know existed, to the bouquet of offerings to deliberate on would have yielded results that would have been far more complimentary than has been the case.

## 5.  The Dying Cadence of the Eastern Melodies

The abrupt introduction by the Military of a unitary system of governing propagated as autonomous and therefore with little emphasis on reference to – indeed a seeming discouragement to previously devised plans - had the drastic effects of jettisoning a coherent plan developed around the most fundamental precepts for success: understanding the needs, appreciating the available resources – including potential to meet the identified needs - and developing the plan to achieve the needs using the available resources and by developing the latent potential – for a less articulate, more fragmented and less coordinated or result-dependent plan.

### 5.1 Preparedness

While that generation of rulers/leaders will always be seen as visionary, patriotic, and selfless, it is my contention that these attributes were largely fueled by a desire to succeed – even if to an extent, for the seemingly selfish reason: of proving themselves right. It is easy to simply attribute the successes of the period to the political will of the ruling class of the time. *But that doesn't tell the entire story* as a quick recollection of the account relayed earlier of the rift in the leadership of the NCNC clearly shows that everyone did not agree on every policy, strategy or ideology.

As is usually the case with all manner of 'battles', the losers' voice and invariably, their story, often seem to get lost – their whimper, overwhelmed *(drowned... subsumed...???)* by the commemorative speeches and triumphant reports, visionary articles, and books that read like ideological manuscripts belittling their (the losers') logic as piles of rubble from the spoils of war would once impressive landscapes; or the confetti from the victors' parade would the daily routine street litter.

The agitation for self-rule and ultimately, independence from colonialism in the years preceding our attainment of Independence was by no means unanimous. Of course, the colonialists did not propose it and were not going to – even if such events as the Constitutional Crisis of 1951-53 - would have presaged its seeming inevitability. Yet, even amongst the most prominent of Nigerian and specifically, Eastern Region leadership, there were those who felt the agitation for immediate independence was ill-thought and misguided. This group of leaders insisted Nigeria was not prepared to independently direct its own affairs as it lacked a sufficiently *(Western-style)* educated populace, the experienced civil service, a developed economy, an industrialized base and a strong middle class – which according to those of the school of thought, were all critical to the success of an independent nation. They felt the march to independence was far too aggressive, the pace too accelerated and argued it ought to be a more gradual and deliberate process.

Their counterparts on the other front – the proponents for independence who were termed the 'fiery brand', condescendingly labelled those who propagated such views, 'apostles of gradualism.' Of course, today – seeing where we are as a country – many wonder if perhaps the so-called 'apostles of gradualism' have indeed been vindicated by history. I would argue that today's failures cannot simply be attributed to such claims – but rather to a lack of 'proper' follow-thru by subsequent leaders, especially as the First Republic started significantly well.

Colonialism was *never* going to develop the proper foundation for building an optimal independent state. One where the colonized's best interests were the paramount objective, as this was contrary to what colonialism represents – that being: to colonize to the benefit of the colonialist government. Thus, no amount of gradualism would have sufficiently prepared us for independence. Rather, the responsibility that came with independence should have been recognized for exactly what it is – the need to devise, develop, drive, and where and when necessary, review and revise an achievable agenda for the growth and sustenance of the Country or Region. That the leadership of the First Republic recognized this is evident - not only as enunciated in such thoroughly developed documents as the Eastern Nigeria Development ... but also in the developments that aligned with such agenda and perhaps most informatively, the results achieved in the short while it existed.

That the 'project' was abruptly truncated and never really restarted, nor a new project or as several states were created from the region, a series of new projects as strategically devised, deliberately initiated and articulately executed are unarguably more appreciable reasons for the subsequent failures than the lame reason that we should have remained colonized longer.                                              ∎

## 5.2   Governance Structure

Many of the voices that today clamour for restructuring highlight the potential benefits that would accrue to the States in a restructured system but do not in so doing speak to the mutuality of benefits of which the Central Government stands to equally benefit.

Because of the Regions' obligatory fiduciary responsibility to the Centre, the Regions' economic success was of vital importance to the Central Government. The Centre therefore was wise to be deliberate in planning 'with' rather than 'for' the Region with the objective of improving the Regions' ability to drive its economy **to the mutual benefit of the Region and the Centre**. So, while the rail system was the Central Government's responsibility, the logical thinking to connect farms to seaports via rail to enhance exports or to provide electricity to industrial areas – in alignment with the State's industrial development plan - would have taken precedence over the need to do same for the personally gratifying reason of building the rail line to the MP's village or not providing to the Region's industrially rich area to instead place it at a destination based on nepotistic preference.

When in most casual conversations, comparisons are made or parallels drawn between then and now, they tend to be in isolation. We speak of the quality of education or the economy or conformity to the right societal values.

The preceding highlights the interdependences that prevailed in the era which many of us so proudly relish and desire to identify with. The economy was developed around the comparative strengths that existed within the region, while education was proactively designed to produce the workforce to drive it. Infrastructure was planned as vehicles to build up, sustain and deliver the outcomes thereof. Government had the responsibility to drive the agenda and politicians were regarded as taskmasters for its execution.

On the COR matter... as a Colony, were we so steeped – all-vested in our fight to be independent that we were blinded to our differences or was the structure indeed workable as thought through and articulated by our founding fathers? To say no to the later would suggest that the only workable situation would be one where there is absolute similarity. Many were rudely awaken to the reality that there is no such thing when the East Central State was split into two states – Anambra and Imo. It seemed that suddenly, Igbos were awoken to their differences. Many of the occurrences that followed were every bit as hostile as the minorities of the Eastern – and indeed, other Regions of the Colony – feared may befall them – their expression of which led to the formation of the afore-mentioned Willink Commission. Today, with 5 Igbo states, there are calls for more primarily based on the same sentiments.

Realistic but rational objectives of wealth creation, equity and fairness developed on a foundation of deliberately formed policies sustained in good governance are more achievable, and sustainable for a larger economy than in the creation of even more unviable states.

Today, countries like Canada, Australia and even the UAE and Botswana have immigration policies intended to bolster their population as they seek the requisite manpower to develop their resources and expand their economies. By maintaining and updating... through continuous assessment and improvements in ....planning.... education, training, the population of the East would have been developed to provide the required human capital to develop the abundance of resources and available potential the region boasted rather than being the threat some feared it portened.

## 5.3 Social Life

The way people live is the ultimate reflection of any society's governance system, its failures and successes are the outcomes of the policies it adopts; the economic agenda it advances; the strategic growth plan it implements.

While some nuances have not entirely been eclipsed, many of the greatest contrasts to be drawn between then and now may be in social lifestyles. In looking back at those times, one can't help but note that the degree to which a seeming blanketing abnormalcy has pervaded our senses is numbing.

Even as cities of Aba, Enugu, Port Harcourt and the like, bustled with activity, residential areas, schools, court and hospital premises remained tranquil zones, their well-maintained yards most, appealingly visible through barbed-wire or picket fences - if any. There was nary the cacophony of generator sounds nor the piercing siren noises that seem only too normal today, rudely disrupting the siesta hour.

Security was all but taken for granted as even young children of the most privileged strolled, ran or cycled from place to place unperturbed and seemingly unaware of the possibilities that dangers may have been lurking.

Sixty- and seventy-year-olds today who would have been teens or younger during the period speak of being sent off to boarding schools - sometimes halfway across the country - by bus or train, unaccompanied. I do not know, nor have I heard, that anyone did not arrive at their destination.

As is the case now, a key aspect of socializing was family-centric celebrations – birthdays, weddings, anniversaries, etc. Despite being nowhere near as ostentatious as we make them today, they were every bit as joyous, exhilarating and entertaining.

The juxtaposing images, often from black and white pictures or 8mm film reels, of people dressed in their traditional outfits and waltzing or twisting to the crooning voices of Nat King Cole, Frank Sinatra and the music of Chubby Checker or swinging to the latest high life beats of Rex "The Cardinal" Lawson, Osita Osadebe, Inyang Henshaw, Bobby Benson, E. T. Mensah and a very young Victor Uwaifo in their western suits and ball gowns, remain cherished nostalgic metaphors from the period.

In most cities, the seemingly obligatory European Clubs (in Enugu, subsequently the Sports Club) and the African Clubs (still operational in Calabar today), which earlier in the colonial era stood out as pejorative icons of segregation, became important symbols of integration, first for the privileged and higher-ups in government, politics and business but eventually, the emerging middle class.

With industrialization came throngs of expatriates of a different ilk – more of them, working and middle class. Their presence in the more industrially advanced areas spurred the demand for a more relaxed and often more adult-oriented entertainment. In places like Port Harcourt which was emerging the Region's industrial centre with the development of the Trans Amadi Industrial Estate and the recent discovery of petroleum reserves, the Silver Valley Club had become emblematic of facilities offering some of the best relaxation to their integrated regaling clientele. By the fifties, Christianity had been largely entrenched in most of the Eastern Region with many families of the period being at least second-generation Christians and proud alumni of the Region's many prominent parochial schools. Religious activities and especially Sunday church attendance in our 'Sunday-best' was largely the norm just as it is today. Of course, the assortment of denominations that exist now were not available then. An innocuous but striking observation is that today, more families though just as smartly dressed are sporting more 'af-fluenced' (African-influenced) outfits than was the case then. I'd opine that the children in particular in their dresses, shirts and ties were every bit as charming then. ∎

## 6. The Finale

A society's reward system cannot be at variance with, rather, it would reflect the values and invariably therefore, the value system of the society.

Many point to differences in the value system that prevailed in the society of the period compared to now. Indeed, they are glaring: Who was highly regarded? What was considered worthy of celebration? How did persons in the various cadres of society relate to others or conduct *(or is it 'comport')* themselves – in public and in their private lives?

Of course, it is great to espouse 'good' values. We may even say it is noble to live by them. But as noble as the intentions may seem, living by values is not independent of rewards. There are immediate-, medium- and long-term benefits to be gained in adopting the values that we choose. We work hard in the hope that we would get promoted; we adopt disciplined eating habits so we can enjoy long, healthy lives and we avoid sin because we want to go to heaven!

So, regardless of how much we pontificate the importance of good values, as a society, the values we adopt (or do not adopt) would tend to speak to the rewards we expect. It should not therefore be unexpected that merit is neither highly sought nor its attainment greatly revered in a society where it is not rewarded. Likewise, it should not seem strange that material wealth is flaunted; and the acquisition there of exalted in a society where its possession – regardless of the means of its attainment - is near universally idolized.

While these examples may seem to reflect personal or individual values, the society is nothing but a collection of these – individuals – and unbiasedly a reflection of their values, which when looked at collectively form 'societal values' and thus are drivers of that society's agenda for development, sustenance, etc.; its way of being and its method of functioning *(or 'dysfunctioning')*.

## Harlem

BY

**LANGSTON HUGHES**

What happens to a dream deferred?

Does it dry up
like a raisin in the sun?
Or fester like a sore—
And then run?
Does it stink like rotten meat?
Or crust and sugar over—
like a syrupy sweet?

Maybe it just sags
like a heavy load.

*Or does it explode?*

## References

Ali, M. A., Abubakar, Y., Ali, H. (2019) The Executive, Legislature and the Judiciary: Toward Democratic Governance in Nigeria Since 1914 (Journal of Economic Info)

Callaway, A. & Musone, A. (1968) Financing Education in Nigeria (UNESCO: International Institute for Education Planning)

Edomah, N., Foulds, C. Jones, A. (2016) Energy Transitions in Nigeria: The Evolution of Energy Infrastructure Provision (1800 – 2015) (Anglia Ruskin University, Cambridge & Pan Atlantic University, Lagos)

Egbe, E. J. (2014) Native Authorities & Local Government Reforms in Nigeria since 1914 (Benue State University)

Falola, T. & Genova, A. (2009) A Historical Dictionary of Nigeria

Floyd, B. (1969) Extract – Industrialization of Eastern Nigeria (Michigan State University)

Hughes, L. (1951) HARLEM - A Dream Deferred (Poem)

Ikpeme, Engr. I. W. (2021) Interview

Imoke, S. E. (1964) Ministerial Broadcasts on Education. Eastern Region (Nigeria). Ministry of Education

Iwuagwu, O. (2006) Rural Development in Eastern Nigeria: An Assessment of Colonial and Post-Colonial Development Plans in the Former Owerri Province, 1946 – 1976 (University of Lagos)

Izuagie, L. (2016) The Willink Minority Commission and Minority Rights in Nigeria (Ambrose Alli University)

Sklar, R. L. (1963) Nigerian Political Parties: Power in an Emergent African Nation (UCLA)

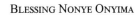
## Ndị Igbo and Inter-Ethnic Stereotyping among Nigerians

## Summary

*This chapter is focused on social constructions of ethnic stereotypes between the Igbo and their immediate neighbors: the Yoruba, Akwa Ibom, Edo, Delta, Cross-River, Bayelsa, North-central and the far North groups among others. Using ethnographic methods and secondary data, this paper discusses types, formation, and maintenance of intra-inter-ethnic stereotypes for the Igbo people among peoples of Nigeria and the sociopsychological implications of these labels. The study found that there are motivational factors like contexts of social learning mainly from family/parents responsible for the formation, fueled and maintained by the media especially social media, with implications like inter-ethnic suspicions, tensions, reinforcing differences between the 'other and self', emotions of anger, fear and, at the extreme, outright conflicts. The Igbo have an array of stereotypes for others and others do the same. These interethnic stereotypes have great implications on intergroup relations and the outcomes are often negative. The paper suggests ways to ameliorate the sociopsychological impact of interethnic stereotypes on social thinking, social behavior and social influences by emphasizing those things that unite Nigerians and encourage unity in diversity.*

## 1. Introduction

STEREOTYPES ARE UBIQUITOUS. Stereotypes are dominant assumptions that shape inter-group encounters and revolves around identity creation which has always been part of the human race. Across the world's continents including African nations like Nigeria, stereotypes are eminent. Stereotypes seem prevalent in heterogenous settings like Nigeria. All ethnic groups in Nigeria, including the three major ones- Yoruba, Hausa and Igbo, are labelled with one stereotype or the other. This highlights the fact that stereotypes are living realities across groups. Stereotypes manifest in diverse forms and shapes across societies and cultures. There are: racial stereotypes (Fernando, 1991; Peffley et al., 1997); national stereotypes (Meed, 1962); regional stereotypes (Gavreliuc et al., 2021; Jost et al., 2005); gender stereotypes (Eagly et al., 2020; Kiaušiene et al., 2011); age stereotypes (Dionigi, 2015; Gázquez et al., 2009); and ethnic stereotypes (Lebedko, 2014; Madon et al., 2001) among others.

The locus of this chapter is therefore inter-ethnic stereotypes with prime focus on stereotypes revolving around the Igbo people, who are known for their entrepreneurial resilience, business skills and trading prowess that gives them the capacity to survive anywhere in the world. The Igbo are mainly found within the five Southeastern states in Nigeria with a few other Igbo people found in neighboring states like Kogi, Akwa-Ibom, Rivers State, Edo, Delta and others. In the recent past, the Igbo were in the center of the Nigerian-Biafran war (1967-1970) and since then, the nature of inter-ethnic relations between the Igbo and others in Nigeria has not been as smooth as it was before the war.

The perception of the Igbo by others is therefore uncertain and vary across ethnic groups in Nigeria. The question of what you think/say of others and what others think/say of you remains salient in the social sciences, behavioral sciences and humanities. Stereotypes bring to fore the 'self-versus others' divide and discourses on these dual opposites constantly crop up in inter-group relations across time and space.

Stereotypes are also manifest in the social world and find expressions during intra-group relations and often trigger emotions serving as defense and justifications for our biases against others.

Stereotypes have been variously defined. According to Lawrence, (2004, p. 251) 'stereotypes are false or misleading generalizations about groups'. To Hilton et al., (1996, p. 240) 'stereotypes are more than just beliefs about groups, they are mental representations of reality and are also theories about how and why certain attributes go together'. However, this idea of 'mental representation' does not address the issue of whether the represented idea might need to be corrected. Hence, this and similar definition tend to portray stereotypes as being cast in stone, though this may not be the case. The United Nations Human Rights, (2014) reports that stereotypes are 'a generalized view or preconception about attributes or characteristics that are or ought to be possessed by members of a particular social group or the roles that are or should be performed by, members of a particular social group'. It is also seen as the 'exaggerated or distorted beliefs about the characteristics, attributes, and behaviors of individuals and communities that categorize individuals and communities into singular, pejorative terms' (Center for the Study of Social Policy, 2019). For the purpose of this chapter, stereotypes are assumed and unsubstantiated judgements or opinions about an individual or group which could be true or untrue, acceptable or unacceptable, favorable or unfavorable to the target group. It implies that there are both negative and positive stereotypes.

It is also pertinent to state that stereotypes are not only unfavorable most times, but they also trigger and sustain prejudices within and outside the targeted group(s). We have *in-group* and *out-group* stereotypes. The *in-group* stereotype seems negative, but is not inherently so; it sometimes tends to be activated to correct deviant behaviors or to maintain social order within the group. The *Out-group* stereotype is often inherently negative towards other groups. Stereotypes as identity issues remain an important discourse because it speaks volumes on the nature of intergroup relations as it determines how humans relate with each other, and who relates with whom. By extension, it brings up identity discourses which also elaborate issues of power relations, access to resources, prestige, and wealth. Stereotypes could either be positive or negative, true or untrue, implicit (covert) or explicit (overt), descriptive or prescriptive, conflict-ridden or peaceful among its other dynamic ways of manifestations. Negative stereotypes most often prevail. The prevalence of negative labels among diverse groups, ethnicities, and nations entrenches different forms of discrimination, marginalization, oppression, among others, as well as expressions of aghast against inequality and inequity. It is worthy of note that every individual or group experiences stereotype, whether the individual or group is in the minority or in the majority. In essence, there are minority group's and majority group's stereotypes, especially in multiethnic or heterogenous countries and nations. In other words, the quality (social status/class) and quantity (population size) of particular group does not immune or exonerate it from being given some stereotypes and labels.

Following from the above issues on stereotypes, this chapter is therefore, focused on exploring the nature of inter-ethnic stereotypes for the Igbos by other ethnics. What names do they call the *Ndị Igbo* and what do the names literally mean in their languages? What are the positive and negative connotations of the name? On the reverse: What name do *Ndị Igbo* have for the same people? What does the name mean in the Igbo language? What is the possible origin of the name? What are the negative and positive connotations of the name? What are the overall psychosocial effects of these names on the intergroup relations?

## 2. Social Learning, Labeling Theories and Stereotypes

The three concepts of *Social learning*, *labelling* and *stereotypes* are so intertwined that it is almost difficult to separate one from the other. The social learning theory, which is associated with Abert Bandura (1925-2021), is a framework for explaining how environmental and cognitive factors interact to influence human learning and behavior (Bandura, 1971; Ramadan & Nazan, 2010). The theory suggests that new behaviors can be learnt by observing and imitating others during social interaction. For instance, aggression, bigotry and ethnocentrism can be learnt by observing and imitating ethnic jingoists. This is known as modelling, and a group can model another group or other groups into developing positive or negative stereotypes towards others. In this vein, this theory proposes five steps/principles for learning social behavior whether they are accepted behaviors or not namely: observation, attention, retention, reproduction and motivation (Stalburg, 2016). The theory is for understanding how individuals/groups learn and form a behavior towards others by observation and modelling/imitation. Stereotypes about others are learnt by observing and imitating older persons who over the years have formulated and recycled stereotypes and labels about other groups. Hence, aggression and negative labeling can be transmitted through observational learning. So, as much as one could learn positive behaviors by observing others, one can also learn negative behaviors or hold negative opinions about others through observation and imitation by recounting such labels. Ethnic stereotypes are circulated and reinforced in the society. For example, people are surrounded by many influential models, such as parents within the family, friends within their peer groups, characters on mass/social media, religions, other members of the society and the schools, all of which may serve as channels for circulating negative stereotypes and labels (Edinyang, 2016).

Labeling theory was developed and popularized by Howard Becker between 1960s and 1970s in his book titled 'Outsiders' and it draws far back from the work of Emile Durkheim's Book on suicide (1897) where he argued that deviant labeling functions to satisfy a society's need to control behaviors (Bernburg, 2009). The theory is also associated with Frank Tanenbaum in his work titled 'Crime and the Community.' George Herbert Mead's work on symbolic interactionism also made contributions to labeling theory that the self is constructed and reconstructed through societal interactions (Lewis, 1976; Stryker, 1987). In essence, labels are creations of powerful interest groups/individuals. The main thrust of the theory is that it 'highlights social responses to crime and deviance and by extensions tries to understand what happens to a person after he/she has been labeled a criminal. It suggests that such criminal behaviors may be heightened after such label. It further suggests that individuals and groups attract labels from how others perceive their behaviors and this also influences how the self relates with others. Labels could refer to acts that are not socially accepted but are not necessarily crimes. Labels sometimes attract social stigma and may assign deviant roles which are by extension sources of negative stereotypes.

Finally, the Igbo people of Southeastern Nigeria, just like all other ethnic groups in Nigeria, are victims of ethnic stereotyping; but again, just like other ethnic groups in the country, they are also guilty of labeling others with diverse stereotypes. The chapter explores the nature, types, formation, and maintenance of these intra-inter-ethnic stereotypes for the Igbo people among peoples of Nigeria and the socio-psychological implications of these labels. Delving into this matter involved the use of predominantly qualitative traditional and digital ethnographic methods (Ardévol & Gómez-Cruz, 2013; Mattern, 2018; Proctor, 2020), secondary data, such as participant observation, and in-depth interviews across internet mediated platforms like Facebook and WhatsApp. My use of internet mediated platforms is necessary because it presents easier access to persons from different parts of Nigeria within the Nigerian social media space; these people would ordinarily not have been reached with the use of traditional ethnography alone. 12 in-depth interviews involving purposively selected 8 males and 4 females who were considered knowledgeable in the research area. In-depth interviews were conducted by contacting the study participants through phones and physically to obtain informed consent after which the interviews were done on WhatsApp chats. This was combined with participating, observing and following social media threads, and posts on stereotypes after permissions to make reference to the posts was obtained from the authors of the social media posts via inbox. These social media posts were identified by doing a *Google* search of such threads as 'stereotypes', 'ethnic stereotypes', 'Nigerian stereotypes', 'abuses and insults', and 'Igbo stereotypes.' At the end of the search, 13 posts met the search criteria and were imported into NVivo R1.5.1 for coding and processing the data. Thematic analysis was employed to elicit emerging themes from the data collected to enable 'thick description', interpretations and extrapolations to be made in line with the study objectives.

## 3. Stereotyping in Nigeria

The findings on the study focus are generally discussed under *common stereotypes, reversed stereotypes* (which are mainly ethnic stereotypes involving Yoruba/Ijebu, South-south stereotypes, Hausa-Fulani stereotypes); *maintenance of stereotypes; motivations, types of stereotypes* and the implications of ethnic stereotypes. More specifically, the findings on 'what other ethnic groups in Nigeria call the Igbo people' revolve around Igbo culture of business/trading, skin color, food types, gender, and in-group stereotypes among others. Some of these stereotypes, as drawn from the data findings, show that some of the stereotypes can be categorized as *traditional* and *modern media-driven* stereotypes, and they are drawn from experiences during inter-ethnic interactions.

3.1 The Common Stereotypes:
What other Ethnic Groups Call Ndị Igbo

*(a) The Traditional/Ancient Stereotypes*

The traditional stereotypes for the Igbo are: 'the Igbo have no king (*Igbo-enwe eze'*)', 'the Igbo are stubborn and strong-headed', 'nyamiri', 'the Igbo eat hard food', and so on. The interview excerpts below show some of these stereotypes:

> *"Ajokuta ma mu omi" is one stereotype. Meaning Igbo people who eat stone without taking water. It is about the solid foods like Eba eaten by the Igbo. They also say the Igbo wake up their father with a kick." Awon mafia Ji baba". 'Ipa' is kick. In a way it depicts stubbornness and disrespect. That they are hard-headed. By interpretation, this means the independence of the Igbo or let me say acephalous system of the Igbo society as evidence of lack of deference to a father or an authority figure. The other part, "okuta" means stone or rock in Yoruba. Like Abeokuta which means "under the rock" in reference to Olumo Rock. Those are the two I can think of right off the bat.*
> *Firstly, we say "Omo a jokuta ma mu mi." (Yoruba people believe that Igbo people like hard food and they can take it without water) This appellation is given to the Igbos in reference to their strength. Secondly, "Yibo feran obe ti ko lepo pupo." (Igbos love soup with little oil). Thirdly, "Yibo feran owo ju emi wan lo." (The Igbos love money more than their lives.) Fourthly, "Yibo feran orisa bibo." (They love idol worshipping) Fifthly, "Awon yibo ma n toju iyawo won ju ara won lo" (The Igbo people love and care for their wives than themselves. (An in-depth interview with a Yoruba study participant, August, 2021).*
> *The Igbo people are perceived by the Yoruba as 'people who*

> *do not have respect for elders and "Ajokuta ma mu omi"-*
> *meaning 'people who eat stone without taking water'. This*
> *is about the solid foods like "Eba" (processed cassava)*
> *eaten by the Igbo while we eat "Amala" (processed*
> *yam/cassava) and you know it is very soft unlike the Igbo*
> *very rocky "fufu" (Personal Communication: August,*
> *2021).* **99**

On the other hand, the Hausa ethnic group identifies the Igbo ethnic group as *"nyamiri"* as shown in the excerpts below:

> **66** *The Hausas call the "Igbos nyamiri do do doya"*
> *(because the Igbos after eating yam demand for*
> *drinking water, they now started calling the Igbos*
> *"nyamiri"- which means "nye m mmiri" in Igbo and in*
> *English, it means 'give me water' (In-depth interview*
> *on WhatsApp, August, 2021).*

> *I've spent most of my life in the north. I can tell you that*
> *many northerners hate that word. Unfortunately, and*
> *curiously, many of them are wont to use ethnic slurs*
> *like 'Nyamiri' for the Igbos. I grew up learning that*
> *'Nyamiri' was the Hausa word for 'Igbo'. (Comment on*
> *a social media post, retrieved in August, 2021).*

> *...Then the Igbos! 'Fondly' called 'okoro' or 'ajokuta ma*
> *m'omi', meaning 'the one who feasts on eba that is as*
> *hard as a rock, without drinking water'. (Comment on*
> *social media posts, retrieved August, 2021).* **99**

*(b) The Modern Media-Driven Stereotypes*
These types of stereotypes are triggered by the media and reinforced in the social media, namely:

> *If some drug guys or a Yahoo boy with Igbo names are caught, for the next week, the news of Igbo bad boys will rent the airwaves. If a robbery or kidnap takes place in the Southeast, it reigns for one week in the media about how Igbos are criminals. (social media post retrieved August, 2021).*

The Igbo are also accused of being involved in circulating some of these modern media-driven stereotypes resulting in a kind of 'in-group modern media-driven stereotypes' for the Igbo as shown here in this comment:

> *The interesting thing is that it is not only non-Igbos that engage in this Igbo hype and stereotyping. Igbos join in it and see it as a matter of "speaking the plain truth and shaming the devil (Comment on social media posts, retrieved August, 2021).*

Many of the comments on the selected social media posts, suggests that the media and particularly Nollywood movies maintain and reinforce these ethnic stereotypes as shown in the excerpts below:

> *That's why I don't watch Nollywood movies. They don't even try to be sensitive about these things. They reinforce all the negative stereotypes that movies should serve to change. From Hausa gatemen, to Igbo lovers of money, to Yoruba "witch" mother-in-laws. No attempt to challenge stereotypes or pursue progressive agendas at all. (Social media comment, retrieved in August, 2021).*

Finally, one interview also drew attention to the fact that the Igbo do not reciprocate when things happen in such a manner that other ethnic groups could also be labelled as a result:

> *Surprisingly, these Igbos don't do this despicable thing when other ethnic groups are involved. When prices of meat rise during Sallah, Igbos conveniently Ignore that. When transport fares rise during Sallah no one discusses the tribe. When there's traffic in Lagos and drivers raise their fares, no one mentions their tribes (Comment on social media posts, retrieved August, 2021).*

### (c) The Gender-Based Stereotypes

Some gender-based stereotypes for the Igbo can just emanate from mere rumour as shown in this social media comment: 'But just a rumour about rape in the Southeast and all hell is let loose about how Igbo men are rapists' (Comment on social media retrieved August, 2021). Others include: 'all Igbo women are light skinned', 'Igbo women are very expensive to marry'.

## 3.2  Common In-Group Stereotypes: What Ndị Igbo Call Themselves

There are many in-group and often derogatory terms that the Igbo call themselves. Some are at the level of village against village, town against town, or even members of a state against members of another state. The most common usually involve the use of town names.

An example is the description of the Mbaise people in Imo State Nigeria. It is often said "when you see an *Mbaise* man and a snake, quickly kill the *Mbaise* man and spare the snake". This means that an *Mbaise* man is dangerous and poisonous to relate with. It is important to state that these stereotypes are baseless and wrong. There is also the assumption that Ngwa people (a group from Abia State, Nigeria) are generally short.

At the state level, the people of Anambra State of Nigeria are erroneously assumed to be commonly involved in money rituals. Interestingly, this is

### 3.3 The Reverse Stereotypes: What Ndị Igbo Call Other Ethnic Groups

The Igbo people also have their own stereotypes for some of the various ethnic groups in Nigeria.

The first is the assumption that all northerners in Nigeria are Hausa-Fulani, 'shoe-shiners (cobblers) and gatemen/Mai-guard.' Fuelled by recent developments in the country is also the assumption that they are hostile, terrorists, cattle herders...'. For the Yoruba, the Igbo refer to them as *ndị ofe mmanu* - meaning 'oily food consumers.' There is also the assumption that the Yoruba mothers-in-laws are witches (this is propagated by the Nigerian *Nollywood* films), etc. Similarly, emergent themes from the study on 'what the Igbo people call other ethnic groups' are: 'The Igbo refer to all Northerners as *aboki* (ordinarily meaning friend) or *Mallam* which is not inherently negative in itself but it is often used with a demeaning and derogatory tone which sometimes angers most Northerners. The excerpts from posts and threads of discussions on social media below explains this stereotype better:

 *Growing up as a Southerner in Nigeria, you learn to think of the Hausa man as an aboki. The term actually means "friend" and its use may have originated from purely innocuous circumstances, but it is invoked in a wide spectrum of situations, from friendly jest to downright insult depending on how derogatory the speaker wants to get. In today's Nigeria, aboki has increasingly become a coded ethnic slur which, placed on a spectrum, may imply anything from a poor working-class northerner to someone stupid, sheep-like or cow-like, ignorant, primitive, and uncivil; an oaf, unable to grasp the complexities of modern life. (From a post made on social media, retrieved August, 2021).*

*"We laugh and dance to every "Aboki, shine my Shoe" that's currently receiving airplay, sung by artists who,*

*no doubt, are born of the same system that sees nothing wrong in stereotyping a region with over 60 different diverse and wonderful tribes. We hear lines like "mallam, pass me the suya", "aboki, change my dollar", and we mouth the same lines without any forethought. (From a post made on social media, retrieved August, 2021).*

*..., Hausa people get offended by it A LOT. I know. I've stayed among them enough to know. Of course, they won't tell you this when they're trying to sell their markets in a society where they're the minority, but trust me, it bothers them. (From a post made on social media, retrieved August, 2021).*

The challenge is also that these stereotypes have become deeply rooted in jokes by comedians, and rhymes and songs in such a way that it has become very difficult to obliterate them from daily interactions.

## 3.4 Stereotyping among Other Ethnic Groups

### (a) What the Yoruba Call Themselves

The Yoruba refer to the *Ijebu* people as misers and ritualists as shown in the interview excerpts below:

*In the old times, the Ijebu of Ogun State, southwest Nigeria, were very industrious and extremely wealthy when weighed against the pervasive poverty of the bygone era. However, their critics don't see industriousness; rather, they accuse them of being involved in money-making rituals. The mindset trails anyone who introduces him/herself as Ijebu up until this moment. Worse, the Ijebu are regarded as miserly. It is common to hear, "Why are you being an*

*Ijebu?" when you try to bargain hard... (In-depth interview, August, 2021).* **99**

### (b) What the Yoruba Call the Hausa-Fulani

Some of the Yoruba stereotypes for the Hausa-Fulani are: 'Hausas are not to be trusted', they sometimes make jest or refer to the Hausa as having dirty kola-nut tinted teeth- meaning that their teeth are brown and unclean. The Yoruba prefer to die than to serve the so-called Gambari (Hausa-Fulani) and the Hausa-Fulani in-group murder/homicide is inconsequential' as shown in the interview excerpts below:

*In fact, the Yoruba people have more stereotypical words for the Hausa than for the Igbo. I don't know why that is anyway. These stereotypes are included even in adages and proverbs. But none for the Igbo in the adages and proverbs. "Gambari pa Fulani, ko le je ninu". Meaning, if a Hausa man kills a Fulani man, there is no case there, because it is a brother killing brother. It's an extension of the otherness. 'We versus them'. They are seen more as an out-group whose plight should not bother them. "Kaka ka dobale fun Gambari, ka Kuku roju Ku". Meaning "Better death, than to 'prostrate' or defer or submit to a Hausa man". Here, "dobale" means to prostrate in deference, like the way Yoruba males greet an elderly person (In-depth interview, August, 2021).*

The interviewer assumed that there seems to have been long years of rivalry between the Yoruba and the Hausa/Fulani. But this study participant thinks otherwise as shown below:

*You know the Hausa/Fulani played a strong role as middlemen to the white slavers. They conquered and kidnapped Yoruba people and sold them to white men.*

*E.g., Bishop Ajayi Crowther was kidnapped by Fulani slavers. This stems from years of slavery. You know the Old Oyo borders Nupe and parts of modern-day Nigeria, most Hausa traders and Fulani herders were able to move and live among the Yoruba. Fulani herdsmen killings/kidnappings did no start today. They could not penetrate the East and the South-South because of the thick rainforest and the fact that Tsetse fly would have decimated their calvaries. Much of northern Yoruba is savannah. That explains why the Oyo were able to build an empire with the aid of horses. (In-depth interview, August, 2021).*

Again, the interviewer further probed if this was as an issue of environmental determinism but the study participant does not think it is as shown below:

*The Hausa/Fulani through Islam also used that to penetrate the Yoruba country. That suspicions have always been there. There was an archival account, I don't know where it is now reported by Toyin Falola on the Ibadan and how they even instructed their women not to sell anything to the Hausa/Fulani during an episode in the 19th century. Gàmbàrí jẹ díẹ̀ l'óbì, kéyín ó tó ó pọ́n meaning "Gambari ate not a few kola nuts before his teeth turned brown". In reference literally to their brown teeth. When Yoruba calls you "Gambari", or "Malaa"- it is the height of insult. (In-depth interview, August, 2021).*

### (c) Some South-South Stereotypes

Some of the peoples of the South-South region of Nigeria also have their stereotypes of other ethnic groups. For example, 'the Yoruba are terrible', 'Ijaw people are strict'. The excerpts of the interview of some persons from the Niger-Delta region of Nigeria show these stereotypes:

Iwho re Yoruba muosho meaning they're terrible while they believe we 419(Urhobo wayo). Iwho re evwere siaro meaning the Ijaws are very strict. (In-depth interview with Study participant from Urhobo in Delta State).

## 4. Implications of Stereotypes and Stereotyping

From all the interviews in section 3 above, it is obvious that the speakers are not sensitive to the implications of stereotypes and stereotyping. The height of such insensitivity is in the use of the labels for pop songs, whereby the singer and the dancer are simply not aware of the negative effect of the song and the ease with which it spreads and consolidates the stereotype. There are many other implications, as can be seen from the excerpts from the interviews below.

"As a people, we have been desensitized to the extent that ethnic bigotry permeates our socio-cultural sphere." (Social media comment, retrieved August, 2021). This implies labeling and stereotypes are prevalent among ethnic groups in Nigeria. Another comment reads "We see nothing wrong with the ethnic labels we've done on people from the north. These things are benign right? It doesn't harm anyone, yeah?" "These stereotypes then hinder the fostering of respect for the minorities" (Social media comment, retrieved August, 2021).

 *Except that, of course, it calcifies our worldview of people from the north as simpletons, hardly capable of being more than cobblers and suya sellers. Marcel Ojinnaka, in his essay "The Worthless Life of an Aboki" made the following observation: We start with seemingly benign ethnic labels. These labels then inform our characterization of a people; usually a minority group in our societies, which in turn*

*reinforces our stereotypes. These stereotypes then hinder the fostering of respect for the minorities (Social media comment, retrieved August, 2021).*

> *We might not immediately feel the impact of this negligence, but if we don't start now to sensitize ourselves and our children, 20 years from now, children in the south will think the north is that place where cattle herders, cobblers and "suya-men" are manufactured (Social media comment, retrieved August, 2021).* "

Gratefully, some social media users are taking a stand against stereotype as it has implications on ethnic cohesion as seen here: "I would not call a Yoruba man anything but his name. I think those tags are unnecessary. A simple 'excuse me' will do instead of calling "aboki' or "okoro". You don't seem to see the deleterious effect these tags have on ethnic cohesion?" Indeed, stereotypes are destructive:

> " *It is naive, self-defeating and self-destructive to accept a negative stereotype of you just because you want to be seen as truthful. It gets you stuck in the stereotype. It doesn't empower you to work on it. You can work on a problem more effectively without a stereotype of yourself but rather proper self-assessment and a determination to deal. The people who push those stereotypes of you aren't helping you but are out to make you feel inferior, helpless and to discriminate against you (Social media comment, retrieved August, 2021).* "

Just as enunciated by the social learning theory (Middleton et al., 2019), we can also model and celebrate the uniqueness of other ethnic groups as rightly captured by this comment: "ridiculing a person or people achieves except creating anger and hatred and quarrels. Every people have something that makes them unique that can be celebrated and even emulated." A good example is the following comment on the Igbo reads:

> *Let's give it to the Igbos, when it comes to business, there is no contest. At major markets, they are dominant. In fact, in places where you do not imagine that you will find them, they are always there. But there is more to this people than business. You find them in politics, literature, education, economy and other sectors. Late Nnamdi Azikiwe, was the first president of Nigeria, a nationalist as well as a journalist. The literary lord, the man of words and the author of the evergreen book-Things Fall Apart that made the world change their perception about African literature, late Chinua Achebe, was not a businessman, same with Chiwetel Ejiofor, and also Chimamanda Adichie. The list is endless. Take it or leave it, no matter the field an Igbo man ventures into, the business trait trails him (Social media post retrieved, August, 2021).*

The commentator is not an Igbo person, but is able to identify something about the Igbo; so also, can the Igbo identify things they can admire and emulate in other groups. A spiral of mutual positive admiration and emulation can only lead to a permanent state of 'striving for improvement' for the whole nation.

# 5. Discussions

From all of the presentations in this chapter, it has become obvious that a lot more needs to be done with regard to stereotypes and stereotyping in Nigeria in general, and not just the Igbo. The two main angles from which this could be broached are the factors that contribute to the maintenance of stereotypes and the psycho-social implications of stereotypes and stereotyping.

On the maintenance of stereotypes, the following themes emerged from the study as factors that contribute to maintaining and reinforcing ethnic stereotypes.

(a) *Parents as Cooks of Stereotypes.* This is not surprising as the home is assumed to be the first agent of socialization where young minds are first introduced to all sorts. Parents end up raising bigoted future generations, disrespectful to other ethnic groups, with calcified worldviews of other ethnic groups outside theirs. This results in the prevalence of very difficult to erase ethnic stereotypes.

(b) *Blind Ethnic Solidarity.*

Clinging blindly to an ethnic group, 'for better for worse', is one of the dangers of stereotyping. See the worst of others forces the person concerned to see the world only from the narrow confines of his ethnic bias and stereotype of other groups. The recognition of this fact should ensure that we treat 'other' people with fairness (Hilton et al., 1996).

(c) *Other Maintenance Sources*

Other means of maintaining stereotypes include careless, thoughtless tags and labels, over-sensitivity, the role of media in maintaining and reinforcing stereotypes, home movies and music industry. **Also,** of relevance here is ignorance and innocence stemming from having little or no exposure to other ethnic groups and cultures (this can be checked by traveling outside our indigenous cultures), and blame-game'. Here is a summary of the implications of seeing stereotyping as 'harmless' or 'not so terrible':

> ❝ *You still don't think this is terrible? Call a random 6-year-old child in the south and point to every barrow pusher, every cobbler, every 'tazarce' wearing person and watch in shock as each one is identified with one word: aboki. The next generation is raised on the back of our stereotypes. (A comment from a post made on social media, retrieved August, 2021).* ❞

The challenge to this stereotype is that it is unintentionally socialized into younger people by adults and the younger people reinforce it daily as they come in contact with Northern Nigerians. "Simple rules such as don't call every northern Nigerian tribe "aboki" should not be hard to obey." (From a post made on social media, retrieved August, 2021). Definitely, we can bridge some of these 'insider-outsider divide, self-versus others' lacuna by encouraging inter-ethnic marriages (Goffman, 1959; Schein et al., 1989; Doki, 2009).

On the socio-psychological Implications of ethnic stereotypes, the following are the main issues. The first is the psychological upheaval it causes through 'stirring up emotions of anger, hatred, ethnic stigma, insensitivity, strife, feeling of inferiority and helplessness, psychiatric illness on the extremes.' These socio-psychological effects come with a lot of ripple effects (Davidson et al., 2015). Stereotypes create divisions with deleterious effects on ethnic cohesion, widen the gap between the minority and the majority, thereby raising more hues and cries of discrimination, marginalization and can lead to a total collapse of social order due to outright conflicts. Then follows the outright exploitation of these names or the emotions associated with them by politicians seeking for votes, and political power thereby creating tensions among the ethnic groups in Nigeria. Politicians must be sensitized to play down on ethnic politics (Ajala, 2009; Ajala, 2016; Ejobowah, 2007; Nolte, 2004; Ukiwo, 2003), because it comes with a lot of clamor for inclusion, violence and disunity among various ethnic groups. There is need for the Igbo to invest in the media which may be employed as platforms for debunking negative stereotypes. ⌐

## 6. Conclusion

In summary, the chapter has been able to explore dimensions of stereotypes associated with the Igbo people and their immediate neighbors. It also captured empirical opinions on how ethnic stereotypes are maintained, the implications of ethnic stereotypes and the solutions to them.

The following solutions have been identified to ameliorate the effects of ethnic stereotypes namely: censuring ethnic bigots, disabusing young minds from ethnic miseducation through the media to ensure emancipation from stereotypes, checkmating and monitoring interactions on social media, and insisting on the engagement of politicians on issue-based and not tribal or ethnically charged discourses. Also, supporting the National Youth Service Corp (NYSC) to ensure inter-ethnic exposures. Others are pursuit of conscious socialization that will engender appropriate socialization and re-socialization of young people by teaching them to be critical of any stereotype by questioning them. On the part of the Igbo, they must learn to invest in the media in order to own and control platforms that can be employed to debunk intra- and inter-ethnic lies, assumptions and overgeneralizations about the Igbo people, resist ethnic supremacists, play down on negative ethnic stereotypes, be less sensitive to differences and learn to appreciate diversities, cease or stop recycling and reacting to ethnic stereotypes about the Igbo people. One thing this study was able to establish is that stereotypes are not static, they are dynamic (Everhart, 1998; Madon et al., 2001). Finally, there is the need to always have before one's gaze the negative effects of stereotyping and to endeavor to always remain psychologically free of them. Positive stereotypes are real and it can heal (Pastner, 1989; McFarlane, 2014), but so also can negative stereotypes be harmful. Hence, focusing on positive stereotypes would do a lot of good to people's psyche. ⌐

## References

Ajala, A. (2016). Yorùbá Elites and Ethnic Politics in Nigeria: Ọbáf. émi Awól. ów. ò and Corporate Agency by Wale Adebanwi. New York: Cambridge University Press, 2014. 312 pp. *American Anthropologist.* http://onlinelibrary.wiley.com/doi/10.111 1/aman.12540/full

Ajala, A. S. (2009). The Yoruba Nationalist Movements, Ethnic Politics and Violence: A Creation from Historical Consciousness and Socio-political Space in South-western Nigeria. *Journal of Alternative Perspectives in the Social Sciences.* http://www.japss.org

Ardévol, E., & Gómez-Cruz, E. (2013). Digital Ethnography and Media Practices. *The International Encyclopedia of Media Studies, VII,* 498–518. https://doi.org/10.1002/9781444361506. wbiems193

Bandura, A. (1971). Social learning: Theory. In *General Learning Press.* General earning Press. https://doi.org/10.1016/B978-0-12-813251-7.00057-2

Bernburg, J. G. (2009). Labeling Theory. In M. D. Krohn, A. Lizotte, & G. P. Hall (Eds.), *Handbook on Crime and Deviance* (Issue November, pp. 187–207). Springer Science + Business Media. https://doi.org/10.1007/978-1-4419-0245-0

Davidson, M. M., Gervais, S. J., & Sherd, L. W. (2015). *The Ripple Effects of Stranger Harassment on Objectification of Self and Others.* 39(1), 53–66.

https://doi.org/10.1177/0361684313514371

Dionigi, R. A. (2015). Stereotypes of Aging: Their Effects on the Health of Older Adults. *Journal of Geriatrics, 2015,* 1–9. https://doi.org/10.1155/2015/954027

Eagly, A. H., Nater, C., Miller, D. I., Kaufmann, M., & Sczesny, S. (2020). Gender stereotypes have changed: A cross-temporal meta-analysis of U.S. public opinion polls from 1946 to 2018. *American Psychologist, 75*(3), 301–315. https://doi.org/10.1037/amp0000494

Edinyang, D. S. (2016). The Significance of Social Learning Theories in The Teaching of Social Studies Education. *International Journal of Sociology and Anthropology Research, 2*(1), 40–45.

Ejobowah, J. B. (2007). Who Owns the Oil? The Politics of Ethnicity in the Niger Delta of Nigeria. *Africa Today, 47*(1), 29–47. https://doi.org/10.1353/at.2000.0011

Everhart, R. (1998). Unraveling the "Model Minority" Stereotype: Listening to Asian American Youth. *Anthropology & Education Quarterly, 29,* 132–133.

Fernando, S. (1991). Racial stereotypes. *British Journal of Psychiatry, 158*(FEB.), 289–290. https://doi.org/10.1192/bjp.158.2.289b

Gavreliuc, A., Gavreliuci, D., & Semenescu, A. (2021). Beyond the facAâde of generosity-Regional stereotypes within the same national culture influence prosocial behaviors. *PLoS ONE, 16*(5 May 2021), 1–26. https://doi.org/10.1371/journal.pone.0250125

Gázquez, J. J., Pérez-Fuentes, C., Fernández, M., González, L., Ruiz, I., & Díaz, A. (2009). Old-age stereotypes related to the gerontology education: an intergenerational study. *European Journal of Education and Psychology N°, 2*(3), 263–273. www.ejep.es

Hilton, J., psychology, W. V. H.-A. review of, & 1996, undefined. (1996). Stereotypes. *Annualreviews.Org, 47*, 237–271. https://doi.org/10.1146/annurev.psych.47.1.237

Jost, J. T., Kivetz, Y., Rubini, M., Guermandi, G., & Mosso, C. (2005). System-justifying functions of complementary regional and ethnic stereotypes: Cross-national evidence. *Social Justice Research, 18*(3), 305–333. https://doi.org/10.1007/s11211-005-6827-z

Kiaušiene, I., Štreimikiene, D., & Grundey, D. (2011). On gender stereotyping and employment assimetries. *Economics and Sociology, 4*(2), 84–97. https://doi.org/10.14254/2071-789X.2011/4-2/8

Lawrence, B. (2004). Stereotypes and stereotyping: A moral analysis. *Philosophical Papers, 33*(3), 251–289.

Lebedko, M. G. (2014). Interaction of Ethnic Stereotypes and Shared Identity in Intercultural Communication. *Procedia - Social and Behavioral Sciences, 154*(October), 179–183. https://doi.org/10.1016/j.sbspro.2014.10.132

Lewis, J. D. (1976). The classic American pragmatists as forerunners to symbolic interactionism. *The Sociological Quarterly, 17*(3), 347–359. http://www.blackwell-synergy.com/doi/abs/10.1111/j.1533-8525.1976.tb00988.x

Madon, S., Guyll, M., Aboufadel, K., Montiel, E., Smith, A., Palumbo, P., & Jussim, L. (2001). Ethnic and national stereotypes: The Princeton trilogy revisited and revised. *Personality and Social Psychology Bulletin, 27*(8), 996–1010. https://doi.org/10.1177/0146167201278007

Mattern, S. (2018). *Toolkit: Digital ethnography*. Designing Methodologies. https://doi.org/http://www.wordsinspace.net/designingmethods/spring2018/2018/01/07/toolkit-digital-ethnography/

McFarlane, D. A. (2014). A Positive Theory of Stereotyping and Stereotypes: Is Stereotyping Useful? *Journal of Studies in Social Sciences, 8*(1), 140–163. https://infinitypress.info/index.php/jsss/article/download/554/353

Meed, M. (1962). National Character and National Stereotypes: A Trend Report Prejared jor the Inlerna- tiolzal Union of Scientijc Philosophy. *American Anthropologist, 64*, 688–690.

Middleton, L., Hall, H., & Raeside, R. (2019). Applications and applicability of Social Cognitive Theory in information science research. *Journal of Librarianship and Information Science, 51*(4), 927–937.

https://doi.org/10.1177/0961000618769985

Nolte, I. (2004). Identity and violence: the politics of youth in Ijebu-Remo, Nigeria. *The Journal of Modern African Studies*, *42*(1), 61–89. https://doi.org/10.1017/S0022278X03004464

Pastner, S. (1989). Good Jew/Bad Jew: Dealing with Informant Stereotypes. *Anthropology and Humanism Quarterly*, *14*(1), 4–9.

Peffley, M., Hurwitz, J., & Sniderman, P. M. (1997). Racial Stereotypes and Whites' Political Views of Blacks in the Context of Welfare and Crime. *American Journal of Political Science*, *41*(1), 30. https://doi.org/10.2307/2111708

Proctor, D. (2020). *So You Want to "Do" Digital Ethnography*. The Geek Anthropologist. https://doi.org/https://thegeekanthropologist.com/2020/03/25/so-you-want-to-do-digital-ethnography/

Ramadan, E., & Nazan, D. (2010). Social Learning Theory (Social Cognitive Theory). In *Learning and Teaching : Theories, Approaches and Models* (pp. 47–59). http://ijonte.org/FileUpload/ks63207/File/chapter_4-_.pdf

Stalburg, C. M. (2016). *Social Learning Theory Apply specific social learning theories to the.*

Stryker, S. (1987). The Vitalization of Symbolic Interactionism. *Social Psychology Quarterly*, *50*(1), 83. https://doi.org/10.2307/2786893

Ukiwo, U. (2003). Politics, ethno-religious conflicts and democratic consolidation in Nigeria. *The Journal of Modern African Studies*, *41*(1), 115–138. https://doi.org/10.1017/S0022278X02004172

United Nations Human Rights. (2014). *Gender stereotypes and Stereotyping and women's rights* (Vol. 17, Issue 2). https://doi.org/10.1007/s00064-005-1126-2

# WRITERS
# &
# CONTRIBUTORS

Mr. Stanley J. Onyemechalu
Department of Archaeology
University of Cambridge
United Kingdom

Dr. J. Kelechi Ugwuanyi
Department of Archaeology and Tourism
University of Nigeria,
Nsukka,
Enugu State

Prof. Onwuka Ndukwe Njoku
Evangel University,
Akaeze,
Ebonyi State

Prof. Austine Uchechukwu Igwe
Department of History and International
Studies, Nnamdi Azikiwe University, Awka,
Anambra State

Mr. Abuoma Agajelu
Department of History and International
Studies, Nnamdi Azikiwe University, Awka,
Anambra State.

Mbanefo Chukwuogor
Department of Linguistics
Nnamdi Azikiwe University,
Awka
Anambra State

Dr. Purity Ada Uchechukwu
Department of Modern European
Languages
Nnamdi Azikiwe University,
Awka
Anambra State

Prof. Chinedu Uchechukwu
Department of Linguistics
Nnamdi Azikiwe University,
Awka
Anambra State

Prof. M. Chibụ Ọnụkawa
Department of Linguistics, Communication
studies/Igbo
Abia State University,
Uturu,
Abia State

Prof. J. Obi Oguejiofor
Department of Philosophy
Nnamdi Azikiwe University,
Awka,
Anambra State

Dr. George C. Odoh
Department of Fine and Applied Arts,
University of Nigeria,
Nsukka,
Enugu State

Dr. Kanayo Nwadialor
Department of Religion and Human
Relations
Nnamdi Azikiwe University, Awka,
Anambra State

Dr. George E. Onwudiwe
Department of Igbo, African and
Communication Studies
Nnamdi Azikiwe University,
Awka,
Anambra State

Prof. Chike Okoye
Department of English Language and
Literature
Nnamdi Azikiwe University, Awka,
Anambra State

Mr. Gerald Eze
Department of Music,
Nnamdi Azikiwe University, Awka,
Anambra State

Dr. Nicholas Chielotam Akas
Department of Theatre and Film
Studies
Nnamdi Azikiwe University,
Awka
Anambra State

Prof. Harry Obi-Nwosu
Department of Psychology
Nnamdi Azikiwe University, Awka,
Anambra State

Dr. Okey Ikechukwu
Executive Director
Development Specs Academy
12 Linda Chalker Crescent, Asokoro
Extension.
Abuja

Prof. Ikechukwu Anthony Kanu
Department of Philosophy and
Religious Studies
Tansian University, Umunya
Anambra State

Dr. Grace Nyetu Malachi Brown
Department of History and Diplomatic
Studies,
Ignatius Ajuru University of Education,
Rumuolumeni,
Port Harcourt
Rivers State

Dr. Michael T.B. Thomas
Department of History and Diplomatic
Studies,
Ignatius Ajuru University of Education,
Rumuolumeni,
Port Harcourt
Rivers State

Prof. Olumide Ekanade
Department of History and International
Studies,
College of Humanities,
Redeemer's University,
Ede,
Osun State,

Dr. Blessing Nonye Onyima
Department of Sociology and
Anthropology
Nnamdi Azikiwe University,
Awka
Anambra State

Mr. Efa Imoke
Managing Director
STRATA Management & Technologies Ltd.
Calabar
Cross River State.